A READER FOR RESEARCH METHODS

LAWRENCE ROSEN
Temple University

and

ROBERT WEST
Temple University

A READER FOR

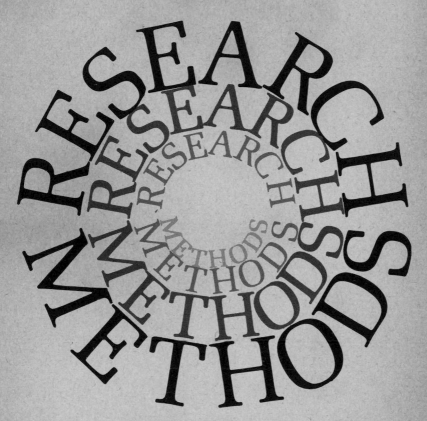

RESEARCH METHODS

Random House   New York

To our respective wives
Sonja and Sarah

Library of Congress Cataloging in Publication Data

Rosen, Lawrence, 1937-   comp.
A reader for research methods.

Includes bibliographies.
1. Social science research—Addresses, essays,
lectures. I. West, Robert, 1935-   joint comp.
II. Title.
H62.R656   300'.1'8   72-12775
ISBN 0-394-31743-2

Manufactured in the United States of America. Composed by Cherry Hill
Composition, Pennsauken, N.J. Printed and bound by Halliday Lithograph Corp.,
West Hanover, Mass.

Design by James M. Wall

First Edition
9 8 7 6 5 4 3 2

Preface

As is the case for many other textbooks and readers, we were motivated
to produce this reader by what we feel is a major gap in the available
pedagogical material for undergraduate courses in methods of social
research. Of course, several fine texts, as well as a few paperbacks on
specialized topics and even a few readers, are available. The latter
invariably consist of papers that discuss methodological issues. All these
sources usually fail to do one simple thing: to present a wide range of
complete and integrated examples of social research. Their approach
usually involves cursory illustrations from "bits and pieces" of several
works. Although such an approach is useful, it falls short of what an
integrated and complete research paper can provide.

To date, if any instructor wants to employ more complete examples of
research for illustration, he has only a few alternatives. First, he can use
a "reader" from a substantive area. Since a large number of papers are
not necessarily included because they illustrate methodological issues,
this usually proves to be inefficient. Second, he can place several papers
and/or monographs on reserve in the library. The problems with this
approach are obvious, especially for large classes. One can choose a
single major research monograph that the student purchases, but this
greatly restricts the range of methodological issues to be illustrated.
Finally, he can select from the Bobbs-Merrill reprint series, one major
disadvantage of which is that optimal papers may not be in the series.
In our view the best solution is a reader consisting of research papers
chosen for the explicit purpose of illustrating the application of research
methodology to substantive areas, and chosen in a way that is understandable to undergraduates. Consequently, we have compiled this
particular reader.

The present collection of papers is not intended to be either a
representative sampling of contemporary sociological research (quite
clearly it is not), or an example of "good" research. Certainly, many fine
papers are not included because of reasons having little to do with
what most professionals consider the dimensions that determine the
"quality" of research. In choosing the papers we attempted to follow the
following criteria:

1. The methodology is sufficiently detailed and clear to enable discussion
   and analysis;
2. The level of difficulty is suitable for undergraduates;
3. A wide variety of data sources and substantive issues is represented.

Although it is impossible to maximize all criteria simultaneously, we
hope that we have been fairly successful in reaching these goals.

We have indicated what this book is. It is also important to say what
this book is not. It is not a methods reader consisting of papers explicitly
concerned with methodological issues, although a few are included.

Nor is it a "mini-text" in methods. The connective material does include a small amount of instructional material, but it is designed only to introduce issues, not to explicate them.

The organization is of course arbitrary. Because most of the articles with the exception of Campbell's are independent of one another, they can be used in any sequence that best fits the needs and purposes of the individual instructor. In addition, most of the papers are complete research reports and can be used to illustrate issues other than those indicated in the text. For such purpose we have provided suggestions in the introduction to each of the sections.

There are several people to whom we are indebted for this project. Foremost, of course, are the many authors of the individual papers. In addition we wish to extend our appreciation to Rose Jackson, Elaine Gordon, Eileen Shellman, and Tonya Johnson. We wish to thank the college staff at Random House, especially Dave Bartlett for his patience for the many delays in this project, and Barbara Conover, and Lynne Farber for their invaluable assistance. Finally, our appreciation to Theodore R. Anderson for his valuable comments.

January 1973

LAWRENCE ROSEN
ROBERT H. WEST

Contents

Contents

INTRODUCTION

■ The student being introduced into methods of social research is not faced with a simple task. Perhaps more than in any other subject matter within sociology he will usually find that, despite repeated readings, textbook discussions of research methods project an abstract quality. Discussions such as what is considered good experimental design, the relative advantages and disadvantages of questionnaires, the limitations of Likert scaling, and so forth, are encountered in practically every text in research methods. However, unless these discussions are expanded with examples of actual research, the beginning student may fail to appreciate their significance. The two most frequently used and effective strategies to counter this tendency toward abstractness are (1) the participation or conduct of research and (2) the reading of published research.

There is a fair amount of consensus among those who teach methods that the experience of conducting research is of immense value. The old homily "experience is the best teacher" rings very true in this particular instance. Research experience not only provides a technical education, but also is very important in generating enthusiasm and respect for empirical sociology. There is little quarrel that the conduct of research should continue to be an integral part of methods instruction. However, complete reliance on actual research experience is not always feasible and in some instances not entirely desirable.

Primary research experience is essential for the student who plans to become a "producer" of research (that is, pursue a career of social research). However, the majority of undergraduate sociology students are far more likely to be "consumers" of research, in the sense that their only contact with social research will be the reading and possible application of research findings. It is for these students that extensive contact with published studies is important in developing the necessary critical skills to evaluate published research, both in terms of substantive issues and methodological adequacy. This is not to argue that the "consumer"-oriented student will not benefit from direct research experience—quite clearly he or she will. Yet complete reliance on a single research project within a single methods course has the tendency to narrow the range of research designs and techniques to which the student will be exposed. For example, it is very unlikely that the student would employ experimental *and* ex post facto survey designs within the same project; nor would he or she experience the problems of cross-cultural research or panel studies. Nevertheless, the sophisticated research "consumer" is required to have some knowledge of a broad spectrum of designs and techniques. The reading and analysis of published studies is one fairly effective device to assist in that endeavor.

Published research is most often found in the form of book-length monographs (for example, W. Whyte, *Street Corner Society*; E. Durkheim, *Suicide*) or research articles in professional journals (see *American Sociological Review, American Journal of Sociology, Social Forces, Social Problems*). Of the two, there is little question that the latter constitutes the bulk of formal sociological knowledge. Despite their importance, the undergraduate, if given the choice, would probably prefer to avoid journal articles. He usually finds them quite imposing because of their emphasis on jargon, use of statistics, and at times excessive brevity (thus projecting to the novice a crypticlike quality). But the serious student of sociology can ill afford to take such a course of action. The purpose of this reader is not only to illustrate the wide range of research designs and techniques utilized in contemporary sociology, but to provide a convenient and structured opportunity to experience professional research articles.

Unlike most readers in sociology, the papers in this anthology have not been selected to explore substantive questions (for example, stratification, race relations, family voting behavior, deviance, and so forth); nor is it a reader composed of papers about methods. Instead, this anthology consists primarily of research papers chosen to exemplify how a variety of techniques and research strategies are applied to substantive questions. The student should also be aware that this book is not intended to be a text in research methods. In other words, it will not stand alone. To be useful and meaningful it should be used in conjunction with a methods text or systematic classroom notes.

In reading the papers in this book, the student should keep in mind that he is being exposed to the researcher's account of his methodology, which tends to be an incomplete and somewhat idealized version of the actual research process. Abraham Kaplan refers to these types of accounts as "reconstructed logic"* and, as he argues, it is problematic to what extent they describe the actual research process (or what Kaplan calls "logic in use"). "Logic in use" is a mixture of formal logic, intuition, implicit generalizing, illogical procedures and processes, and so forth, that we are often unable to completely formalize or even make explicit. In addition, decisions about how much space to devote to discussion of procedures as well as what to discuss are governed very much by the style and editorial policies of the journal. For these reasons we shall probably never become good researchers simply by reading texts or published accounts of research. There is still an element of art to social research, and like other arts it has never been possible to completely describe in explicit and precise terms how one becomes a good artist. However, the concept of the "reconstructed logic" is still of value in helping to develop the critical skills of evaluating research.

Attempts to compartmentalize the research process into stages (problem selection, data collection, measurement, analysis, and so forth) are in a sense somewhat misleading. They often give the impression that all research proceeds in a fixed temporal sequence, and that one stage is not begun until the previous one is ended. Those who have conducted research will usually indicate that this is not always the case, nor should all research be forced into this mold. Therefore we have decided not to organize this book in terms of sequential stages. Instead we have selected four major methodological areas or concerns that involve some of the major decisions of the research process and in no way imply stages of research. These areas are (1) data sources (where and how will the data be collected?), (2) measurement (how shall we translate our theoretical concepts into research operations?), (3) data analysis (what analytical procedures shall we employ to make sense of the data?), and

* Abraham Kaplan, *The Conduct of Inquiry* (San Francisco: Chandler, 1964), Chapter 1.

(4) research design (how shall we handle the variable of time? What degree of control do we have over the research variables? How do we control for certain variables? And so forth). For the most part, the papers in each of these sections illustrate the application of selected techniques within each of these areas. Because most of the papers employ a full-scale research design (from selection of the problem to interpretation of findings), they exemplify research issues beyond the one for which the paper was chosen. Consequently, almost all of the papers can serve many purposes. In each of the brief introductions to the major sections we have provided some suggestions for further use of these papers.

The first two papers in this reader serve as a guide and overview of the "world of journal sociology." The Knop article provides suggestions for careful and systematic reading of journal articles, whereas the Brown and Gilmartin selection attempts to describe empirically the important trends emphasized by the two major journals in American sociology.

Understanding Journal Sociology
EDWARD KNOP

The reading of professional research journal articles is for most undergraduates
an arduous task. Facility with technical papers usually requires a fair number
of years of experience—experience not normally available to the undergraduate.
Consequently some assistance is usually needed to help guide the novice to a
comprehensive, systematic reading and understanding of journal articles. One
such device is offered in the following paper by Knop. Because the bulk
of the articles in this anthology are research journal articles, we strongly
recommend that the student use Knop's suggestion in reading this book.

■ A general set of instructions as these will best serve as guides for the
student who has some knowledge of research methods, statistics, and
theory, but who is not especially familiar with the literature contained in
the discipline's research journals. Thus, this paper is intended to (1) orient
the student to orthodox methods and organization of research presentations, and (2) to aid him in understanding the content of specific articles
which interest him. Several prerequisites to journal comprehension include
(1) knowledge of the professional vocabulary, (2) knowledge of standard
research methods, and (3) knowledge from the body of theory which gives
guidance to each research study. If the student should find himself poorly
prepared in any of these respects, a conscientious effort should be made
to improve himself in the area of his deficiency. (A time-tested method for
such self-improvement involves regular notebook entries of vocabulary
which is problemsome, notation of methods with which he is unfamiliar,
and a rigid reading schedule from sources frequently noted in journal
footnotes. A portion of the self-improvement notebook might profitably be
devoted to brief biographical sketches of the most prominent names in the
field—those which most consistently appear in footnote references—along
with a listing of their most pertinent contributions.) All of this is to say, a
person's ability to comprehend and profit from journal presentations is
directly contingent on his knowledge of general sociology; and familiarity
with journal articles—through a regular and conscientious journal reading
program—will serve to increase the person's knowledge of general sociology, and prove to be an index of his sociological maturity.

In an introductory context, it should be noted that one of the most valuable aids to the student is development of and proficiency with a system
of abbreviations or shorthand symbols which should regularly be used to
diagram relationships between variables.[1] Such diagrams are a quick and
handy method of ensuring clearer personal understanding, and are invaluable in demonstrating a given set of interrelationships to others. As with
any endeavor, accomplishment of a given task is most quickly and easily
achieved by a *systematic* approach to that end. Thus, it is the intention of

Reprinted from *The American Sociologist* 2 (1967), 90–92, with permission of The American Sociological Association. (Formerly titled, "Suggestions to Aid the Student in Systematic Interpretation and Analysis of Empirical Sociological Journal Presentations.")

this paper to provide a systematic framework for understanding and interpreting research presentations in the sociological journals.

Articles in the journals of the profession vary greatly in style of writing, type of organization, and methods of arriving at conclusions. Also, each of the journals has an editorial policy which makes articles in a source rather typical of that journal in style and method as well as content. It is to the student's advantage to survey each of the major journals in an attempt to characterize the kinds of presentations which are typical of each of those sources.

It is assumed that even the beginning journal reader needs no particular help in understanding and analyzing descriptive or narrative presentations such as those typical of *Transaction* or *The Annals,* save when the vocabulary problem is operant. Quite another case is represented by *Public Opinion Quarterly* or the *American Sociological Review,* for these typically contain presentations of sophisticated sociological research, usually in hyper-concise form. For this reason, it is here intended to present a frame of reference for understanding and evaluating this second kind of journal presentation.

This framework must necessarily be that of the model research project. Although there will be considerable deviation in forms of organization and styles of presentation, all research should contain the same basic elements, and progress through the same general phases. Preliminary research reports may not be completed through the final stages, and thus must be understood in the context of the model project only partially completed or reported. Any social research methods book will offer the same basic anatomy of the research project.[2] Keeping in mind that shorthand and diagrams of relationships between variables are extremely handy tools of the journal reader, the following general analysis form might be of considerable aid to the beginning journal reader because such would serve to systematize the article in the form of the model research project, and call to the reader's attention any shortcomings of a given research report.

To benefit most from the presentation, the reader should first read the abstract when such is provided, and the first few paragraphs of the article so that a general understanding of the research area is obtained. Then a quick glance at the middle pages will tell the reader the kinds of data which are used as proof for the author's purpose. A cursory reading of the summary section will further orient the reader to content and conclusions of the research. He should then read the article from title to closing sentence, marking key statements for future reference. It is only after this complete reading that the article should be carefully analyzed in terms of the model project. Shorthand entries in the appropriate sections of an analysis form such as the one included here will give systematic form to the procedures, purposes, and problems of the presentation. Certain standard conceptual and procedural questions should be raised about each stage of the project. These include the following (see Figure 1):

I. Conceptualization.
    A. What is the research problem or general area of research?
    B. What does the author list as the major references? Does he cite enough sources so that the theoretical basis for his conceptual position can be traced to more complete discussions?

Title _____ : Author _____ : Source _____

I. CONCEPTUALIZATION:
A. Research Area of Problem:

B. Most Pertinent Literature:

C. Major Concepts Defined:

D. Basic Hypothesis: Major Concepts (Variables) Related:

E. Subhypotheses:

V_i Relationship V_d

1.
2.
3.
4.
5.

COMMENTS ON THE CONCEPTUALIZATION:
Is author's "thinking" clear?

Suggestions for a more adequate conceptualization:

II. RESEARCH DESIGN:
A. Technique of Observation:
1. Instrument:
2. Reliability:
3. Validity:
B. Design of Proof:
C. Sample:
1. Size: (Adequate)
2. Method of Selection: (Representative?)

F. Operational Definitions:

V_i Relationship V_d

1.
2.
3.
4.
5.

COMMENTS ON THE RESEARCH DESIGN:
Is all of the design the most appropriate?

Suggestions for a more adequate research design:

III. IMPLEMENTATION OF RESEARCH:
A. Collection of Data: (Time, Place, by Whom, etc.)

B. Data Processing Techniques:

C. Presentation of Data:
1. Method:

2. Levels of Significance:

3. Levels of Generalization:

D. Findings:

1.
2.
3.
4.
5.

E. Explanation of Deviance:

1.
2.
3.
4.
5.

CONCLUSIONS:
Is basic hypotheses supported?

Suggestions for further research:

Is research: well presented? Why? convincing? Why?

FIGURE 1: Suggested schema for analyzing research articles.

C. What are the major concepts he uses as variables, and how does he define each of them?

D. Is it relatively easy to see how the author relates these key concepts to form one or several basic or guiding hypotheses? Diagram the relationship between these variables at the most general (abstract) level used by the author; this is his conceptual model.

E. Note how the author reduced the generality of the guiding hypothesis to form more specific subhypotheses or "working hypotheses." Identify the independent and dependent variables (and intervening, control, or antecedent if these are evident) and diagram the relationship between them to represent each of the subhypotheses.[3] (These variables are easily identifiable in each of the tables if they are not clearly presented in the text of the article.)

F. How does the author operationally define each of the variables stated in the subhypotheses? Diagram each of the subhypotheses in terms of the operational definitions. Are the author's empirical referents for each of the key concepts valid indicators of the variables he seeks to represent?

Comments on the Conceptualization: Is the author's conceptual thinking clear—that is, are there any logical fallacies or conceptual contradictions in his formation of the guiding hypothesis and its reduction to more specific working hypotheses? Could you offer any suggestions for strengthening his conceptualization?

II. Research Design.

A. What is the method of observation? Is it the most appropriate for this research situation? How clearly are its components derived from variables of the subhypotheses? What does the author say about the level and method of ascertaining the reliability of this instrument? Does he offer some evidence of validity other than "face validity"?

B. How close does his method of proof come to the ideal "classical" method?[4] Diagram his method of proof.

C. Is the sample he uses adequate for the purposes of his research? Is the sample size large enough and so chosen to warrant the generalizations he derives and the methods of data processing he uses? Does his purpose require a randomly selected sample? How adequate is his method of selecting the sample?

Comments on the Research Design: Does it appear that the author had his study thoroughly planned prior to collection of data? Did he employ pretest precautions? How could the author's research design be improved?

III. Implementation of Research.

A. Does the author specify when, where, and by whom his observations were collected?

B. What steps did he go through in the preparation of his data for presentation—that is, did he make mention of coding and tabulating procedures? Make special note of any processing procedure that is unique.

C. Does the author rely on conventional contingency tables for presentation of his data? Does he use percentages when his number of cases is large enough? Is the method of data presentation the most adequate for offering evidence to support his hypotheses in the context of his method of proof? If tables are used are they internally consistent, and do they meet other tabular criteria such as mutually exclusive categories arranged in logical order, inclusive in range of responses, and are all cases accounted for? Are variables controlled for when this seems warranted and size of the sample allows? Are levels of significance noted, are these realistically set, and is one predetermined critical value used for accepting hypotheses throughout the paper?[5] What does he say about the level of generalization which may be safely assumed in the context of his research design?

D. Do his data clearly support his hypotheses? Does he seem to "bend over backwards" to prove himself wrong before accepting hypotheses?

E. If his hypotheses are not all accepted, does he make some effort to explain why there is deviance from the expected results?

Conclusions. Are you left with the feeling that his basic hypothesis has been satisfactorily documented? In general, are his findings convincing? If not, why? What does he suggest as appropriate supplemental research? What could you suggest in this regard?

The student must be cautioned to a typical reaction of the beginning journal reader. If at first it might seem that too many errors were committed by the author, it should be remembered that the quality journals have high editorial standards which are ostensibly met by all articles which pass editorial inspection. Because they must be presented in very concise fashion, however, some of the procedures undertaken might escape explicit mention, and many of the implied methods may not be detected by the inexperienced journal reader. Because sociology is a relatively new endeavor in human understanding, many articles are included in the professional periodicals not because they are excellent examples of orthodox research techniques, but rather because they are quality efforts to apply new or seldom-used techniques so to complement the procedures of the discipline.

In summary, then, the student will benefit most by a conscientious and systematic study of the articles in the sociological journals, for this will not only give him knowledge of the most current activities in the discipline, but also serve as a realistic indicator of his sociological maturity, and function as a guide to self-improvement in deficient areas of knowledge.

NOTES

1. For instance, a series of hypotheses from the Deutsch and Collins "Interracial Housing" classic (in William Peterson, ed., *American Social Patterns*, Garden City, N.Y.: Doubleday and Co., 1956, pp. 7–61, quote from p. 11) reads as follows: "(1) The amount of contact between any two persons will increase as the distance between their places of residence decreases; and (2) as the amount of contact between any two persons increases, they will tend to like each other more. From these hypotheses we expected that (1) there will be more frequent and more intimate contacts between Negro and white families in an integrated than in a segregated project; and (2) a prejudiced white person who moves into an integrated project, if he stays long enough, is more likely to develop friendly feelings toward the Negroes in the project than if he were to move into a segregated project." This series of propositions can be diagrammed as follows:

1. HYP gen: $\downarrow$ Dp $\longrightarrow$ $\uparrow$ $\leftarrow$ I $\rightarrow$ $\longrightarrow$ $\uparrow$ "LIKING"

2. A. HYP sub: R seg = $\uparrow$ Dp $\longrightarrow$ $\downarrow$ $\leftarrow$ I $\rightarrow$ $-\parallel$ $\rightarrow$ $\uparrow$ "LIKING" N by WH

   B. HYP sub: R int = $\downarrow$ Dp $\longrightarrow$ $\uparrow$ $\leftarrow$ I $\rightarrow$ $\longrightarrow$ $\uparrow$ "LIKING" N by WH

where: capital letters indicate nouns (variables), while small letters indicate adjunctive subscripts; and where: HYP=hypothesis, gen=general, $\downarrow$=decrease, D=distance, p=physical, $\longrightarrow$=yields, $\uparrow$=increase, $\leftarrow$ I $\rightarrow$=interaction as a variable, R=residence, seg=segregated, int=integrated, $-\parallel\rightarrow$=does not yield, N=Negro, WH=white. Notice how the subhypotheses are derived from the general or guiding hypothesis.

2. The present author considers the following to be especially good sources in this regard: (1) William Goode and Paul Hatt, *Methods in Social Research*, New York: McGraw-Hill, 1952; (2) Claire Selltiz, et al., *Research Methods in Social Relations*, New York: Henry Holt Co., 1960; (3) Leon Festinger and Daniel Katz, *Research Methods in the Behavioral Sciences*, New York: Holt, Rinehart and Winston, 1953. Other related sources which the student may find especially useful include: (4) Hans Zetterberg, *On Theory and Verification in Sociology*, Totowa, N.J.: Bedminster Press, 1965; (5) R. V. Bowers, "Conceptual Integration and Social Research," *American Sociological Review*, 3 (June, 1938), pp. 307–319; (6) Hubert Blalock, *Social Statistics*, New York: McGraw-Hill, 1954; (7) Sidney Siegel, *Nonparametric Statistics for the Behavioral Sciences*, New York: McGraw-Hill, 1956; (8) J. P. Guilford, *Psychometric Methods*, New York: McGraw-Hill, 1954.

3. For further explanation see William Goode and Paul Hatt, *op. cit.*, pp. 353–385.

4. *Ibid.*, pp. 74–90, or Samuel Stouffer, "Some Observations on Study Design," in Thomas Lasswell, et al., *Life in Society*, Chicago: Scott, Foresman and Co., pp. 13–18. See also Hans Zetterberg, *op. cit.*, pp. 111–156.

5. See Hubert Blalock, *op. cit.*, pp. 89–96, and William Goode and Paul Hatt, *op. cit.*, chapter 7.

Sociology Today: Lacunae, Emphases, and Surfeits

JULIA S. BROWN and BRIAN G. GILMARTIN

Before exploring a few of the many methodological issues and concerns encountered in contemporary sociological research, it is useful to provide some indication about the nature of current research. In the following article, Brown and Gilmartin's analysis of a sample of research papers published in two major journals of sociology (American Sociological Review and American Journal of Sociology) provides us with a fairly good indication of the predominant research trends and practices in American sociology.

In addition to having such concerns as what major substantive fields are researched, the time and spatial locus of the research, and the nature of the research unit, the reader should pay special attention to the findings about data sources. The authors have indicated that, despite the attention paid in methods textbooks to a broad spectrum of data-collecting techniques, sociology has actually increased its reliance on interviews and questionnaires. This trend has important implications, not only in terms of the research questions that sociology explores, but also for the kinds of theoretical models that can be considered. As the authors conclude, ". . . sociology is becoming the study of verbally expressed sentiments and feelings, rather than an analysis of human performance."

This paper also demonstrates very well that sociological research is "fair game" for research itself. In other words, social research is amenable to empirical investigation, and statements about the trends and nature of the field are best offered on the basis of empirical findings rather than on "arm chair" speculation.

■ In sociology today, as in other sciences, the professional journals serve as major channels for the dissemination of ideas and information. The papers presented in the principal periodicals reach a wide audience among sociologists, are acknowledged as the best work, and stand as models for all who aspire to success. The viewpoints, conceptual schemes, interests, and methodologies reflected in these articles are therefore significant influences on both the current character and the future development of our discipline.

The present writers have selected for analysis a sample of contributions to two prestigious journals, the American Sociological Review and the American Journal of Sociology. Included in this survey are the 202 articles published in the two periodicals during 1965 and 1966, and the 200 papers published in 1940 and 1941.[1] It is hoped that an examination of the form and content of this literature will increase our knowledge of the present nature of, and continuing trends in, sociology.

Reprinted from The American Sociologist 4 (1969), 283–291, with permission of the American Sociological Association. (Editorial adaptations.)

TABLE 1. Articles Published in the American Sociological Review and the American Journal of Sociology in the Years 1940, 1941, 1965, and 1966, by Subject

Journal and Year	Substantive Research			Methodology				Theory					Miscel-laneous	Total Articles
	(1)	(2)	(3)	(4)	(5)	(6)	(7)	(8)	(9)	(10)	(11)	(12)	(13)	(14)
AJS														
1940	19	13	6	5	2	1	2	10	1	1	1	7	0	34
1941	21	18	3	4	0	2	2	25	2	0	10	13	5	55
ASR														
1940	37	35	2	5	2	2	1	11	0	0	0	11	5	58
1941	24	19	5	10	0	5	5	16	5	1	0	10	3	53
Total	101			24				62					13	200
Per cent	50.5%			12%				31%					6.5%	100%
AJS														
1965	31	29	2	7	0	5	2	5	0	2	0	3	1	44
1966	36	35	1	2	0	0	2	5	0	0	3	2	0	43
ASR														
1965	32	32	0	12	1	7	4	14	4	2	0	8	0	58
1966	42	40	2	7	1	3	3	8	0	0	1	7	0	57
Total	141			28				32					1	202
Per cent	69.8%			13.9%				15.8%					5.5%	100%

Note: Column numbers refer to:

1 = Total substantive articles (sum of columns 2 and 3)
2 = Studies presenting substantive research
3 = Papers reviewing research or offering suggestions for future research
4 = Total methodological articles (sum of columns 5, 6, and 7)
5 = Articles concerning general methodological issues
6 = Specific tests and techniques
7 = Papers concerning the development, reliability and validity of specific measures and scales
8 = Total theoretical papers (sum of columns 9, 10, 11, and 12)
9 = History and status of sociology
10 = Discussions of classical theories
11 = Social commentary, speculative essays, impressionistic analyses
12 = Discussions of concepts and general theoretical schema
13 = Miscellaneous articles. Save for two bibliographies, all of these were appeals and suggestions for specific social actions and policies.
14 = Total articles in the periodical specified for period specified.

GENERAL CONCERNS

As a point of departure, we consider first the relative space devoted to papers on theory, methodology, and substantive research. In Table 1 a breakdown of articles into these three broad categories is presented.[2] The term "substantive research" is employed to refer both to studies presenting empirical data on social phenomena and to papers reviewing past research or proposing new directions for inquiry. Classed under methodology are all articles dealing with the basic assumptions of science, with the limitations and potentialities of specific methods, with the development, validity, and reliability of specific scales and measures, and with various statistical and mathematical devices and techniques. Included under the umbrella of theory is a mélange of papers, some exploring the history and scope of sociology; some expounding and expanding classical theories; others proposing, clarifying, and assessing concepts; and a few articulating systematically the linkages of variables. Also included among works on theory is the "wisdom" literature, drawing upon the general knowledge, personal experience, and Verstehen of individual authors in an attempt to illumine the social scene.

Inspection of Table 1 reveals that a greater proportion of journal space is allocated today to substantive research than in 1940–41, about the same proportion to methodology, and a lesser amount to theory. In both periods, empirical studies outnumbered theoretical essays. In 1940–41, the American Journal of Sociology was the more theoretical of the two periodicals, a somewhat surprising finding in view of its stereotype as the vehicle of the atheoretical Chicago school. Today, however, the American Sociological Review appears somewhat more partial to theory than does the Journal.

The conclusion seems warranted that American sociology has been empirically oriented throughout its recent history.[3] It is even possible that substantive research has prospered at the expense of theory over the past quarter-century, but the more probable explanation is that theory-building now is less likely to be an isolated activity, and is more frequently incorporated into the discussion and interpretation sections of empirical papers. Likewise, methodological advances may be presented as part of research articles rather than separately.

It is also of interest to examine the selected articles for answers to the questions: Which areas are of central concern to contemporary sociologists? Which subfields have endured, which are in decline, which are on the rise? To answer these questions, sheer number of publications may again be taken as indicative of the relative importance and prestige of an area.

A topical distribution of all articles is presented in Table 2. A classification problem arose when the author's expressed purpose was to explore the relation of two or more variables representing differing sociological subfields. This problem was solved arbitrarily by classifying each such paper according to the nature of the dependent variable. As an example, a study of the effect of social class on aspirational level would be tallied under the heading of social psychology rather than stratification.

It is apparent from Table 2 that the subfield of social psychology occupies first place today among sociologists, just as it did in 1940–41. In

TABLE 2. Distribution Among Special Interest Areas of All Articles Published in the 1940, 1941, 1965, and 1966 Issues of the *American Sociological Review* and the *American Journal of Sociology*

Special Interest Area	1940 and 1941	1965 and 1966
Social psychology	29 (46)[a]	22 (37)[a]
Formal organizations	1 (2)	18 (27)
Work and occupations	3 (7)	17 (28)
Political sociology	8 (9)	17 (20)
Family	22 (23)	15 (17)
Deviant behavior[b]	6	13
Stratification and social mobility	6 (8)	11 (33)
Juvenile delinquency and crime	9	9 (10)
Urban sociology and community	22 (27)	8 (18)
Religion	5 (9)	7 (12)
Education	0	6 (9)
Social change	4 (5)	6
Race and ethnic relations	4	5 (14)
Demography	14 (17)	5 (10)
Miscellaneous minor interests		
Values, norms, culture	5 (7)	4
Sociology of knowledge and science	4	3
Small-groups analysis	3	2
Collective behavior	0	2
Social ethics	10 (11)	1
Communication and public opinion	5 (6)	1
Medicine	1 (2)	1
Law	1	1
Recreation and play	1	1
War	15 (18)	0
General theory and methods (not classifiable otherwise)	22	27
Total	200	202

[a] Parenthetical figures represent the number of articles in a specific category when classification is made with respect to the nature of the independent variable as well as the nature of the dependent variable. See text for further explanation.

[b] This category includes articles relating to social psychiatry.

those years, the second and third major specialties were urban or community sociology and the family. Today, the study of organizations constitutes the second most popular subarea. Then follow the sociology of work and occupations, political sociology, and the family. However, if articles are classified not only on the basis of the nature of the dependent variable but on that of the independent variable as well, then the number of stratification studies swells to a total second only to that noted for social psychology. In both periods, some interests remained peripheral, such as the study of small groups, collective behavior, the study of values and norms, communication and public opinion, social change, medical sociology, religion, and the sociologies of law, recreation, science, and knowledge.

Since 1940 there has been a decline in sociologists' concern with the community and with demography, and a virtual disappearance of the sociology of war. Interest has increased in the areas of organizations, work, and the polity. Although emphasis on social psychology has continued, important changes in conceptual focuses have occurred. Thus, in 1940–41 there were twenty-two papers on morale. In 1965–66 there were no papers on morale but seven on alienation.

Finally, our data support the claim made by Popovich (1966) that certain problems, such as social change, that are rated as of vital importance by leading sociologists are in fact among those least subjected to research today.

THE CHARACTER OF
SUBSTANTIVE RESEARCH

Using as our guide the paradigm for research outlined in Table 3, our findings may be elaborated as follows:

TIME FACTOR AND SETTING   Substantive research in our journals is today even more culture-bound and time-bound than in 1940–41. Three-fourths of today's research has its setting in the United States, and 85 per cent refers to only one point in time, usually the present. Furthermore, very few studies are concerned with change through time, or with process as such. These two findings support our earlier contentions that sociologists tend to provincialism, and that they do not always study the topics (for example, social change) that they verbally pronounce to be important.

BASIC ORIENTATION   The orientation of the published research is quantitative rather than descriptive.[4] This was clearly perceptible twenty-five years ago and is becoming continually more pervasive, so that today quantitative data are reported in 85 per cent of the inquiries examined. In addition, whereas in 1940–41 authors were content with simple enumerations and tabulations, today more sophisticated statistical treatments of data have become the rule. Thus, in the earlier period statistical manipulations (other than calculating means or percentages) were performed for only 20 per cent of the articles; in 1965–66 the figure is 71 per cent.

SOURCE OF DATA   The sociologist of today is more likely than his counterpart of yesteryear to collect primary data for the express purpose at hand. The use of secondary data, i.e., information collected for a purpose other than that of the immediate researcher, has declined from 61 per cent in 1940–41 to 47 per cent in 1965–66. Moreover, the secondary materials used today differ in nature from those of twenty-five years ago. A shift has occurred away from the use of literature, historical documents, and journalistic accounts to the use of the empirical facts gathered by other scientific investigators, frequently by means of survey interviews.

In collecting his data, the sociologist employs a remarkably narrow range of techniques. Apparently, the detailed discussions presented in many of our texts regarding the virtues and limitations of specific techniques are

TABLE 3. Distribution of Research Articles Published in the *American Sociological Review* and the *American Journal of Sociology* in the Periods 1940–1941 and 1965–1966, According to Selected Aspects of Their Research Design

Characteristic of Research	1940–1941		1965–1966	
	Number (N=85)	Per Cent	Number (N=136)	Cent Per
Time factor				
Synchronic	54	63.5	115	84.6
Diachronic	31	36.5	21	15.4
Stressing change and process	21	24.7	21	15.4
Setting				
United States	52	61.2	102	75.0
Other	33	38.8	34	25.0
Comparative	10	11.8	12	8.9
Basic orientation				
Descriptive	40	47.0	21	15.4
Quantitative	45	53.0	115	84.6
Source of data				
Primary	33	38.8	72	53.0
Systematic observation	0	—	0	—
Impressionistic observation	2	—	0	—
Participant observation	9	—	6	—
Questionnaire	6	—	30	—
Interview	15	—	32	—
Both interview and questionnaire	1	—	4	—
Secondary	52	61.2	64	47.0
Census	15	—	16	—
History, literature, press	19	—	13	—
Records	13	—	8	—
Other scientific investigators' data	5	—	27	—

purely academic exercises, for most of the tools in the sociologist's armamentarium are seldom employed. Content analysis was performed in only 6 of the 136 research studies reported in 1965 and 1966. Six inquiries were based on participant observation, but in almost every instance the investigators felt compelled to add supplementary facts from structured interviews to bolster their conclusions. Other anthropological techniques were completely ignored. Life histories and personal documents were seldom gathered. "Unobtrusive" measures remained completely untapped as sources of information regarding social phenomena. Not a single study in either period was based on systematic observation, i.e., the recording or tallying of specific types of behavior according to a pre-determined schedule. There were only two panel studies with before-and-after measures on a given group. And only one piece of research approximated the classical experimental design.[5] The fear of some sociologists that artificial laboratory experimentation will take over our science to the detriment of in-depth, naturalistic studies appears completely without foundation. It would seem that more, not less, experimental research is in order.

In actual practice, the sociologist today limits himself rather generally

Characteristic of Research	1940–1941		1965–1966	
	Number (N=85)	Per Cent	Number (N=136)	Per Cent
Type of case				
Individual	31	36.5	73	53.7
Primary group	10	11.8	3	2.2
Formal organization	2	2.3	23	16.9
Occupational and ethnic categories	0	—	8	5.9
Community	18	21.1	14	10.3
Society	22	25.9	12	8.8
Other[a]	2	2.4	3	2.2
Number of cases				
One only	27	31.8	19	13.9
Few (2–10)	15	17.6	16	11.8
Large sample	43	50.6	101	74.3
General purpose				
Fact finding	21	24.7	16	11.8
Exploration, understanding	25	29.4	27	19.8
Hypothesis testing	39	45.9	93	68.4
Type of variables analyzed				
Individual	12	30.9	34	36.5
Individual-group[b]	13	33.2	30	32.3
Group	14	35.9	29	31.2

[a] Studies using as their cases dyads, institutions, cultural traits, events like race riots, etc.

[b] In research papers testing hypotheses, sometimes the variables selected all pertain to the individual, sometimes all to a group, and sometimes one variable pertains to the individual and another variable pertains to a group of which the individual is a part. See text for fuller explanation.

to the construction and conduct of questionnaires and interviews.[6] In 1940–41, 25 per cent of the 85 empirical studies depended on interviews and questionnaires for their data; in 1965–66, 48 per cent did. However, if we also consider studies based on secondary data that, in turn, derived from interviews, then 64 per cent of the total 136 research papers in the latter two years were based on such verbal reports.

Increasingly, these verbal reports are limited to the expression of attitudes, feelings, and opinions rather than to factual accounts of past behavior and interactions. In 1940–41, 8 of the 22 studies using questionnaires and interviews obtained statements about opinions or feelings, 6 focused on actual behavior, and 8 gathered information about both past behavior and attitudes. In 1965–66, 49 of 66 studies in which interviews were collected dealt only with opinions and sentiments, 6 with behavior, and 8 with both behavior and attitudes. It would seem that our colleagues tend to ignore actual behavioral patterns and also fail to come to grips with the fundamental problem of the relation of attitudes and sentiments to behavior. To an ever greater extent, sociology is becoming the study of verbally expressed sentiments and feelings, rather than an analysis of human performance.

TYPE OF CASE   Considering now the subject of the focus of research, what conclusions may be reached concerning the type and number of cases involved in substantive studies today? From Table 3 it would appear that the "case" most frequently researched today is the individual (in 54 per cent of the 136 studies). When the focus of interest is a collectivity, it is more likely to be the formal organization than the family, the friendship group, the informal interactional network, the community, or the total society. The increased contemporary tendency to focus on the individual is attributable in part to the intensity of the social-psychological orientation of sociology, and in part to the fact that the use of the interview technique implicitly assumes that the individual is the basic unit for analysis.

NUMBER OF CASES   The number of cases taken under analysis is typically larger today than formerly. Case studies comprised 32 per cent of all empirical investigations in 1940–41, but only 13 per cent in 1965–66. A tendency to large samples, sometimes in excess of the thousand mark, may be accounted for in terms of the access of modern sociologists to large research centers with funds and personnel to engage in large-scale surveys.

GENERAL PURPOSE   The purpose of research today is shifting away from fact finding and exploration toward the testing of hypotheses. However, even today, authors frequently fail to state their hypotheses formally and explicitly, leaving to their readers the task of deciding whether a point of fact is being ascertained or a more general relationship is being tested. The following statements by authors as to the purpose of their inquiry may serve to illustrate the nature of this quandary.

. . . to assess the importance of talent and achievement relative to that of academic environment [in determining scientific productivity] (Crane, 1965:700).

. . . to assess roughly the proportions of managers with upward and downward career orientations and to explain variations in terms of other variables (Tausky and Dubin, 1965:726).

Occupational and municipal government characteristics influence the occurrence of riots; demographic and housing characteristics do not (Lieberson and Silverman, 1965:887).

. . . we wished to investigate the extent to which varying self-concepts are a function of the consistency of self-definitions given to the boys by significant others, as those definitions are perceived by the boys themselves, and to determine, as far as possible, who the significant others really are (Schwartz and Tangri, 1965:924).

In each of the above instances, and in some twenty-one other similar cases, the present analysts were able to conclude that a hypothesis was being tested only after a laborious examination of the context. To us, at least, it seems clear that a more explicit rendering of one's general hypothesis would be highly desirable.[7]

TYPES OF VARIABLES ANALYZED   Finally, let us analyze the nature of the variables or properties that are related hypothetically. In some studies, the hypothesis relates one variable (or set of variables) pertaining to the individual to another variable (or set of variables) pertaining to the same person. The mode of analysis applicable to such a situation is sometimes called "individual analysis" (Riley, 1964), for example, a study purporting to relate the individual's voting preferences to the size of his income. In a second set of studies, all the variables under analysis refer to group characteristics, for example, a study that attempts to relate the literacy rate of a society to its degree of industrialization. In a third set of studies, the purpose is to demonstrate an association between one or more group variables and one or more individual variables,[8] for example, an investigation relating the amount of psychological stress of an individual to the degree of integration of the group to which he belongs.

According to our estimates, the total research in each of the two periods under examination was divided about evenly among these three types of study. One final point might be mentioned here. Few were the studies that dealt immediately and directly with reciprocal interactions among individuals or collectivities. Only two studies related a variable pertaining to one individual to a variable pertaining to another individual in a dyadic situation (for example, the relation between a son's educational attainment and his father's F-score). And no study was encountered that related a variable or property of one group to a variable or property of another group. We offer as a mythical example of such a study one which tests the hypothesis that the size of the army of a country is directly proportional to the size of the army of its nearest neighbor. It would seem that the whole field of intergroup relations has lain fallow and should prove highly fertile ground for future exploration.

IMPLICATIONS AND CONCLUSIONS

Among the characteristics of sociology that have persisted over the past quarter-century may be noted a preference for empirical inquiry as against theory, a strong interest in social-psychological issues, and an abiding commitment to quantification and statistical analysis. Continuing also has been a trend to specialization, with the development of several new substantive areas, including political sociology, industrial sociology, and the study of formal organizations. Another enduring trait, though one of more questionable value, has been sociology's provincialism. The culture-bound and time-bound nature of sociological research, being limited largely to present-day American society, constitutes evidence for this charge. Still further evidence is provided by the tendency of sociologists to confine their attention almost entirely to the work of colleagues who have published in the two principal journals within a five-year time span, while ignoring earlier work, foreign research, papers in the minor sociological journals, and papers in the journals of allied behavioral sciences.*

While sociology as a science has experienced considerable expansion in recent years, its growth has been somewhat uneven. Marked advances have been made in some areas, but in others the problems and methods have suffered neglect. Thus, this analysis revealed few inquiries involving macroscopic, grand-scale problems, such as long-term evolutionary trends, wars and revolutions, or the rise and fall of institutions, ideologies, cultures, and nations. Also rarely encountered in our sample were intensive investigations of specific, concrete social situations. Running accounts of current events, customs, rituals, and practices and first-hand naturalistic descriptions of such social groups as families, gangs, schools, and religious fellowships seem to be vanishing. When today's sociologist seeks out man in his natural habitat, he is less likely to come as participant observer and ethnographic recorder than as opinion sampler, questionnaire in hand.

These findings would indicate that two of the three general sociological orientations distinguished by Schellenberg (1957) and Williams (1958), the "historical and cultural" and the "concrete and clinical," have been declining, while the third has come to dominate the sociological scene. This last approach is dedicated to the construction and testing of predictive hypotheses concerning the interrelations of abstract variables. It was termed "logico-experimental" by the aforementioned authors, an unfortunate label in our opinion, since experimentation is seldom employed today in sociological variable analysis. Where controls are needed, they are provided by statistical manipulations rather than by laboratory procedures.

Lack of interest in macroscopic problems and in concrete cases has led to decreased use of the techniques particularly appropriate to their study, specifically, historical and library research, the life history, the unstructured interview, and participant observation. Yet there has been, as well, a neglect of some of the techniques presumably well suited to the type of sociological investigation so frequently conducted today. Archives, systematic tallies of coded behaviors, sociographic and sociometric tests, laboratory experiments, content analyses, all can provide data for testing hypotheses but are rarely exploited. Instead, sociologists tend more and more to restrict their choice of method to the structured survey interview or questionnaire.

The widespread acceptance of the interview as the major method of sociology means that research has become increasingly limited to what is researchable by that means, namely, verbal behavior. Nonverbal behavior is likely to pass unexamined, along with the crucial issue of the correspondence between what is said and what is done.

There are also theoretical ramifications to the limitation of methods in the sociologists' repertoire. Each sociological technique or method necessarily involves certain philosophical assumptions as to the nature of man, of society, and of scientific truth.[9] Since these assumptions vary from method to method, maintaining a variety of techniques has the advantage of providing alternative theoretical models of man and society for consideration.

* [Editor's note: The data supporting this conclusion are contained in the original article.]

In view of the preeminent position of the interview method in sociological research today, it would seem fruitful to clarify its epistemological and scientific presuppositions. However, to date, sociologists who favor this technique have generally failed to reveal their underlying assumptions regarding the relation of verbal behavior to the subject's consciousness, to his veridicality, to his rationality, to his feelings and motives, and to his nonverbal and verbal performance in other social situations. Only when these assumptions are explicitly stated can a full understanding of the virtues and limitations of the interview method be achieved so that it can be placed in proper perspective relative to other methods and their theoretical implications.

In summary, if a more balanced sociology is desirable, then existing excesses might be curbed and neglects rectified. More effort might be expended on the systematic formulation of coherent sets of empirical generalizations into theory. More attention might be paid to such topics as social change, integration, collective behavior, communication, and values and norms. If sociology is to transcend American national culture and become truly general, then more cross-cultural and historical research is in order. If sociology is indeed a "science of society" or a "study of social groups," as our texts inform us, then more studies might focus on the society, and on intergroup and intersocietal relations. If sociology is the "scientific study of human social behavior," then behavior other than verbal statements of opinions and feelings warrants intensive investigation. If sociology is not to become the slave of a single method, then a wide variety of techniques should be exploited. And, finally, if adequate theories of man and society are to be developed, then the interplay between theory and method needs to be consistently probed and explicated.

NOTES

1. Excluded from this analysis are letters, commentaries, and professional news and announcements.

The fact that this project was initiated in 1967 accounts for the selection for analysis of the 1965 and 1966 volumes of the journals. The 1940 and 1941 volumes were chosen because it was felt that a twenty-five-year interval would provide an adequate basis for calculating long-term trends, continuities, and changes in sociology. It was also felt that the papers published in those years would be more representative of sociology than the papers appearing during or immediately following American involvement in World War II.

2. Independent classifications by the two authors resulted in agreement in all but 19 of the 402 instances. In those 19 cases, consensus was reached through discussion.

3. This accords with the expressed view of a number of leading sociologists either exclusively or in combination with cardinal data.

4. In this report, the term "quantitative data" refers to data handled numerically in any fashion, even by simple counting. Our usage does not accord with that of some sociologists (see Gold, 1957) who reserve the adjective "quantitative" for equal-interval data and designate as "qualitative" all nominal and ordinal data. As a matter of fact, our analysis revealed that 73 per cent of the studies in

1940–41 and 93 per cent of the studies in 1965–66 used nominal or ordinal data interviewed by Mihailo Popovich (1966).

5. Stuart Chapin (1940) conducted a projective experimental study. However, even this study deviated from the classical experimental paradigm in that Chapin himself did not manipulate the experimental condition and lacked control over the assignment of cases to his "experimental" and "control" groups. In addition to Chapin's research, two ex post facto studies were published in the *American Sociological Review* in 1940. Most of the research papers examined proved to be either correlational in form, interrelating various characteristics of individuals or of collectivities, or cross-sectional in design, comparing the responses or characteristics of various categories or groups (such as men vs. women, Negroes vs. whites, scientists from major universities vs. those from minor universities, managers vs. entrepreneurs, agrarian communities vs. industrial communities, etc.).

6. Conrad (1952), in a systematic analysis of research in the area of the sociology of education from 1940 to 1950, noted the absence of a variety of research methods, such as observational or experimental studies, and the strong reliance on opinion questionnaires.

7. Conrad (1952) noted that only 1 of 16 articles on the sociology of education published in the *American Sociological Review* during the period 1940–51 stated and tested a hypothesis.

8. Riley (1964) distinguishes between two modes of analysis for this set of studies, the "contextual," which focuses on the individual, and the "structural," which focuses on the group. In attempting to apply her analytical scheme, the present investigators ran into difficulties. It was often next to impossible to determine which was the focus, individual or group. To us it often seemed that the focus was the relation itself.

9. Bruyn (1966) has faced up admirably to the problem of the theoretical implications of the method of participant observation. Similar analyses are needed for other methods.

REFERENCES

BROADUS, R. N. 1952. "An analysis of literature cited in the American Sociological Review." *American Sociological Review* 17 (June):355–357.

———— 1967. "A citation study for sociology." *American Sociologist* 2 (February):19–20.

BRUYN, SEVERYN T. 1966. *The Human Perspective in Sociology.* Englewood Cliffs, N.J.: Prentice-Hall.

CHAPIN, F. S. 1940. "An experiment on the social effects of good housing." *American Sociological Review* 5 (December):868–879.

CONRAD, R. 1952. "A systematic analysis of current researches in the sociology of education." *American Sociological Review* 17 (June):351–355.

CRANE, D. 1965. "Scientists at major and minor universities: a study of productivity and recognition." *American Sociological Review* 30 (October): 699–714.

GOLD, D. 1957. "A note on statistical analysis in the American Sociological Review." *American Sociological Review* 22 (June):332–333.

LIEBERSON, S., and A. R. SILVERMAN. 1965. "The precipitants and underlying conditions of race riots." *American Sociological Review* 30 (December): 887–898.

OROMANER, M. J. 1968. "The most cited sociologists: an analysis of introductory text citations." *American Sociologist* 3 (May):124–126.

POPOVICH, M. 1966. "What the American sociologists think about their science and its problems." *American Sociologist* 1 (May):133–135.

RILEY, M. W. 1964. "Sources and types of sociological data." Pp. 978–1026 in Robert E. L. Faris (ed.), *Handbook of Modern Sociology*. Chicago: Rand McNally.

SCHELLENBERG, J. A. 1957. "Divisions of general sociology." *American Sociological Review* 22 (December):660–663.

SCHWARTZ, M., and S. S. TANGRI. 1965. "A note on self-concept as an insulator against delinquency." *American Sociological Review* 20 (December): 922–926.

TAUSKY, C., and R. DUBIN. 1965. "Career anchorage: managerial mobility motivations." *American Sociological Review* 30 (October):725–735.

WILLIAMS, R. M., Jr. 1958. "Continuity and change in sociological study." *American Sociological Review* 33 (December):619–633.

SUGGESTED READINGS

HAMMOND, PHILLIP E., ed. *Sociologists at Work: Essays on the Craft of Social Research*. New York: Basic Books, 1964.

KAPLAN, ABRAHAM. *The Conduct of Inquiry*, Chapters 1–4. San Francisco: Chandler Publishing Co., 1964.

LAZARSFELD, PAUL F. *Qualitative Analysis: Historical and Critical Essays*. Boston: Allyn and Bacon, 1972.

MADGE, JOHN. *The Origins of Scientific Sociology*. New York: The Free Press, 1962.

REYNOLDS, LARRY T., and REYNOLDS, JANICE M., eds. *The Sociology of Sociology*. New York: David McKay Co., 1970.

■ The sources of data that are available to social scientists are numerous
and varied. Perhaps the most important distinction that can be made in
this context is that between primary and secondary sources. "Primary
data" refers to information that is collected primarily for the original
researcher's own research objectives; "secondary data" is information
that was collected by others for purposes that were invariably different
from those of the secondary researcher. Secondary data may have
originated from other researchers for the primary purpose of answering
social science questions and are usually very similar to primary data.
However, in many instances secondary data stem from nonscientific
sources (for example, transcripts of court hearings, school records,
among others).

The primary data collection techniques that have been traditionally used
in social research are of two major types: observation of behavior, and
questioning of respondents. "Behavioral observation" refers to procedures
for the *direct* observation and recording by trained observers of behavior
in specified social situations. The social settings can be natural ones
(for example, P.T.A. meetings, football crowds, or classrooms) or artificial
ones (such as small groups in a laboratory setting). Questioning of
respondents involves either *interviews* (a verbal exchange between a
respondent and interrogator) or *questionnaires* (a subject recording his
own responses to series of questions).

Three major types of secondary data are: (1) previous social science
research, (2) societal records, and (3) communication media. Material from
previous social science research is readily available from "data banks"
(facilities housing large volumes of data) and provides a major source of
inexpensive and relatively good quality data for the contemporary
researcher. "Societal records" refers to written records of various public
and private organizations, agencies, and institutions. Major sources of
such data have been the U.S. Bureau of the Census, police and court
records, marriage license applications, voting records, school records, and
membership directories of banks, corporations, and other business
concerns.

"Communication media" refers to sources that are used to communicate
ideas, thoughts, descriptions of events, and so forth, to others. If such
transactions are recorded in one form or another they can be used as a
source of data. Communication media on an intimate scale (that is, the
involvement of only a few people) are referred to as "personal documents"
(letters and diaries, for example). For the most part, personal documents
are rarely used in contemporary sociological research. Transmission to
large numbers of people is called "mass media" and is used with far
greater frequency than personal documents. Mass media includes, among
other things, books, magazines, newspapers, and television.

In the first article of this section Feest utilizes direct observation of
behavior to explore some aspects of normative behavior. Schuman and
Mercer and Butler address themselves to various issues and problems of
questioning techniques. Schuman suggests a technique for validation of
close-ended questions. The problem of respondent cooperation is explored
in the Mercer and Butler article. Secondary analyses of three previous
social science surveys are utilized by Hyman and Reed to research the

issue of the relative likelihood of matriarchy among blacks and whites. The "accuracy" of the U.S. Census and National Vital Statistics is investigated in the article by Farley. Schwartz and Miller provide an example of previous social science research (ethnographic reports) and at the same time give us some indication of the kinds of problems involved in doing cross-cultural research. Books that report statistics on baseball may not seem a likely source of social science data, but Grusky illustrates that the richness of a data source depends upon the imagination and resourcefulness of the researcher. The final article in this section, by Donley and Winter, uses as its data source materials from communication media.

The data sources employed in the remaining papers in this reader are listed in the following table:

Data Source	Paper Numbers
Behavioral observation	15, 22, 25
Interviews or questionnaires	11, 12, 13, 14, 19, 23
Societal records	16, 17, 20, 21
Communication media	2, 18, 24

Compliance with Legal Regulations:
Observation of Stop Sign Behavior
JOHANNES FEEST

A good portion of sociological research has been primarily concerned with such mental phenomena as attitudes, opinions, values, beliefs, ideas, and so forth. One reason for this may be that it is often easier to utilize verbal responses that have been collected with interviews or questionnaires than it is to analyze observed behavior. However, whatever the reasons for this tendency, there is little question that the bulk of sociological data relates more to mental phenomena than to behavior (see Brown and Gilmartin, article 2). This state of affairs raises many important questions about what sociologists are actually studying, rather than about what they say they are studying. There are many who view sociology as the study of behavior and as a consequence believe that sociological data should be concerned more with behavior than with the mental states of research subjects.

In researching behavior, usually only two approaches can be used. Either one can ask the respondent to act as his own observer, recounting past events (by asking such questions as: Did you vote? Have you ever taken anything of value?, for example), or one can directly observe the behavior of others. The latter strategy has many advantages. For one, it avoids the problems of selective recall on the part of the respondent. Secondly, if the researcher remains "hidden" it reduces the likelihood that the research subject will alter his behavior as a direct result of the data collection process. However, in many instances direct behavioral observation cannot be employed and alternative means must be used. These include, for example, instances of past behavior and situations where it is difficult or impossible to gain access (bedrooms, executive sessions of decision-making bodies).

The Feest study provides an illustration of direct behavioral observation in a natural setting (as contrasted to a small group laboratory) where the researcher successfully remains hidden from the research subjects. Although the behavior being investigated is of a relatively simple nature (drivers stopping at stop signs), the problems of connecting the observations to the theoretical issue of "conformity to legal norms" are far from simple.

THEORETICAL FRAMEWORK

ASSESSING THE IMPACT OF LEGAL REGULATIONS   There is an age-old controversy over the relative importance and feasibility of formal and informal controls of human behavior. One body of theory, most notably the Sumner tradition, has held that control by formal laws is unimportant and dependent compared to controls by other means: "Acts of legislation come out of the mores. . . . Things which have been in the mores are put under police regulation and later under positive law. . . . The regu-

Reprinted from *Law and Society Review* 2 (1968), 447–461, with permission of the Law and Society Association.

lations must conform to the mores, so that the public will not think them too lax or too strict."[1]

Others have argued, that formal law can and does increasingly become an agent of social control. Gunnar Myrdal has voiced "grave scepticism" toward Sumner's approach[2] and Edwin Lemert has contrasted Sumner's "passive" social controls with "active" social control.[3] There have been, however, relatively few attempts to discover the actual impact of formal legal regulations.[4] The main reason for this seems to be that it is extremely difficult to assess the net impact of such regulations. In most everyday life situations, legal norms carry a social stigma, *i.e.*, they are paralleled and backed by nonlegal norms. But there are also certain legal regulations which carry little or no such social stigma. As a consequence they are backed only or at least mainly by legal sanctions. Their violation has been labeled "folk crime," which includes all "illegal acts which are not stigmatized by the public as criminal."[5] Typically, these are regulations of technical character and recent origin. Examples are: traffic violations, white collar crimes, and chiseling in unemployment compensation. The regulations that "create" folk crime have not yet received an overall name. Because of their supposed lack of social stigma, I will refer to them as "unstigmatic" regulations. Unstigmatic regulations offer a chance to measure the effect which formal legal regulations per se have on human behavior.

COMPLIANCE WITH LEGAL REGULATIONS   Compliance, as it is understood here, is more than outward conformity with a regulation. Behavior which externally (objectively) conforms with a certain regulation may not coincide with internal (subjective) intention to conform. In performing the prescribed behavior, the actor may not be aware of the existence of the regulation, or he may be forced to conform for reasons that have nothing to do with the norm or its sanctions. The concept of compliance has, therefore, three essential elements: (a) norm-awareness, (b) intention to conform, and (c) conforming behavior.

Norm-awareness cannot always be assumed to exist. Especially at times when the law is constantly changing, many people will not know of the existence and/or the content of a particular regulation. Norm-awareness can, however, be assumed in the case of self-explicatory signs, announcing the content of the regulation. With respect to the intention to conform, two reasons can be distinguished: the actor may have internalized the norm (compliance for its own sake) or he may fear sanctions (enforced compliance). Both are included in the concept of compliance as it is used here. There will be a few remarks on the special problems of enforced compliance at the end of this paper.

OBSERVATION OF STOP SIGN BEHAVIOR   Of the many possible unstigmatic regulations, I have selected stop signs for study. They are easily observable and quite self-explicatory. The language of the sign is simply and unambiguously "Stop," and frequently a white line indicates where to perform the required act. In California, where I made the observations for this study,[6] the relevant legal regulation is the California Vehicle Code Section 22450. All California drivers must have come across the pamphlet *California Vehicle Code Summary*, since it is distributed to everybody who wants to take the driver's examination.[7] In three different paragraphs of this pamphlet, the driver is told to bring his car to a "full stop back of the limit line."

I have distinguished above between compliance and conformity. As an observer, however, I had to use conformity as an indicator for compliance.[8] But I tried to make this indicator more sensitive by excluding some typical cases in which norm-awareness or the intention to conform are highly doubtful. With respect to stop signs such cases are:

1. *Stopping during cross traffic.* In such a case, it is unclear whether the regulation or the perceived "impossibility" to proceed makes the driver stop. I have excluded all cars that stopped or slowed down during cross traffic (*i.e.,* all cars that let cross traffic cars pass before they themselves proceeded). This method has one shortcoming: it may exclude cars driven by overcautious drivers, who stop and wait until finally cross traffic appears. The number of strict conformers will be slightly reduced by this method.

2. *Stopping for staying.* Some people stop at stop signs in order to stay there rather than to cross the intersection. They are usually easy to distinguish from the true compliers, and can be excluded from the sample.

3. *No stopping because stop sign has been overlooked.* This is much harder to distinguish. I saw only one case where the observable evidence could be most easily interpreted that way (relatively high speed; near collision with cross traffic; double check and slow proceeding).

The most severe limitations of the so specified indicator of conformity are the following two:

1. Some people may slow down or stop neither because of the sign nor because of actual cross traffic, but because they anticipate cross traffic. The ideal research design would be the following: to observe the patterns of behavior before and after the regulatory sign has been installed. This turned out to be impossible in the present study because the Berkeley Department of Public Works informed me that no new stop signs were to be installed during this period.

2. Although the stop sign regulation is extremely clear, there may still be differential perceptions or interpretations as to what the norm prescribes. The people who violate the strict official interpretation of the norm may, in doing so, comply with a less strict interpretation which they regard as the relevant one. This limitation is, however, less damaging for my present purposes, since I am interested in the amount of compliance with the regulation-as-announced. More important is a variation of this same limitation: some drivers may experience their maneuver as a full stop. This possibility cannot be excluded, and will again reduce the number of observed compliers.

PRESENTATION OF FINDINGS

The only empirical data on stop sign behavior published to date were published in 1934 by Floyd H. Allport in a paper on conforming behavior.[9] These data have been reprinted in at least one major textbook as an example for the generalization that "the majority of persons conform to the prescribed standard and that small deviations are more frequent than large deviations. This generalization appears to hold true for many kinds of social behavior."[10] Whatever may be true for other kinds of social behavior, this generalization is not supported by the data gathered here for stop sign behavior, if we separate cross traffic from other sorts of traffic. Table 1 compares Allport's data

TABLE 1. Cross Traffic and Stop Sign Behavior

	Type of Traffic Included			
	Cross Traffic Only		Total Traffic Including Cross Traffic	Total Traffic Excluding Cross Traffic
Type of Stop	Allport %	Feest %	Feest %	Feest %
Full stop (Stop)*	75.5	78	34	15
Rolling stop (Very slow)	22.0	21	47	58
Half stop (Slightly slow)	2.0	1	16	22
No stop (Same speed)	0.5	0	3	5
N	2114	72	241	169

* The categories in parentheses are Allport's.

with equivalent data from my sample. He used only such cases "where there was traffic coming at right angles to the direction of travel of the motorists concerned; so that a double incentive to stop was presented in the possibility of a collision and the presence of the stop sign."[11] Such a procedure, as I have discussed above, obscures completely the subjective side of the compliance with a norm. The conformity figures will rise and fall with the amount of cross traffic. When I follow Allport's procedure of data collection (Column 2), my results are strikingly similar to his. But when I use my own procedure, compliance with the norm (i.e., a full stop in the absence of cross traffic) goes down from 78 per cent to 15 per cent.

My complete data on compliance, i.e., with cross traffic always excluded, are shown in Table 2. Table 2 shows that 14 per cent of the observed drivers bring their cars to a full stop without being forced to do so by cross traffic (i.e., regardless of whether the driver makes a right or left turn or whether he goes straight on). The type of crossing makes a difference only when the car is not brought to a full stop. Left turners are least likely and right turners are most likely to make a half stop or no stop at all. This can presumably be explained by the fact that such maneuvers are most risky in left turns and least risky in right turns. An additional factor may be the California Vehicle Code Section 21453 which permits right turns against red lights. I think that these variations can be seen quite independently from compliance or non-compliance with the stop regulation. It is not surprising that the number of stop violators goes up in locations with a good range of vision (field of sight). It is also more puzzling

TABLE 2. Stop Sign Behavior at Three Berkeley Stop Signs

	Location of Stop Sign			Type of Crossing			
Type of Stop	Russell & Ellsworth %	Rose & Shattuck %	Russell & Adeline %	Left Turn %	Straight On %	Right Turn %	Grand Total %
Full stop	11	15	20	16	14	14	14
Rolling stop	72	50	50	75	63	46	62
Half stop	16	28	25	9	19	32	21
No stop	1	8	4	—	8	8	4
N	227	99	68	68	246	77	391

that the number of strict compliers varies directly with range of vision: from 11 per cent at Russell and Ellsworth (smallest range of vision) to 20 per cent at Russell and Adeline (widest range of vision). But I think the explanation is as follows: In order to see into the cross street at Russell and Ellsworth one has to proceed deeply into the intersection, while at Russell and Adeline one can get a fairly good view into the cross street right from the stop sign (see Appendix).

I expected lower compliance during the night hours, because the drivers might feel less observed and inhibited by official and unofficial law enforcers. This turned out to be only partly true (see Table 3): the number

TABLE 3. Stop Sign Behavior: Day and Night; Accompanied and Single

	Day			Night			Total	
Type of Stop	Single %	Accom-panied %	Total %	Single %	Accom-panied %	Total %	Single %	Accom-panied %
Full stop	9	20	13	17	24	20	10	21
Rolling stop	70	62	66	48	41	45	66	57
Half and no stop	22	18	21	36	35	35	24	22
N	227	84	311	48	29	77	275	113

of half stops and no stops goes up, but so does the number of full stops (Columns 3 and 6). I tried to reduce the latter phenomenon to the different composition of the population of nightly drivers. Night drivers are more likely than day drivers to be young, male, and accompanied, but neither of these differences explains the decrease in compliance. My best guess is that at night the cautious are even more cautious and the daring even more daring.

Much clearer results derive from a comparison of single and accompanied drivers: Accompanied drivers are consistently more norm-abiding than unaccompanied ones. This can be interpreted as a measure of social pressure, and it could show that the stop regulation is not purely unstigmatic. The difference between single and accompanied drivers is more marked during daytime than at night. This again seems to indicate that there are factors operating at night that do not show up in this analysis. Because of this, and because of the relatively small number of night cases, I have excluded the nightly stop sign behavior from the following tabulations. Since, on the other hand, the single-accompanied distinction seems to yield fruitful results, I have retained it throughout the following tables. Official statistics have often been quoted to the effect that the Negro crime rate is higher than that of whites. One of the exceptions to this rule is drunken driving, where whites predominate, but with respect to all other traffic regulations Negroes are supposed to be more often delinquent than whites.[12] But official statistics refer only to the number of arrests and convictions, not to the number of actual violations. Our data indicate that whites predominate among the stop sign offenders. Table 4 shows that

TABLE 4. Stop Sign Behavior by Race and SES

	Low SES*			High SES			Total	
	(1) Negro %	(2) White %	(3) Total %	(4) Negro %	(5) White %	(6) Total %	Negro %	White %
Type of Stop								
Full stop	30	12	18	4	11	10	15	11
Rolling stop	65	74	71	76	63	64	72	66
Half stop and no stop	5	14	11	20	26	26	13	23
N	20	42	62	25	199	224	46	268

* Indicated by cars which I classified as "old."

23 per cent of whites and only 13 per cent Negroes are in clear violation of the norm. If that is true not only for Berkeley but for the United States, and if the official statistics are correct, this could only be interpreted as a case of differential law enforcement along racial lines. In accordance with previous studies,[13] Table 4 indicates that "folk criminality" is associated with high rather than with low social standing (Columns 3 and 6).

Wholesale compliance was observed by 18 per cent of drivers with low socioeconomic status as opposed to only 10 per cent of those with higher status. There is a question whether the relationship between race and compliance can be reduced to one between class and compliance. Table 4 offers no clear evidence on that point. With respect to Negroes, the factor class makes a big difference: while only 4 per cent with high SES show strict compliance, the percentage for those with low SES is 30. With respect to whites the factor class does not seem to make much of a difference: strict compliance of those with old cars is about as frequent as of those with new cars. This could be interpreted to mean that class makes a difference only with respect to Negroes: one could speculate about "ritualism" on the part of lower class Negroes, and about "successful integration" on the part of middle class Negroes. But I am more inclined to think that the age-of-car indicator for social class, valid as it may be for Negroes, is quite misleading among whites in Berkeley. There are not too many lower class whites in Berkeley, but there are many middle class students with old cars. The relationship between race and compliance is modified considerably by introduction of the single-accompanied variable. It turns out that social pressure (as distinct from legal pressure) makes a considerable difference for Negroes while it hardly makes any difference for whites (see Table 5). This lends some empirical support to my assumption

TABLE 5. Stop Sign Behavior by Race and Social Pressure

	Single		Accompanied		Total	
Type of Stop	Negro %	White %	Negro %	White %	Negro %	White %
Full stop	0	10	41	13	15	11
Rolling stop	87	68	53	66	75	67
Half stop and no stop	13	22	7	21	11	22
N	30	194	17	70	47	264

that stop signs are unstigmatic norms; at the same time the assumption is shown to be correct for whites only.

Table 6 shows that women consistently comply more strictly with the

TABLE 6. Stop Sign Behavior by Sex and Social Pressure

	Single		Accompanied		Total	
Type of Stop	Male %	Female %	Male %	Female %	Male %	Female %
Full stop	6	12	18	25	9	16
Rolling stop	73	65	60	63	70	64
Half stop and no stop	21	23	22	12	21	20
N	130	96	50	40	180	136

legal regulation than men do. Social pressure (indicated by the single-accompanied variable) seems to have about the same influence on men as it has on women as far as strict compliance is concerned.

Table 7 shows that the age of the driver consistently makes a difference with respect to compliance. The youngest and the oldest drivers are more likely than others to comply strictly with the stop regulation. At the same time, however, we find a positive relationship between age and the clearer types of violation. One can speculate that age indicates two quite different things; on the one hand younger people may be more daring, on the other hand they have learned the legal norm more recently and may not yet have reinterpreted it. This would seem to be confirmed by the breakdown in single and accompanied drivers. Single drivers under thirty are much more likely than accompanied ones to go through stop signs. There is no difference for older drivers in this respect.

TABLE 7. Stop Sign Behavior by Age of Driver and Social Pressure

	Single			Accompanied			Total		
Type of Stop	-30 %	35-55 %	60- %	-30 %	35-55 %	60- %	-30 %	35-55 %	60- %
Full stop	11	6	16	29	18	(17)	17	9	16
Rolling stop	59	74	64	54	61	(75)	57	70	68
Half stop and no stop	30	19	20	18	20	(8)	26	20	16
N	54	144	25	28	49	12	82	193	57

SUMMARY   The data presented above indicate that the number of people who strictly comply with the formal legal regulation is about 15 per cent. This figure is subject to some variation relative to time, place, and the type of people involved.

It seems likely that the number of strict compliers is slightly higher than the data would indicate. . . . But the fact that more than four-fifths of the people observed violate the legal norm (in its strict, official interpretation) is certainly striking. We have to consider, however, two things:

1. The official enforcement of stop sign regulations appears to be rather lax in Berkeley.[14] The police, more concerned with speeding, apparently cite stop sign violators mainly in connection with other violations, and particularly as a result of accidents.

2. The data indicate, that most people (62 per cent) make a rolling stop, and one can very well argue that the "living law" permits this type of behavior. This would bring the number of people who comply, to some extent, with the law to 76 per cent (79 per cent during daytime). Only 4 per cent (2 per cent during daytime) go through stop signs in a truly reckless manner ("No Stop"). While this may be reassuring, it does not invalidate my findings which are concerned with the regulation as it is announced and reiterated, rather than with the "living law."

ON THE GENERALIZABILITY
OF THE REPORTED DATA

The data presented in this paper can hardly be generalized even for Berkeley, since they stem from observation of only three arbitrarily chosen intersections. But how far could data of this kind be generalized if their reliability were beyond doubt? Three factors seem to make generalizations even to other "folk crimes" difficult and hazardous:

1. We have already mentioned the problem of enforcement. This is of particular importance for unstigmatic norms as the one here under consideration. Clearly, our results cannot be generalized to regulations that are more strongly enforced. For the purposes of generalization and comparison it will be necessary to devise some sort of "enforcement coefficient."[15]

2. Another decisive variable is norm-awareness. With respect to stop signs, we have assumed that knowledge of the regulation is relatively high. This is certainly true in the sense that the norm is clearly announced and propagated. Our results cannot be generalized to norms where this is not the case. On the other hand, I suspect that even very clearly announced regulations can be reinterpreted or misinterpreted by those to whom they apply if enforcement is lax.

3. The last factor is the perceived reasonableness of the norm. Our data indicate that most drivers regard the strict version of the stop regulation as unreasonable. In order to see whether there is any danger, the driver has to proceed into the intersection, and if there is no visible danger, there is no good reason to stop. The perceived unreasonableness is more marked in locations where the limit line is drawn too far back, and the driver's field of vision is very limited (see Table 2).

Widespread violation is less likely in the case of norms that have all the trappings of reasonableness. In order to be able to generalize from our results to other types of folk crime, we would have to know how reasonable the different norms are supposed to be from the point of view of a certain population.

APPENDIX

Collection of Data

1. Time and Places of Observation
Stop sign behavior was observed at three stop signs in Berkeley:
a. Shattuck and Rose

2/13/67	11:30 a.m.–12:30 p.m.
2/13/67	3:30 p.m.– 4:30 p.m.
2/16/67	midnight
2/17/67	midnight

b. Russell and Adeline

2/27/67	3:00 p.m.– 5:00 p.m.
2/27/67	9:00 p.m.–10:00 p.m.

c. Russell and Ellsworth

3/2/67	9:00 a.m.–11:00 a.m.
3/2/67	2:15 p.m.– 4:15 p.m.
3/6/67	9:00 a.m.–12:00 p.m.
3/6/67	5:30 p.m.– 6:30 p.m.
3/8/67	9:30 p.m.–10:00 p.m.

2. Recording of Observations
I recorded the following informations on the cars that passed the stop signs under observation:
a. Type of car
b. Estimated age of car: old (ten years and older); middle; new (last two to three years)
c. Sex of driver
d. Race: Caucasian, Negro, Oriental
e. Estimated age: 20, 25, 30

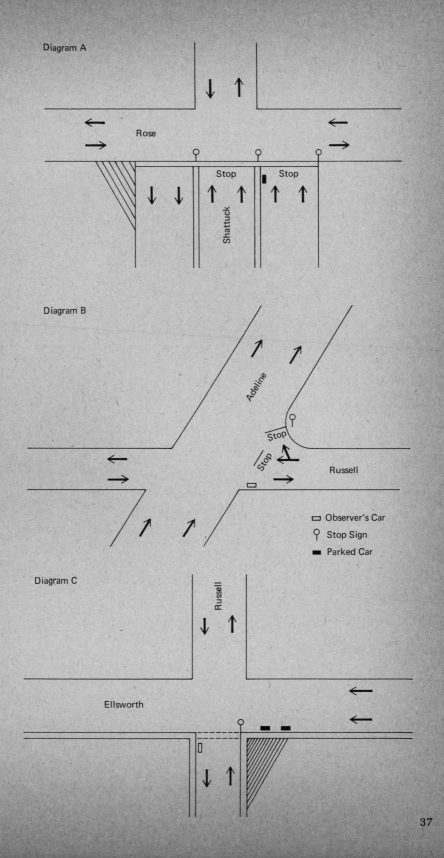

Diagram A

Rose

Stop   Stop

Shattuck

Diagram B

Adeline

Stop

Stop

Russell

⬜ Observer's Car
♀ Stop Sign
▬ Parked Car

Diagram C

Russell

Ellsworth

37

f. Single/accompanied

g. Type of stop (see below, 3)

h. Type of crossing intersection: left turn, straight on, right turn

3. Types of Stop

The police brochure *Required Stops*[16] defines "Stop" as "cessation of all forward motion." "A cessation of forward movement even though it is momentary will satisfy the legal requirements." The brochure advises police officers to watch the wheels of the vehicle: "If they do not cease their motion at any time, your testimony to this effect will usually be sufficient."[17]

The brochure lists 5 types of "stops":

a. Complete stop. Vehicle comes to a full stop before proceeding.

b. Rolling stop, in which the vehicle goes through the stop zone at 2–10 mph.

c. Half stop, in which vehicle slows but goes through stop zone at 10–20 mph.

d. No stop. Vehicle does not slow but continues on through the stop zone at a constant rate.

e. Over speed limit. Vehicle goes through stop zone in excess of the speed limit.[18]

4. Sampling

a. Cars

I have attempted to observe and report the stop sign behavior of all cars that passed the sign during the time of observation. This was not always possible, e.g., when more than one car approached the intersection. In such cases, I made it a rule to take the first one, and to disregard all others until I had finished recording the information on it. At one point, I tried to replace this somewhat unsystematic procedure by recording only every third car. This worked well, but I dropped it because it took too much time.

b. Intersections

I did not sample intersections. The three intersections which I observed were chosen for the following reasons: Rose and Shattuck because it gives the driver a relatively wide range of vision (field of sight); Ellsworth and Russell, since it gives the driver relatively little range of vision; Russell and Adeline, to make up for the total lack of Negroes at Rose and Shattuck.

5. Unobtrusiveness

Ideally, one should presumably stay at some distance from the stop sign and use binoculars. I observed the cars from within my own car which I had parked near the stop sign. I do not think, however, that my approach was in any way obtrusive, since I was just another person sitting in a parked car. The only "danger" was to come into eye-contact with the approaching drivers. This can, however, be avoided by choosing a good location (see maps of intersections, Diagrams A, B, and C, on page 37).

NOTES

1. W. G. Sumner, Folkways 55 (1906).

2. G. Myrdal, An American Dilemma 1031ff., 1048ff. (1964).

3. E. Lemert, *Social Structure, Social Control, and Deviation,* in Anomie and Deviant Behavior 88ff. (M. B. Clinard ed. 1964). *See also The Folkways and Social Control,* 7 Am. Sociological Rev. 394–99 (1942).

4. Recently, interesting attempts have been made by so-called legal "impact studies" along quasi-experimental lines. These studies involve the comparison between actual behavior patterns in jurisdictions having a certain law, and the behavior patterns which would have existed in those same jurisdictions had the law in question never been enacted. The main flaw in the ingenious research designs developed is that they rely mainly on official statistics. *See* R. Lempert, *Strategies of Research Design in the Legal Impact Study,* 1 L. & Soc'y Rev. 111ff. (Nov. 1966).

5. H. L. Ross, *Traffic Law Violations: A Folk Crime,* 8 Social Problems 232 (1961).

6. For details on the collection of data see Appendix.

7. Department of Motor Vehicles (ed.), 1966, at 54. Section 22450 reads:

The driver of any vehicle upon approaching any entrance of a highway or inter-section, or railroad grade crossing signposted with a stop sign provided in this code, except as otherwise permitted or denoted in this code, shall stop:
(a) At a limit line, if marked, otherwise before entering the crosswalk on the near side of the intersection or, if not, then before entering the highway or intersection.

Comparable regulations are assumed to exist in other states and thus, they are likely to be familiar to out-of-state drivers.

8. Another indicator, but again only an indicator, would be a statement of the actor as to whether he knew the norm and/or conformed voluntarily.

9. F. H. Allport, *The J-Curve Hypothesis of Conforming Behavior,* 5 J. Soc. Psych. 141–83 (1934). Quoted after the abridged version in Readings in Social Psychology, 55–67 (Newcomb *et al.,* eds. 1947).

10. G. A. Lundbert, *et al.,* Sociology 344 (1958).

11. F. H. Allport, *supra* note 9, at 57.

12. G. Myrdal, *supra* note 2, at 973.

13. *See* H. L. Ross, *supra* note 5, at 233.

14. Out of a total of 22,158 moving violations in Berkeley, which resulted in cita-tions during 1966, only 617 were stop sign violations.

15. Some such measures for traffic law enforcement have been devised by John A. Gardiner. As to the impact of enforcement, however, he claims that "while few empirical studies have been made on this point, there is some evidence that police enforcement rates have *no* influence whatsoever on the rate of traffic violations . . ." in Police Enforcement of Traffic Laws: A Comparative Analysis, Sept. 1966, at 17 (paper presented at the Annual Meeting of the American Politi-cal Science Association, New York).

Data Sources

16. Traffic Institute of Northwestern University, Required Stops (Traffic Law Enforcement Series, Pub. No. 2541, 1958).

17. *Id.* at 5.

18. *Id.* at 10.

QUESTIONS

1. Is the author interested in mental phenomena as well as in overt behavior? If he is, how does he attempt to use behavioral observations to make statements about mental phenomena? Can you construct alternative ways of researching the mental phenomena?
2. Two key terms utilized in this study are "compliance" and "conformity." How are they related to and used in the observational process? What research strategy did Feest employ to enhance the congruity between the two concepts? Can you conceive of other ways of dealing with this problem?
3. Are there other characteristics of the social situation (including the driver) that the author may have been able to observe and that would have been of some theoretical importance?
4. Discuss the problems that might have ensued if the drivers were aware that they were being studied.
5. Using the Feest research strategy as a model, attempt to construct your own research project of a behavioral situation involving adherence to a legal norm.

The Random Probe:
A Technique for Evaluating the
Validity of Closed Questions
HOWARD SCHUMAN

Questions constitute the building blocks of interviews and questionnaires, and as such they can be analyzed and discussed independently of how they are used (as in face-to-face interviews, self-administered questionnaires, and so forth). For example, it is possible to classify questions according to their degree of structuring. At one end of the spectrum are the "close-ended" questions calling for answers in the form of fixed alternatives (agree or disagree, yes or no, among others). On the other end are "open-ended" questions requiring the respondent to use his own discretion about what he decides to communicate to the researcher (for example, "If you have ever smoked

Reprinted from *American Sociological Review* 31 (1966), 218–222, with permission of The American Sociological Society.

marijuana, describe the circumstances of, and your reactions to, your first experience with marijuana").

As one can imagine there is some controversy over the relative merits of each type of question. The proponents of "close-ended" questions argue that they are easier and cheaper to administer, and are standardized, which allows for greater reliability. The critics of this type of question, on the other hand, contend that its validity is uncertain because the question does not necessarily have the same meaning for the respondent as it does for the researcher. "Open-ended" questions, they argue, provide the opportunity for the respondent to qualify his answers and thus give a more adequate indication of how he interprets the question.

Very often the debate is never settled because only in rare instances does either side bring evidence to bear on the issue. Instead, they are content simply to assume the correctness of their respective positions. In the following article Howard Schuman has proposed a technique for systematically evaluating the validity of close-ended questions, a technique that requires that randomly selected close-ended questions be explored or "probed" in greater depth.

■ Important sociological analysis is often based on a small number of "closed" survey questions.[1] To the survey analyst, and perhaps even more to the non-survey-oriented sociologist, doubts sometimes arise about whether a question carries the same meaning for respondents as for the social scientist who constructed it. This is particularly true when the respondents differ greatly from the investigator in education, cultural characteristics, or life chances. True, the process of analysis itself is intended to elucidate the sense of data, yet there is often a need on the part of both investigator and reader to hear the respondent's own voice, and this is doubtless an important reason why surveys make use of open-ended questions and why free responses often make up a significant part of survey reports.

As surveys are increasingly undertaken in non-Western countries the problem becomes both more salient and more important. Questions framed in English by middle-class American professors are translated into Bengali and put in formal fashion by educated and urbanized Pakistani students to illiterate peasants in East Pakistan. Is this a reasonable endeavor? The survey researcher, accustomed to being told "it can't be done," plunges ahead boldly, but even he at times must wonder whether his tables really mean what he thinks they mean. If he himself has wrestled with problems of translation, and realized the ease with which unwanted connotations are added and wanted connotations lost, he cannot help but be aware that wording can be equally meaningful to both parties without that meaning being shared.

One solution is to work largely with open-ended questions. But in addition to immense problems of translation and coding when large-scale surveys are involved, it is difficult to obtain sufficiently rich responses from individuals who are both uneducated and unused to expressing opinions. Moreover, the very variety of frames of reference produced by open-ended questions changes from asset to liability when one is attempting to classify all respondents in terms of single variables. Because of these difficulties, surveys continue to rely heavily on closed multiple-choice questions even in settings very different from the United States.[2]

In this paper I would like to suggest a simple technique for obtaining on a routine basis both qualitative and quantitative information on the meaningfulness and meaning of responses to closed survey questions. The approach is an obvious extension of interviewer probing, traditionally used in surveys to encourage more detailed answers to *open*-ended questions. Such probing has undoubtedly been used in pre-testing closed questions and perhaps has been tried in regular surveys; but it seems never to have been developed and applied systematically. The technique is direct and simple: each interviewer is required to carry out follow-up probes for a set of closed items *randomly* selected from the interview schedule for *each* of his respondents. The probe does not replace the regular closed question in any way, but follows immediately after the respondent's choice of an alternative. Using non-directive phrases, the interviewer simply asks the respondent to "explain a little" of what he had in mind in making his choice.[3] The recorded comments (or occasionally lack of comments) are used by the investigator to compare the intended purpose of the question and chosen alternative with its meaning as perceived and acted on by the respondent.

Both the randomization method and its usefulness will be illustrated by describing its application in a complex attitude survey of 1000 factory workers and cultivators in East Pakistan in 1964. In addition to background and open-ended questions, the schedule consisted of 200 closed and quasi-closed items, mostly in the form of two to four forced alternatives.[4] Each interviewer was given a list of these 200 questions and shown how to select by a chance method ten items from the list prior to each interview. He was to probe these ten questions *regardless* of the respondent's general or specific level of understanding. (Interviewers were also instructed to probe under certain other circumstances, but different symbols distinguished random from other probes.) The essence of the method is to obtain probe material on a *random* sample of the 200,000 closed responses expected in the survey.

The selection of ten questions per interview results in a sample of ten explanations by *each respondent,* and these can be evaluated to provide a measure of his ability to understand the questionnaire as a whole. From exactly the same item evaluations, we simultaneously obtain on the average fifty randomly probed responses for *each question;* working with these across individuals gives us an evaluation for each of the 200 items, indicative of how well *they* are understood.[5]

EVALUATING THE RANDOM
PROBES QUANTITATIVELY

The Pakistan random probe material has been evaluated question by question on a five-point scale by regular coders who first read the follow-up material blind, then used it to predict the respondent's original closed alternative, and finally evaluated the total "fit" between probe explanation and chosen alternative. The evaluation code, explanations, and point equivalents are shown below.

Code	Interpretation	Points
A	Explanation is quite clear and leads to accurate prediction of closed choice.	1
B	Explanation of marginal clarity and leads to accurate prediction of closed choice.	2
C	Explanation very unclear; cannot make any prediction about closed choice.	4
D	1. Explanation seems clear, but leads to wrong prediction of closed choice; 2. Respondent was unable to give any explanation of his closed choice ("don't know"); 3. Respondent in course of explanation shifted his closed choice away from original.	5
(R)	(Explanation is simply literal repetition of closed choice; cannot judge respondent's understanding of question.)	(omit)

The point gap between "B" and "C" reflects the fact that "B" is close to "A" in meaning and implication, while "C" points to an essentially unsatisfactory explanation. The symbol "R" really indicates inadequate probing by the interviewer, since rote repetition of a chosen alternative by the respondent does not allow us to judge his understanding one way or the other. Such repetitions are excluded from score computations, but a separate count of them can be kept for both individuals and questions. In general, the evaluation scheme is conservative: some of the responses coded "C" may be due to inadequate probing or translation, and some proportion of the responses coded "D" for incorrect prediction may actually have involved mis-check during the interview.[6]

To obtain quantitative indices, the numerical scores for separate responses are summed separately for each individual and for each question, and the sums are divided by the number of scorable probes available in each case. The resulting averages constitute 1000 individual probe scores and 200 question probe scores.[7] For the Pakistan survey, the reliability of the scoring was estimated by having the necessary responses reevaluated independently for a random sample of 30 individuals and a random sample of 30 questions. Product moment correlations of 0.75 and 0.92, respectively, were obtained, indicating satisfactory scoring reliabilities for both types of scores. The higher question reliability is due to the larger number of responses on which question scores are based.

Both individual and question scores can be interpreted directly in terms of the meanings used in the original evaluation procedure. For example, a mean score of 3, whether for an individual or for a question, indicates understanding half way between the "B" and "C" levels. If an individual score, it becomes a signal that the respondent probably had a generally low understanding. This supplements interviewer comments and ratings with a more objective measure of comprehension. But the more important warning is a high *question* probe score, for it suggests ambiguity, lack of clarity, or unintended meaning for the question over the entire sample.

This provides information not ordinarily obtained from interviewers, especially newly trained interviewers in developing countries.

In the Pakistan study the median question probe score is 1.4; 87 per cent of the closed questions have mean scores between 1.0 ("A" understanding) and 2.0 ("B" understanding). Thus most but not all of the questions fall within what would appear to be an acceptable range. On an individual basis, the median score is 1.4, and 87 per cent of the respondents average between 1.0 and 2.0. A small but significant minority of respondents thus seem to have real difficulties with the questions—not surprising for a sample with generally low education—although it should also be noted that within the sample the correlation between individual probe scores and schooling is trivial (-0.10), and between the same scores and a verbal aptitude measure the relation is not much greater (-0.23). There are a few individuals with such low scores as to suggest that they contribute mostly random error to the study (22 persons score 3.0 or greater), but to a considerable extent error seems to be concentrated in a few questions. Questions and individuals are inextricably related, of course, because the unit of analysis is the single response to a single question, but it is of some significance that more than half the responses rated "C" or "D" are concentrated in only one-fifth of the questions.

QUALITATIVE USE OF RANDOM PROBES

Formal numerical scoring provides only a rough index of the general value of an item. The qualitative understanding gained by reading 50 responses to a question offers a much richer source of information on the way the question was perceived and the meaning of the closed responses it evoked.[8] The kinds of elucidation provided will be illustrated by several examples from a set of questions on religion.

In the Pakistan study two questions were included to determine whether Islamic religious obligations are interpreted by various sample groups to include achievement-related effort as an end in itself. The answers to these questions show excellent variation, intercorrelate well, are significantly related to a number of background variables, and are relevant to an important hypothesis. But the random probes suggest that the questions were reasonably well understood by less than half the sample. Most respondents reinterpreted them in ways that had little to do with their original purpose. This question, with a mean probe score of 2.3, is an example:

Do you think that whether a man works diligently every day is:

1. An absolutely essential part of religion,
2. An important but not essential part of religion, or
3. Of little importance to religion.

A common interpretation is represented by the following probe response from a man who had chosen the first alternative: "My family depends on me. If there is no food and empty stomachs [because of laziness], then I cannot give attention to prayer." Respondents who chose the third alternative tended to give even more distant explanations, for example: "It is not good to work hard every day. It will ruin the health."

The minority of probed respondents (about two-fifths) who did appear to understand the question in the intended frame of reference (e.g., "Allah has written in the Koran that men should work hard each day") were more educated than average, as would be expected. For them the question can certainly be used. For the less educated in the sample, however, the question must at the very least be treated with caution, and empirical relationships discoverable with it should be subjected to special scrutiny before final interpretation is made. Indeed, some researchers may prefer to drop such a question altogether.

Quite the opposite type of case is provided by the following yes-or-no question, intended to determine whether ethical actions and religious actions are conceived as separable by certain of the groups studied:

Do you think a man can be truly good who has no religion at all?

When this question was first presented to local translators and interviewers, their reaction was unanimously negative. No ordinary man would understand the point of the question, they felt. Whatever might be the case among Westerners or among the university-educated, the average Pakistani Muslim would certainly see a non-religious man as by definition devoid of goodness. All agreed that the question could not lead to meaningful responses and should not be included.

It was included, however, and in fact produced about one-third "yes" and two-thirds "no" choices. But was the question perhaps misinterpreted in some way? The random probes indicate that understanding was very good indeed (mean score 1.1). A typical probe explanation for a "yes" response was: "He may not believe any religion, yet he can render good offices to the people of the land." Another man said: "He may be good and his heart may be very pure, and he can help people anyway." The "no" responses were also to the point: "The man who has no faith has no idea of good and bad, so he cannot be good." "The person who has no religion, what good thing may be in him? He is wretched." More generally, of the 52 probes to this question, only one was coded as confused. It therefore seems quite reasonable to interpret Pakistani response patterns for the question much as one would for ordinary Americans.

The two questions discussed thus far have shown the usefulness of random probe material in reaching decisions about the inclusion or exclusion of questions for analysis. But probably the greatest value of this additional material comes from making the analyst aware of subtle changes in meaning that have occurred between question formulation and tabular analysis. Usually it is not a case of rejecting a question, but rather of bringing into clearer focus the impact the wording had upon respondents and thus interpreting response patterns in a more accurate way.

The following forced-choice question, for example, was intended to contrast material striving with concern for more spiritual ideals:

Some people say that the more things a man possesses—like new clothes, furniture, and conveniences—the happier he is.

Others say that whatever material things a man may possess, his happiness depends upon something else beyond those.

What is your opinion?

This question produced a wide distribution of responses and was understood without difficulty. However, the Bengali phrase for "something else beyond those" was interpreted in a broader way than the limited religious idea conceived in constructing the question and attempted in translation. Those who chose the second alternative sometimes gave religious justification ("It depends upon God's blessing"), but even more frequently they gave other sensible non-material explanations for their responses:

Suppose a man has no child, whereas he has all other things; then he is not happy.

It depends on one's wife. If she is not good, one is not happy.

I may have much wealth but there are many enemies against me.

Clearly the question was well understood. But just as clearly it would be incorrect to use the question as a direct indicator of religious versus secular orientation. The probe material here helps the analyst to understand more precisely what it is he has measured—which is, after all, the final goal of "validity."

This last illustration also indicates why the quantitative evaluation described earlier must remain a relatively crude index. For each question that was not understood exactly as originally intended, it becomes a matter first of judgment and then of convention whether the question is being "misinterpreted" or simply differently interpreted. In practice the decision is seldom difficult, but occasionally a set of scores would be considerably altered had a different convention been established.

CONCLUSION

Through qualitative and quantitative review of random probe responses the survey researcher has an opportunity to increase his own sensitivity to what his questions mean to actual respondents, and thereby improve his comprehension of the resulting data. At the same time, quotations become available that can offer emotional insight into a table representing answers from people he and his readers are attempting to understand.

Of course, the addition of random probes to a survey is no panacea. It does not reduce the need for careful pre-testing, or solve the problems of survey analysis, but it is a simple, inexpensive, and natural way of obtaining valuable free response material on a systematic basis. In research in other cultures—and under some conditions in one's own culture—it forms a useful supplement to standard attitude survey methods.

NOTES

1. One among many examples is the use of a single question on aspirations in Alan B. Wilson, "Class Segregation and Aspirations of Youth," *American Sociological Review,* 24 (December, 1959), pp. 836–845. One solution to the problem discussed here leads of course toward scaling, but few exploratory cross-cultural surveys develop unidimensional or even adequately reliable Likert scales. More often the focus is on individual questions or on small sets of very modestly intercorrelated items. There are few "scales" in the sociological literature for which the problem raised here would not be relevant.

2. Cf., Gabriel A. Almond and S. Verba, *The Civic Culture,* Princeton University Press, 1963, p. 46, where approximately 90 per cent of the questions are closed. For a full discussion of the advantages of both open and closed questions, see P. F. Lazarsfeld, "The Controversy over Detailed Interviews—An Offer for Negotiations," reprinted in Daniel Katz *et al., Public Opinion and Propaganda,* The Dryden Press, 1954.

3. Phrases used by the interviewer are: "Would you give me an example of what you mean?"; "I see—why do you say that?"; "Could you tell me a little more about that?"; As with most probes, the exact wording is less important than the manner in which it is made. It is particularly important that the respondent's closed choice not seem challenged.

4. Not all of the questions probed were completely closed. Some required brief free replies which were highly constrained by the form of the question (e.g., "Generally, how often during a day do you pray?"). Still others involved quite free responses (e.g., ten sentence completion items). In these latter it also seemed desirable to obtain probe material on a random basis to clarify the sometimes cryptic patterns of answers. Such open and quasi-closed questions are involved in the random selection procedure but are generally excluded from the quantitative scoring to be discussed here. Scoring was applied to 175 questions.

5. To obtain similar follow-up qualitative information, Almond and Verba, *op. cit.,* reinterviewed in depth a 10 per cent sub-sample of their original survey respondents. Their method has the advantage of allowing construction of a stratified rather than simple random sample, thus insuring better representation for infrequent responses. On the other hand, it is very costly in time and money, and it may also lead to over-probing and to "second-thought" explanations rather different from those a respondent might have given in the original interview. Our method involves only slight additional costs in interviewing time and provides a more natural inflow of information for all questions and for all individuals.

6. The major limitation of the quantitative evaluation scheme is its inapplicability to subtle grades of intensity. In general, on items that ask a person not only to select among qualitatively different alternatives but also to indicate his strength of feeling, only the former can be evaluated readily from probe material. Thus a response is evaluated as "A" if it is spontaneously worded, clear in meaning, and correctly predicts the respondent's basic closed choice among two or more possibilities—even though his intensity of feeling cannot be predicted.

7. Since only ten out of two hundred responses were probed in each interview,

there is sampling error in the sense that a given individual may have been probed by chance on a particularly easy or difficult set of items. Sampling error by question is less, since 50 respondents were probed on each question. The number of questions probed is limited not only by cost of evaluation (the present ratio produced $10 \times 1000 = 10,000$ free responses) but also by the need to avoid questioning too frequently a respondent's choices.

8. In the Pakistan analysis, coders not only provided a score for each individual response but also wrote a brief holistic evaluation of each question on the basis of having read all fifty responses to it.

QUESTIONS

1. Schuman has described the application of the random probe for interview situations. Discuss the possibility and feasibility of using the procedure for self-administered questionnaires.
2. If a researcher were to take the time and effort to utilize the random probe procedure, why would he not probe every question for every respondent?
3. Are there any types of questions that could not be effectively evaluated by the random probe technique? If not, why? (See note 6 in article 4.)

Disengagement of the Aged Population and Response Differentials in Survey Research

JANE R. MERCER and EDGAR W. BUTLER

One of the necessary conditions for a successful interview is that the roles of interviewer and interviewee be played within certain limits. Perhaps the most basic consideration is that the participants must first *agree* to play their respective roles. Although there are times when an interviewer refuses to play his role, a more frequent and critical problem is the noncooperative interviewee. Every survey has its percentage of nonrespondents, and most researchers attempt to keep this figure as small as possible. Although various devices are employed to reduce the rate of nonparticipation, it is highly unlikely that the problem of the nonrespondent will be completely eliminated. Therefore, some attempt must be made to determine what differences of any consequence may exist between the respondent and the nonrespondent. For if there are

Reprinted from *Social Forces* 46 (1967), 89–96, with permission of The University of North Carolina Press.

differences of consequence, there is a strong possibility that the interview will be biased in critical ways.

In following article the authors attempt empirically to access possible differences between participants and nonparticipants. Even though they are primarily concerned with a specific population (persons over age fifty), the approach can be used with almost any population.

■ Cumming and Henry proposed the hypothesis that aging involves a gradual "disengagement" from many social systems both by decreasing the amount of interaction and by relinquishing some social roles altogether. When the disengagement process is complete, a new equilibrium is established characterized by greater social distance. This process will be manifested by changes in the number of persons habitually interacted with, by a reduction in the amount of interaction with those with whom he continues to interact, and by increasing preoccupation with the self.[1] Additionally, Cumming and Henry hypothesize a decrease in the intensity of interaction.

Since the most intense social interactions ordinarily take place within the family, the type of family structure can serve as one index of both extent and intensity of interaction. Other indices of social participation are the extent to which persons visit friends and co-workers (or if they work at all) and whether they participate in the life of the community.

Another measure of disengagement is willingness to engage in social interaction with representatives of the outside world, and it seems reasonable that disengaged older persons might resist the intrusion of a survey interviewer. Therefore, the possibility that older persons refusing to be interviewed might be more disengaged than those cooperating is explored in this paper.

It has been reported in the literature for field work in the United States and elsewhere that older persons are more likely to refuse to be interviewed than are younger persons.[2] When this differential exists, it raises two issues in interpretation. The first issue is estimating the extent of error produced by underrepresentation of older persons when the researcher is attempting to estimate the size of various aggregates. The second issue arises when an attempt is made to determine the nature of biases introduced by nonparticipation. The latter issue becomes central when a study is focusing specifically on an analysis of the aged population. For example, in a longitudinal study of the aging process using a sample of persons between the ages of 50 and 70, 17 percent of the respondents selected for study refused the initial interview.[3] While this rate of refusal is comparable with other studies, estimating the characteristics of the aged population becomes quite precarious when the refusal rate is this high if those who refuse are systematically different from those who cooperate. For these reasons, an intensive analysis of the characteristics of those who refused to participate in a sample survey was undertaken following the completion of field work in a study conducted in a southern California community.

METHOD

The sample for the field work consisted of 10.5 percent of the housing units of the city. The sample was stratified so that all geographic areas and socioeconomic levels of the community were represented proportionately. Field work, conducted in the summer of 1963, was preceded by newspaper publicity and a letter to each sample household describing the survey as a study of chronic handicaps with emphasis on mental retardation. Any member of the household, eighteen years of age or over, was acceptable as a respondent for facts about other household members related to him, although the spouse of the head was interviewed when a choice was available. Interviews averaged an hour and fifteen minutes in length. Socio-developmental information was gathered for every member of the household,[4] and interviews were completed in 90.7 percent of the approximately 3,000 occupied housing units.[5] Eighty-eight and one-half percent were interviewed with no refusals, and an additional 2.2 percent of the respondents were interviewed after refusing in a previous contact. However, 1.4 percent of the households were lost to the study because it was impossible to contact a qualified respondent and 7.9 percent were never interviewed because of refusal.

Interviewers were instructed to complete a report form for every refusal. This form recorded the estimated age, sex, and ethnic group of the respondent, respondent's reason for refusal, condition, type and size of the housing unit, family structure, and any other information gained from observation of the respondent. In addition, the city directory provided information on occupation, the United States Census provided information on the median value of housing on the block, voter registration rolls contained additional information on occupation as well as political affiliation and voting frequency. Power company rolls yielded length of residence data.[6]

FINDINGS

Refusals were compared with respondents who either granted an interview or an interview appointment on the first contact. The comparison group varies slightly from table to table depending upon availability of information.

ERRORS IN ESTIMATING AGGREGATES   Table 1 shows that the tendency to refuse to be interviewed increases with the age of respondents.[7] The refusal rate ranged from almost 16 percent for respondents between 60 and 69 years of age to a low of under 2 percent for respondents 16 to 19. This differential poses the problem of estimating the extent to which older persons will be underrepresented and younger persons will be overrepresented when estimates of aggregates by age are made from the sample. This question was approached empirically.

Using information about refusals gained from the reports of interviewers, the household composition by age was determined for 82 percent of the refusals. For the remaining 18 percent, household composition

TABLE 1. Age of Eligible Respondents and Willingness to Grant an Interview[a]

Age	Interviewed	Refusals	Total Respondents	Refusal Rate per 1,000
16–19	63	1	64	15.6
20–29	489	24	513	46.8
30–39	584	44	628	70.0
40–49	562	64	626	102.2
50–59	384	54	438	123.3
60–69	280	53	333	159.2
70–79	208	29	237	122.4
80 and over	56	9	65	138.5
Unknown	5	21	26	
Total	2631	299	2930	

[a] The t-test of differences between uncorrelated means was used. $p < .001$.

was estimated using the mean number of persons per household in that age group for the census block. This approach produced a very close approximation to the "actual" number of persons in each age group living in the households which refused to participate.

This actual number was then compared to the number of persons in each age group which would have been estimated as living in the households which refused if there had been no information available on actual composition. This estimate was based on the usual procedure of extrapolating from information gained about households in which an interview was completed to households on the same block in which the respondent refused to be interviewed. Again, the mean for cooperative households on each block was projected as the value for refusing households.

TABLE 2. Comparison of "Actual" Age Composition of Refusing Households with "Estimated" Age Composition Using the Mean of Interviewed Households on Each Block as Basis for Estimate

Age Composition	Actual Number in Ref. Hsehlds. (A)	Estim. Number in Ref. Hsehlds. (B)	Aggreg. Estimate Based on Actual Number (C)	Aggreg. Estimate Based on Mean Value (D)	% Error Based on Actual Number $\left(\dfrac{D-C}{C}\right)$
0–15	150.7	272.1	29,943	31,106	+3.88%
16–49	252.4	398.2	40,579	41,970	+3.43%
50 and over	235.7	182.8	18,927	18,421	−2.67%

The aggregate estimate was obtained by adding the actual number of persons in the refusing households in each age group and the estimated number of persons in the refusing households in each age group, respectively, to the total persons in each age group as found in the completed interviews and then multiplying by the sampling ratio of 9.53.

Table 2 shows that the actual number of children and middle-aged adults in the refusing households was less than would have been estimated using block means as the basis for allocation and the actual number of persons 50 years of age and older was more than would have been estimated. When the sample estimates are multiplied by the sampling ratio, 9.53, this produced two estimates of the total number of persons in each age group in the city. For persons under 15 years of age, the population estimate using "actual" knowledge of the household composition is 1,163 persons less than that which results from using the mean of households on the block in which interviews were completed as the basis for determining household composition of refusing households. This is an overrepresentation error of 3.88 percent. For persons 16 through 49 years of age, the comparable figure is 1,391, an overrepresentation error of 3.43 percent, and for persons 50 years of age and older, the difference is 506 individuals, an underrepresentation error of 2.67 percent.

Probably the most significant feature of these findings is due to the fact that households containing persons over 50 years of age are smaller in size. Therefore, failure to count such persons in the proper age category causes a smaller error than the complementary error of projecting the mean number of children and middle-aged adults per housing unit into refusing households because these younger cooperating persons tend to live in larger household units.

ERRORS IN ESTIMATING SOCIAL CHARACTERISTICS OF THE POPULATION   The second issue raised by higher rates of refusal is that of determining the characteristics of persons who refuse to participate in order to estimate systematic biases which may be introduced as a result of nonparticipation. In this analysis, therefore, focus was specifically on a comparison of persons over 50 who did and did not participate.

Socioeconomic characteristics of the refusing households in the older group were rated, using occupation of the head, median value of housing on the block, presence of a telephone, and condition of housing. Although older persons were significantly more likely to rate lower in socioeconomic level, socioeconomic characteristics did not differentiate refusing from cooperative respondents.[8] Negro and Mexican-American households were assigned to Negro and Mexican-American interviewers, and there was no difference in response rate by ethnic group. Also, the sex of the respondent was likewise found to be unrelated to the probability of refusing, as was length of residence in the community.

As shown in Table 3, refusers were more likely to come from households with no children. In addition, when refusers with children were compared to refusers without children, it was found that those without children were significantly more likely to refuse abruptly, allowing minimal contact, while those with children were more communicative when approached. Both results tend to support the hypothesis that refusers over 50 may be more disengaged than cooperative respondents over 50.

In addition, refusers were more likely to live in small housing units and in multiple family type units than were cooperatives. Since living in a small housing unit and multiple type dwelling is correlated with having no children, it may be that type of dwelling unit is not significant in its own right. However, since all persons studied were over 50 years of age and most of them have probably completed rearing their families, it is possible

TABLE 3. Family Structure and Housing Unit Characteristics of Persons 50 and
Over Comparing Cooperatives with Refusers

Variables	Cooperatives (N=928) Percent	Refusers (N=145) Percent	Significance Level[a]
Family Structure			
No Children Present	70.5	86.0	
Children Present	29.5	14.0	p < .01
Type Housing Unit			
Single Family Unit	86.2	74.5	
Multiple Type Unit	13.8	25.5	p < .01
Size Housing Unit			
1–3 Rooms	18.1	16.9	
4–5 Rooms	46.6	67.6	p < .01
6+ Rooms	35.3	15.5	

[a] The chi-square test of significance of difference between two independent samples was used.

that many of the older persons who lived in multiple family units have moved to them from former homes and neighborhoods. In such cases, residence in a multiple family unit could be evidence of disengagement from former neighborhood associations. In addition, multiple units have high occupancy turnover, a condition likely to produce anonymity and less involvement in a neighborhood social system. In this context, residence in a multiple family unit may be interpreted as an indirect measure of disengagement.

Table 4 presents information from the voting register on the extent of participation in the political life of the community for refusers and a random sample of 197 of the cooperatives. In addition to recording party affiliation and voting behavior, the register notes the number of petitions signed for the purpose of placing various propositions on the ballot. Contrary to the disengagement hypothesis, older persons were more likely to be registered voters and to sign petitions than persons under 50. Although a study done in France found refusers slightly less interested in politics than persons who responded favorably to survey research, Table 4 shows no difference between the level of political activity of persons refusing and persons cooperating.[9] Lowe and McCormick likewise found no association between refusing to be interviewed and voting in elections.[10]

Table 5 presents additional evidence on social participation. In this table, respondents are compared with persons who refused the first contact but later granted an interview, the only group for whom detailed social participation information was available. When persons 49 and under were compared with those 50 and over, older persons were less likely to have an occupational role, and less likely to be married and living with spouse. Furthermore, they were less likely to report frequent visits with friends and co-workers. On the other hand, frequency of visiting neighbors and relatives and of attending organizational meetings and religious activities was approximately the same for both age groups. This pattern of participation diminution is similar to that reported by Cumming

TABLE 4. Political Affiliation and Activity of a Sample of Cooperative Households and Refusing Households[a]

	49 and Under		50 and Over		Significance Level			
Variable	Cooperatives (N=118) Percent	Refusers (N=113) Percent	Cooperatives (N=79) Percent	Refusers (N=145) Percent	49 and Under vs. 50 and Over	Coop. vs. Ref.	49 and Under Coop. vs. Ref.	50 and Over Coop. vs. Ref.
Political Affiliation[b]								
Democrat	25.4	21.1	17.7	16.6				
Republican	17.8	24.1	40.5	35.9	p < .01	NS	NS	NS
Not Declared or Independent	5.9	5.3	7.6	9.0				
Not Registered	50.8	49.6	34.2	38.6				
Number of Petitions Signed by Head[c]								
0	73.7	76.7	51.9	59.3				
1-2	22.1	16.5	26.6	22.1	p < .01	NS	NS	NS
3 or More	4.2	6.8	21.5	18.6				
Total Registered Voters in Household[c]								
0	50.8	49.6	34.2	38.6				
1	8.5	15.0	24.1	19.3	p < .01	NS	NS	NS
2 or More	40.7	35.3	41.8	42.1				

[a] A pure random sample of 197 households from the completed interviews was selected for investigation of voting registration rolls because it was not feasible to investigate the registration for every household in the survey.

[b] The chi-square test of two independent samples was used.

[c] The Kolmogorov-Smirnov test of two independent samples was used.

TABLE 5. Social Participation of Respondents Who Were Cooperative When First Contacted with Respondents Who Refused the First Contact but Accepted the Second, Relative to Age Status[a]

Involvement	49 and Under		50 and Over		Significance Level[b]			
	Cooperatives (N=1698) Percent	Refusers (N=34) Percent	Cooperatives (N=928) Percent	Refusers (N=31) Percent	49 and Under vs. 50 and Over	Coop. vs. Ref.	49 and Under Coop. vs. Ref.	50 and Over Coop. vs. Ref.
Occupational Role								
Retired	0.0	0.0	29.8	35.5	p < .01	NS	NS	NS
Not Retired	100.0	100.0	70.2	64.5		NS	NS	NS
Marital Status								
Married, Living with Spouse	81.4	88.2	62.0	54.8	p < .001	NS	NS	NS
Single, Divorced, Separated, Widowed	18.6	11.8	38.0	45.2	p < .001	NS	NS	NS
Social Activities[c]								
Visit Friends	71.6	79.4	60.0	67.7	p < .001	NS	NS	NS
Visit Neighbors	66.4	73.5	59.7	48.4	NS	NS	NS	NS
Visit Relatives	45.2	41.2	39.9	45.2	NS	NS	NS	NS
Visit Co-workers	27.3	17.6	15.6	6.5	p < .001	NS	NS	NS
Attend Organizations	19.7	20.6	19.7	19.4	NS	NS	NS	NS
Religious Activities[c]								
Attend Church	43.3	41.2	42.0	48.4	NS	NS	NS	NS

[a] Age was unknown in 21 refusal cases and five cooperative cases.
[b] The chi-square test of two independent samples was used.
[c] Frequency of once a week or more.

and Henry who also found that occupational and marital role losses were the most prominent in the aging process.[11] However, there were no significant differences in social participation when cooperatives were compared with refusers.

TABLE 6. Role Count Index Comparing Respondents Who Were Cooperative When First Contacted with Respondents Who Refused the First Contact but Accepted the Second, Relative to Age

	49 and Under		50 and Over	
Role Count Index	Cooperatives (N=1698) Percent	Refusers (N=34) Percent	Cooperatives (N=928) Percent	Refusers (N=31) Percent
0	0	0	2.3	0
1	1.1	0	7.0	12.9
2	7.8	2.9	14.7	12.9
3	16.9	20.6	21.5	25.8
4	23.3	14.7	21.4	19.3
5	25.0	32.3	16.7	12.9
6	16.8	26.5	11.1	16.1
7	7.8	2.9	4.8	0
8	1.2	0	.4	0

49 and Under vs. 50 and Over, $p < .0001$ using Kolmogorov-Smirnov test.

Cooperatives vs. Refusers, Not Significant using Kolmogorov-Smirnov test.

49 and Under, Cooperatives vs. Refusers, Not Significant using Kolmogorov-Smirnov test.

50 and Over, Cooperatives vs. Refusers, Not Significant using Kolmogorov-Smirnov test.

In Table 6 the various indicators shown in Table 5 were combined into a role count index approximating that used in the Cumming and Henry study.[12] Each individual was given a score, ranging from zero to seven, based on the extent of social participation. Although persons over 50 participated significantly less than those under 50, the index did not differentiate cooperative respondents from those who refused to grant an interview on the first contact but later agreed to an interview. It may be that the individual who refuses at first but later agrees to participate is more like the respondent who is initially cooperative than the respondent who remains adamant in refusing. It is not possible to answer that question with the present data.

SUMMARY AND CONCLUSIONS

This paper fits into a disengagement framework the higher than usual refusal rates of older people in social surveys. Refusals by the aged are of concern on two accounts: the extent to which the higher refusal rate for persons over 50 biases estimates of population aggregates and the extent to which older persons who refuse to participate in survey research are systematically different from those who are cooperative.

It was shown that the underrepresentation of persons over 50 produced an estimate of 2.67 percent fewer persons in that age group than would have resulted if estimates were based on the actual number. Nevertheless, this error was smaller than the complementary error of overestimating the number of persons in the population under 50 years of age, an error of 3.88 percent for persons under 15 and an error of 3.43 percent for persons 16 to 49. This suggests that a correction factor for age bias should be used when precise estimates are needed.

Analysis of the extent to which older persons who refuse to participate in survey research are systematically different from those who cooperate revealed that refusers are more likely to live in households in which there are no children and in dwellings which are small, multiple type units. This finding tended to support the hypothesis that older persons who refuse may be more disengaged than those who cooperate. However, no difference was found in the extent to which refusers participate in political activities nor in their level of social participation in general.

Consequently, the findings on the relationship between disengagement and refusal to participate in survey research are equivocable. The evidence generally supports the conclusion that differences between cooperative and refusing respondents are minimal, except for age. If adjustments are made for age, then socioeconomic, social participation, and political participation differences are relatively minor.

NOTES

1. Elaine Cumming and William E. Henry, *Growing Old: The Process of Disengagement* (New York: Basic Books, 1961), p. 234.

2. Nonresponse ranged from 2.3 percent for persons in their twenties to 17.3 percent for persons over 70 in a study conducted in Madison, Wisconsin. Francis E. Lowe and Thomas E. McCormick, "Some Survey Sampling Biases," *Public Opinion Quarterly*, 19 (Fall 1955), pp. 303–315. In an analysis of nonresponse to the 1956–58 Detroit Area Study Surveys, 91 percent of the adults 21 to 34 years of age granted an interview while only 78 percent of those over 60 years of age were interviewed. Although mental and physical incapacity were factors in the nonresponse, refusals were significantly higher in spite of the fact that older people were easier to contact on the first call. Harry Sharp and Allan Feldt, "Some Factors in a Probability Sample Survey of a Metropolitan Community," *American Sociological Review*, 24 (October 1959), pp. 650–661. Analysis of persons refusing to be interviewed in the election study done in Elmira, New York, in 1948, indicated that persons who refused the first interview were older than those who granted an interview. Reported in Frederick F. Stephen and Philip J. McCarthy, *Sampling Opinions* (New York: John Wiley & Sons, 1958), p. 264.

For a foreign example, success rates were highest for the age group 25 to 44 in a health study conducted on a housing estate near London and declined with increasing age. Ann Cartwright, "Families and Individuals Who Did Not Cooperate on a Sample Survey," *Milbank Memorial Fund Quarterly*, 47 (October 1959), pp. 347–360.

3. Cumming and Henry, *op. cit.*, p. 234.

4. For a discussion of the theoretical framework and development of these scales, see Jane R. Mercer, Edgar W. Butler, and Harvey F. Dingman, "The Relationship Between Social Developmental Performance and Mental Ability," *American Journal of Mental Deficiency,* 69 (September 1964), pp. 195–205.

5. We wish to thank Dr. Raymond Jessen, School of Business Administration, University of California, Los Angeles, who developed the sampling design and served as sampling consultant throughout the study.

6. For a more complete description of this research, see Jane R. Mercer, Harvey F. Dingman, and George Tarjan, "Involvement, Feedback and Mutuality: Principles for Conducting Mental Health Research in the Community," *The American Journal of Psychiatry,* 121 (September 1964), pp. 228–237.

7. See Lowe and McCormick, *op. cit.*, p. 310, for similar rates.

8. For a similar example, see Sharp and Feldt, *op. cit.*, p. 662.

9. Elmo C. Wilson, "Adapting Probability Sampling to Western Europe," *Public Opinion Quarterly,* 14 (1950), pp. 215–223.

10. Lowe and McCormick, *op. cit.*, p. 310.

11. Cumming and Henry, *op. cit.*, p. 45.

12. *Ibid.*, pp. 38–44.

QUESTIONS

1. In this particular study very few differences of consequence were noted between participants and nonparticipants. Can you think of specific social issues where nonresponse might introduce a sizeable error?
2. Suggest specific strategies that might be employed to reduce the refusal rate.
3. Compare the potential for nonresponse among the following data sources:

   a. Mailed questionnaires,
   b. Questionnaires completed in a classroom,
   c. Telephone interviews,
   d. Lost-letter technique (see Milgram, Mann, and Harter, article 25),
   e. Behavioral observation.

4. Select a research article from a journal employing interviews or questionnaires and analyze how the author handles the nonresponse problem.

"Black Matriarchy" Reconsidered: Evidence from Secondary Analysis of Sample Surveys

HERBERT H. HYMAN and JOHN SHELTON REED

When data are collected firsthand by the researcher, they are usually referred to as "primary" data. In contrast, "secondary" data have been collected by previous researchers, often for purposes that differed from that of their second use. Very often, secondary data have originated from social scientific studies and as a result are very similar to primary data. However, in many instances secondary data stem from such nonscientific sources as school records, transcripts of court hearings, crime reports, and so forth. Irrespective of the original reasons for which the data were collected, however, secondary sources have proved themselves to be quite valuable to social science.

Hyman and Reed provide us with an example of secondary data from previous social science research. Data from three separate survey projects are utilized to make some empirical assessment of the relative tendencies for matriarchal family patterns among whites and blacks.

■ The American Negro family has been characterized as a *matriarchy* so often that the assertion is widely accepted as a truth rather than a proposition still in need of empirical evidence and critical analysis. Moynihan was only a recent, albeit prominent, example of the many scholars, both Negro and white, who have contributed to the growth of such belief.[1] Is it not significant that most critics of his report attacked what they took to be its policy implications or implicit moral judgments, rather than its factual content?[2]

If the conception of a matriarchy referred solely to the physical datum, father's absence from the family, adequate evidence could be extracted from the Census, although its proper interpretation is not so simple. The fact is indisputable that father-absent families are relatively more frequent among Negroes. But how common does the situation have to be, and how much more frequent among Negroes than whites, perhaps of equivalent status, for the characterization to be valid and peculiarly applicable to the Negro family?[3]

The conception, however, usually implies that even when a father is present, the mother is the dominant member of the intact Negro family. Evidence adequate to support this more subtle aspect of the concept is much harder to find.[4] To be sure, many Negroes believe this to be true of the Negro family. In 1966 Louis Harris asked a national sample of Negroes: "In most Negro families do you think the mother or the father is usually the one who teaches the children to behave right?" Fifty-one per cent

Reprinted from *Public Opinion Quarterly* 33 (1969), 346–354, with permission of Columbia University Press.

replied that the mother is; only 6 per cent said the father. But this may be unfounded belief—perhaps even a *stereotype*—rather than a knowledgeable report, let alone proof. Among the small sample of "Negro community leaders" whom Harris also questioned, 60 per cent mentioned the mother, but this group may not be fully knowledgeable about the situation that prevails in the general population, although it may be highly informed by the literature on the subject.[5]

On this aspect of the problem more searching inquiry of a social psychological nature is needed which adequately samples the general population. In the absence of such a specially designed study, we present a secondary analysis of three existing surveys which fortunately contained relevant data. The major limitation of these surveys is that the samples, although national in scope, include only small numbers of Negro respondents. But for reasons which will become dramatically clear, the large numbers of white respondents are a most valuable resource. Apart from the efficiency and economy of secondary analysis, we also benefit from the replication of our findings over three independent studies, from the fact that several aspects of the broad domain within which maternal dominance might operate are covered by the various questions, and from the fact that the observations are not drawn from one narrow point in time.[6] Some brief description of the three studies from which we have drawn our data is essential background.

For the larger cross-national inquiry on *The Civic Culture* by Almond and Verba, the National Opinion Research Center interviewed in 1960 a probability sample of Americans over the age of eighteen. The sample of approximately 1,000 individuals included about 100 Negro respondents. All were asked in the course of the inquiry who had made each of a number of decisions in their families of origin, and, if married, whether they or their spouses made each of the decisions. In the South, interviewers and respondents were explicitly matched racially; elsewhere, interviewer assignment patterns made such matching quite likely, although not certain. The total sample agrees very closely with census estimates on population in metropolitan areas, population with little schooling, and is slightly overweighted on low-income families, the very stratum in which matriarchy is supposed to be most prevalent.[7]

The second survey was a Gallup Poll conducted in 1951 in which a national sample of about 1,400 adults (21 and older) was interviewed and asked one general question on which parent had been most influential during their childhood. The sample was drawn by quota control methods, and included about eighty Negro respondents, of whom an undeterminable number were interviewed by Negro interviewers.[8]

In 1965 the Survey Research Center conducted a series of studies directed by Kent Jennings of political socialization among national samples of high school seniors. Our data are drawn from a self-administered questionnaire taken by almost 20,000 students. To test one aspect of the theory of matriarchy we have limited ourselves to the smaller group of about 2,500 students, including some 150 Negro youth, who live in intact families where the father and mother have definite and different political party loyalties, as perceived and reported by the student. Since the youth also reported on their own political preferences, the relative influence of the two parents on this dimension of political socialization can be deter-mined and regarded as one test of a theory of matriarchy.[9]

All three surveys were selected for secondary analysis without any prior knowledge of the relevant results, thus providing a fair test.

Given the ages spanned by the samples, the timing of the inquiries, and the retrospective nature of the questioning, the Gallup Poll reconstructs the family patterns that prevailed in a much earlier era and one battery in the Almond and Verba survey re-creates the patterns of a somewhat more recent, but still distant, past. Their other battery of questions and the Jennings inquiry explore the contemporary situation. The data are summarized in Table 1, and the limitations specific to each inquiry will be treated below.

We urge the reader to imagine the primary survey he might well have undertaken to explore the problem of matriarchy in which he invested all of his resources in the study of a large, and exclusively Negro, sample. He might then have generated only the column of figures for Negro respondents presented in Table 1. Note that an examination limited to those data might have given considerable support to the theory. Women's influence exceeds that of men in a number of instances. Even in the area of politics, where male dominance has long been assumed, Negro children are more likely to side with the mother when the parents disagree on party choice. But the phenomenon of a "Black Matriarchy" revealed in the several areas is seen to be an illusion when viewed in the perspective of the second column of findings on white respondents. It appeared as a product of what Hyman has called elsewhere the "pseudo-comparative design" or fictitious comparison," in which the comparative data, in this case for whites, are imputed on the basis of the analyst's beliefs rather than by measurement.[10]

The actual white pattern, contrary to expectation, is almost identical to that for Negro families. The plausible notion that the father dominates the transmission of party preference has been cast into serious doubt by a number of studies, and is demonstrated in the Jennings inquiry not to apply to the aggregate sample.[11]

Over the three studies and all the aspects examined, the differences be-tween white and Negro respondents are small and inconsistent. When the Almond and Verba data are arranged in terms of their temporal reference to past or present, there is some suggestion that matriarchal power has grown in the recent era, but if true, this applies to both Negro and white families. There seems to be little evidence for any social-psychological pattern of matriarchy peculiarly characteristic of the Negro family, on the basis of which social theorizing or social policy could be formulated.

This evidence goes so contrary to the literature that one must examine it most critically. Certainly, one must be tentative in light of the small number of Negro respondents in each of the samples—no smaller indi-vidually, however, than the statistical base of the Detroit study of the problem cited earlier, and considerably larger when pooled. The small numbers prevent an examination of the pattern separately for such sub-groups as the urban lower classes, where matriarchy is supposed to be most prevalent. But, as was noted earlier, such subgroups are strongly represented in the Negro sample, whereas the white respondents tend to

Data Sources

TABLE 1. Patterns of Male and Female Influence in Negro and White Families

Surveys and Questions		Negro	White
GALLUP—1951[a]			
Per cent reporting that most important influence on them when growing up was			
Father		27%	31%
Mother		73	69
	N=	(68)	(1,367)
NORC (Almond and Verba)—1960[b]			
Per cent reporting that the important family decisions were made by			
Father		28	23
Mother		14	13
	N=	(93)	(858)
Per cent reporting that decisions about child discipline were made by			
Father		16	19
Mother		28	25
	N=	(97)	(855)
Per cent of married respondents reporting that important family decisions are made by			
Husband		9	6
Wife		10	7
	N=	(67)	(628)
Per cent of married respondents with children reporting that decisions about child discipline are made by			
Husband		4	7
Wife		37	28
	N=	(56)	(474)
Per cent reporting that decision as to how husband and wife vote are made by			
Husband		11	7
Wife		2	—
	N=	(66)	(627)
JENNINGS—1965[c]			
Per cent of youth from politically divided homes who agree with			
Father		32	34
Mother		40	40
	N=	(151)	(2,384)

[a] Negro respondents were considerably less likely to *volunteer* "both parents equally." Those who gave this response have been excluded from this table.
[b] Other possible responses were "Both . . . *together*" and "Each . . . *individually*."
[c] A "politically divided home" is one in which the child reported one parent Democrat and the other Republican or one "Independent" and the other partisan.

be drawn from higher strata. Thus the gross comparisons in Table 1 probably overstate the differences that would be found if whites and Negroes were equated in class position.

One must also entertain the possibility of response error. In the instance of the Gallup and the Almond and Verba surveys, the respondent is cast in the role of an *informant* about the family. The hypothesis immediately suggested is that the *sex* of the respondent making that report is relevant. Women might be inclined to inflate their own power when reporting on the battle of the sexes. And the lady survey analyst might add: men would be inclined to an equivalent self-aggrandizement.[12] But as will be recalled, the sex distribution in the Almond and Verba study is almost 50-50 in both the Negro and the white samples. Any bias of report would presumably be balanced out and would not obscure the racial comparison.

In the Gallup survey, the situation is not so fortunate. Women constitute a considerably higher proportion of the Negro sample than men, whereas there is parity in the white sample. An ideal test of bias would be to obtain independent reports from a sample of husbands and wives from the same family units, or from male and female offspring of the same families. An approximate test was made by comparing the answers of men and women in the Gallup survey. The numbers are very small and too few to equate the informants in social characteristics to ensure that they are describing the patterns in families from the same stratum. Among the white respondents, the sex of the informant clearly made no difference. Among Negro respondents, differences by sex could easily be due to sampling variation.

The findings must also be interpreted in relation to one other feature of the surveys. Families where there was prolonged father-absence cannot be eliminated from the Gallup data, nor from the Almond and Verba data pertaining to patterns in the families of origin. Thus any evidence of matriarchy in these data reflects two phenomena: objective absence of father plus his low power, when present. Since father absence is more frequent among Negroes, it seems a reasonable inference that the racial comparison presented overstates the Negro-white difference in maternal power in intact families.

The Jennings data (and the Almond and Verba data on the contemporary situation) describe the balance of power in intact families. However, the sample of high school seniors obviously excludes academic dropouts, who are known to come disproportionately from poorer households. The findings must be qualified in light of this restriction on the universe.[13]

Our evidence is tentative, but it certainly casts the issue into doubt. If the concept of a culturally linked Negro-white difference in family organization has been weighty enough to generate debate about social policy and action, it deserves the conclusive evidence that primary research could provide.[14] We hope our secondary analysis will give guidance in the design of such research and impetus for it to be undertaken. Although the economy of secondary analysis will have to be forsaken, there is a halfway strategy to be recommended. Since race and family composition are routine fact-sheet items in surveys, a few indicators of the balance of power can be "piggy-backed" or "hitchhiked" onto surveys of the general population. Provided some basic cautions are observed, the pool of data will soon grow large enough to permit substantial and sound analysis at modest cost.

NOTES

1. For example, Hortense Powdermaker concluded from her field work in rural Mississippi in the 1930's that "among the middle- and lower-class Negroes . . . , the woman is usually the head of the house in importance and authority." (After Freedom: A Cultural Study in the Deep South, New York, Atheneum Reprint NL3, 1968; p. 145.) E. Franklin Frazier also dealt with this theme, drawing on his field work in Chicago and on documentary census sources. (See his chapter "The Matriarchate" in The Negro Family in the United States, Chicago, University of Chicago Press, 1939, pp. 125–145. See also pp. 108–124, 325–357.) In the same period, Charles Johnson, in The Shadow of the Plantation, Chicago, University of Chicago Press, 1966, pp. 35–39, reached similar conclusions. (See also his Growing Up in The Black Belt, New York, Schocken Books, 1967.)

More recently, matriarchal organization of the Negro family has been discussed by, among others, Abram Kardiner and Lionel Ovesey, in The Mark of Oppression: Explorations in the Personality of the American Negro, Cleveland Meridian Books, 1962, pp. 60 ff.; Kenneth Clark, in Dark Ghetto: Dilemmas of Social Power, New York, Harper and Row, 1965, pp. 70–74; and Whitney M. Young, Jr., To Be Equal, New York, McGraw-Hill, 1964, pp. 174–175. Billingsley's recent essay reviews critically these and other scholarly works on the Negro family. (Andrew Billingsley, Black Families in White America, Englewood Cliffs, Prentice-Hall, 1968, pp. 197–215.)

Data on father-absence can be found in Lee Rainwater, "Crucible of Identity: The Negro Lower Class Family," Daedalus, Vol. 95, No. 1, 1966, p. 181, and in Martin Deutsch and Bert Brown, "Social Influences in Negro-White Intelligence Differences," Journal of Social Issues, Vol. 20, No. 2, 1964, p. 28. Leonard Broom and Norval Glenn also note the high frequency of father-absent Negro families, but their treatment is highly qualified and their observation that "the stereotype is grossly inaccurate when generally applied, since Negro families are now as varied as white families" is worth repeating (The Transformation of the Negro American, New York, Harper Colophon CN117, 1967, p. 15). For a thoughtful critique of the concept and fruitful analysis of the data, see also Jessie Bernard, Marriage and Family among Negroes, Englewood Cliffs, Prentice-Hall, 1966, especially pp. 21–23, 83–84. Another researcher who questions the accuracy of the matriarchal image, on the basis of intensive study of ten families, is David A. Schulz, in "Variations in the Father Role in Complete Families of the Negro Lower Class," Social Science Quarterly, Vol. 49, 1968, pp. 651–659.

The celebrated "Moynihan Report" (Daniel Patrick Moynihan, The Negro Family: The Case for National Action, Washington, U. S. Department of Labor, Office of Policy Planning and Research, 1965) is reprinted in full, with its original pagination, in Lee Rainwater and William L. Yancey, The Moynihan Report and the Politics of Controversy, Cambridge, M.I.T. Press, 1967.

2. See Rainwater and Yancey, op. cit., pp. 185–186, 195–200, 215–219, 235–236, et passim.

3. A paper by Lee Rainwater illustrates the complexity of interpretation. Data from the Census of 1960 are presented showing that among urban Negroes (nonwhites) with incomes under $3,000, 47 per cent of the families with children have female heads. Rainwater stresses the consequences of such a "matriarchal" situation, but makes no reference in his text to the finding he presents in the

same table that in the equivalent white stratum, 38 per cent of the families have female heads, a difference of 9 percentage points. In the other strata table, the differences between Negroes and whites are less than 5 per cent and the matriarchal pattern is exceedingly rare (loc. cit.). Moynihan charts trends in this datum from census sources (op. cit., p. 11). For data on the situation as recently as 1966, see Report of the National Advisory Commission on Civil Disorders, Washington, U. S. Government Printing Office, 1967, pp. 129, 337–338. The Commission is careful to emphasize that most Negro families are headed by men.

4. On this score, it should be stressed that although the Moynihan Report provides most elaborate statistical evidence on the physical datum, father-absence, the only empirical evidence presented on the psychological datum, husband's subordination to the wife, is one study conducted in Detroit in 1955. The wives in a sample of 103 Negro families and 554 white families answered a series of questions on who made the decisions in each of 8 spheres. A scale score of 10 indicates that power lies completely in the hands of the husband, and a score of 4 indicates that husband and wife share equally in power. While the distribution can be examined in various ways, and cut at different points to define particular types of family structure, it should be noted that the mean score for whites was 5.2 and for Negroes 4.4. A not unreasonable interpretation of these findings is that the average white family studied was slightly patriarchal, and the Negro family equalitarian, rather than matriarchal in pattern. For the data and the authors' somewhat different appraisal, see Robert O. Blood, Jr., and Donald M. Wolfe, Husbands and Wives, New York, Free Press, 1960, pp. 22–36. The other evidence Moynihan summarized on this aspect is in the nature simply of learned opinions or generalizations (op. cit., pp. 30, 34). That "harder" evidence is very rare cannot be doubted. And the kind of evidence required for a test of theories of matriarchy that would convince all advocates would be even more difficult to collect, given the elusive nature of the argument. Highly aggressive behavior within the family is sometimes regarded as a defense or reaction on the part of the Negro male to his inferior status. If both submission and ascendance can be regarded as indicators of the feeling of subordination, it is hard to see how the theory could ever be refuted. On such psychodynamic consequences of inferior status, see Whitney Young, op. cit., pp. 174–175, or Kenneth Clark, op. cit., p. 70.

5. William Brink and Louis Harris, Black and White, New York, Simon and Schuster, 1967, pp. 268–269. The authors apparently share this belief, referring in the text to "the matriarchal character of Negro society today . . ." (p. 150). That the leaders were not reflecting their higher socioeconomic status and the corresponding circles in which they move is suggested by the fact that higher income respondents in the general sample were less likely to credit the mothers with dominance.

6. That social change might operate in this sphere is likely as one realizes that rising economic position and educational level might affect the dominance of one or another parent and the prevalence of matriarchy in the particular population.

7. G. Almond and S. Verba, The Civic Culture, Princeton, Princeton University Press, 1963, pp. 519–522. From a secondary analysis of the Negro sample reported by Marvick, we may add that 57 per cent of the Negro respondents reported family incomes less than $5,000 a year; 37 per cent were unskilled

workers and 39 per cent operatives and service workers; 89 per cent were born in the South; 37 per cent reported only some grammar school, and another 19 per cent had completed only grammar school; 53 per cent lived in big cities. The white respondents, as Marvick reports, were considerably less likely to be big city dwellers, poor, in low occupations, or poorly educated. Relevant to our later discussion is the fact that 49 per cent of the Negro sample and 47 per cent of the white sample were male. See D. Marvick, "The Political Socialization of the American Negro," *Annals*, Vol. 361, 1965, p. 116. The data were made available to us through the courtesy of the Inter-University Consortium for Political Research, Ann Arbor.

8. Of the Negro respondents, 19 per cent were unskilled or domestic workers, 49 per cent semi-skilled or service workers, and 4 per cent skilled workers; 30 per cent resided in the South; 53 per cent reported education of eight grades or less; 53 per cent lived in cities of over 100,000 population. The white respondents were considerably less likely to be southern, poorly educated, big city residents, and in low-status occupations. The data for these analyses were provided by the Roper Center for Public Opinion Research, whose cooperation is gratefully acknowledged. They are from the American Institute of Public Opinion (Gallup) Poll 478K.

9. These unpublished data were kindly made available to us by M. Kent Jennings and are gratefully acknowledged. For some of his basic findings on political socialization see, for example, M. Kent Jennings and R. G. Niemi, "Patterns of Political Learning," *Harvard Educational Review*, Vol. 38, 1968, pp. 443–467.

10. Herbert H. Hyman, "Research Design," ch. 8 of Robert E. Ward, ed., *Studying Politics Abroad: Field Research in the Developing Areas*, Boston, Little, Brown, 1964, p. 162. Cross-national data from the Almond and Verba study also show that American white and Negro families are more like each other in respect to family decision-making than either is like the more patriarchal German family, but even in the German family, maternal dominance is evident in some areas of family life. (We shall not present these data, but they were made available to us by the Inter-University Consortium for Political Research.)

11. Herbert H. Hyman, *Political Socialization: A Study in the Psychology of Political Behavior*, New York, Free Press, 1959, pp. 82–84; John Shelton Reed, "The Transmission of Party Preference by Identification," paper read at the conference of the American Association for Public Opinion Research, Santa Barbara, California, May 11, 1968; M. Kent Jennings and Kenneth P. Langton, "Mothers versus Fathers: The Formation of Political Orientations among Pre-Adults," mimeographed, University of Michigan, March 1968. In an inquiry into political socialization among college students in Puerto Rico, drawn mainly from the urban middle classes, it was found that 40 per cent of the sample deviated from the party preferences of their fathers. This finding was most unexpected, not only because of the usual theory, but because the culture is presumed to produce a strong propensity to defer to authority generally, and to paternal authority in particular. See P. Bachrach, "Attitude toward Authority and Party Preference in Puerto Rico," *Public Opinion Quarterly*, Vol. 22, 1958, pp. 68–73.

12. The analyst of a psychoanalytical persuasion might prefer an Oedipal model of such response error, suggesting that the daughter would inflate the power of the father, and the son the mother. In any case, the sex of the informant would be at issue. [Findings from a study of 179 couples, in which the husbands and

wives were questioned separately, were reported in the summer issue of the *Quarterly,* after the present article was received. Each partner tended to attribute more importance to his or her own role in disciplining their child than was attributed to it by the spouse. See John A. Ballweg, "Husband-Wife Response Similarities on Evaluative and Non-Evaluative Survey Questions," *Public Opinion Quarterly,* Vol. 33, 1969, pp. 249–254. *Editor's Note.*]

13. The analysis was also restricted to those students who were able to report a political position for *both* parents. Since it was not possible unambiguously to separate "Don't know" responses due to parent absence from those attributable to other causes, all cases where such a response was given for either parent were excluded. It is possible that differential awareness of parental political positions could be an indicator of a subtle aspect of relative parental influence which has eluded us.

14. Several surveys conducted by the National Opinion Research Center in 1966 for the U. S. Civil Rights Commission, but not as yet published, may provide additional data on the phenomenon.

QUESTIONS

1. What advantages have Hyman and Reed gained by utilizing previous social science research?
2. What are some of the limitations to the use of secondary data in this study? How have the authors attempted to handle these limitations?
3. Discuss the implications of the authors' statement that the matriarchy issue "deserves the conclusive evidence that primary research could provide." Describe what the major features (including questions to be asked) of that primary research might be.

The Quality of Demographic Data for Nonwhites
REYNOLDS FARLEY

Perhaps the major source of secondary data for the social sciences in the United States is the information collected on a routine basis by the United States government. One important agency in this regard is the Bureau of the Census, which has been collecting data on the U. S. population since 1790, both in the form of a complete census of the population every ten years (as required by law) and a series of yearly studies of representative samples of the population (published as the *Current Population Reports*). Another important agency is the National Vital Statistics Division, which collects, collates, and

Reprinted from *Demography* 5 (1968), 1–10, with permission of the Population Association of America. (Editorial adaptations.)

analyses data supplied through a system of continuous registration of vital events (births, deaths, accidents, and so forth). The data from both of these agencies are readily available to the social scientist in the form of either published reports or computer tapes.

The intelligent user of such data sources should be aware of the limitations and errors in the data so that he can assess their effects on his conclusions. This awareness includes, among other things, being knowledgeable of the definitions of terms and concepts being employed, of the devices and procedures used to collect the basic information, and of the comprehensiveness or completeness of the coverage. For example, if we want to determine the trend over time of maternal mortality, we must be certain that the definition of maternal mortality remains fairly constant. Or if we are interested in the relative fertility of whites and blacks we should pay some attention to the relative accuracy of the birth registration systems of both populations.

In the following article Farley investigates both census and vital statistics data for nonwhites. Note that Farley is interested not only in what the errors are, but also in how they may effect any conclusions based upon such data.

PROBLEMS OF UNDERREGISTRATION
AND UNDERCOUNT

Demographers who describe the nonwhite population of the United States frequently compute rates and then note that these rates may be inaccurate because the data are deficient. However, few people explore the prevalence or magnitude of these deficiencies. This paper delineates some of the most obvious errors in census and vital statistics data for nonwhites and assesses the effect that these errors have on the analysis of data.

EARLY INVESTIGATIONS   The first deficiency which must be investigated is that of underregistration or undercount. Each census misses some people who should be enumerated, and every vital statistics system fails to register all births and deaths. For a long time there has been suspicion about the accuracy of the census count of Negroes. The Census of 1870 was thought to be particularly erroneous, for in that year the Census Office had no control over enumerators or enumeration districts and very little control over enumeration procedures.[1] The Census of 1890 also apparently undercounted Negroes, for tallies from that census did not seem reasonable in comparison to tallies from the censuses of 1880 and 1900.[2]

Early in this century the Bureau of the Census corrected the 1870 and 1890 counts of Negroes by making assumptions about decennial growth rates. It was estimated that Negroes were undercounted by 10 percent in 1870 and by 5 percent in 1890.[3]

MORE RECENT INVESTIGATIONS   The development of more sophisticated techniques for estimating net census undercount depended upon the emergence of a system for registering vital events. In 1933 Texas joined the registration area affecting national coverage. In conjunction with the Census of 1940, a test was conducted to determine the completeness of birth registration in the United States. Each census taker was given special forms to fill out for every infant less than five months old at the time of enumeration, and an extensive search procedure was followed to locate birth certificates for all these infants. This test indicated that 94 percent of the white and 82 percent of the nonwhite births were registered.[4]

An analogous test was carried out in conjunction with the Census of 1950. The registration of births improved during the 1940's, for the 1950 test discovered that 99 percent of the white and 93 percent of the nonwhite births were registered.[5]

Results from these birth registration tests have been used to estimate the total number of births that occurred in the United States each year from 1935 to the present. These corrected estimates of births can, then, be used to investigate census undercount; that is, births in a given year can be survived to a census date to estimate the number of people who should have been enumerated. The actual number counted by the census may be compared to the expected number, and the difference between these numbers represents net census undercount.[6]

If undercount rates for young ages are known for one census date, assumptions can be made about similar patterns of undercount in previous censuses. An iterative technique can then be used to derive estimates of undercount at older ages, and summing these estimates for all age groups produces an estimate of undercount for the entire census.

This approach has been used a number of times, employing slightly different assumptions about the pattern of census errors.[7] These techniques estimate that net census undercount of nonwhite men ranged from a high of 20 percent to a low of 11 percent in the censuses of 1940, 1950, and 1960. However, there is evidence of improvement: each of the estimates indicates that undercount of males was less in 1960 than in 1950 or in 1940. For nonwhite women, estimates of undercount ranged from a high of 12 percent to a low of 7 percent in the last three censuses. Again, there are indications of improvement, for undercount was lower in 1960 than in the earlier censuses.

THE EFFECT OF UNDERCOUNT ON VITAL RATES   What effects do errors in census data and birth registration have on the demographic parameters of the nonwhite population? To answer this question, a variety of demographic rates have been computed for 1950 and 1960 based on different assumptions about the data. These are shown in Table 1.

The first column of Table 1 presents rates computed from the published tabulations; that is, these rates have been computed from data which have not been adjusted or corrected in any fashion.

The second column contains rates calculated from data which have been adjusted for both the underregistration of births and for net census undercount. The birth figures were adjusted in line with the results of the 1940 and 1950 tests of birth registration completeness. The denominators for these rates have been corrected by using estimates of net census undercount contained in the *Current Population Report*.[8] It must be very clearly noted that these estimates of undercount are in no way an official Bureau

Data Sources

TABLE 1. Demographic Rates of the Nonwhite Population, for the United States, 1950 and 1960

Year and Rate	Rates Calculated from		
	Uncorrected Data	Data Corrected for Under-enumeration of Population and Under-registration of Births	Data Corrected for Under-registration of Births Only
1950			
Crude birth rate	31.0	29.6	33.1
Crude death rate	11.1	9.9	—
Rate of natural increase	19.9	19.7	—
Gross reproduction rate	1.81	1.83	1.93
Net reproduction rate	1.65	1.68	1.77
Expectation of life at births (years)			
Males	58.7	60.3	—
Females	62.4	64.5	—
Intrinsic rates of female population			
Birth rate	29.4	29.4	31.4
Death rate	7.5	7.0	6.8
Growth rate (percent)	2.19	2.24	2.46
1960			
Crude birth rate	32.1	30.2	33.3
Crude death rate	6.2	5.6	—
Rate of natural increase	25.9	24.6	—
Gross reproduction rate	2.23	2.15	2.32
Net reproduction rate	2.09	2.02	2.17
Expectation of life at births (years)			
Males	61.2	62.6	—
Females	66.2	67.6	—
Intrinsic rates of female population			
Birth rate	35.4	33.8	36.5
Death rate	5.1	5.2	4.8
Growth rate (percent)	3.03	2.86	3.17

Source: Population: United States Bureau of the Census, "Estimates of the Population of the United States and Components of Change, by Age, Color and Sex, 1950 to 1960," *Current Population Reports*, Series P-25, No. 310 (June 30, 1965).

Births: United States National Office of Vital Statistics, *Vital Statistics of the United States, 1950,* Vol. II, Table 21; United States National Vital Statistics Division, *Vital Statistics of the United States, 1960,* Vol. I, Table 2-16.

Deaths: United States National Office of Vital Statistics, *Vital Statistics of the United States, 1950,* III, Table 56; United States National Vital Statistics Division, *Vital Statistics of the United States, 1960,* Vol. II, Part A, Table 5-12.

of the Census estimate of census deficiencies; they merely represent the results of one study of census accuracy.

The third column of Table 1 shows certain rates computed from data which have been corrected for the underregistration of nonwhite births. However, no adjustment has been made for census undercount.

Figures in columns one and two may be compared first. Rates computed from published data overestimate both the birth and death rates of the nonwhite population by 1 or 2 points. Moreover, they overestimate the rate of natural increase, but by a smaller margin.

In 1950 births were underregistered to a greater degree than women of childbearing age were undercounted. As a consequence, the reproduction rates computed from uncorrected data underestimated the growth of the population. Between 1950 and 1960 the pattern of underregistration of births and undercount of women changed, so that, in 1960, reproduction rates computed from uncorrected data overestimated population growth.

The tabulated figures produce estimates of the life span of nonwhites that are about two years shorter than the life span estimated from data corrected for census undercount. In 1960 national life tables indicated that there was a gap of about eight years between the life span of white and nonwhite females.[9] For males the gap was five years. Each of the investigations of census errors has found that errors are much less significant for the white than for the nonwhite population. In essence, undercount has little effect on the estimated life span of whites.[10] Thus, we can conclude that about one-quarter of the white-nonwhite gap in life expectation is a result of nonwhites' being less well enumerated than whites.[11]

In 1959 the National Vital Statistics Division ceased publishing fertility rates which were corrected only for the underregistration of births. This is a very sound policy: the rates in column three of Table 1 indicate that a correction for deficiencies in birth registration leads to particularly erroneous estimates of fertility and population growth.

THE UNDERCOUNT OF NEGRO MALES   While the various tests of census accuracy suggest an improvement in the overall enumeration of nonwhites during the years 1940–60, this may not characterize all age groups. There is one age group which appears to be increasingly less well counted—young nonwhite men. Unless there has been a war or catastrophe, the number of young adult men in an age group should be roughly equal to the number of females in the same age group. The ratios of nonwhite men to nonwhite women in the age range 20–39 years, for the census dates 1910–60, are shown in the accompanying tabulation.[12]

Nonwhite Males per 100
Nonwhite Females Aged 20–39 Years

Census Date	Ratio
1910	99.7
1920	93.0
1930	93.8
1940	90.5
1950	89.0
1960	87.8
Nonwhite Life Tables, 1940	98.9

The decline in the sex ratio suggests this age group of men is less well enumerated now than in the past. It may be that, with urbanization, nonwhite males become more and more elusive.

PROBLEMS OF INACCURATE RESPONSES   In addition to errors that arise from omissions, the information provided by respondents may be erroneous. Some people report their age incorrectly; others may forget their birth dates, may exaggerate their educational attainment, or misreport their marital status or income.

AGE DATA   The accuracy of age reporting can be studied easily by examining the internal consistency of census returns. The Myers blended index provides a concise measure of age reporting.[13] If many people misreport their age (that is, if many people claim to be at ages ending in particular digits), the Myers index takes on a high value. On the other hand, a low value suggests that age is accurately reported. Myers blended indices of age heaping, for nonwhites for the census dates 1880–1960 and for whites for 1960, are shown in the accompanying tabulation.[14]

Census Nonwhites	Index
1880	36.40
1890	26.81
1900	20.45
1910	18.29
1920	15.78
1930	18.76
1940	11.89
1950	8.19
1960	3.42
Whites 1960	0.95

These Myers indices demonstrate a trend toward more accurate reporting of age by nonwhites. Much of the improvement in 1960 can be attributed to the rephrasing of the age question. The Census of 1960 was the first to ask year of birth rather than year of age.[15] However, it is clear that nonwhites do not report their ages as accurately as whites. An examination of data reveals that an unusually large number of nonwhites reported in 1960 that they were born in 1910, 1900, or 1890.

EDUCATIONAL ATTAINMENT   Nathan Hare suggests there is a tendency for Negroes to overreport their educational attainment as they grow older.[16] This may be investigated by using figures from recent census and Current Population Surveys to compare the educational attainment reported by the identical cohort at two or more census dates. In the United States relatively few people aged over 25 years attend "regular" school.[17]

Thus, for most of the population, educational attainment is a characteristic which is fixed by age 25 years.

We could begin with the cohort of nonwhite males aged 30–39 years in 1940 and look at their educational attainment reported in the Census of 1940. Survivors of this cohort were aged 40–49 years in 1950, 50–59 years in 1960, and 55–64 years in 1965. The educational attainment reported by these men at each of these dates may be compared to the educational attainment they reported in 1940 in order to see if there has been any change.

Table 2 presents information for a series of cohorts of nonwhite and white men. This table shows the reported percentage of high-school graduates and the average years of school completed. Also shown are Gini indices which compare the reported educational attainment distributions in later years with the attainment reported in the first year for which data are available. Finally, there are indices of dissimilarity comparing the educational attainment reported by whites and nonwhites at the same date.

Figures in Table 2 indicate that reported educational attainment rises as a cohort ages. This is true for whites as well as for nonwhites, and some of this may be attributed to selective mortality or may result from differential census coverage. However, it appears that overreporting of education is an important component of this change.

Increases over time in reported educational attainment are much greater for nonwhites than for whites. Consequently, the gap between the educational attainment of whites and nonwhites diminishes as a cohort ages. The decrease over time in the indices of dissimilarity suggests the gradual convergence of reported educational attainment.

It is not clear how educational data might be corrected for this bias. Hare made the assumption that education is most accurately reported when the cohort is youngest.[18] Folger and Nam suggest using figures from post-enumeration studies to correct for this bias.[19] In any case, a user of these data needs to be aware of this trend toward overreporting.

THE USE OF SURVEY DATA
TO STUDY CENSUS ACCURACY

The results of an independent survey may be compared to census results to ascertain the accuracy of census data. One technique is to compare the net results of each study. This involves comparing the marginal distributions obtained from each source. A more thorough study of errors may be conducted if a sample of people included in the census is reinterviewed, using questions similar to those of the census. Respondents' answers to census questions can then be compared to the answers they gave interviewers. In 1950 a Post Enumeration Survey (PES) was conducted for this purpose, and in 1960 a reinterview study—called the Content Evaluation Study (CES)—was carried out.[20] Both in 1950 and in 1960, moreover, census responses were compared to those obtained in the Current Population Survey (CPS) taken in the same month for those individuals included in both the census and the Current Population Survey.[21]

TABLE 2. Changes over Time in the Reporting of Educational Attainment for Selected Cohorts of White and Nonwhite Males, for the United States, 1940–65

Age	Year Data Collected	Nonwhite			White			Index of Dissimilarity Comparing White and Nonwhite Distributions
		Percentage High School Graduates	Mean Years Completed	Gini Index[a]	Percentage High School Graduates	Mean Years Completed	Gini Index[a]	
Born 1900–09								
30–39 years	1940	7.8	5.8	—	30.0	9.5	—	49
40–49 years	1950	10.1	6.1	+ 4.0	32.9	9.6	+ 1.6	43
50–59 years	1960	11.3	6.2	+ 4.7	31.5	9.5	− 0.3	40
55–64 years	1965	11.4	6.3	+ 7.3	35.0	9.7	+ 4.1	38
Born 1910–14								
25–29 years	1940	10.4	6.3	—	38.9	10.1	—	49
35–39 years	1950	13.9	6.8	+ 6.7	41.7	10.2	+ 2.3	42
45–49 years	1960	15.5	7.0	+10.0	41.4	10.2	+ 2.1	38
Born 1910–19								
30–39 years	1950	16.1	7.1	—	45.5	10.4	—	40
40–49 years	1960	18.5	7.4	+ 4.6	45.8	10.4	+ 0.6	35
45–54 years	1965	26.6	8.6	+22.4	50.2	10.7	+ 5.3	26
Born 1920–24								
25–29 years	1950	21.4	7.9	—	53.9	11.0	—	34
35–39 years	1960	26.8	8.5	+ 9.2	55.8	11.2	+ 3.3	29
Born 1930–34								
25–29 years	1960	36.2	9.6	—	62.8	11.7	—	27
30–34 years	1965	43.8	10.2	+ 8.7	69.3	12.0	+ 6.1	26

[a] The Gini Index compares the reported educational attainment in later years with the attainment reported at the earliest date listed. Positive values indicate and measure apparent overreporting.

Source: United States Bureau of the Census, Census of Population: 1950, P-C1, Table 115; Census of Population: 1960, PC(1)-1D, Table 173; "Educational Attainment: March, 1966 and 1965," Current Population Reports, Series P-25, No. 158 (December 19, 1966), Table 4.

74

Before the results of these sample surveys can be used to adjust census data for nonwhites, three questions must be answered. First, it must be asked whether the individuals included in the sample surveys are indeed a representative sample of all people included in the census. Table 3

TABLE 3. Comparison of Census and Survey Age Data for Nonwhites, for the United States, 1950 and 1960

Age	1960 Census Tabulations	Age as Reported to the Census for Matched Individuals Included in:		1950 Census Tabulations	Age as Reported to the Census for Matched Individuals Included in the 1950 Post-enumeration Survey
		March, 1960 CPS	Reinterview Study, 1960		
Total	100.0	100.0	100.0	100.0	100.0
0–4 years	14.5	13.6	15.3	12.6	12.5
5–14 years	23.2	24.6	26.1	19.2	19.3
15–24 years	14.4	13.8	14.0	16.5	16.4
25–34 years	13.0	12.7	11.5	15.8	15.7
35–44 years	12.2	11.1	11.6	13.9	14.0
45–54 years	9.8	11.3	10.0	10.3	10.4
55–64 years	6.8	6.6	5.8	6.0	6.0
65 years and over	6.1	6.3	5.7	5.7	5.7

Indices of dissimilarity
1960 Census vs. CPS   3.1
1960 Census vs. reinterview 3.9
1960 CPS vs. reinterview   3.9
1950 Census vs. post-enumeration 0.3

Source: United States Bureau of the Census, Census of Population: 1960, PC(1)-1B, Table 47; "Accuracy of Data on Population Characteristics as Measured by CPS-Census Match," Evaluation and Research Program of the U.S. Censuses of Population and Housing: 1960, Series ER-60, No. 5, Table 6; "Accuracy of Data on Population Characteristics as Measured by Reinterview," Series ER-60, No. 4, Tables 7 and 8; "The Post-Enumeration Survey," Technical Paper No. 4 (1960), Tables 1C and 1D.

presents data pertinent to this question. The first column shows the age distribution of all nonwhites included in the Census of 1960; the second column shows age as reported to the census for those nonwhites included in the March, 1960 CPS; and the third column shows age as reported to the census for nonwhites included in the 1960 CES. A similar comparison for 1950 is shown in the fourth and fifth columns.

An examination of figures in the first three columns of Table 3 shows, on the one hand, that the 1960 CES and the March, 1960 CPS overrepresented the young (aged 5–14 years) nonwhite population. On the other hand, these studies underrepresented the nonwhite population aged 15–44 years—an age group which seems particularly difficult to enumerate.

These difficulties suggest that the March, 1960 CPS and the 1960 CES represent a population slightly different from that included in the Census of 1960. Thus, it would be inappropriate to take the age distribution reported in the 1960 CES as the accurate age distribution and adjust census data accordingly. The final columns of Table 3 indicate that the 1950 PES did represent the nonwhite population included in the Census of 1950.

The second question concerns the accuracy of responses. Most respondents provide the same answer to the census and survey queries, but some people give discrepant answers. It is ordinarily assumed that responses to surveys are more accurate than census responses, since survey interviewers are more rigorously trained than census takers. In addition, the 1950 PES and the 1960 CES attempted to reconcile discrepant answers.[22] Only if this is carefully done can we be certain survey answers are correct.

The third question concerns the availability of data. Few tabulations have been published for nonwhites. Many surveys involve relatively small numbers of respondents. As a consequence, it is feasible to publish results only for the total population. Age data, for example, are the principle figures shown separately for nonwhites from the 1950 PES.

Reinterview surveys are potentially valuable for determining errors in census data. However, at present they are of limited value if one is interested in characteristics of the nonwhite population.

CONCLUSIONS

Demographers who are concerned about the validity of data for nonwhites have one great asset: the officials of agencies which collect and publish these data have been the individuals who have worried most about the quality of data. The long series of methodological reports and investigations, dating back to the last century, bears witness to this concern.

NOTES

1. Francis Walker, Superintendent of the Census of 1870, termed the count "inadequate, partial and inaccurate, often in a shameful degree." Francis A. Walker, "Statistics of the Colored Race in the United States," *Publications of the American Statistical Association,* II (September–December, 1890), 97.

2. United States Bureau of the Census, *Negro Population, 1790–1915* (Washington: Government Printing Office, 1918), pp. 26–29.

3. *Ibid.*

4. Robert D. Grove, *Studies in the Completeness of Birth Registration* (Special Report Series, XVIII, 18 [United States Public Health Service, April 20, 1943]).

5. United States National Office of Vital Statistics, *Vital Statistics of the United States, 1950,* Vol. I, pp. 108–33.

6. This methodology is most clearly explained in Ansley J. Coale, "The Population of the United States in 1950 Classified by Age, Sex, and Color—A Revision

of Census Figures," *Journal of the American Statistical Association,* L, 269 (March, 1955), 16–54.

7. United States Bureau of the Census, "Estimates of the Population of the United States and Components of Change, by Age, Color and Sex, 1950 to 1960," *Current Population Reports,* Series P-25, No. 310, June 30, 1965; Jacob S. Siegel and Melvin Zelnick, "An Evaluation of Coverage in the 1960 Census of Population by Techniques of Demographic Analysis and Composite Methods" (paper presented to American Statistical Association [Los Angeles, August, 1966]); and Ansley J. Coale, *op. cit.*

8. United States Bureau of the Census, "Estimates of the Population . . . 1950 to 1960," *op. cit.*

9. United States National Vital Statistics Division, *Vital Statistics of the United States, 1964,* Vol. II, Part A, Table 55.

10. Life tables for whites for 1960 were also computed using adjusted and unadjusted data. The results are shown in the accompanying tabulation.

	Life Expectation at Birth (Years)	
	Males	Females
Enumerated population	67.5	74.1
Corrected for net census undercount	67.6	74.4

The sources were the same as those used for nonwhites.

11. For a more complete discussion of how census errors may influence death rates for nonwhites see Richard F. Romasson, "Bias in Estimates of the U.S. Non-white Population as Indicated by Trends in Death Rates," *Journal of the American Statistical Association,* LVI, 293 (March, 1961), 44–51.

12. United States Bureau of the Census, *Census of Population: 1960,* PC(1)81B, Table 47; *Sixteenth Census of the United States: 1940,* United States Life and Actuarial Tables, 1939–41, Tables 8 and 9.

13. Paul J. Myers, "Errors and Bias in the Reporting of Ages in Census Data," *Transactions of the Actuarial Society of America,* XLI, Part 2, No. 104 (October, 1940), 411–15.

14. United States Bureau of the Census, *Census of Population: 1960,* PC(1)-1D, Table 155; *Census of Population: 1950,* P-C1, Table 94; *Sixteenth Census of the United States: 1940,* Population, Vol. IV, Part 1, Table 1; *Negro Population, 1790–1915,* Chapter X, Table 2; and United States Census Office, *Eleventh Census: 1890,* "Report on the Population of the United States," Part II, Age, Table 1.

15. In 1890 the census asked age at nearest birthday. In 1900 enumerators were instructed to first ask year of birth. If the respondent could not answer this question accurately, enumerators were to ask the age at most recent birthday. Problems with the year of birth question led the Census Bureau to ask current age until 1960. United States Bureau of the Census, *Twelfth Census of the United States: 1900,* Supplementary Analysis and Derivative Tables, Age, p. 131.

16. Nathan Hare, "Recent Trends in the Occupational Mobility of Negroes, 1930–1960: An Intra-cohort Analysis," *Social Forces,* LVIV, 2 (December, 1965), 171.

17. " 'Regular' schooling is that which may advance a person toward an elementary school certificate, or high school diploma, or a college, university or professional degree." United States Bureau of the Census, *Census of Population: 1950,* PC(1)-1D, p. xvi.

18. Hare, *op. cit.*

19. John F. Folger and Charles B. Nam, "Educational Trends from Census Data," *Demography,* I, 1 (1964), 255.

20. United States Bureau of the Census, "The Post Enumeration Survey: 1950," *Technical Paper No. 4 (1960);* "Accuracy of Data on Population Characteristics as Measured by Reinterviews," *Evaluation and Research Program of the U.S., Censuses of Population and Housing:* 1960, Series ER-60, No. 5.

21. Gertrude Bancroft, *The American Labor Force* (New York: John Wiley and Sons, 1958), pp. 161–75. United States Bureau of the Census, *Evaluation and Research Program of the U.S. Censuses of Population and Housing: 1960,* "Accuracy of Data on Population Characteristics as Measured by CPS-Census Match," ER-60, No. 5.

22. The sample design did not permit reconciliation in about one-third of the households included in the 1960 CES. United States Bureau of the Census, "Accuracy of Data on Population Characteristics Measured by Reinterviews," *op. cit.,* p. 6.

QUESTIONS

1. The researcher has three choices after becoming aware that there are limitations or errors in secondary data: (1) not to use the data; (2) simply to make the reader aware of what the errors are; and (3) attempt to assess their effects on the conclusions of the study. Discuss the implications of each of these strategies.
2. What possible difficulties might be encountered in using census data and/or vital statistics to make comparisons: (1) over time within a single country, and (2) between countries?
3. Compile a list of government sources of data that are easily accessible (state, local, and federal) and suggest some research questions that might be answered by such data.
4. Realizing that the Bureau of the Census uses a combination of interviews and self-administered questionnaires to collect data, comment on how important it is for those who report and interpret census findings to the public (journalists, editors, news analysts, and so forth) to have some knowledge of data-collecting techniques.

Legal Evolution
and Societal Complexity
RICHARD D. SCHWARTZ and JAMES C. MILLER

The major portion of published sociological research is based on data collected from a single society in a relatively short span of time; namely, the United States from 1920 to the present. One good consequence of this is that we have a fairly intensive and extensive knowledge of our own society. However, many social scientists are more interested in developing a general science of human societies, which necessitates collecting data from other cultures as well.

Cross-cultural research is far from a simple venture. For one, if primary data are desired, fairly large investments of money are usually needed. In addition special problems are added to the already numerous difficulties in conducting research in general. These include, among other things, the difficulty of obtaining equivalent meanings across different languages. (This is especially true when questionnaires and interviews are used.)

Fortunately, a major secondary source of cross-cultural data is readily available, the Human Relations Area File (H.R.A.F.). The file consists of detailed ethnographic descriptions of a sample of societies (which numbered 250 as of 1964). The primary data are research findings of numerous investigators, most of whom are professional anthropologists. These findings are organized, classified, and cross-indexed according to approximately twenty subject categories (economy, family, religion, communication, and so forth).

As with all data sources researchers must consider major limitations when using the H.R.A.F. A few are:

1. Societies for which no adequate research exists are excluded from the sample.
2. The extent or amount of the coverage varies from society to society. Thus it is difficult to determine if an issue not discussed (for example, sibling rivalry) is omitted because of its absence in that culture or because the researcher for one reason or another failed to report it. It seems that the smaller, simpler societies are more adequately documented.
3. The primary sources of data are quite variable in quality.

[For a more detailed discussion of H.R.A.F. see Robert W. Marsh, *Comparative Sociology* (New York: Harcourt Brace Jovanovich, 1967), pp. 261–270.]

In the following paper, data from the H.R.A.F. are used to test the theoretical idea that legal institutions develop in a regular sequential pattern.

■ The study of legal evolution has traditionally commended itself to scholars in a variety of fields. To mention only a few, it has been a concern in sociology of Weber[1] and Durkheim;[2] in jurisprudence of Dicey,[3] Holmes,[4] Pound,[5] and Llewellyn;[6] in anthropology of Maine[7] and Hoebel;[8] in legal history of Savigny[9] and Vinogradoff.[10]

There are theoretical and practical reasons for this interest. Legal

Reprinted from *American Journal of Sociology* 70 (1964), 159–169, with permission of The University of Chicago Press.

evolution[11] provides an opportunity to investigate the relations between law and other major aspects and institutions of society. Thus Maine explained the rise of contract in terms of the declining role of kinship as an exclusive basis of social organization. Durkheim saw restitutive sanctions replacing repressive ones as a result of the growth of the division of labor and the corresponding shift from mechanical to organic solidarity. Dicey traced the growth of statutory lawmaking in terms of the increasing articulateness and power of public opinion. Weber viewed the development of formal legal rationality as an expression of, and precondition for, the growth of modern capitalism.

For the most part, these writers were interested in the development of legal norms and not in the evolution of legal organization. The latter subject warrants attention for several reasons. As the mechanism through which substantive law is formulated, invoked, and administered, legal organization is of primary importance for understanding the process by which legal norms are evolved and implemented. Moreover, legal organization seems to develop with a degree of regularity that in itself invites attention and explanation. The present study suggests that elements of legal organization emerge in a sequence, such that each constitutes a necessary condition for the next. A second type of regularity appears in the relationship between changes in legal organization and other aspects of social organization, notably the division of labor.

By exploring such regularities intensively, it may be possible to learn more about the dynamics of institutional differentiation. Legal organization is a particularly promising subject from this point of view. It tends toward a unified, easily identifiable structure in any given society. Its form and procedures are likely to be explicitly stated. Its central function, legitimation, promotes cross-culturally recurrent instances of conflict with, and adaptation to, other institutional systems such as religion, polity, economy, and family. Before these relationships can be adequately explored, however, certain gross regularities of development should be noted and it is with these that the present paper is primarily concerned.

This paper reports preliminary findings from cross-cultural research that show a rather startling consistency in the pattern of legal evolution. In a sample of fifty-one societies, compensatory damages and mediation of disputes were found in every society having specialized legal counsel. In addition, a large majority (85 per cent) of societies that develop specialized police also employ damages and mediation. These findings suggest a variety of explanations. It may be necessary, for instance, for a society to accept the principles of mediation and compensation before formalized agencies of adjudication and control can be evolved. Alternatively or concurrently, non-legal changes may explain the results. A formalized means of exchange, some degree of specialization, and writing appear almost universally to follow certain of these legal developments and to precede others. If such sequences are inevitable, they suggest theoretically interesting causative relationships and provide a possible basis for assigning priorities in stimulating the evolution of complex legal institutions in the contemporary world.

METHOD

This research employed a method used by Freeman and Winch in their analysis of societal complexity.[12] Studying a sample of forty-eight societies, they noted a Guttman-scale relationship among six items associated with the folk-urban continuum. The following items were found to fall in a single dimension ranging, the authors suggest, from simple to complex: a symbolic medium of exchange; punishment of crime through government action; religious, educational, and government specialization; and writing.[13]

To permit the location of legal characteristics on the Freeman-Winch scale, substantially the same sample was used in this study. Three societies were dropped because of uncertainty as to date and source of description[14] or because of inadequate material on legal characteristics.[15] Six societies were added, three to cover the legally developed societies more adequately[16] and three to permit the inclusion of certain well-described control systems.[17]

Several characteristics of a fully developed legal system were isolated for purposes of study. These included counsel, mediation, and police. These three characteristics, which will constitute the focus of the present [article],[18] are defined as follows:

Counsel: regular use of specialized non-kin advocates in the settlement of disputes

Mediation: regular use of non-kin third party intervention in dispute settlement

Police: specialized armed force used partially or wholly for norm enforcement

These three items, all referring to specialized roles relevant to dispute resolution, were found to fall in a near-perfect Guttman scale. Before the central findings are described and discussed, several methodological limitations should be noted.

First, despite efforts by Murdock[19] and others, no wholly satisfactory method has been devised for obtaining a representative sample of the world's societies. Since the universe of separate societies has not been adequately defined, much less enumerated, the representativeness of the sample cannot be ascertained. Nevertheless, an effort has been made to include societies drawn from the major culture areas and from diverse stages of technological development.

Second, societies have been selected in terms of the availability of adequate ethnographic reports. As a result, a bias may have entered the sample through the selection of societies that were particularly accessible —and hospitable—to anthropological observers. Such societies may differ in their patterns of development from societies that have been less well studied.

Third, despite the selection of relatively well-studied societies, the the quality of reports varies widely. Like the preceding limitations, this problem is common to all cross-cultural comparisons. The difficulty is mitigated, however, by the fact that the results of this study are positive. The effect of poor reporting should generally be to randomize the apparent

Data Sources

TABLE 1. Scale of Legal Characteristics

Society	Counsel	Police	Mediation	Errors	Legal Scale Type	Freeman-Winch Scale Type
Cambodians	x	x	x		3	*
Czechs	x	x	x		3	6
Elizabethan English	x	x	x		3	6
Imperial Romans	x	x	x		3	6
Indonesians	x	x	x		3	*
Syrians	x	x	x		3	*
Ukrainians	x	x	x		3	6
Ashanti		x	x		2	5
Cheyenne		x	x		2	*
Creek		x	x		2	5
Cuna		x	x		2	4
Crow		x		1	2	0
Hopi		x	x		2	5
Iranians		x	x		2	6
Koreans		x	x		2	6
Lapps		x	x		2	6
Maori		x	x		2	4
Riffians		x	x		2	6
Thonga		x		1	2	2
Vietnamese		x	x		2	6
Andamanese		x			1	0
Azande		x			1	0
Balinese		x			1	4
Cayapa		x			1	2
Chagga		x			1	4
Formosan aborigines		x			1	0
Hottentot		x			1	0

occurrence of the variables studied. Where systematic patterns of relationship emerge, as they do in the present research, it would seem to indicate considerable accuracy in the original reports.[20]

Fourth, this study deals with characteristics whose presence or absence can be determined with relative accuracy. In so doing, it may neglect elements of fundamental importance to the basic inquiry. Thus no effort is made to observe the presence of such important phenomena as respect for law, the use of generalized norms, and the pervasiveness of deviance-induced disturbance. Although all of these should be included in a comprehensive theory of legal evolution, they are omitted here in the interest of observational reliability.[21]

Fifth, the Guttman scale is here pressed into service beyond that for which it was developed. Originally conceived as a technique for the isolation of uni-dimensional attitudes, it has also been used as a means of studying the interrelationship of behavior patterns. It should be particularly valuable, however, in testing hypotheses concerning developmental sequences, whether in individuals or in societies.[22] Thus, if we hypothesize that A must precede B, supporting data should show three scale types: neither A nor B, A but not B, and A and B. All instances of B

Society	Counsel	Police	Mediation	Errors	Legal Scale Type	Freeman-Winch Scale Type
Ifugao			x		1	0
Lakher			x		1	2
Lepcha			x		1	3
Menomini			x		1	0
Mbundu			x		1	3
Navaho			x		1	5
Ossett			x		1	1
Siwans			x		1	1
Trobrianders			x		1	*
Tupinamba			x		1	0
Venda			x		1	5
Woleaians			x		1	0
Yakut			x		1	1
Aranda					0	0
Buka					0	0
Chukchee					0	0
Comanche					0	*
Copper Eskimo					0	0
Jivaro					0	0
Kababish					0	1
Kazak					0	0
Siriono					0	0
Yaruro					0	0
Yurok					0	1

* Not included in Freeman-Winch sample.

Coefficient of reproducibility $= 1 - 2/153 = .987$; coefficient of scalability $= 1 - 2/153 - 120 = .94$; Kendall's tau $= +.68$.

occurring without A represent errors which lower the reproducibility of the scale and, by the same token, throw doubt in measurable degree on the developmental hypothesis.[23] Although the occurrence of developmental sequences ultimately requires verification by the observation of historic changes in given units, substantiating evidence can be derived from the comparative study of units at varying stages of development. The Guttman scale seems an appropriate quantitative instrument for this purpose.

FINDINGS

In the fifty-one societies studied, as indicated in Table 1, four scale types emerged. Eleven societies showed none of the three characteristics; twenty had only mediation; eleven had only mediation and police; and seven had mediation, police, and specialized counsel. Two societies departed from these patterns: the Crow and the Thonga had police, but showed no evidence of mediation. While these deviant cases merit detailed study, they reduce the reproducibility of the scale by less than 2 per cent, leaving the coefficient at the extraordinarily high level of better than .98.[24] Each characteristic of legal organization may now be discussed in terms of the sociolegal conditions in which it is found.

MEDIATION   Societies that lack mediation, constituting less than a third of the entire sample, appear to be the simplest societies. None of them has writing or any substantial degree of specialization.[25] Only three of the thirteen (Yurok, Kababish, and Thonga) use money, whereas almost three-fourths of the societies with mediation have a symbolic means of exchange. We can only speculate at present on the reasons why mediation is absent in these societies. Data on size, using Naroll's definition of the social unit,[26] indicate that the maximum community size of societies without mediation is substantially smaller than that of societies with mediation.[27] Because of their small size, mediationless societies may have fewer disputes and thus have less opportunity to evolve regularized patterns of dispute settlement. Moreover, smaller societies may be better able to develop mores and informal controls which tend to prevent the occurrence of disputes. Also, the usually desperate struggle for existence of such societies may strengthen the common goal of survival and thus produce a lessening of intragroup hostility.

The lack of money and substantial property may also help to explain the absence of mediation in these societies. There is much evidence to support the hypothesis that property provides something to quarrel about. In addition, it seems to provide something to mediate with as well. Where private property is extremely limited, one would be less likely to find a concept of damages, that is, property payments in lieu of other sanctions. The development of a concept of damages should greatly increase the range of alternative settlements. This in turn might be expected to create a place for the mediator as a person charged with locating a settlement point satisfactory to the parties and the society.

This hypothesis derives support from the data in Table 2. The concept

TABLE 2. Damages in Relation to Legal Functionaries

	No Mediation	Mediation Only	Mediation and Police	Mediation, Police, and Counsel	Total
Damages	7	17	10	7	41
No damages	6*	3	1	0	10
Total	13	20	11	7	51

*Includes Thonga, who have neither mediation nor damages, but have police.

of damages occurs in all but four of the thirty-eight societies that have mediation and thus appears to be virtually a precondition for mediation. It should be noted, however, that damages are also found in several (seven of thirteen) of the societies that lack mediation. The relationship that emerges is one of damages as a necessary but not sufficient condition for mediation. At present it is impossible to ascertain whether the absence of mediation in societies having the damage concept results from a simple time lag or whether some other factor, not considered in this study, distinguishes these societies from those that have developed mediation.

POLICE   Twenty societies in the sample had police—that is, a specialized armed force available for norm enforcement. As noted, all of these but the Crow and Thonga had the concept of damages and some kind of mediation as well. Nevertheless, the occurrence of twenty societies with mediation but without police makes it clear that mediation is not inevitably accompanied by the systematic enforcement of decisions. The separability of these two characteristics is graphically illustrated in ethnographic reports. A striking instance is found among the Albanian tribesmen whose elaborately developed code for settling disputes, Lek's Kanun, was used for centuries as a basis for mediation. But in the absence of mutual agreements by the disputants, feuds often began immediately after adjudication and continued unhampered by any constituted police.[28]

From the data it is possible to determine some of the characteristics of societies that develop police. Eighteen of the twenty in our sample are economically advanced enough to use money. They also have a substantial degree of specialization, with full-time priests and teachers found in all but three (Cheyenne, Thonga, and Crow), and full-time governmental officials, not mere relatives of the chief, present in all but four (Cuna, Maori, Thonga, and Crow).

Superficially at least, these findings seem directly contradictory to Durkheim's major thesis in *The Division of Labor in Society*. He hypothesized that penal law—the effort of the organized society to punish offenses against itself—occurs in societies with the simplest division of labor. As indicated, however, our data show that police are found only in association with a substantial degree of division of labor. Even the practice of governmental punishment for wrongs against the society (as noted by Freeman and Winch) does not appear in simpler societies. By contrast, restitutive sanctions—damages and mediation—which Durkheim believed to be associated with an increasing division of labor, are found in many societies that lack even rudimentary specialization. Thus Durkheim's hypothesis seems the reverse of the empirical situation in the range of societies studied here.[29]

Counsel   Seven societies in the sample employ specialized advocates in the settlement of disputes. As noted, all of these societies also use mediation. There are, however, another thirty-one societies that have mediation but do not employ specialized counsel. It is a striking feature of the data that damages and mediation are characteristic of the simplest (as well as the most complex) societies, while legal counsel are found only in the most complex. The societies with counsel also have, without exception, not only damages, mediation, and police but, in addition, all of the complexity characteristics identified by Freeman and Winch.

It is not surprising that mediation is not universally associated with counsel. In many mediation systems the parties are expected to speak for themselves. The mediator tends to perform a variety of functions, questioning disputants as well as deciding on the facts and interpreting the law. Such a system is found even in complex societies, such as Imperial

China. There the prefect acted as counsel, judge, and jury, using a whip to wring the truth from the parties who were assumed a priori to be lying.[30] To serve as counsel in that setting would have been painful as well as superfluous. Even where specialized counsel emerge, their role tends to be ambiguous. In ancient Greece, for instance, counsel acted principally as advisors on strategy. Upon appearance in court they sought to conceal the fact that they were specialists in legal matters, presenting themselves merely as friends of the parties or even on occasion assuming the identity of the parties themselves.[31]

At all events, lawyers are here found only in quite urbanized societies, all of which are based upon fully developed agricultural economies. The data suggest at least two possible explanations. First, all of the sample societies with counsel have a substantial division of labor, including priests, teachers, police, and government officials. This implies an economic base strong enough to support a variety of secondary and tertiary occupations as well as an understanding of the advantages of specialization. Eleven societies in the sample, however, have all of these specialized statuses but lack specialized counsel. What distinguishes the societies that develop counsel? Literacy would seem to be an important factor. Only five of the twelve literate societies in the sample do not have counsel. Writing, of course, makes possible the formulation of a legal code with its advantages of forewarning the violator and promoting uniformity in judicial administration. The need to interpret a legal code provides a niche for specialized counsel, especially where a substantial segment of the population is illiterate.[32]

CONCLUSIONS

These data, taken as a whole, lend support to the belief that an evolutionary sequence occurs in the development of legal institutions. Alternative interpretations are, to be sure, not precluded. The scale analysis might fail to discern short-lived occurrences of items. For instance, counsel might regularly develop as a variation in simple societies even before police, only to drop out rapidly enough so that the sample picks up no such instances. Even though this is a possibility in principle, no cases of this kind have come to the authors' attention.

Another and more realistic possibility is that the sequence noted in this sample does not occur in societies in a state of rapid transition. Developing societies undergoing intensive cultural contact might provide an economic and social basis for specialized lawyers, even in the absence of police or dispute mediation. Until such societies are included in the sample, these findings must be limited to relatively isolated, slowly changing societies.

The study also raises but does not answer questions concerning the evolution of an international legal order. It would be foolhardy to generalize from the primitive world directly to the international scene and to assume that the same sequences must occur here as there. There is no certainty that subtribal units can be analogized to nations, because the latter tend to be so much more powerful, independent, and relatively deficient in common culture and interests. In other ways, the individual nations are farther along the path of legal development than subtribal units because all of them have their own domestic systems of mediation, police, and counsel. This state of affairs might well provide a basis for short-circuiting an evolutionary tendency operative in primitive societies. Then too, the emergent world order appears to lack the incentive of common interest against a hostile environment that gave primitive societies a motive for legal control. Even though the survival value of a legal system may be fully as great for today's world as for primitive societies, the existence of multiple units in the latter case permitted selection for survival of those societies that had developed the adaptive characteristic. The same principle cannot be expected to operate where the existence of "one world" permits no opportunity for variation and consequent selection.

Nonetheless, it is worth speculating that some of the same forces may operate in both situations.[33] We have seen that damages and mediation almost always precede police in the primitive world. This sequence could result from the need to build certain cultural foundations in the community before a central regime of control, as reflected in a police force, can develop. Hypothetically, this cultural foundation might include a determination to avoid disputes, an appreciation of the value of third-party intervention, and the development of a set of norms both for preventive purposes and as a basis for allocating blame and punishment when disputes arise. Compensation by damages and the use of mediators might well contribute to the development of such a cultural foundation, as well as reflecting its growth. If so, their occurrence prior to specialized police would be understandable. This raises the question as to whether the same kind of cultural foundation is not a necessary condition for the establishment of an effective world police force and whether, in the interest of that objective, it might not be appropriate to stress the principles of compensatory damages and mediation as preconditions for the growth of a world rule of law.

NOTES

1. Max Weber, *Law in Economy and Society,* ed. Max Rheinstein (Cambridge, Mass.: Harvard University Press, 1954). For a discussion and development of Weber's thinking on legal evolution, see Talcott Parsons, "Evolutionary Universals in Society," *American Sociological Review,* XXIX (June, 1964), 350–53.

2. Emile Durkheim, *The Division of Labor in Society,* trans. George Simpson (Glencoe, Ill.: Free Press, 1947).

3. A. V. Dicey, *Lectures on the Relation between Law and Public Opinion in England during the Nineteenth Century* (London: Macmillan Co., 1905).

4. Oliver Wendell Holmes, Jr., *The Common Law* (Boston: Little, Brown & Co., 1881). Holmes's discussion of the place and limitations of historical analysis provides an appropriate background for the present study. "The law embodies the story of a nation's development through many centuries, and it cannot be dealt with as if it contained only the axioms and corollaries of a book of mathematics. In order to know what it is, we must know what it has been, and what

it tends to become. But the most difficult labor will be to understand the combination of the two into new products at every stage. The substance of the law at any given time pretty nearly corresponds, so far as it goes, with what is then understood to be convenient; but its form and machinery, and the degree to which it is able to work out desired results depend very much on its past" (pp. 1–2). In stressing history as providing an explanation for procedure rather than substance, Holmes points to those aspects of legal development that—in the present study at least—appear to follow highly uniform sequences of change.

5. Roscoe Pound, "Limits of Effective Legal Action," *International Journal of Ethics,* XXVII (1917), 150–65; and *Outlines of Lectures on Jurisprudence* (5th ed.; Cambridge, Mass.: Harvard University Press, 1943). See also his *Interpretations of Legal History* (London: Macmillan Co., 1930).

6. Karl N. Llewellyn, *The Common Law Tradition: Deciding Appeals* (Boston: Little, Brown & Co., 1960).

7. Sir Henry Maine, *Ancient Law* (London: J. M. Dent, 1917).

8. E. Adamson Hoebel, *The Law of Primitive Man* (Cambridge, Mass.: Harvard University Press, 1954).

9. Frederick van Savigny, *Of the Vacation of Our Age for Legislation and Jurisprudence,* trans. Abraham Hayward (London: Littlewood & Co., 1831).

10. Paul Vinogradoff, *Outlines of Historical Jurisprudence,* Vols. I and II (London: Oxford University Press, 1920–22).

11. The term "evolution" is used here in the minimal sense of a regular sequence of changes over time in a given type of unit, in this case, societies. This usage neither implies nor precludes causal links among the items in the sequence. For a discussion of diverse uses of, and reactions to, the term "evolution," see Sol Tax (ed.), *Issues in Evolution* (Chicago: University of Chicago Press, 1960).

12. Linton C. Freeman and Robert F. Winch, "Societal Complexity: An Empirical Test of a Typology of Societies," *American Journal of Sociology,* LXII (March, 1957), 461–66.

13. This ordering has not been reproduced in other studies that followed similar procedures. Freeman repeated the study on another sample and included four of the six items used in the first study. They scaled in a markedly different order, from simple to complex: government specialization, religious specialization, symbolic medium of exchange, writing. The marked change in position of the first and third items appears attributable to changes in definition for these terms (Linton C. Freeman, "An Empirical Test of Folk-Urbanism" [unpublished Ph.D. dissertation, Northwestern University, 1957], pp. 45, 49–50, 80–83). Young and Young studied all six items in a cross-cultural sample of communities, changing only the definition of punishment. Their ordering is somewhat closer to, but not identical with, that found by Freeman and Winch *(op. cit.).* From simple to complex, the items were ordered as follows: punishment, symbolic medium of exchange, governmental specialization, religious specialization, writing, educational specialization (Frank W. and Ruth C. Young, "The Sequence and Direction of Community Growth: A Cross-Cultural Generalization," *Rural Sociology,* XXVII [December, 1962], 374–86, esp. 378–79).

In the present study, we will rely on the Freeman-Winch ratings and orderings, since the samples overlap so heavily. The reader should bear in mind, however, that the order is tentative and contingent upon the specific definitions used in that study.

14. Southeastern American Negroes and ancient Hebrews.

15. Sanpoil.

16. Three societies—Cambodian, Indonesian, and Syrian—were selected from the Human Relations Area Files to increase the number of societies with counsel. The procedure for selection consisted of a random ordering of the societies in the Human Relations Area Files until three with counsel were located in geographically separate regions. These were then examined to determine the presence or absence of other legal characteristics. The random search eliminated the possibility of a bias in favor of societies conforming to the scale type.

The three societies were quota sampled by region to represent a randomly determined three of the following six regions: Asia, Africa, the Middle East, North America, South America, and Oceania. Purposely omitted from the sample were Europe and Russia because they were already represented in the "counsel" type in the Freeman-Winch sample. Selection from different regions was designed to avoid the problem, first noted by Francis Galton, that cross-cultural regularities might be due to diffusion rather than to functional interrelationships. For a discussion of the problem and evidence of the importance of geographical separateness in sampling, see Raoul Naroll, "Two Solutions to Galton's Problem," *Philosophy of Science,* XXVIII (1961), 15–39; Raoul Naroll and Roy G. D'Andrade, "Two Further Solutions to Galton's Problem," *American Anthropologist,* LXV (October, 1963), 1053–67; and Raoul Naroll, "A Fifth Solution to Galton's Problem," *American Anthropologist,* LXVI (forthcoming).

17. These three—Cheyenne, Comanche, and Trobrianders—were selected by James C. Miller before the hypothesis was known to him. Selection of both the Comanche and Cheyenne is subject to some criticism on the grounds that they were prone to diffusion, but this hardly seems a serious difficulty in view of the difference in their scale positions. At all events, the coefficients of reproducibility and scalability would not be seriously lowered by eliminating one of the two.

18. The original study also included damages, imprisonment, and execution. These were dropped from the present analysis, even though this unfortunately limited the scale to three items, to permit focus on statuses rather than sanction. Data on damages will be introduced, however, where relevant to the discussion of restitution.

19. George Peter Murdock, "World Ethnographic Sample," *American Anthropologist,* LIX (August, 1957), 664–87.

20. On this point see Donald T. Campbell, "The Mutual Methodological Relevance of Anthropology and Psychology," in Francis L. K. Hsu (ed.), *Psychological Anthropology* (Homewood, Ill.: Dorsey Press, 1961), p. 347. This inference should be treated with caution, however, in light of Raoul Naroll's observation that systematic observer bias can lead to spurious correlations (*Data Quality Control: A New Research Technique* [New York: Free Press of Glencoe, 1962]).

21. Determination of the presence of a characteristic was made after a detailed search by Miller of the materials on each society in the Human Relations Area Files. His search began with a thorough reading for all societies of the material

filed under category 18, "total culture." (All categories used are described in detail in George P. Murdock *et al., Outline of Cultural Materials* [4th rev. ed.; New Haven, Conn.: Human Relations Area Files, 1961].) This was followed by a search of the annotated bibliography (category 111) to locate any works specifically dealing with legal or dispute settling processes. When found, works of this kind were examined in detail. In addition, materials filed under the following categories were read: community structure (621), headmen (622), councils (623), police (625), informal in-group justice (627), intercommunity relations (628), territorial hierarchy (631), legal norms (671), liability (672), offenses and sanctions (68), litigation (691), judicial authority (692), legal and judicial personnel (693), initiation of judicial proceedings (694), trial procedure (695), execution of justice (696), prisons and jails (697), and special courts (698). If this search did not reveal the presence of the practice or status under investigation, it was assumed absent. . . .

A reliability check on Miller's judgments was provided by Robert C. Scholl, to whom the writers are indebted. Working independently and without knowledge of the hypotheses, Scholl examined a randomly selected third of the total sample. His judgments agreed with those of Miller 88 per cent, disagreed 4 per cent, and he was unable to reach conclusions on 8 per cent of the items. If the inconclusive judgments are excluded, the reliability reaches the remarkable level of 96 per cent.

The use of a single person to check reliability falls short of the desired standard. In a more detailed and extensive projected study of the relationships reported here, we plan to use a set of three independent naïve judges. For discussion of the problems involved in judging cross-cultural materials see John W. M. Whiting and Irvin L. Child, *Child Training and Personality* (New Haven, Conn.: Yale University Press, 1953), pp. 39–62; and Guy E. Swanson, *The Birth of the Gods* (Ann Arbor: Michigan University Press, 1960), pp. 32–54.

22. The use of the Guttman scale is extensively treated by Robert L. Carneiro in "Scale Analysis as an Instrument for the Study of Cultural Evolution," *Southwestern Journal of Anthropology,* XVIII (1962), 149–69. In a sophisticated critique of the Carneiro paper, Ward L. Goodenough suggests that quasi-scales may be needed for charting general evolutionary trends and for treating the traits that develop and then fail to persist because they are superseded by functional equivalents ("Some Applications of Guttman Scale Analysis to Ethnography and Culture Theory," *Southwestern Journal of Anthropology,* XIX [Autumn, 1963], 235–50). While the quasi-scale is a desirable instrument for analyzing supersedence, Goodenough appears unduly pessimistic about the possible occurrence of approximately perfect scales, see p. 246. Studies that obtained such scales, in addition to the one reported here, include Freeman and Winch, *op. cit.;* Stanley H. Udy, " 'Bureaucratic' Elements in Organizations: Some Research Findings," *American Sociological Review,* XXII (1958), 415–18; Frank W. and Ruth C. Young, "Social Integration and Change in Twenty-four Mexican Villages," *Economic Development and Cultural Change,* VIII (July, 1960), 366–77; and Robert L. Carneiro and Stephen L. Tobias, "The Application of Scale Analysis to the Study of Cultural Evolution," *Transactions of the New York Academy of Sciences,* Series II, XXVI (1963), 196–207.

The suggestion that Guttman scales could be used for discovering and testing temporal sequences was made earlier by Norman G. Hawkins and Joan K. Jackson in "Scale Analysis and the Prediction of Life Processes," *American*

Sociological Review, XXII (1957), 579–81. Their proposal referred, however, to individuals rather than societies.

23. The developmental inference does not preclude the possibility of reversal of the usual sequence. It merely indicates which item will be added if any is acquired. Cf. S. N. Eisenstadt, "Social Change, Differentiation and Evolution," *American Sociological Review,* XXIX (June, 1964), 378–81. The finding of a scale also does not rule out the possibility that two items may sometimes occur simultaneously, although the existence of all possible scale types indicates that no two items invariably occur simultaneously and that when they occur separately one regularly precedes the other.

24. This coefficient of reproducibility far exceeds the .90 level suggested by Guttman as an "efficient approximation . . . of perfect scales" (Samuel Stouffer [ed.], *Measurement and Prediction* [Princeton, N.J.: Princeton University Press, 1950]). The coefficient of scalability, designed by Menzel to take account of extremeness in the distribution of items and individuals, far exceeds the .65 level that he generated from a scalability analysis of Guttman's American Soldier data. Herbert A. Menzel, "A New Coefficient for Scalogram Analysis," *Public Opinion Quarterly,* XVII (Summer, 1953), 268–80, esp. 276. The problem of determining goodness of fit for the Guttman scale has still not been satisfactorily resolved (see W. S. Torgerson, *Theory and Methods of Scaling* [New York: John Wiley & Sons, 1958], esp. p. 324). A method utilizing χ^2 to test the hypothesis that observed scale frequencies deviate from a rectangular distribution no more than would be expected by chance is suggested by Karl F. Schuessler, "A Note on Statistical Significance of Scalogram," *Sociometry,* XXIV (September, 1961), 312–18. Applied to these data, Schuessler's Test II permits the rejection of the chance hypothesis at the .001 level. $\chi^2 = 60.985$ $(7df)$.

25. Statements of this type are based on the ratings in the Freeman-Winch study, as noted in n. 13 above. For societies that did not appear in their sample, we have made our own ratings on the basis of their definitions.

26. Raoul Naroll, "A Preliminary Index of Social Development," *America Anthropologist,* LVIII (August, 1956), 687–720.

27. Data were obtained for thirty-nine of the fifty-one societies in the sample on the size of their largest settlement. Societies with mediation have a median largest settlement size of 1,000, while those without mediation have a median of 346. Even eliminating the societies with developed cities, the median largest settlement size remains above 500 for societies with mediation.

28. Margaret Hasluck, *The Unwritten Law in Albania* (Cambridge: Cambridge University Press, 1954).

29. A basic difficulty in testing Durkheim's thesis arises from his manner of formulating it. His principal interest, as we understand it, was to show the relationship between division of labor and type of sanction (using type of solidarity as the intervening variable). However, in distinguishing systems of law, he added the criterion of organization. The difficulty is that he was very broad in his criterion of organization required for penal law, but quite narrow in describing the kind of organization needed for non-penal law. For the former, the "assembly of the whole people" sufficed (*op. cit.,* p. 76); for the latter, on the other hand, he suggested the following criteria: "restitutive law creates organs which are more and more specialized: consular tribunals, councils of arbitration, administrative tribunals of every sort. Even in its most general part, that which

pertains to civil law, it is exercised only through particular functionaries: magistrates, lawyers, etc., who have become apt in this role because of very special training" (p. 113). In thus suggesting that restitutive law exists only with highly complex organizational forms, Durkheim virtually insured that his thesis would be proven—that restitutive law would be found only in complex societies.

Such a "proof," however, would miss the major point of his argument. In testing the main hypothesis it would seem preferable, therefore, to specify a common and minimal organizational criterion, such as public support. Then the key question might be phrased: Is there a tendency toward restitutive rather than repressive sanctions which develops as an increasing function of the division of labor? Although our present data are not conclusive, the finding of damages and mediation in societies with minimal division of labor implies a negative answer. This suggests that the restitutive principle is not contingent on social heterogeneity or that heterogeneity is not contingent on the division of labor.

30. Sybille van der Sprenkel, *Legal Institutions in Manchu China* (London: Athlone Press, 1962). See also Ch'ü T'ung-tsu, *Law and Society in Traditional China* (Vancouver, B.C.: Institute of Pacific Relations, 1961).

31. A. H. Chroust, "The Legal Profession in Ancient Athens," *Notre Dame Law Review*, XXIX (Spring, 1954), 339–89.

32. Throughout the discussion, two sets of explanatory factors have been utilized. The observed pattern could be due to an internal process inherent in legal control systems, or it could be dependent upon the emergence of urban characteristics. It does seem clear, however, that the legal developments coincide to a considerable extent with increased "urbanism" as measured by Freeman and Winch. Evidence for this assertion is to be found in the correlation between the Freeman-Winch data and the legal scale types discerned. For the forty-five societies appearing in both samples, the rank correlation coefficient (Kendall's tau) between positions on the legal and urbanism scales is $+ .68$. While this coefficient suggests a close relationship between the two processes, it does not justify the assertion that legal evolution is wholly determined by increasing urbanism. A scatter diagram of the interrelationship reveals that legal characteristics tend to straddle the regression line for five of the seven folk-urban scale positions, omitting only scale types 2 (punishment) and 3 (religious specialization). This suggests that some other factor might emerge upon further analysis that would explain why roughly half of the societies at each stage of urbanism appear to have gone on to the next stage of legal evolution while the others lag behind. A promising candidate for such a factor is the one located by Gouldner and Peterson in their cross-cultural factor analysis of Simmons' data and described by them as "Apollonianism" or "Norm-sending" (Alvin W. Gouldner and Richard A. Peterson, *Technology and the Moral Order* [Indianapolis: Bobbs-Merrill Co., 1962], pp. 30–53).

To test whether the legal sequence has a "dynamic of its own," it would seem necessary to examine the growth of legal systems independent of folk-urban changes, as in subsystems or in societies where the process of urbanization has already occurred. The data covered here do not permit such a test.

33. For an interesting attempt to develop a general theory of legal control, applicable both to discrete societies and to the international order, see Kenneth S. Carlston, *Law and Organization in World Society* (Urbana: University of Illinois Press, 1962).

QUESTIONS

1. Can the theoretical ideas being explored by Schwartz and Miller be tested by simply utilizing data from the contemporary United States? Why, or why not?
2. Have the authors made the reader aware of the possible limitations of their data? If they did, how have they dealt with these limitations? (Pay careful attention to the notes.)
3. If you were to replicate this study by using primary data, discuss the problems you might encounter.

Managerial Succession and Organizational Effectiveness
OSCAR GRUSKY

Data often stem from very unlikely sources. How many of us would, for example, view the published "won and lost" records of professional sports teams as data that might be used to test social science hypotheses? Yet this is exactly what Grusky has done in the following paper.

Public documents, not unlike other data sources, vary a great deal in quality. Some agencies have been known to distort or actually falsify their published documents in order to create an image of a successful organization. The more public the criteria of success and the accounting system of critical events, the more difficult it is for an agency to falsify its published statistics. It would seem that the documents employed by Grusky are at the extreme "public" end of the continuum; consequently, one can have a fair amount of confidence in their accuracy. Contrast this with statistics released by police departments, social welfare agencies, and courts.

This study also provides us with an example of research involving organizations as the basic research unit, and as such it stands in sharp contrast to the bulk of contemporary sociological research.

As often happens with papers in professional journals, controversy has been generated over Grusky's article. The reader may be interested in pursuing the subsequent exchange of letters that the article produced (American Journal of Sociology 70 [1964], 69–76).

■ The major purpose of this study was to test two related hypotheses: (1) that rates of administrative succession and degree of organizational effectiveness are negatively correlated, and (2) that a change in the rate of administrative succession is negatively correlated with a change in

Reprinted from American Journal of Sociology 69 (1963), 21–31, with permission of The University of Chicago Press. (Editorial adaptations.)

organizational effectiveness.[1] The hypotheses are deliberately stated so as
not to attribute causality solely to either succession or effectiveness. We
assumed that the variables induce reciprocal effects. High rates of succession should produce declining organizational effectiveness, and low
effectiveness should encourage high rates of administrative succession.

To obtain anything resembling an adequate field test of these hypotheses required a substantial number of formal organizations that, ideally,
were identical in official goals, size, and authority structure. If the objectives of the organizations were not similar, then obviously it would not be
feasible to compare their relative effectiveness, since this concept refers
to the extent to which an organization is able to move toward the
accomplishment of its official aims. We know that for business organizations and certain public agencies, and perhaps for other kinds as well,
rates of succession are positively related to organizational size.[2] Therefore,
we sought a sample of organizations of similar size.

There is some evidence, although it is highly limited, that organizations
with different types of authority structures respond in very different ways
to personnel changes at top levels in the hierarchy.[3] Hence, organizations
with similar types of structures of authority were desirable.

In addition, a relatively "clean" field test of the hypotheses demanded
reliable and valid measures of rates of administrative succession and
organizational effectiveness. Since the sixteen organizations selected for
study, professional baseball teams, met all the relatively stringent requirements described, a second objective of this research was to illustrate
some of the potentialities of sports organizations as objects of sociological
investigation.

METHODS AND FINDINGS

All data for this study were gathered by
means of secondary analysis of published documents.[4] Baseball teams
and, in fact, most professional sports clubs offer the research advantages
of public records of team personnel and team performance. This fact, as
we shall see, also has important implications for the behavior of the
organization.

Two time periods, 1921–41 and 1951–58, were selected for study. It
was deemed wise to skip the World War II and immediate post–World
War II periods.

The structure of baseball organizations is such that ultimate responsibility for the performance of the team is almost always fixed on one position, that of field manager. At the same time, official authority is generally
concentrated in this position. Therefore, it was clear that personnel
changes among field managers rather than club presidents, general managers, or team captains were central to the study. The number of managerial changes for each time period or the average length of managerial
tenure constituted the rate of succession for each team.

The measure of organizational effectiveness was team standing, based
on the number of games won and lost at the completion of the season.
This might be considered analogous in some respects to productivity in

industrial organizations. Georgopoulos and Tannenbaum's study of thirty-two similar suborganizations or stations demonstrated significant correlations between their various measures of organizational effectiveness: expert assessment of station effectiveness, productivity, intragroup strain, and flexibility.[5] It would certainly be safe to say that, among baseball experts, team standing is the most widely accepted criterion of effectiveness. Financial profit is also an important criterion. It would appear that the profitability of a baseball club is highly related to its team standing. Consistent with this assumption, we found a strong positive correlation between team standing and yearly attendance.[6]

TABLE 1. Measures of Succession and Effectiveness for Sixteen Professional Baseball Organizations over Two Time Periods*

Team	No. of Successions			Average Team Standing†		
	Period I (1)	Period II (2)	Periods I and II (3)	Period I (4)	Period II (5)	Periods I and II (6)
Phillies	7	3	10	7.2	4.8	6.5
Giants	1	1	2	2.7	3.4	2.9
Cardinals	10	4	14	3.0	3.8	3.2
Braves	7	3	10	6.3	6.9	5.3
Pirates	6	3	9	3.2	6.9	4.2
Cubs	8	3	11	3.5	6.2	4.4
Dodgers	4	1	5	4.9	2.2	4.2
Reds	7	3	10	4.9	4.9	4.9
Athletics	0	4	4	4.8	6.6	5.3
Nats	6	3	9	4.2	6.8	4.9
Yankees	2	0	2	1.8	1.2	1.6
White Sox	8	2	10	5.6	2.9	4.9
Red Sox	8	2	10	6.0	3.9	5.4
Indians	6	1	7	3.9	2.6	3.6
Browns (Orioles)	9	5	14	5.6	6.8	5.9
Tigers	4	4	8	3.9	5.4	4.3

* Period I, 1921–41; Period II, 1951–58. Rank-order correlations (Kendall's tau) and one-tail p values are: cols. (1) and (4), $-.40$ ($p < .02$); cols. (2) and (5), $-.60$ ($p < .001$); and cols. (3) and (6), $-.43$ ($p < .001$).

† A numerically high team standing meant low effectiveness.

Table 1 presents the basic data of the study. The data for Periods I and II taken separately or together strongly supported the hypothesized negative correlation between rates of managerial succession and organizational effectiveness. The correlations were considerably greater in the second time period, 1951–58, than in the earlier one. Rates of succession and team standing correlated $-.40$ in the first period and $-.60$ in the second. One team that contributed to the lower correlation in the earlier period was the Philadelphia Athletics. Despite the fact that the team consistently finished in the second division between 1921 and 1941, no managerial successions took place during this period. Undoubtedly, manager Connie Mack's ownership of the club assisted his long tenure. The Athletics experienced frequent managerial succession during 1951–58 with the departure of Mack from the scene.

In contrast, the Yankees, as Table 1 suggests, contributed to the magnitude of the correlation in both time periods. Not only were they highly effective, but they also experienced few managerial changes.

The second hypothesis was tested by examining the relationship between changes from Period I to Period II in the average length of time a manager retained his position with a team and changes in the team's standing. That is, we wanted to see if teams that kept their managers for shorter periods (experienced more succession) in Period II than they had in Period I were less effective in the later period and vice versa. In fact, the average tenure for managers declined in Period II for all but two clubs. As Table 2 demonstrates, our hypothesis was again strongly supported.[7]

TABLE 2. Relationship Between Change in Average Length of Managerial Tenure and Average Team Standing from Period I to Period II for Fifteen Professional Baseball Teams*

| | Change in Average Team Standing | |
Change in Average Managerial Tenure	Increased Effectiveness	Decreased Effectiveness
Tenure longer	2	0
Tenure about same†	4	1
Tenure much shorter	0	8

* $P = .0014$ by Fisher's Exact Test if the categories "Longer tenure" and "Tenure about same" are combined. One team (Reds) that did not change its average team standing was excluded.

† Defined as a decrease of 0.3 year or less.

All eight teams that increased considerably their rate of managerial succession over that of the earlier period experienced a decline in average team standing. Moreover, the two clubs that decreased their rate of succession increased their effectiveness. However, it was evident that those teams that had experienced frequent and infrequent succession in the original period needed to be analyzed separately. Therefore, we controlled for average length of managerial tenure in Period I (a control for average team standing in Period I also would have been desirable, but we did not have a sufficient number of cases). The hypothesis was supported when the relationship was examined separately for teams that were below and above the median with respect to rates of succession in the first period (Table 3). Moreover, it should be noted that the single deviant case in Table 3 (the St. Louis Cardinals) was the team with the *lowest managerial tenure of any team in Period I*. This low rate remained about the same in Period II, although team effectiveness declined somewhat. We might speculate that perhaps (1) the very slight alteration of the club's policy of frequent succession was not above the threshold necessary to raise the organization's effectiveness, and/or (2) the slight decrease in the club's effectiveness did not encourage the owners to alter their policy of frequent succession.

TABLE 3. Relationship Between Change in Average Length of Managerial Tenure and Average Team Standing from Period I to Period II for Fifteen Professional Baseball Teams, Controlling for Average Length of Managerial Tenure in Period I*

| | Change in Average Team Standing | | One-Tail |
Change in Average Managerial Tenure	Increased Effectiveness	Decreased Effectiveness	p Level†
A. Short tenure in Period I (below median)			
Tenure longer or about same‡	3	1	
			.11
Tenure much shorter	0	3	
B. Long tenure in Period I (above median)			
Tenure longer or about same	3	0	
			.018
Tenure much shorter	0	5	

* One team (Reds) that did not change its average team standing was excluded.
† By Fisher's Exact Test.
‡ "About same" was defined as a decrease of 0.3 year or less.

The findings of this study may be compared with a recent laboratory investigation by Trow.[8] Using Leavitt's Common-Symbol problem and the five-position chain organizational network, Trow found no significant linear relationship between mean rate of succession and long-run organizational performance. He did find that the mean performance of the twelve teams with the lowest replacement rates was significantly superior to the mean performance of the twelve teams with the highest rates of succession. Trow discovered that *variability* in the rate of succession was a more important factor in team performance, noting that "whatever the average rate of succession, an increase in the rate, i.e., a temporal clustering of succession, tends to bring about a decrease in the level of organizational performance." In addition, he found that ability of the successor was a major factor in organizational performance. Thus, despite considerable differences between the techniques of secondary analysis and contrived experimentation, the findings of the two studies appear to be consistent at least with respect to the second hypothesis.

SUCCESSION AND EFFECTIVENESS   It is apparent that theoretical explanations for the findings of this study may be pursued from two opposite directions; it may be assumed that either effectiveness or succession functions as the primary independent variable. Our data demonstrate only the existence of an association, not its cause. Logic or common knowledge will not permit us to decide the issue. However, there is no intrinsic reason why a particular variable, such as rate of succession, could not be *both* a cause and an effect of effectiveness. This may very well be so in this instance.

A common-sense explanation for our results might suggest that effectiveness alone is the cause. The manager is fired because the team performs badly. Not only is the simplicity of this explanation appealing, but the negative correlation between succession and effectiveness is fully consistent with it. However, if taken by itself, this approach possesses all the deficiencies properly attributed to orientations that rest only on common knowledge: they typically do not stimulate careful empirical test; they typically do not suggest additional propositions which might be worthy of examination; they typically do not fit in systematically to a comprehensive body of generalizations in the field of interest. Naturally, we prefer explanations that can meet these and other criteria described by Nagel somewhat more adequately.[9]

If we assume that effectiveness and succession influence each other by contributing to managerial role strain, it is possible to formulate an alternative explanation for the major findings, one that ties in with a growing body of theory and research. It was this assumption that originally provoked this study. Succession, because it represents a universal organizational process, and effectiveness, because all formal organizations tend to strive toward the attainment of their official objectives, are strategic concepts for studying organizations within a comparative framework. Numerous studies conducted in the laboratory as well as in the field suggest that these variables produce reciprocal effects. For example, both Gouldner's and Guest's field research as well as Trow's experiment indicate that succession influences organizational effectivness.[10] On the other hand, Hamblin's laboratory study suggests that the ineffectiveness of the group contributes to high rates of succession among the leaders. When the leader could not solve a crisis problem confronting the group, he was replaced.[11] Accordingly, the relationship between rates of succession and organizational effectiveness was analyzed within the context of a conceptual scheme that focused on their interrelationships with a number of other variables: managerial (or executive) role strain, expectation of replacement, style of supervision, subgroup stability, morale, clientele support, degree of discrepancy between managerial authority and responsibility, and availability of objective assessment of organizational performance.* The methodological weaknesses of studies such as the present one, based wholly on official documents, should not be underestimated. Clearly, such inquiries are not adequate substitutes for well-designed field and laboratory investigations. Systematic research examining, for example, the nature of the relationship between morale and effectiveness in baseball teams (morale and productivity studies of industrial organizations have produced contradictory findings[12]), morale and strength of clientele support, and managerial role strain and team effectiveness would be highly desirable.

Several years ago Herbert A. Simon pointed out that the problem of organizational effectiveness was essentially an empirical one. He observes: "What is needed is empirical research and experimentation to determine the relative desirability of alternative administrative arrangements."[13] In

---

[*Editors' note: An extended discussion of some ten variables, of which the two researched here are part, is contained in the original paper.]

addition, he emphasized two canons of research design: "First, it is necessary that the objectives of the administrative organization under study be defined in concrete terms so that results, expressed in terms of these objectives, may be accurately measured. Second, it is necessary that sufficient experimental control be exercised."[14] As an approximation to these principles, this study, by means of secondary analysis of published documents, has, in effect, compared the performance of professional baseball teams operating under contrasting administrative arrangements, the conditions of frequent and relatively infrequent managerial succession.

NOTES

1. This hypothesis was discussed in my "Administrative Succession in Formal Organizations," *Social Forces,* XXXIX (December, 1960), 105–15.

2. See my "Corporate Size, Bureaucratization, and Managerial Succession," *American Journal of Sociology,* LXVII (November, 1961), 261–69, and L. Kriesberg, "Careers, Organization Size, and Succession," *American Journal of Sociology,* LXVIII (November, 1962), 355–59. For a comprehensive discussion of other variables related to size see T. Caplow, "Organizational Size," *Administrative Science Quarterly,* II (March, 1957), 484–505.

3. D. M. Sills, *The Volunteers* (Glencoe, Ill.: Free Press, 1957); W. A. Lunden, "The Tenure and Turnover of State Prison Wardens," *American Journal of Corrections,* XIX (November–December, 1957), 14–15; and A. Etzioni, "Authority Structure and Organizational Effectiveness," *Administrative Science Quarterly,* IV (June, 1959), 43–67.

4. H. Hurkin and S. C. Thompson, *The Official Encyclopedia of Baseball* (2d rev. ed.; New York: A. S. Barnes & Co., 1959); H. Johnson, *Who's Who in Baseball* (New York: Buston Publishing Co., 1953); F. Menke, *The Encyclopedia of Sports* (2d rev. ed.; New York: A. S. Barnes & Co., 1960); *1958 Baseball Guide and Record Book* (St. Louis, Mo.: Sporting News, 1958); T. Spink and Son, *Baseball Register,* compiled by T. Spink and P. Rickart (St. Louis, Mo.: Sporting News, 1940–41, 1951–58).

5. B. S. Georgopoulos and A. S. Tannenbaum, "A Study of Organizational Effectiveness," *American Sociological Review,* XXII (October, 1957), 534–40.

6. Profitability, attendance, and effectiveness are related in part because prolonged increases in profits tend to yield increases in organizational control over the market for new talent and therefore tend to produce a more effective farm system. Interpretation of the correlation between team standing and attendance should be approached cautiously. Attendance may also be a function of variables such as the total population of the metropolitan area, its particular age and sex distribution, and, of course, the number of professional baseball teams in the community.

7. We realize some of the interpretative limitations of utilizing team averages as measures of succession. A study comparing the "effectiveness" and length of tenure of the successor and his managerial predecessor is in progress. In this investigation the object of study is the manager and not the team. Some limitations in our measure of effectiveness also should be noted. Team standing may not reflect perfectly the ability of the team, just as fielding and batting averages

are not ideal measures of individual performance. E.g., a team may improve over the course of a season and because of a poor start finish only second, although it is the best team by other standards. And the bias of the official scorer has a lot to do with the players' fielding and batting averages.

8. D. B. Trow, "Membership Succession and Team Performance," *Human Relations*, XIII, No. 3 (1960), 259–68. An immediate problem in making such a contrast is the critical difference in the objects of study. Trow applies his findings to "self-organizing" groups and points out several limitations of the experimental situation relevant to generalizing the findings. Formal organizations typically possess properties that laboratory organizations such as Trow's do not possess, such as: a formal system of authority, at least three levels of authority, and planned task differentiation. Moreover, when laboratory investigations have attempted to manipulate some of these differentiating variables, important results have been indicated. Hence, H. H. Kelley found that the existence of a hierarchy influenced communication ("Communication in Experimentally Created Hierarchies," *Human Relations*, IV [1951], 39–56), and I. D. Steiner and W. I. Field found that the assignment of roles to persons in laboratory groups affected persons' perceptions of and reactions to one another ("Role Assignment and Interpersonal Influence," *Journal of Abnormal and Social Psychology*, LX, No. 2 [1960], 239–45). Of course, there are outstanding examples of experimental studies that have attempted to establish structures which legitimately could be called formal organizations. See, e.g., W. M. Evan and M. Zelditch, Jr., "A Laboratory Study on Bureaucratic Authority," *American Sociological Review*, XXVI, No. 6 (1961), 883–93.

9. Ernest Nagel in a recent book provides an excellent discussion of the elements of the scientific and common sense approaches. He observed that "the sciences seek to discover and to formulate in general terms the conditions under which events of various sorts occur, the corresponding happenings. This goal can be achieved only by distinguishing or isolating certain properties in the subject matter studied and by ascertaining the repeatable patterns of dependence in which these properties stand to one another. In consequence, when the inquiry is successful, propositions that hitherto appeared to be quite unrelated are exhibited as linked to each other in determinate ways by virtue of their place in a system of explanation" (*The Structure of Science* [New York: Harcourt, Brace & World, 1961], p. 4).

10. A. Gouldner, *Patterns of Industrial Bureaucracy* (Glencoe, Ill.: Free Press, 1954); R. H. Guest, *Organizational Change* (Homewood, Ill.: Dorsey Press, 1962); and Trow, *op. cit.* See also W. F. Whyte, "The Social Structure of the Restaurant Industry," *American Journal of Sociology*, LIV (January, 1949), 302–10; C. R. Christiansen, *Management Succession in Small and Growing Enterprises* (Boston: Graduate School of Business Administration, Harvard University, 1953); E. Dale, "Du Pont: Pioneer in Systematic Management," *Administrative Science Quarterly*, II (June, 1957), 26–30; O. Grusky, "Role Conflict in Organization: A Study of Prison Camp Officials," *Administrative Science Quarterly*, III (March, 1959), 463–67; and R. H. McCleery, *Policy Change in Prison Management* (East Lansing: Michigan State University, 1957), pp. 10–27.

11. R. L. Hamblin, "Leadership and Crisis," *Sociometry*, XXI (December, 1958), 322–35.

12. E.g., R. L. Kahn and N. C. Morse, "The Relationship of Productivity to

Morale," *Journal of Social Issues,* VII, No. 3 (1951), 8–17; D. Katz, N. Maccoby, and N. C. Morse, *Productivity, Supervision and Morale in an Office Situation* (Ann Arbor, Mich.: Institute of Social Research, 1950); D. Katz, N. Maccoby, and L. G. Floor, *Productivity, Satisfaction and Morale among Railroad Workers* (Ann Arbor, Mich.: Institute of Social Research, 1951); and N. C. Morse, *Satisfactions in the White-Collar Job* (Ann Arbor, Mich.: Institute for Social Research, 1953); H. Wilensky's paper in C. Arensberg *et al.* (eds.) *Research in Industrial Human Relations: A Critical Appraisal* (New York: Harper & Bros., 1957), pp. 25–50.

13. *Administrative Behavior* (2d ed.; New York: The Macmillan Co., 1958), p. 42.

14. *Ibid.*

QUESTIONS

1. Discuss the importance of baseball team data in selecting data for the "critical" test of Grusky hypothesis.
2. Can Grusky's study be easily replicated by an undergraduate student? Why? (If you answer "yes," you might undertake such a project.)
3. Are there any other issues or hypotheses that can be explored with the same type of data source?
4. How does Grusky operationalize the concepts of occupational effectiveness and managerial succession? Have you any quarrel with these measurements?
5. How does Grusky handle data that does not support his hypothesis (for example, Philadelphia Athletics)?
6. How are the two distinct time periods used differently in testing each of the two hypotheses noted in the first paragraph of the paper?
7. What are the advantages and disadvantages of a field study compared to a lab study in testing Grusky's hypotheses? Attempt to analyze the research design employed by Grusky in terms of the types of designs discussed by Campbell (article 21).

Measuring the Motives of Public Officials at a Distance: An Exploratory Study of American Presidents

RICHARD E. DONLEY and DAVID G. WINTER

An important and often overlooked data source for the social sciences is communication media, which vary from personal documents (letters, diaries, suicide notes, and so forth) to mass media (books, magazines, newspapers, television, among others). The latter sources are often readily available and provide a fairly inexpensive source of data for the social researcher. The

Reprinted from *Behavioral Science* 15 (1970), 227–236, with permission of James G. Miller, M.D., Ph.D., Editor.

principle sociological use of these materials has been for research on the values, ideas, and beliefs of relatively large social categories (nations and social classes, for example), very often over fairly large periods of time.

A specialized set of techniques usually referred to as "content analysis" has been developed over the last thirty years for the specific purpose of analyzing communication media.

The primary reasons for using communication media as a data source are:

1. The unavailability of other sources of data and the inability (outright refusal or death) to gain access to research subjects;
2. Validation of data collected by other means (for example, attitudes toward premarital sex researched by means of a public opinion poll might be partially validated by a content analysis of love stories in popular magazine fiction).

Some of the issues that have been researched by means of data from the communication media are:

1. Cultural values of different nations expressed in songs and popular literature;
2. Suicidal motivations expressed in suicide notes;
3. Generalized attitudes toward minority groups in popular magazine fiction;
4. The relationship between "need achievement" and child-rearing techniques as reflected in folk tales;
5. Trends in sexual techniques and values as seen in marriage manuals;
6. Legitimation of violence as expressed in television programs.

In the following article, Donley and Winter have explored selected psychological dimensions of U.S. presidents by means of a content analysis of their inaugural speeches. Besides the intrinsic interest of the topic, this study is an excellent example of how content analysis can be used to research what would have been practically impossible to explore by more direct means.

INTRODUCTION

Many contemporary theories recognize that the personality dispositions of individual actors can be important factors in explaining social and political action, but systematic research on the relationships between individual personality and political action has been hampered by the lack of precise techniques for measuring the motives and other personality characteristics of really significant actors. Persons of historical importance are dead; significant contemporary actors are, by virtue of their official position, usually unavailable for the administering of most psychological assessment techniques. Thus researchers have had to rely on two alternative strategies: (1) Speculative clinical interpretation of known biographical facts (for example, Lasswell, 1936; Freud and Bullitt, 1967). Such interpretations are often sensitive and sometimes brilliant, but they are of necessity *post hoc* explanations. Moreover, they usually do not use standard quantifiable measures, so that there is no way to compare precisely the personality of one actor with that of another. (2) Systematic testing of persons at lower levels in the political hierarchy, with implicit extrapolation to actors at higher levels (for example, Kaltenbach and McClelland, 1958; Browning and Jacob, 1964). Such testing contributes to our understanding of political actors; yet we simply do not know whether the results hold true for actors at the higher levels.

The American Presidency is an excellent case in point. At any one time, only a few Presidents and former Presidents are alive. Moreover, it would be rather unrealistic for even the most ambitious social scientist to seek an hour of the President's time to administer a Thematic Apperception Test or a questionnaire. Most of the same difficulties confront the social scientist who would study lesser officials, or politicians and administrators from other countries. Without direct access, therefore, how can we hope to carry out systematic research on personality and political action at the significant, national levels of decision-making? Quite accurate records of the speeches and public statements of such men are available. Normally, of course, such speeches are analyzed only for overt statements of policy and program: a foreign policy, a plan for transportation, a proposal for tax changes, or even some suggestion of a change in political alliances. The nuances, the style, and the psychological imagery of such speeches are usually dismissed as unimportant, or else as being of only literary interest. Since, as Barber (1968a, p. 938) points out, our predictions about a man's political style and performance have so often been wrong, perhaps it is worthwhile to examine the psychological imagery of political speeches.

This study is a first attempt to apply to such speeches a systematic, objective, and quantified method of measuring human motives through techniques that have been carefully validated in the psychological laboratory (summarized in Atkinson, 1958, and Heckhausen, 1967). Specifically, this study reports levels of achievement and power motives (n Achievement and n Power) in the inaugural speeches of American Presidents from 1905 to 1969. However, the method used here can readily be applied to records of verbal and written material of any kind, from political actors of any historical period.

PREVIOUS STUDIES OF AMERICAN PRESIDENTS

There is certainly no lack of historical accounts of Presidential administrations, political analyses of Presidential accomplishments, and studies of the powers and limitations of the Presidential role and institutional aspects of the Presidency. There are some interpretations of individual Presidents that make use of impressionistic psychological data and elements of psychological theory. Perhaps the Georges' study of Woodrow Wilson and Colonel House is the most comprehensive recent example (George and George, 1956), while the works mentioned above of Lasswell and Freud and Bullitt are earlier examples. Other noteworthy studies by Hargrove (1966) and Barber (1968a, b) combine personality theory with consideration of the President's adult political style. While these studies may be provocative and illuminating, they suffer from the inherent defect that it is always possible and sometimes superficially easy to find, after the fact, some early biographical data that, with the aid of some psychological theory, will "explain" later political actions.

Is there any scientific pay-off to the study of the President's personality as a factor in his political actions? Does personality significantly affect performances that are so obviously shaped by the external problems that the President faces, by the balance of political forces that he confronts, and by the range and quality of advice that he receives? Greenstein (1967) argues that whether individual actors affect events or whether personal variability affects political behavior is likely to depend on circumstances such as the following: Does the environment admit of restructuring? Are there elaborate fixed conventional expectations or mental sets concerning performance? Is the situation ambiguous (new, complex, or contradictory)? Is the individual actor in a "strategic" location? Clearly there are times when all of the above conditions prevail with respect to the Presidency; at such times we should expect the President's personality to have relatively greater impact on his political actions. For example, as is well known, Franklin Roosevelt had great personal impact during the first one-hundred days of the New Deal. This argument that both personality and circumstances affect action is also reflected in current motivation theory and research, which suggest that motives interact with expectancies and incentives to produce behavior that cannot be predicted from knowing either the motives (personality) or the expectancies and incentives (situation) alone (Atkinson and Feather, 1966).

THE CONTENT ANALYSIS OF
INAUGURAL SPEECHES

In this study we apply a technique of content analysis that was devised by McClelland, Atkinson, Clark, and Lowell (1953) for scoring human motives from Thematic Apperception Test (TAT) protocols. Essentially the researcher measures a motive with a scoring system that is developed through arousing the motive experimentally, and then noting its effects on imaginative thought. Such scoring systems are further validated through research on the action correlates and developmental origins of the motive. Often motives scored in this way do not correlate highly with a person's conscious report of what his motives are, but they do relate to important patterns of his action (McClelland, 1966; Heckhausen, 1967, pp. 7–9). The human motive most thoroughly studied in this manner is the achievement motive (n Achievement), which has been shown to have extensive relationships to economic development and entrepreneurial success (McClelland, 1961). In the course of this research, the n Achievement scoring system originally designed for analyzing TATs has been successfully applied to children's readers (deCharms and Moeller, 1962); to folktales (Child, Storm, and Veroff, 1958); to writings of classical authors, popular dramatists, and diaries (McClelland, 1961); and even to reported dreams of Nigerian school children (LeVine, 1966). Hence it is clear that the method can be used to analyze written or verbal records that are quite different from the spontaneous unconstrained associations that are typically manifested in the TAT. In fact it appears to be appropriate for application to any written sequence that is at least partly imaginative—in the sense that the sequence describes some kind of action, real or imagined—rather than purely factual.

Is it a sound procedure to apply such a scoring system to Presidential inaugural speeches? They do contain a good deal of strictly factual material; yet as the first official statement of a President, they also make many references to the intended or projected action of "this people" or "this administration." They record the President's fundamental concerns, his hopes and fears, and his aspirations. They establish a distinctive tone and atmosphere for the incoming administration. Naturally the projected actions and atmosphere are calculated to appeal to popular sentiment and social constraints; in this sense the speeches are carefully worded. (In psychological terms, they contain defenses as well as needs.) However, such "manifest" alterations and adjustments are not likely to have great effect on the results of the motive scoring, since these scoring systems are sensitive to variations in the quality of imagery and metaphor, the specificity and elaboration of goals, the expression of affect or emotion, and the force of language. The inaugural speeches differ among themselves enormously in these ways; in fact, such aspects may well be a more reliable indication of Presidential personality than are abstract outlines of issues and policies, which can be so easily calculated or modified. In any case, the issue of whether motive scoring systems can usefully be applied to the inaugural speeches will be resolved only by trying them. In Table 2 below, we will present passages dealing with the same issues and goals, but taken from different speeches. The corresponding differences in motive scores are great. Thus it seems clear that the topics, issues, or policies of a speech do not necessarily determine its motive content.

Granted that the speeches may reflect valid motive imagery, do they reflect the motive imagery of the President or of the persons who wrote the speeches? There is evidence that some Presidents wrote their own inaugural speeches (see Pringle, 1939; Schlesinger, 1957; Israel, 1965). Undoubtedly all Presidents retain great control over the content of their inaugural speeches: they select the writers; they give ideas; they approve or disapprove of wording; and they add the final touches, phrasing, and imagery. In any case, the action and impact of the Presidency are derived from both the President and those who shape his image, including close advisors and speechwriters.

ACHIEVEMENT AND POWER AS PRESIDENTIAL ATTRIBUTES AND AS MOTIVES

Why select the achievement and power motives for analysis? Achievement and power appear to be central to the Presidency—indeed, central to all aspects of political life. Parsons (1952) points out that any social system has two important tasks: goal-attainment (achievement) and system-maintenance (external and internal control or power). More specifically, Burns (1966) describes the way in which achievement is important to success in the Presidential role:

Better than any other human instrumentality he [the President] can order the relations of his ends and means, alter existing institutions and procedures or create new ones, calculate the consequences of different policies, experiment with various methods, control the timing of action, anticipate the reactions of affected interests, and conciliate them or at least mediate among them. (p. 339)

The President must choose among different degrees of risk; he must take personal responsibility for his actions; and he must pay attention to the results of those actions, modifying his future performance accordingly, if he wishes to retain his effectiveness. As societies grow in complexity, executive power appears to have greater inherent freedom, flexibility, and scope than does legislative or judicial power.

There can be little doubt that power is equally as important as is achievement to the Presidential role: the President must have power in order to be elected, and in order to secure adoption, implementation, and continuous execution of his programs. Weber (1948) goes so far as to define the politician as a power-seeker:

He who is active in politics strives for power either as a means in serving other aims, ideal or egoistic, or as "power for power's sake," that is, in order to enjoy the prestige-feeling that power gives. . . . The career of politics grants a feeling of power. The knowledge of influencing men, of participating in power over them, and above all, the feeling of holding in one's hands a nerve fiber of historically important events. . . . (pp. 78, 115)

Hargrove contends that "the first requisite for doing these tasks well is a sense of personal—and thus, Presidential—power."

There is considerable evidence that the behaviors associated with n Achievement and n Power are directly related to the kinds of achievement and power behaviors that we have postulated as necessary for the successful President. McClelland (1961, Chapter 6) points out that n Achievement is associated with moderate risk-taking, acceptance of personal responsibility, and the use of concrete feedback or knowledge of results to improve performance. Thus n Achievement leads to success in an entrepreneurial or innovating role. Our measure of n Power is taken from the research of Winter (1968, 1969), who revised an earlier measure developed by Veroff (1957), which was used in a study of local politicians conducted by Browning and Jacob. While the new measure of n Power has not been as thoroughly studied as has n Achievement, it appears to have several action correlates that are related to the Presidential role: it is associated with holding office; with argumentativeness and trying to convince or manipulate others; and with a concern about prestige, especially as reflected in ownership of prestigeful possessions. Both of the motive-scoring measures are reliable, objective, and quantified. They can readily be learned by a previously inexperienced scorer.[1] For all of these reasons, we felt justified in employing them in the present study.

HYPOTHESES: A TYPOLOGY OF PRESIDENTIAL LEADERSHIP

In advance of the scoring of inaugural speeches, we constructed a typology of American Presidents who served from 1905 to 1968 along the dimensions of achievement and power, as shown in Table 1. Combining the two dimensions gives four basic types of President.[2] We placed each President in a cell of the table according to our overall impression of his performance in office. We were guided by a survey of Presidential biographies, comparative analyses of Presidents, and the historical record of accomplishments, innovations, and changes made during the various administrations.[3] Each cell can be described briefly in terms of the Presidents placed there.

TABLE 1. American Presidents, 1905–1964, Classified According to the Dimensions of Achievement and Power Behavior in Office

		Power Behavior (and hypothesized need for Power)	
		high	low
Achievement Behavior (and hypothesized need for Achievement)	high	Theodore Roosevelt Woodrow Wilson Franklin Roosevelt John Kennedy Lyndon Johnson	Herbert Hoover
	low		William Howard Taft Warren Harding Calvin Coolidge Dwight Eisenhower

Note: No predictions were made for Harry Truman.

1. The high achievement/high power President is likely to be strong and active; he will try to give his administration a record of accomplishments; he will be led to acquire the political influence that is necessary for these accomplishments. He may even be considered as ruthless or too powerful by some. Of the twentieth century Presidents, Theodore Roosevelt, Woodrow Wilson, Franklin Roosevelt, John Kennedy, and Lyndon Johnson appear to fit this category. They are usually considered to have been among the strongest Presidents.

2. The high achievement/low power President will try to bring about substantive accomplishments, but he will lack the political skills necessary to bring them about in the office of President. Given his energy and resolve, he might have been more successful in business. Herbert Hoover appears to belong to this category. Prior to 1928, he accomplished much; but as President he seemed to lack a "political sense," and his administration seemed unable to rally public support (Barber, 1968b, p. 59).

3. The high power/low achievement President would seek office for his own prestige and personal ends, rather than for achieving any lasting accomplishments. We did not hypothesize that any twentieth century President was of this type, although it is likely that some nineteenth century American Presidents, and other kinds of politicians and chief executives may fit here.

4. The low achievement/low power President will not try to achieve any major accomplishments, nor will he live up to the power potential of the Presidential role. He may not be especially happy as President. It is even likely that he was chosen by his party for its own reasons, rather than having actively pursued the office. Depending on the situation and the times, he may be seen either as "acceptable" or as "inactive." We hypothesized that William Howard Taft, Warren Harding, Calvin Coolidge, and Dwight Eisenhower fit this pattern.[4]

Our typology is an hypothetical arrangement of the twentieth century Presidents based on their *actions* as President. Our hypothesis is that their patterns of achievement and power motives will be consistent with these groupings.

METHODS AND RESULTS

The first task was to obtain accurate and complete records of the inaugural speeches, which were taken from a collection compiled by F. Israel.[5] Next, the scoring procedures had to be modified somewhat to take account of the great difference between the individual TAT stories for which they were originally intended and the public speeches to which they would be applied.[6] First, only Achievement Imagery and Power Imagery were scored; the various related subcategories were ignored because a single speech has no clearly defined break, as does a TAT protocol. Second, each sentence was considered as a unit of scoring, with the reservation that two consecutive sentences with the same kind of Imagery were counted as only one sentence. These changes are similar to those made by Berlew (reported in McClelland, 1958), who adapted the n Achievement system for use in scoring classical Greek texts. Finally, certain slight changes were made in the definition of Achievement and Power Imagery. These changes were quite consistent with the original systems, and were designed to make more precise the definition of a "character" and of "action" in the context of an inaugural speech. The speeches were then scored for n Achievement and n Power by one of us (RED). It was not possible to score the speeches "blind," because most of them contained specific identifying details, as well as words which have become famous phrases, all of which could not be effectively changed or disguised. Therefore, as a check on reliability and in an attempt to eliminate bias, both authors reviewed a large sample of scoring decisions, using only the actual phrase that had been scored or not scored, taken out of the larger context. Units were then scored blind by DGW, and the percentage category agreement was 85 percent, which seems acceptable for this kind of research, given the problems of adapting the systems to scoring speeches (see Atkinson, p. 688).

One additional problem was the length of speech, which varied from 970 words to 5,570 words. Some kind of correction for length is needed; yet there is no general agreement as to the appropriate procedure (Atkinson, p. 837). We adopted the simplest method, which was to divide the total score by the number of words and then to multiply by 1,000, in order to get a corrected score of imagery per thousand words. Table 2 presents samples of various speeches, arranged in pairs; both passages in a pair deal with the same general issue, but one is scored for n Achievement or n Power and the other is not. It is hoped that the reader will be convinced of the reality of differences in motive imagery, independent of the particular topic; more generally, that the expression of Presidential personality is not completely determined by the situation and issues that confront the President.

Table 3 presents the principal findings: the raw scores for Achievement and Power Imagery, word lengths, and corrected Imagery scores.[7] In general, the findings confirm our hypotheses about the motive patterns of the various Presidents, as these hypotheses were summarized in Table 1. Interestingly enough, Woodrow Wilson appears to contradict our hypothesis, in that he appears as high in n Power and low in n Achievement (although close to the median in both cases). This finding appears to be related to the interpretation of George and George (p. 320), which holds

TABLE 2. Samples from Various Inaugural Speeches Scored and Not Scored for Motive-Related Imagery

---

1. *On Legislation*

"To render the reform lasting, however . . . further legislative and executive action are needed."

Taft; not scored.

"To consider these evils, to find their remedy, is the most sore necessity of our times."

Hoover; scored for *n* Achievement.

2. *On Man's Condition*

"We dedicated ourselves to the fulfillment of a vision—to speed the time when there would be for all the people that security and peace essential to the pursuit of happiness."

F. Roosevelt (2nd); not scored.

"We are beginning to wipe out the line that divides the practical from the ideal; and in so doing we are fashioning an instrument of unimagined power for the establishment of a morally better world."

F. Roosevelt (2nd); scored for *n* Achievement.

3. *On Enacting Legislation*

"I wish to say that insofar as I can I hope to promote the enactment of further legislation of this character." [Refers to specific legislation on injury-compensation.]

Taft; not scored.

"These are the lines of attack. I shall presently urge upon a new Congress in special session detailed measures for their fulfillment."

F. Roosevelt (1st); scored for *n* Power.

4. *On Defense*

"The strong man must at all times be alert to the attack of insidious disease."

Hoover; not scored.

"[We must be prepared] in order to prevent other nations from taking advantage of us and of our inability to defend our interests—and assert our rights with a strong hand."

Taft; scored for *n* Power.

5. *On Assisting Other Nations*

"We have emerged from the losses of the Great War and the reconstruction following it with increased virility and strength. From this strength we have contributed to the recovery and progress of the world."

Hoover; not scored.

"If we fail, the cause of free self-government throughout the world will rock to its foundations, and therefore our responsibility is heavy, to ourselves, to the world as it is today, and to the generations yet unborn."

T. Roosevelt; scored for *n* Achievement and *n* Power.

---

that Wilson's concern for achievement was less an internalized motive than it was a defense or "purifying" mask for his great power needs.

A further interesting observation is that the four Presidents who have had attempts made on their lives are higher in *n* Power ($p = .012$, Mann-Whitney U test, 2-tailed) and in *n* Achievement ($p = .072$, Mann-Whitney U test, 2-tailed) than those who have not. Since *n* Power and *n* Achievement are highly correlated (rho $= +.70$, $p = .01$), it is impossible to determine which motive is truly associated with assassination attempts. It may be that "vigorous" Presidents, who are high in both motives, arouse more hostility in potential assassins, or it may be that such Presidents simply

TABLE 3. Achievement and n Power Scores of Presidential Inaugural Speeches

President	Approximate number of words	Raw n Ach. score	n Ach. per 1,000 words	Raw n Power score	n Power per 1,000 words
T. Roosevelt (1905)	970	6	6.2+	8	8.3+
W. H. Taft (1909)	5570	5	.9−	11	2.0−
W. Wilson (1st–1913)	1670	5	3.0−	9	5.4+
W. Harding (1921)	3540	8	2.3−	13	3.4−
C. Coolidge (1925)	4200	7	1.7−	13	3.1−
H. Hoover (1929)	3960	16	4.0+	12	3.0−
F. Roosevelt (1st–1933)	1900	10	5.2⎱ +	12	6.3⎱ +,
F. Roosevelt (2nd–1937)	1870	8	4.3⎰	12	6.4⎰
H. Truman (1949)	2460	10	4.1+	18	7.3+
D. Eisenhower (1st–1953)	2460	7	2.8−	10	4.1−
J. Kennedy (1961)	1320	9	6.8+	11	8.3+
L. Johnson (1965)	1460	11	7.5+	10	6.8+
R. Nixon (1969)	2130	18	8.5+	11	5.1−

+ = Rated as high among the group of Presidents.
− = Rated as low among the group of Presidents.
Cutting points were set at the median for n Power, and at the point of greatest natural break near the median for n Ach. Actually, Hoover, Truman, and F. Roosevelt (2nd) could be classified as low in n Achievement, except that this might unnecessarily presuppose an upward secular trend in Presidential n Achievement.

exposed themselves more to the public. This finding could be checked and extended by studying speeches of series of leaders in other countries, some of whom have been attacked or killed.

In general, the motive levels expressed in a particular President's inaugural speech are closely related to the overall record of that President's term of office, regardless of the particular issues, crises, or political situation that confront the President. In terms of psychological theory, verbal measures of motives are related to long-term trends of choice and action, even in very complex situations. Would we have obtained similar results had we been able to question Presidents directly about their concerns—for example by giving them questionnaires measuring "Patriotism," "Achievement values," or "Belief in leadership"? Probably not. Very likely most citizens—even Presidents—would be constrained by public opinion and popular values to give very similar answers to such questions. In other words, the indirect method of assessing motives is not only feasible, but also more sensitive and more revealing.

While the differences among the Presidents do fit our hypotheses, it may seem unfair to compare men from such different time periods. Thus William Howard Taft and Franklin Roosevelt are separated from each other by almost twenty-five years, a war and a depression, and enormous changes in American social and political life. We therefore decided to make a finer comparison of three pairs of contiguous Presidents: Theodore Roosevelt and William Howard Taft; Herbert Hoover and Franklin Roosevelt; and Dwight Eisenhower and John F. Kennedy. Our predictions were that T. Roosevelt would score higher than Taft in both n Achievement and n Power; that F. Roosevelt would score higher than Hoover in n Power but not in n Achievement; and that Kennedy would score higher than Eisenhower in both motives. Table 4 shows the results of these more precise comparisons. All of the predicted differences held up, although in some cases the difference was not quite significant at usual levels of statistical significance. However, the combined probability estimate for each motive was highly significant, using the method for combining probability estimates that is described by Mosteller and Bush (1954). These significances are conservatively estimated, since the Chi-Square statistics were computed only on the basis of presence of motive-related imagery, in 2×1 tables. Of course, the "units" of a given speech are not fully independent, as the Chi-Square test requires, and so the significance may thereby be elevated.

For these reasons, as well as because of the small sample of cases, the

TABLE 4. Comparison of n Achievement and n Power Scores Between Selected Pairs of Presidential Inaugural Speeches

President	Number of Words	n Achievement		n Power	
		Observed[a]	Expected[b]	Observed[a]	Expected[b]
T. Roosevelt	972	6	1.6	8	2.8
W. H. Taft	5568	5	9.4	11	16.2
Total		11	11.0	19	19.0
		$\chi^2 = 14.16$		$\chi^2 = 11.41$	
		$d.f. = 1$		$d.f. = 1$	
		$p < .001$		$p < .001$	
H. Hoover	3960	16	17.5	12	16.2
F. Roosevelt (1st)	1908	10	8.5	12	7.8
Total		26	26.0	24	24.0
		$\chi^2 = 0.39$		$\chi^2 = 3.34$	
		$d.f. = 1$		$d.f. = 1$	
		p n.s.		$p < .10$	
D. Eisenhower (1st)	2460	7	10.6	10	13.7
J. Kennedy	1320	9	5.4	11	7.3
Total		16	16.0	21	21.0
		$\chi^2 = 3.62$		$\chi^2 = 2.88$	
		$d.f. = 1$		$d.f. = 1$	
		$p < .10$		$p < .10$	
		Combined $\chi^2 = 17.78$[a]		Combined $\chi^2 = 17.63$	
		$d.f. = 2$		$d.f. = 3$	
		$p < .001$		$p < .001$	

[a] Observed = the actual number of motive-related images in the speech.

[b] Expected = the number of images expected, assuming the total number of images for the pair to be distributed in proportion to the relative speech lengths of each (i.e., assuming no difference in image frequency).

[c] Only the T. Roosevelt/W. Taft and the Eisenhower/Kennedy comparisons were combined, since no differences were hypothesized between F. Roosevelt and Hoover in n Achievement.

results should be regarded as tentative. Indeed, the point of the study is not so much to find out something that is not already known about American Presidents as it is to demonstrate the practicability and usefulness of the method of scoring speeches for motives.

It is interesting to note the relationship between our results and an earlier study by Smith, Stone, and Glenn (1966) of nomination acceptance speeches by Republican and Democratic Presidential candidates from 1928 through 1964. Smith et al. used the General Inquirer, which is a computer system of content analysis that uses the "tag," or group of words assumed to be synonymous, as the basis of analysis, rather than the more complex "themes" derived from experimental arousal that constitute the motive scoring systems. Of course, the two studies are not directly comparable, since nomination speeches are written for very different occasions and purposes than are inaugural speeches. However we did take the seven inaugural speeches (six men) for which we had motive scores, and compared them to the data from the corresponding previous acceptance speeches. With only seven cases, it was not surprising to find that none of the correlations was significant. N Power did have a rank-order correlation of $+.39$ with Factor I, which Smith et al. label "Universalistic Leadership," and describe as a shift from formal, legal power to a more generalized urging and influence. It is reasonable and certainly interesting that n Power is especially related to influence and urging, rather than only formal power structures. Nevertheless even this correlation is not statistically significant with the small number of cases.

CONCLUSIONS

We have demonstrated that Presidential inaugural speeches can reliably be scored for n Achievement and n Power, using objective and readily applied measures. We have made a preliminary demonstration that these scores relate rather well to the overall records of action, innovation, power, and general success of the Presidents. Our principal conclusion is that the method itself can be of great value and use in assessing the personality of important political leaders about whom, for a variety of reasons, it is very difficult or impossible to gather the usual information and personality data. Political speeches are normally thought of as obvious and open statements of policy and intent. Perhaps for this reason they are usually widely distributed and carefully recorded, yet assumed to be of little psychological interest. However they can be analyzed to determine the underlying motives of the speaker or political actor, motives which may have a very great role in determining the future political behavior of that actor. The scope for application of this relatively easy method of obtaining otherwise inaccessible information should be apparent. One can make analyses of the speeches of political actors while they are seeking office, or before they assume office.[8] One can make a psychological analysis of speeches of leaders about whom more obvious information is unavailable. For example, it may be very important to have some way of estimating the motives of leaders or leadership groups in different countries, in order to get a reliable estimate of their subsequent policy. Such an estimate would, of course, have to take into account a variety of other factors. Thus in analyzing speeches of leaders in developing countries, one would have to have some idea of what motives are required for successful leadership in a particular country before one ventures to predict which leaders would bring about accomplishments or hold power. Finally, these techniques may be applied to leaders of the past. At what point, for example, did speeches of leaders in ancient Greece or Victorian England show a decline in n Achievement? (McClelland, 1961, Chapter 4) In the historical sense, who were the really significant leaders—that is, the men whose motive patterns presaged important social and political developments in their countries? In any case, the techniques described here provide a measure of motives that is independent from observations of overt action, so that historical and political psychology can avoid fruitless statements of the type that "Napoleon must have had a high need for power, because he was a very powerful man."

NOTES

1. Those researchers desiring to learn the use of the scoring system should consult Atkinson (1958, Appendix I) for n Achievement, and should write to the second author of this study for learning and practice materials for the revised n Power scoring system used in this study.

2. It seems to us that these two dimensions crosscut the dimensions of *activity-passivity* and *positive-negative affect* proposed by Barber (1968b). N Achievement and n Power may both involve activity, and n Power is probably related to positive affect. Yet it is not clear that all low n Achievement/low n Power Presidents had negative affect for what they were called upon to do.

3. Sources consulted include: Bailey (1966); Barber (1968a, 1968b); Blum (1966); Burns (1956); George and George (1956); Mowry (1958); Newstadt (1956); Pollard (1947); Pringle (1939); Rossiter (1956); Schlesinger, Sr. (1962); and Schlesinger, Jr. (1957).

4. No predictions were made for Harry Truman.

5. The Nixon inaugural speech was taken from the text printed in *The New York Times*, January 21, 1969.

6. See Donley (1968, Chapter 4) for the details of these modifications.

7. Only the first inaugural speech of each President was scored, except in the case of Franklin Roosevelt, whose first two speeches were scored. The rationale for this procedure is that a President's first inaugural speech is the most likely to represent aspirations and goals, uncontaminated by specific issues arising from his actual performance in the Presidency.

8. Ways in which such a motive assessment technique could be incorporated into a general model for predicting of office-seeking are discussed in Browning (1968).

REFERENCES

ATKINSON, J. W. (ed.). *Motives in fantasy, action, and society*. Princeton: Van Nostrand, 1958.

ATKINSON, J. W., and FEATHER, N. T. *A theory of achievement motivation*. New York: John Wiley & Sons, 1966.

Data Sources

BAILEY, T. A. *Presidential greatness: the image and the man from George Washington to the present.* New York: Appleton-Century-Crofts, 1966.

BARBER, J. D. Adult identity and presidential style: the rhetorical emphasis. *Daedalus,* 1968, 97, 938–968. *(a)*

BARBAR, J. D. Classifying and predicting Presidential styles: two "weak" Presidents. *J. soc. Issues,* 1968, 24, 3, 51–80. *(b)*

BLUM, J. M. *The Republican Roosevelt.* New York: Atheneum, 1966.

BROWNING, R. P. The interaction of personality and political system in decisions to run for office: some data and a simulation technique. *J. soc. Issues,* 1968, 24, 3, 93–109.

BROWNING, R. P., and JACOB, H. Power motivation and the political personality. *Pub. opin. Quart.,* 1964, 28, 75–90.

BURNS, J. M. *Roosevelt: the lion and the fox.* New York: Harcourt Brace, 1956.

BURNS, J. M. *Presidential government: the crucible of leadership.* Boston: Houghton Mifflin, 1966.

CHILD I., STORM, T., and VEROFF, J. Achievement themes in folk tales related to socialization practice. In J. W. Atkinson (Ed.), *Motives in fantasy, action, and society.* Princeton: Van Nostrand, 1958, Pp. 479–492.

deCHARMS, R., and MOELLER, G. H. Values expressed in American children's readers: 1800–1950. *J. abnor. soc. Psychol.,* 1962, 64, 136–142.

DONLEY, R. E. Psychological motives and the American Presidency. Unpublished A.B. thesis. Wesleyan University, 1968.

FREUD, S., and BULLITT, W. C. *Thomas Woodrow Wilson: A psychological study.* Boston: Houghton Mifflin, 1967.

GEORGE, A., and GEORGE, J. *Woodrow Wilson and Colonel House: A personality study.* New York: John Day, 1956.

GREENSTEIN, F. I. The impact of personality on politics: an attempt to clear away underbrush. *Amer. polit. sci. Rev.,* 1967, 61, 629–641.

HARGROVE, E. C. *Presidential leadership: Personality and political style.* New York: Macmillan, 1966.

HECKHAUSEN, H. *The anatomy of achievement motivation.* New York: Academic Press, 1967.

ISRAEL, F. *The Chief executive: Inaugural addresses of the presidents of the United States from George Washington to Lyndon B. Johnson.* New York: Crown, 1965.

KALTENBACH, J. E., and McCLELLAND, D. C. Achievement and social status in three small communities. In D. C. McClelland et al. (Eds.), *Talent and society.* Princeton: Van Nostrand, 1958.

LASSWELL, H. *Politics: Who gets what, when, how.* New York: McGraw-Hill, 1936.

LeVINE, R. *Dreams and deeds: achievement motivation in Nigeria.* Chicago: University of Chicago Press, 1966.

McCLELLAND, D. C. The use of measures of human motivation in the study of society. In J. W. Atkinson (Ed.), *Motives in fantasy, action, and society.* Princeton: Van Nostrand, 1958, Pp. 518–552.

McCLELLAND, D. C. *The achieving society.* Princeton: Van Nostrand, 1961.

McCLELLAND, D. C. Longitudinal trends in the relation of thought to action. *J. consult. Psychol.*, 1966, 30, 479–483.

McCLELLAND, D. C., ATKINSON, J. W., CLARK, R. A. and LOWELL, E. L. *The achievement motive.* New York: Appleton-Century-Crofts, 1953.

MOWRY, G. E. *The era of Theodore Roosevelt and the birth of modern America: 1900–1912.* New York: Harper & Row, 1958.

MOSTELLER, F., and BUSH, R. R. Selected quantitative techniques. In G. Lindzey (Ed.), *Handbook of social psychology.* Reading, Mass.: Addison-Wesley, 1954, Vol. 1, Pp. 328–331.

NEUSTADT, R. E. *Presidential power: the politics of leadership.* New York: John Wiley & Son, 1960.

PARSONS, T. *The social system.* New York: The Free Press, 1952.

POLLARD, J. E. *The Presidents and the press.* New York: Macmillan, 1947.

PRINGLE, H. F. *The life and times of William Howard Taft: A biography.* New York: Farrar & Rinehart, 1939.

ROSSITER, C. *The American Presidency* (2nd rev. ed.). New York: Harcourt, Brace, & World, 1956.

SCHLESINGER, A. M., SR. Our Presidents: a rating by seventy-five historians. *New York Times Magazine,* July 29, 1962, 12–14.

SCHLESINGER, A. M., JR. *The age of Roosevelt: Crises of the old order.* Boston: Houghton Mifflin, 1957.

SMITH, M. S., STONE, P. J., and GLENN, E. N. A content analysis of twenty presidential nominating speeches. In P. J. Stone, D. C. Dunphy, M. S. Smith, and D. M. Ogilvie (Eds.), *The General Inquirer; A computer approach to content analysis in the behavioral sciences.* Cambridge: M.I.T. Press, 1966, Pp. 359–400.

VEROFF, J. Development and validation of a projective measure of power motivation. *J. abnor. soc. Psychol.*, 1957, 54, 1–8.

WEBER, M. Politics as a vocation. In H. H. Gerth and C. W. Mills (Eds.), *From Max Weber—Essays in sociology.* London: Routledge Kegan Paul, 1948.

WINTER, D. G. Need for power in thought and action. *Proceed. 76th Ann. Con. Amer. Psychol. Assoc., 1968.* Washington: Amer. Psychol. Assoc., 1968, Pp. 429–430.

WINTER, D. G. Studies in the need for power. Paper presented at the East. Psychol. Assoc. Convention, April, 1969.

QUESTIONS

1. Would you say that the primary concern of this study was latent content or manifest content of speeches? What are some other issues (manifest or latent) that might be pursued utilizing the same speeches?
2. Need the speeches have been used exclusively to ascertain the characteristics of the presidents? If not, what other purposes might they have served? Give examples.
3. Why did the authors choose to study only inaugural speeches? What are some advantages in using speeches other than the inaugural addresses?

SUGGESTED READINGS

HYMAN, HERBERT H., et al. *Interviewing in Social Research*. Glenwood, Ill.: Free Press, 1955.

LOFLAND, JOHN. *Analyzing Social Settings: A Guide to Qualitative Observation and Analysis*. Belmont, Calif.: Wadsworth Publishing Co., 1971. Chapters 4 and 5.

OPPENHEIM, A. N. *Questionnaire Design and Attitude Measurement*. New York: Basic Books, 1966.

PAYNE, S. L. *The Art of Asking Questions*. Princeton, N.J.: Princeton University Press, 1951.

PHILLIPS, DEREK L. *Knowledge from What?: Theories and Methods in Social Research*. Chicago: Rand McNally, 1971.

REISS, ALBERT J., Jr. "Systematic Observation of Natural Social Phenomena." In *Sociological Methodology 1971*, edited by Herbert L. Costner. San Francisco, Calif.: Jossey-Bass, Inc., 1971.

RICHARDSON, STEPHEN A., et al. *Interviewing: Its Forms and Functions*. New York: Basic Books, 1965.

Survey Research Center. *Interviewer's Manual*. Ann Arbor, Mich.: Institute for Social Research, University of Michigan, 1969.

WEBB, EUGENE J., et al. *Unobtrusive Measures: Nonreactive Research in the Social Sciences*. Chicago: Rand McNally, 1966.

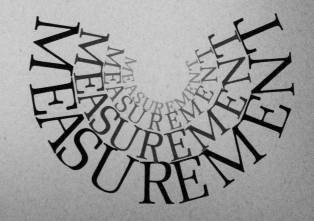

■ Contained in this section are four articles illustrating the construction of measuring instruments by four different techniques. No one of these articles is sufficient in instructional detail to enable the naïve reader to set off on his own to build a measuring instrument. Yet each article does give more detail on constructing a measurement instrument than is found in the typical research article. Each article leads the reader from the concept formation stage (what it is that we are trying to measure), through the item search and selection stage (what operational elements reflect the concepts we are interested in), to the actual production of scale values.

The four articles represent three different levels of measurement:
1. Nominal scaling is illustrated in the Rollins and Feldman article;
2. Ordinal scaling is found in the Smith and Inkeles selection (using Likert techniques) and in the Stephenson article (using a Guttman technique);
3. Ratio scaling is attempted in the Akman, Normandeau, and Turner article.

As you read each of these articles, ask yourself what operational steps are involved in the production of a final scale value; what assumptions are made in moving from one step to the next. Certainly, in those articles that are "self-consciously" concerned with measurement it should be fairly easy to find answers. Then, when you read other articles where distinctions are made between objects, challenge your understanding of how the scale values come about.

Because all empirical research must involve measurement, every one of the selections in this reader can be analyzed for its measurement procedures. However, three articles in particular may be of special interest because they employ measurement techniques that are not explored in the set of papers in this section. For one, an *ad hoc* summated scale (similar to a Likert scale) is used in the Mercer and Butler study (selection 5), and it would be instructive to compare it to the procedures outlined in the Smith and Inkeles article (selection 11). Another illustration of a Guttman technique is offered in the article by Schwartz and Miller (selection 8), but this time the research units are societies and not individuals. Finally, Donley and Winter (selection 10) use a measurement procedure that quantifies data that, on the surface, seem to be qualitative in nature.

118

The OM Scale: A Comparative Socio-Psychological Measure of Individual Modernity

DAVID HORTON SMITH and ALEX INKELES

It is sometimes desirable to have a single measure of a rather complex set of characteristics. In attaining a single measure, the researcher must often make decisions of how to combine the several characteristics and which of several criteria for composition is to be emphasized. The following article is an example of the use of Likert-type scale construction in the development of a cross-national instrument for measuring "modernity." The authors display the steps of scale construction and the several scales they develop in a particularly explicit fashion, allowing the reader to understand better the advantages and limitations of each of the several scales that they construct.

■ The concept of modernity has emerged as one of the central themes in social analysis, not only among sociologists, but also in the work of economists, historians, and political scientists. In the next decade it seems destined to assume an even more prominent place in the thinking of behavioral scientists. The term may refer to two quite different objects. As used to describe a society, "modern" generally means a national state characterized by a complex of traits including urbanization, high levels of education, industrialization, extensive mechanization, high rates of social mobility, and the like. When applied to individuals, it refers to a set of attitudes, values, and ways of feeling and acting, presumably of the sort either generated by or required for effective participation in a modern society. In this report we deal only with *individual* modernity, that is, with a socio-psychological rather than an exclusively sociological problem.

As is true of so many important concepts, individual modernity is more often defined than measured. On the occasions when it is measured, it is generally done on an *ad hoc* basis, separately by each team going into the field. This consumes much energy for a task which may be incidental to the main interest of the various projects. The venture is, furthermore, inherently fraught with much risk of failure. Even when the effort is successful, the lack of comparability of one's new measure with the measures of modernity used in other studies greatly reduces its contribution to cumulative social science knowledge.

As a by-product of a large scale comparative study of modernization in six developing countries we believe we have been able to devise a brief, reliable, valid, and cross-culturally useful measure of the relative standing of individuals on a scale of modernity. We feel this scale has potential for use not only in research, but . . . in developing countries as a practical personnel screening device to aid in the selection of indi-

Reprinted from *Sociometry* 29 (1966), 353–377, with permission of The American Sociological Association.

viduals for training or employment, or for selecting communities which might or should be prime targets for community development programs. In this paper we present the scale we have devised, and explain very briefly the research operations by which we arrived at it.

After reviewing the literature and defining our own theoretical position we identified some thirty topics, themes, areas, or issues which seemed relevant to a definition of modernity. The complete list is given in Chart 1. In this paper, unfortunately, we lack space either to define the

CHART 1. Major Themes Explored in Defining Psycho-Social Modernity

Project Code	Descriptive Title of Theme	Project Code	Descriptive Title of Theme
AC	Political Activism	GO(1)	Growth of Opinion Awareness
AG	Role of Aged	GO(2)	Growth of Opinion Valuation
AS(1)*	Education Aspirations	ID	Political Identification
AS(2)	Occupational Aspirations	KO(1)	Extended Kinship Obligations
CA(1)	Calculability of People's Dependability	KO(2)	Kinship Obligation to Parental Authority
CA(2)	Calculability of People's Honesty	MM	Mass Media Valuation
CH	Change Perception and Valuation	NE(1)	Openness to New Experience —Places
CI	Citizens Political Reference Groups	NE(2)	Openness to New Experience —People
CO(1)	Consumption Aspirations	PA	Particularism-Universalism
CO(2)	Consumer Values	PL	Planning Valuation
DI	Dignity Valuation	RE(1)	Religious Causality
EF(1)	General Efficacy	RE(2)	Religious-Secular Orientation
EF(2)	Efficacy and Opportunity in Life Chances	SC	Social Class Attitudes
EF(3)	Efficacy of Science and Medicine	TI	Time (Punctuality) Valuation
		TS	Technical Skill Valuation
FS(1)	Family Size—Attitudes	WR(1)	Women's Rights
FS(2)	Family Size—Birth Control	WR(2)	Co-ed Work and School
		IN	Information Eliciting Questions
		**	Behavioral Measures

* Some of the larger and more complex theme areas identified by a single code have been broken into two or more subthemes for this analysis. To indicate this, the code letters are followed by a number in parentheses to identify which subtheme it is.
** All but the last two codes (information and behavior) refer to attitude areas. There was no single code designation for behavioral measures. In addition, a question falling mainly in one of the attitudinal realms might be coded not for attitudinal content, but as a behavior item.

content of any of these attitude and behavior realms or to indicate the reasons why we considered them relevant.[1] We hope, however, that the brief descriptive titles we have presented will somewhat explain and justify the themes selected. Basically, we assumed that modernity would emerge as a complex but coherent set of psychic dispositions manifested in general qualities such as a sense of efficacy, readiness for new experience, and interest in planning, linked, in turn, to certain dispositions to act in institutional relations—as in being an active citizen, valuing science, maintaining one's autonomy in kinship matters, and accepting birth control. As indicated above, we assumed these personal qualities would be the end product of certain early and late socialization experiences such as education, urban experience, and work in modern organizations such as the factory.

To measure each of these themes we devised a long series of questionnaire-interview items, largely of the fixed-alternative type, but including a number of open-ended questions. More than 60 of the questions are presented, albeit in highly abbreviated form, in Table 1, with code designations which permit them to be related to the themes described in Chart 1. Some of these items we borrowed from prior or concurrent studies of modernization, but the majority we created ourselves.[2] By avoiding an agree-disagree format, we attempted to develop an instrument that would not be susceptible to acquiescence response set. We also strove to avoid social desirability response set by presenting item alternatives of balanced desirability. After careful pretesting of our initial pool of items over a two year period, first in Puerto Rico and then in three of the field stations, our original interview with sixteen hours of questions was boiled down to a more manageable, though still quite lengthy, four hours of average interviewing time. The principal bases of selection used for deriving the final set of items were (a) that an item measure a theoretically important aspect of one or more of our themes, (b) that every theme be measured by at least two items, (c) that none of the themes be measured by more items than the complexity and importance of the theme demanded, (d) that the question deal with general human situations, understandable in other cultures and accessible to men of little or no formal education, (e) that the item be readily translatable into other languages than English without substantially changing its meaning or intent, and (f) that the pretest results show the item had elicited a good range or distribution of responses in each of the countries in which it was tested.

The same pool of items used to derive some more selective measure may yield quite a different set of items depending partly on the procedure used to extract the final set, and partly on the nature of the samples to which the questions were presented. The samples studied were chosen to answer certain analytic questions of concern to the larger project. They were, therefore, highly selective, rather than representative or random. Yet they were, we believe, sufficiently diverse to insure that the final distillate of our procedures for screening items from the larger pool cannot be assumed to be mainly, or even very largely, shaped by the peculiar or distinctive characteristics of our sample. We have samples from six different countries, which are all in the classification "under-developed" but range from those with predominantly European culture such as Argentina and Israel through Chile to the relatively "exotic" cultures of India, Pakistan and Nigeria. Any scale which works with samples from such a range of countries must be general indeed.

So far as the samples within each country are concerned, while not covering the full range of variation, they do deal with representatives from a large proportion of the main population groups in each. Our samples are focused on the common man in a range of settings—the peasants (or cultivators, to use a less value-laden term) represent the traditional, base-line culture in the several societies. The urban non-industrial

TABLE 1. Abbreviated Questions and Item-to-Scale Correlations for Six Scales Measuring Individual Modernity (OM)

Code Number	Abbreviated Version of Questions[a] (Italic Alternative Indicates Modern End of Scale)	Six Country Average Item-to-Scale Pearsonian r in Form[b]						
		Long[c]	Short 1	Short 2	Short 3	Short 4	Short 5	Short 6
AC-1, 2	Number of organizations you belong to: *low to high number*	d						.315
AC-6	Wanted to do something about public issue: *frequently/seldom/never*	.245	.299	.290	.312	.296	.401	.412
AG-2	Does boy learn most truth from: *old people/both/books and school*	.192		.216				
AG-3	How do you feel about growing old: *want/don't care/dread*	.059				.145		
AS-5	What is ideal amount schooling for children like yours: *low to high years*	.269	.311	.315	.321	.313	.426	.386
AS-7	For person like you what is best job to be hoped for: *low to high status*	.259	.293	.261	.340	.306		
AS-8	If money no problem toward what work should father guide son: *low to high status*	.217	.270		.290			
CA-3	Which more useful: *schooling/good head*	.165	.188			.229		
CA-6	Most important quality in fellow workers: *friendly/respected/reliable*	.142				.156		
CA-7	Would you treat a stranger with: *trust/caution/distrust*	.092						
CA-8	Will relatives exploit knowledge of your personal affairs: *yes/unlikely/no*	.019		.154				
CA-11	Do merchants give you honest merchandise: *always/usually/seldom/never*	.102		.188	.050			
CH-3	How often should irresponsible boy be excused: *always/seldom/never*	.148	.308	.311	.304	.304	.427	.382
CI-2	If boy suggests new idea for farming should father: *approve/disapprove*	.273	.300			.323		
CI-7	What would you do about proposed unjust law: *action to inaction*	.249	.358	.342				
CI-9	Would you give most weight to advice of: *church/government*	.304	.254	.268	.258	.264	.352	.293
CI-13	Would you give most weight to advice of: *political party/tribal council (or boss)*	.232		.250	.254			
CI-14	Which should most qualify man for high office: *education/popularity/family/tradition*	.227			.183	.175		
CO-4	Government official should grant petition of man with: *right/influence/most need*	.194	.202	.216				
CO-5	Is this (picture of radio shown) something you want: *much/little/none*	.184		.169				
CO-8	Is this (picture of camera shown) something you want: *much/little/none*	.196			.293	.199		
CO-9	Is striving for money over and above comfortable living: *good/bad*	.139						
DI-8	Does a man's happiness depend on: *material possessions/other things*	.083		.233		.252		
DI-11	How would you treat defeated people who had attacked you: *kindly or harshly*	.194			.246			
EF-1	Should a person consider feelings of: *self always to others always*	.178	.183					
EF-2	Poor but ambitious and hardworking man will: *fail always to succeed always*	.183	.338		.334			
EF-4	Accident prevention at work depends on: *luck always to care always*	.303	.386	.368	.368	.362		
EF-8	Man's position in life depends on: *fate always to own effort always*	.344	.266					
EF-11	Can able, smart, industrious, ambitious boy succeed against fate: *completely/partly/no*	.234	.335		.332			
EF-13	Do you prefer job with *many/few/no responsibilities*	.294	.434	.425	.420	.428	.483	.456
EF-14	Which is most important for future of country: *work/gov't planning/God/luck*	.373	.319					
	Will man someday understand nature: *fully/never can*	.286						
	If man explores nature's secrets (by science) is it: *good/bad (ungodly)*	.335						
FS-1	What is ideal number of children for man like yourself: *low to high number*	.218	.388	.378	.363	.378	.467	.417
FS-3	Limiting size of family is: *necessary/wrong*	.315	.370	.280	.281	.296		
FS-4	Is harmless pill contraceptive for wife: *good/bad*	.263	.338	.318	.321	.325	.394	.347
FS-5	Should people take government advice on family size: *yes/no*	.213	.278					
GO-2	What are biggest problems facing your country: *few to many problems*	d				.152		
GO-4	Are the opinions of other people different from yours: *many/few/none*	.090		.157				.356

122

TABLE 1. Abbreviated Questions and Item-to-Scale Correlations for Six Scales Measuring Individual Modernity (OM) (Continued)

Code Number	Abbreviated Version of Questions[a] (Italic Alternative Indicates Modern End of Scale)	Six Country Average Item-to-Scale Pearsonian r in Form[b]						
		Long[c]	Short 1	Short 2	Short 3	Short 4	Short 5	Short 6
GO-5	Who should speak for family: husband only/both/*wife too*	.187	—	.233	—	—	—	—
GO-6	Should one pay more attention to opinion of: *people*/both equally/leaders only	.140	—	—	.222	.222	—	—
ID-1	Do you consider yourself primarily citizen of: *nation*/region/state/city	.279	.323	.339	—	.342	—	.559
IN-6 or 7	Where is Washington (or Moscow): *correct*/incorrect	d	—	—	—	—	—	—
KO-1	Should man feel closer to: *wife*/other family member (e.g. mother, father, brother)	.152	—	.206	.207	.222	—	—
KO-2	Should man choose job preferred by: *himself*/parents	.242	.282	—	.255	.305	—	—
MM-5	How often do you get news from newspapers: *daily/often*/rarely/never	d	—	—	—	—	—	.520
MM-6	What sources do you trust most for world news: *mass media*/non-mass media	.236	.261	—	.267	—	—	—
MM-10	What news interests you most: *world/nation*/village/sports/religion	.294	.350	.350	.340	.356	.440	.399
NE-1	If you could improve standard of living 100% would you: *be willing to move*/prefer not	.152	—	.206	—	—	—	—
NE-2	Want to know stranger with different customs, speech or religion: *well*/prefer not	.255	.309	—	.293	—	—	—
NE-3	In meeting people do you prefer: *to meet new people*/see familiar ones	.272	.310	—	.318	—	—	—
NE-4	Could you understand thinking of man of different religion: *yes*/no	.284	.353	—	.379	—	—	—
NE-5	Could you understand thinking of man from distant country: *yes*/no	.278	.352	.350	.372	.351	.424	.404
NE-7	Would you prefer *rural*/urban life	.150	—	—	.216	.203	—	—
PL-4	Do you prefer to plan affairs in advance: *mostly*/sometimes/never	.244	.262	.249	—	.234	—	—
RE-8	Who do you admire most: monk/both/*factory owner*	.250	.303	.262	—	—	—	—
RE-9	Who has done more for his country: monk/both/*factory owner*	.231	.290	—	—	—	—	—
RE-10	Which has best lived up to his religion: monk/both/*factory owner*	.200	—	—	—	.232	—	—
RE-11	Most important in caring for sick person: prayer/both/*medical care*	.305	.359	—	.327	—	—	—
RE-12	Can man be good without religion: *yes*/no	.260	.326	.328	.342	.331	.436	.390
RE-14	A man should give to the poor because of: fear of God/*generosity*	.266	.298	—	—	—	—	—
TI-5	After how many minutes would you consider pal late for date: few to *many minutes*	.205	—	.278	.281	.284	—	—
TS-12	Best way to increase factory output: more workers/*more training for workers*	.204	—	.247	.245	.239	—	—
WC-2	Kind of work you would prefer: low to *high status*	.173	—	—	.296	—	—	—
WR-7	If women do same work as men pay should be: *same*/less/much less	.216	.250	.288	—	.291	—	—
WR-9	If family has both boy & girl children prefer next child: boy/girl/*either*	.105	—	—	.159	—	—	—
WR-11	Choose spouse to suit: parents always to *self always*	.244	.286	.304	.307	—	—	—
WR-13	Worry about illicit relations if men and women work together: lot/little/*none*	.163	—	.205	—	.214	—	—

[a] In this compressed form the original question is often necessarily poorly represented. The exact text of each question should be consulted in the (Document #9133) American Documentation Institute, Washington, D. C., where the Questionnaire, Project Description, Sampling Design, Behavioral Measures, and OM lists are on file.

[b] The Long Form included 119 attitudinal items, but for lack of space we have given here the correlation of the item to the Long Form scale only for the 64 items which also appeared in one of the Short Forms 1–6.

[c] In each column, the figures entered give the correlation of the abbreviated question on the left to the modernity scale form identified at the head of the column averaged for six countries. A blank cell in any column indicates that the question was not included in the given scale form.

[d] Four items were not included in the Long Form. A fuller explanation is given in footnotes 34 and 35 of the text.

workers represent men who either migrated to the city from the country-side, or who were born in the city but who have not been exposed to factory work or any other large bureaucratic work setting. The industrial workers were selected purposively from a variety of modern and traditional factories to include one-third to one-half as many new (less than 6 months experience) as experienced (3 years or more) factory men. The industrial worker and urban non-industrial worker samples include men of urban and rural origin who have recently been exposed to both the city and the factory as modernizing social influences. Because we were working mainly with the common man, the educational range in our samples was limited, running in most cases, from illiteracy to 6 or 8 years of schooling. In each country, however, we added a special sample of highly educated workers, and this increased the range to 12 or even 14 years of schooling.[3]

Because we were studying modernization as a process, we conducted our research in developing countries, rather than in fully developed, industrialized nations. To avoid the danger of false generalizations based on the special cultural or social structural attributes of a single country, we decided to collect samples from several quite different developing countries. Both theoretical and practical considerations we cannot explain here led us to work, finally, in Chile, Argentina, Pakistan, India, Nigeria, and Israel. We do not claim our samples are representative of any of these countries, especially in the cases of Pakistan, India, and Nigeria where all of our respondents are drawn from relatively homogeneous cultural-linguistic subareas, rather than from the nation as a whole.[4] But for purposes of deriving a measure of modernity the requirement of representativeness is clearly not critical. Our objective is to devise a measure which has general applicability. Diversity is therefore more important than representativeness, and we feel that a measure based on samples as diverse as are ours, both within and across countries, meets this objective very well. We believe the measures we have devised will work well in almost any developing country and probably in more advanced countries as well.[5] Although the instrument is designed with the common man in mind, it can, with some upward adjustment in the scale of alternatives, be easily adapted for use with highly educated men.[6]

Our four hour interview went through extensive translation, retranslation and pretesting in each country. When finally ready, it was administered by native language interviewers, usually social workers or college students whose social origins were the same as those of the interviewees. The samples included the following numbers of young men between the ages of 18 and 32: Argentina, 817; Chile, 931; India, 1300; Israel, 739; Nigeria, 721; and Pakistan, 1001. In each case the total was made up of approximately 15% cultivators, 15% urban nonindustrial workers, and 70% urban industrial workers.

As a result of these procedures we are left with the data for some 5500 men in six countries responding to 159 different interview items measuring attitudes, information, and behavior conceived to be relevant to our theoretical conception of modernity.[7] Of these 159 items, 119 we consider to be measures of attitudes, values and opinions, 17 measures of self-reported behavior, and 23 tests of information or verbal fluency.[8] Our attention will be given mainly to the attitudinal items, and, while we make some use here of the behavioral and information items, we leave for a later report a more complete discussion of them.[9]

There are many possible types of analysis one could perform on this large and complex set of attitudinal items, but two principal analytic approaches merit our consideration. The first, followed in this [article], seeks to create a general summary index score that represents the degree to which a man possesses the attitudes measured by these items. Insofar as the set of items measures "psychological modernity," this summary index may be called a measure of Overall Modernity ("OM"). The second general analytic approach, reported elsewhere, treats these items as defining a multi-dimensional property space and analyzes the results for each individual in terms of profiles of many different characteristics, rather than in terms of a single summary score.[10]

Given that we have chosen here to develop a summary modernity score, rather than to develop a detailed modernity profile, there are still two different analytic approaches we might follow, and several methodological varieties within each of these. The two broad approaches are the *item analysis* and the *criterion group* methods. Rather than follow one exclusively, we chose to use both approaches including sub-varieties, and then to compose the results in a highly compact final distillate. In this way, we hope to avoid some of the arbitrariness that is so often manifested when new scales are proposed. Both the item analysis and the criterion group methods for deriving the short scale of individual modernity rest on the fundamental assumption that the larger pool of items from which they are derived is adequate to support the operations which lead to the short scale. But what is an adequate basis?

One test of adequacy is purely theoretical. If our conception of modernity is profoundly different from the reader's, then whatever the procedures we use, the final product will not be accepted. Although we cannot here take space to support our argument, we note the following points: (1) our conception of modernity rests on thoroughly elaborated theory as to the qualities which modern settings are likely to generate, as well as consideration of personal attributes which are likely to best adapt a man to life in such institutional settings; (2) we checked this conception against numerous theoretical and empirical studies of modernization, and found that almost without exception, our basic themes were also commonly cited by other students of the problem; (3) in the interest of the broadest testing of ideas we incorporated many themes which were not central to our original conception, but which had been cited with sufficient frequency in the literature to warrant inclusion in the set we studied. We believe, therefore, that our list of themes is quite comprehensive, certainly as much as, and probably more so than, any other which has been used up to this time in any substantial research in modernity.[11]

A second test of adequacy is empirical. One way of assuring that our set of items does indeed measure modernity is to examine the relation of the individual scale scores to social indices which are generally acknowledged to be associated with modernity. Each person in our samples was assigned a summary modernity score based on his answers to the entire set of 119 attitudinal questions, by procedures described in the next paragraph. The individual scores were then correlated with social factors presumed to be associated with modernity. These independent variables did indeed correlate significantly and substantially with the over-all modernization score.[12] We were therefore quite certain that this was a set of items which seemed definitely to reflect empirically what theory indicated it should measure, namely the amount of modernizing influences to which a man had been subjected.

Mention of this *summary attitudinal* measure of modernization provides an opportunity to review certain decisions concerning our procedure which are relevant to almost everything that follows. The 119 items used were, as we noted, those which, in our judgment, measured attitudes *and* could be unambiguously scored as having a "modern" vs. "traditional" answer. To avoid making too many judgments, however, we arbitrarily and sometimes forcefully, drew in every item which was not a background, intervening variable, or psychological test item. In the analysis presented here we largely restrict ourselves to the *attitudinal* items available in all six countries. Each item was dichotomized as close to the median as possible,[13] but this was done separately for each country.[14] One part of the dichotomy was classified as the "modern" answer, the other as the "traditional."[15] Traditional answers were scored 1, modern 2, so that the minimum score was in effect 1.00 and the maximum 2.00, a result given us forthwith by a basic computer operation which *averaged* the answers a man gave to all 119 questions.[16] The result we call the Long Form of the overall modernity score (OM).[17] Since it is based on the largest appropriate pool of attitudinal items, we consider it in principle our most reliable measure of any individual's attitudinal modernity, and in our Project analysis we will use mainly this score.[18] Yet the fact that an individual must answer 119 questions to be rated makes it clearly desirable that we use our data and experience to derive for others some short forms for measuring individual modernity.

DERIVATION OF SHORT FORM VIA ITEM ANALYSIS METHOD

The derivation of short forms via the item analysis method rests on a simple principle. Using the OM Long Form score based on all items as a standard, we ask what sub-set from the larger pool has the strongest relation to the overall score.[19] But since everything depends first on having the complete Long Form and a measure of the relation of each item to the total score, let us turn to consider that set of relationships.

We may note, first that the Long Form proved to have much the same characteristics in all the countries in mean (about 1.54), in median (1.55), in range (about 1.20 to 1.80) and in standard deviation (about .07). Since the items were the same in each country, and the procedure used to derive the scores was also identical, this result is no surprise. A standard procedure for interpreting the internal consistency and coherence of a scale such as OM uses the Spearman-Brown formula.[20] Calculations reported in Table 2 show that for each of our countries the Long Form OM scale has

TABLE 2. Average Item-to-Scale Correlations and Scale Reliabilities for Six Scales of Modernity (OM), by Country and Scale

Country	Long	Short 1	Short 2	Short 3	Short 4	Short 5	Short 6
Pakistan: Mean R	.167	.299	.250	.251	.237	.391	.361
Reliability		.767	.774	.685	.685	.653	.622	.660
India: Mean R	.235	.372	.334	.323	.314	.466	.438
Reliability		.873	.852	.808	.792	.784	.736	.769
Nigeria: Mean R	.151	.279	.244	.254	.228	.403	.394
Reliability		.732	.759	.678	.702	.697	.659	.719
Chile: Mean R	.158	.291	.268	.261	.265	.422	.411
Reliability		.754	.779	.721	.713	.713	.685	.741
Argentina: Mean R	.165	.290	.272	.287	.284	.436	.415
Reliability		.767	.770	.724	.752	.744	.701	.744
Israel: Mean R	.170	.297	.266	.265	.252	.428	.395
Reliability		.779	.782	.709	.719	.688	.691	.719

test reliability coefficients of .73 or higher. Considering that the Long Form OM measures so complex and multi-dimensional a concept as individual modernity, the similarity from country to country of the reliability levels, and of the item to test correlations on which they are based, is quite notable. Many widely used scales devised to measure one single attitude or trait do not do much better, and for a scale measuring a multi-faceted personal property the Long Form OM achieves a level of internal consistency which is quite respectable indeed.[21]

There is, then, substantial reason to conclude that the Long Form OM scales for each country are internally consistent and coherent to a significant and substantial degree. We take this to be evidence that there is an underlying dimension of psychological modernity pervading our set of 119 attitude items.[22] This heightens the justification for using the items in the OM Long Form, and particularly their relation to the summary score, as a basis for deriving a short form of the scale.

Having established the character and quality of the Long Form OM, we may now return to the procedures for deriving the short forms.

Our first method was maximally empirical, that is, it required and allowed us minimal opportunity to exercise our judgment to influence which particular items entered into the short form. For each country separately, we simply listed the 50 items with the highest correlations of item to Long Form OM score. Any item which appeared on top in four countries out of six was automatically judged to have survived the competition. Thirty-eight items met this stringent test, and taken together they constitute our OM Short Form 1.[23] The items which compose the scale may be identified by the entry of an item-to-scale correlation coefficient in the cells of the second column, headed "Short 1" of Table 1.[24] The fact that there is so much overlap among the top 50 items in our six countries indicates a great deal of underlying similarity in the meaning of psychological modernity across our samples.

While Short Form 1 has the virtue of being untouched by human hands (beyond the decisions involved in selecting the initial item pool) it has the defects of all scales derived purely empirically. In the larger pool some areas may be represented by more items than others. In addition, some one or two closely related sets of items may cohere so well and relate so strongly to the larger scale as to crowd out items representing many other sub-scale areas. The victorious set of items may then represent a coherent scale, but one which no longer so well represents the universe—in this case, modernity—which the scale was originally designed to measure. That has happened, to some extent, with Short Form 1. The questionnaire contains more items testing efficacy (EF) than any other area, and they generally cohere quite well as a set. We must, therefore, take note that of the 38 items in Short Form 1, there are 8, or more than 20 per cent, from the efficacy area alone. All 4 questionnaire items which test *openness to new experience* with people (NE, 2–5) made it. When to these are added the items on birth control (FS, 3–5) and similar items, it seems that the Short Form 1 is heavily weighted toward what Parsons calls "instrumental activism." If one insists that the modernity measure give weight to other themes as well, Short Form 1 will not serve. It taps too few of the dimensions, and is too dominated by a few others.

To represent other areas more properly we imposed an additional content qualification for the selection of items. We selected from within each of our theoretically defined major attitudinal themes as listed in Chart 1, the single item which best represented the theme in all countries. For all themes, only *one* item was selected.[25] No matter how low the item-to-total score correlations were on a particular theme, we nevertheless selected one question from the area. And no matter how high the item-to-scale correlations were, no more than one item was selected for any one of our 33 themes. When two items were equally good candidates from a given area (in terms of item-to-scale correlations), preference was given to what we judged to be the more general and theoretically more relevant item. This derivation procedure, therefore, combined both subjective and objective item-selection criteria in what we felt was a reasonable compromise. Its end product was a coherent 33-item scale of psychological modernity that included representatives from all of our theoretically defined attitudinal themes.

This scale, which we designate OM Short Form 2, is internally consistent in all six countries by a variety of tests presented in Table 2. The average item-to-scale correlations of Short Form 2 are somewhat lower than for Form 1, because of the selection procedure which required the inclusion of some items with relatively low correlations with the Long Form. Nevertheless, the average item-to-scale correlations of OM Short Form 2 for each country are quite a bit greater than the corresponding average correlations for the OM Long Form, even though their *test reliability coefficients* are quite similar. The reason for this is that the increase in the average item-to-scale correlation in Short Form 2 is compensated for by a large decrease in the number of items it contains when compared to the Long Form OM.

On balance, Short Form 2 will probably be the most generally useful and cross-culturally applicable, purely attitudinal measure of psychological modernity that we can suggest on the basis of our theory as it is disciplined by our data. It strikes a balance between the undue length of the long form and undue brevity of later short forms of OM yet to be described, and between the purely theoretical and more or less purely empirical mode of derivation such as was used for Short Form 1. The overall picture that Short Form 2 gives of the modern man may be obtained at a glance by reading off the questions identified by the entry of an item-to-scale correlation figure in the cells of the third column in Table 1. Each of these 33 items should be considered as *representatives* of their respective theme or sub-theme areas, rather than as absolutes in any sense. For each there are one or more "back-up" items which might have been selected in some cases were the countries in our sample different.

The OM Short Forms 1 and 2 share 19 items, and it is therefore not surprising as indicated in Table 3, that they correlate .80 and above in all six countries. Both are highly related to the Long Form (correlation of .80 or above) and in much the same way in each country. Because Short Form 2 is just about as good a representative of the Long Form as is Short Form 1, and since it also has the other virtues we have indicated (primarily, theoretical breadth), we would prefer it in competition with Short Form 1.

THE CRITERION GROUP METHOD OF OM SCALE DERIVATION

The principal alternative to coherence methods of deriving a reduced scale for rating overall psychological modernity is the criterion group method. This involves selecting items from the larger pool of 119 attitudinal modernity items on the basis of their power in differentiating known criterion groups. This method has the defect of precluding unbiased subsequent analysis of the relationships of independent variables to the resulting reduced version of OM. Once OM is derived by this method, then only in a new and separate sample can one freely analyze the relationships of these independent variables to the reduced OM scale. But anyone else's sample other than our own six is, for this purpose, a "new and separate" sample.[26] In our own Project analysis, we will use the theoretically derived Long Form only, but we can draw on our experience with it to derive for others a short form based on the criterion group method of derivation.

In a review of the literature we had identified education, urban experience, and occupation (especially industrial experience) as three of the most powerful influences determining individual modernity. In our study these were measured by years of formal education; urban vs. rural origin and years of urban residence since age 15 (for those of rural origin); and years of factory work (for factory workers only). Our criterion group procedure therefore was to determine, for each of the 119 Long Form OM items, the correlation with each of these three independent variables (treating the two urbanization measures combined as one variable).[27] For this purpose we used not dichotomies, as in the item-analysis or "coherence" derivation, but rather the raw, uncorrected data. Since this method did not require prejudging which end of the answer continuum was modern or traditional, the criterion group approach allowed the very few items which earlier suffered from our having misjudged their direction in

TABLE 3. Inter-correlations of Modernity Scales, by Scale and Country

Form	Country	Short Form 1	Short Form 2	Short Form 3	Short Form 4	Short Form 5	Short Form 6
Long	Pakistan	.861	.805	.789	.786	.619	.626
Form OM	India	.910	.903	.886	.880	.790	.813
	Nigeria	.836	.811	.804	.775	.635	.617
	Chile	.837	.837	.797	.803	.699	.686
	Argentina	.832	.814	.813	.796	.638	.651
	Israel	.863	.832	.803	.784	.650	.648
Short	Pakistan	—	.806	.827	.775	.739	.722
Form 1	India	—	.898	.896	.875	.859	.852
	Nigeria	—	.808	.837	.762	.776	.747
	Chile	—	.836	.841	.824	.822	.790
	Argentina	—	.839	.869	.834	.791	.783
	Israel	—	.839	.861	.789	.776	.765
Short	Pakistan	—	—	.773	.859	.706	.701
Form 2	India	—	—	.880	.914	.847	.855
	Nigeria	—	—	.791	.867	.769	.736
	Chile	—	—	.805	.894	.795	.755
	Argentina	—	—	.825	.891	.778	.763
	Israel	—	—	.817	.874	.763	.736
Short	Pakistan	—	—	—	.813	.700	.705
Form 3	India	—	—	—	.899	.847	.857
	Nigeria	—	—	—	.835	.760	.743
	Chile	—	—	—	.851	.808	.786
	Argentina	—	—	—	.874	.806	.801
	Israel	—	—	—	.849	.784	.764
Short	Pakistan	—	—	—	—	.703	.685
Form 4	India	—	—	—	—	.842	.842
	Nigeria	—	—	—	—	.756	.725
	Chile	—	—	—	—	.808	.779
	Argentina	—	—	—	—	.806	.796
	Israel	—	—	—	—	.774	.738
Short	Pakistan	—	—	—	—	—	.892
Form 5	India	—	—	—	—	—	.940
	Nigeria	—	—	—	—	—	.908
	Chile	—	—	—	—	—	.917
	Argentina	—	—	—	—	—	.923
	Israel	—	—	—	—	—	.913

the item analysis now to enter freely into competition for high standing as indicators of individual modernity.

In each country, for the same basic set of 119 attitudinal items, we computed the Pearsonian correlation of the item with each of the three independent variables in turn. Then we selected in each country the top 50 items in terms of the average of their correlations with the three criterion variables—education, urban experience, and industrial work experience. Finally, the six lists of 50 were compared, and all items noted which appeared on the list of at least four countries. There were 34 items which survived this additional test. Taken together they constitute Short Form 3.[28]

Short Form 3 is our first *criterion group derived* scale. Its content may be discerned by reading the list of items in Table 1 with entries in the column headed "Form 3." Since Form 3 is arrived at almost entirely by objectively defined operations (as was Form 1), it will appeal to those who prefer a scale in which the scalemaker is kept by his procedures from suiting the items to his conscious or unconscious propensities. As a criterion group derived scale, of course, it gains its validity not from the theoretical integrity conferred by an independent concept of modernity, but rather from its empirical or predictive relation to categories of people assumed to be modern. It gives heavy weight, as did Short Form 1, to the single area of Efficacy,[29] but this may be compensated for by very broad representation of other themes. Twenty-four areas are represented, only 9 less than the maximum possible number of 33 themes.[30] Short Form 3, therefore, has much to recommend it.

Finally, we derived a Short Form 4 by again (as in Short Form 2) placing the "theme constraint" on item selection, but now using the criterion group method. That is, we selected one item from each of the 33 theme areas to best represent that theme in terms of its average correlation with the three criterion variables. The questions constituting the resultant 33-item scale may be identified by the column entries under "Form 4" in Table 1.[31] In all six countries Form 4 correlates well with Form 3 (.81 or above) and with the Long Form OM (.77 or better). Note that there are 22 items in common between Short Form 3 and 4. Again, on the grounds that it is more theoretically based, we recommend Short Form 4 over Short Form 3 for those who prefer a criterion group derived scale rather than an item analysis derived scale for measuring overall modernity.

A MINIMUM SCALE OF ATTITUDINAL MODERNITY

Even a 33-item scale limited to measuring attitudes may be too long for the purpose of many potential users. For them we can recommend a scale which gets down to the bare minimum.

Again there are many paths one might follow in pursuit of that end. The formula we chose was a composite procedure designed simultaneously to satisfy a number of requirements. First, we felt objective procedures should serve as a screen, to permit only those items with a truly outstanding record to be in the competition. To that end we selected any item which appeared on all four short forms discussed above. This gave us a pool of 12 items. Second, we reviewed this list to discard items which could not be coded more or less automatically in the field directly by the interviewer. Finally, we reviewed the content of each item, to identify those which seemed to overlap most—either in the area they dealt with (such as religion), the relationship they concerned (such as teacher-pupil), or the psychological quality they reflected (such as efficacy). Using these standards we worked toward a final list of not more than 10 items which we designate Short Form 5.[32]

Since this brief attitudinal modernity scale is the final distillate of our successive efforts, and we hope it will be widely used, we present in Chart 2 the exact wording of the questions, both for their theoretical inter-

CHART 2. Minimum Scale of Individual Modernity: Short Forms 5 and 6

A. Purely Attitudinal Items (Form 5)

AC-6   Have you ever (thought over much) gotten so highly concerned (involved) regarding some public issue (such as . . .) that you really wanted to do something about it?
1. Frequently   2. Few times   3. Never

AS-1   If schooling is freely available (if there were no kinds of obstacles) how much schooling (reading and writing) do you think children (the son) of people like yourself should have?

CH-3   Two twelve-year-old boys took time out from their work in the corn (rice) fields. They were trying to figure out a way to grow the same amount of corn (rice) with fewer hours of work.
1. The father of one boy said: "That is a good thing to think about. Tell me your thoughts about how we should change our ways of growing corn (rice)."
2. The father of the other boy said: "The way to grow corn (rice) is the way we have always done it. Talk about change will waste time but not help!"
Which father said the wiser words?

CI-13   What should most qualify a man to hold high office?
1. Coming from (right, distinguished or high) family background
2. Devotion to the old and (revered) time-honored ways
3. Being the most popular among the people
4. High education and special knowledge

EF-11, 12   Which is most important for the future of (this country)?
1. The hard work of the people
2. Good planning on the part of government
3. God's help
4. Good luck

EF-14   Learned men (scholars, scientists) in the universities are studying such things as what determines whether a baby is a boy or girl and how it is that a seed turns into a plant.
Do you think that these investigations (studies) are:
1. All very good (beneficial)   2. All somewhat good (beneficial)
3. All somewhat harmful   4. All very harmful

FS-3   1. Some people say that it is necessary for a man and his wife to limit the number of children to be born so they can take better care of those they do have (already have).
2. Others say that it is wrong for a man and wife purposely (voluntarily) to limit the number of children to be born.
Which of these opinions do you agree with more?

MM-10-12   Which one of these (following) kinds of news interests you most?
1. World events (happenings in other countries)
2. The nation
3. Your home town (or village)
4. Sports
5. Religious (or tribal, cultural) events (ceremonies) or festivals

NE-5   If you were to meet a person who lives in another country a long way off (thousands of kilometers away), could you understand his way of thinking?
1. Yes   2. No

RE-12   Do you think a man can be truly good without having any religion at all?
1. Yes   2. No

B. *Behavior-Information Items (added to above=Form 6)*

AC-1, 2	Do you belong to any organization (associations, clubs), such as, for example, social clubs, unions, church organizations, political groups, or other groups? If "Yes," what are the names of all the organizations you belong to? (Scored for number of organizations)
GO-2	Would you tell me what are the biggest problems you see facing (your country)? (Scored for number of problems or words in answer)
IN-6 or 7	Where is (in what country is the city of) Washington/Moscow? (Scored correct or incorrect)
MM-5	How often do you (usually) get news and information from newspapers? 1. Every day 2. Few times a week 3. Occasionally (rarely) 4. Never

Note: Words in parentheses are alternative phrasing for aid in translation. In every case the items should be adapted to make sense in the particular culture. See Chart 1 for parallel attitude items and codes.

est and as an encouragement to further use. We have also prepared a set of coding instructions and a set of comparably tested alternatives for items which might prove especially sensitive or would pose coding problems too severe for the given field conditions of many investigations. . . .

Since our items are complex in content it becomes almost impossible to develop even a short scale in which each question involves absolutely no similarity in any attribute to some other item. We feel, however, that this scale maximizes the range of material covered within the limits of size and the objective criteria we have established. In terms of area or topic covered, it includes religion, strangers, change, mass media, birth control, education, the family, science, and government. The particular relationships the questions treat are almost as diverse, including man and God, native and foreigner, self and information media, man and wife, boy and school, man and knowledge, citizen and government, and official and public office. The particular qualities or personal attributes dealt with include openness to new people, acceptance of new ideas and practices, trust, aspiration, efficacy and civic mindedness or political activism. Even if it seems immodest to say so, we do not see how one could do better within the limits we imposed.

Since it is so highly selective, Form 5 has lower correlations with the Long Form OM, but it still represents it reasonably well as reflected (in Table 3) in correlations between .619 and .790. Despite the diversity of material represented, the scale shows quite high average item-to-scale correlations (Table 2), although this is facilitated by the limited number of questions used. Perhaps more important, despite the great diversity of content included in the questions, the scale continues to have reliabilities close to .7, falling to .622 only in Pakistan (Table 2).

INFORMATION AND BEHAVIORAL ITEMS
IN THE MEASURE OF MODERNITY

In the analysis presented above we focused exclusively on the 119 items we considered attitudinal. We thereby excluded from consideration 23 items which test our respondent's ability to produce various types of information, and 17 items in which he describes his behavior rather than attitudes. We thought it wise to keep them apart for several reasons. For one thing, the sheer amount of information a person possessed might reflect not so much his interest in the world around him as his basic intelligence. We saw no reason to classify a man as modern simply because he was smart. For another, we knew from experience that the information items, although numerous, correlated very highly with one another. Allowed to enter a pool of items used to derive an OM scale, therefore, they might well crowd out other items and overweight the end product in the direction of this one area. So far as the behavioral items are concerned, the case is similar but with reversed emphasis. We had little independent experience in working with them, but assumed because of their experimental character and diverse content they might not correlate well with each other nor be able to survive in a completely open competition with a large set of powerful attitudinal items. Yet we felt that a strong case could be made for considering what a man actually does, or at least says he does, as important an indicator of modernity as what he feels or believes. We wished, therefore, to give these behavioral items a special analysis shelter much like that given an infant industry by means of protective tariffs or tax relief.

Since a definite theoretical case could be made for the relation of both information levels and behavior to individual modernity, and since the answers to the relevant questions could unambiguously be scored as having a modern and traditional direction, we decided to broaden further the base of our most distilled attitudinal scale, Short Form 5, by adding two items from the information set and two from the behavioral set. This final summary measure, including all of Short Form 5 and four informational-behavioral items, we designate Short Form 6.[33]

In deciding which information and behavior items to use, we followed the same basic procedure already familiar as the "item-analysis method" for deriving short forms from the long form. Items were screened first by item analysis for their ability to "work" simultaneously in 5 or 6 of the six countries.[34] From this set we selected those which gave us the widest theme representation and promised to be simple to code in the field if necessary. In the information area, questions requiring the respondent to identify correctly a public figure of world prominence such as Kennedy or Nehru, or a national leader of his own country, proved very effective, as did questions about important distant places such as Washington or Moscow. These questions were consistently among those with the strongest items to overall scale correlations we observed. For example, the item to Long Form OM correlation for the question on Nehru ranged from .458 in Pakistan to .649 in India.[35] Since the information questions were numerous, this seemed to justify our earlier having segregated them in computing the attitudinal OM. But we now also felt the case was clear for adding at least one such information-soliciting item to the final short form of the modernity scale. A second and distinct type of information-soliciting item was the type that asked the respondent to give his opinions freely on some topic, to name a series of things he wanted to own, to name some books or newspapers he had read, and so forth. Of these verbal fluency items, the all around best item to emerge asked the respondent to name what he considered to be the main problems facing his country. When coded for the number of problems cited, without probing by the interviewer, this item shows excellent results both by the item analysis and by the criterion group method.

The situation of the behavioral items is somewhat different. As we expected, the fact that they dealt with behavior—even though reported by the respondent rather than being observed by us[36]—meant that they related less strongly to the total pool of items than did the attitude questions on the very same topic. For example, the question which asked whether the respondent had ever *actually* written to or otherwise actively contacted a public official (AC-4), had much lower correlation with the overall OM score than did the item which asked only whether he had ever felt so concerned about a public issue that he merely *wanted* to do something about it (AC-6).

Two different behavioral items, however, emerged quite unambiguously in all countries as strongly related to both the sub-set of behavioral items and the larger pool of attitudinal items. The first item (AC-1, 2) asked whether the individual belonged to any voluntary organizations and if so, how many. It thus tested in part the degree of active, or realized, interest in public and community affairs, although our denotative definition of voluntary organization permitted social clubs and the like to be counted here also. In addition, we found the question on how often a man read or was exposed to a newspaper to be a very powerful indicator in all countries; hence we included it as the second behavioral item.

When the informational and behavioral attitudinal items are added in the second part of Chart 2 to the attitudinal items previously selected to make up Form 5, the result is a 14-item scale we designate Form 6,[37] which gives a broad base for judging individual modernity. The proportional weight of attitudinal vs. informational *and* behavioral measures in Form 6 is, of course, quite arbitrary, and we make no special theoretical case for it. We can see how some might insist on giving equal weight to all three types of question—attitudinal, informational and behavioral. Further experience with these measures will help reach a decision on empirical grounds, although the ultimate balance anyone establishes will be in large degree a matter of personal preference. For now we offer Form 6 as a highly serviceable start toward devising the "ultimate" measure of individual modernity. This is no ordinary stopgap we offer, since it has the virtue of having questions which have run an exceptional gauntlet of tests by both the item and criterion method of selection in six countries. It is broadly based, catholic in conception to weigh not only attitudes by behavior and information levels. It represents the Long Form OM even better than did Form 5, as may be seen from the correlation coefficients in Table 3. In reliability, Form 6 is also superior, as indicated in Table 2, going below .7 only in Pakistan.

CONCLUSION

With the presentation of Short Form 6 in Chart 2, we complete our formal assignment to devise a theoretically broad, empirically tight, administratively simple measure of individual modernity which has been widely tested cross-nationally and can be used with little or no adaptation under all field conditions in either research or practical work which requires one to judge the modernity of individuals or groups in developing countries. To take account of personal preferences, theoretical and methodological, for one or another type of scale, and in response to the fact that some will have time and energy to use longer, but others only shorter tests, we have not restricted ourselves to developing only one scale. We have, rather, presented several, indeed a battery, of measures of psychological modernity. Within the severe space limits under which we operate, we sought to give the fullest and frankest account of our method, so that others may check, or even seek to replicate, our efforts, and so that the intellectual and technical ground on which the end product rests will be reasonably clear.

Of course there are many alternatives to paths we took which we know of and could not mention, and no doubt there are others we never imagined. Certainly even within the broad course we followed, there were by-paths we pursued but could not describe, and there were detours and short-cuts as well as pit-falls of which we may not even be aware. Our continuing analysis experience and the critical discussion of our work by others will presumably bring all that out. We limit ourselves here to stating our opinion that the final product of most efforts broadly similar to ours in conception would be unlikely to yield results really fundamentally different from the scales presented. Certainly the set of themes and topical areas could be somewhat different, but only within modest limits. Many an item could perhaps be substituted for one we recommend, but this would not make a structural change. Different sub-samples of the national populations should be studied, and another set of countries might certainly make a difference in the outcome, but we doubt the differences would be profound. Only experience will tell.

We cannot leave the subject, however, without noting that from some points of view the derivation of a short scale to test modernity, however practically useful, is of only limited importance compared to some of the things we may note only in passing. To us the most fundamental of these observations lies in the evidence we find of the trans-cultural nature of the human psyche. We consider it notable in the highest degree that a pool of some 119 attitude questions and some 40 related informational and behavioral items should show such extraordinarily similar structure in six such diverse countries—and even more than that number of cultural groups.[38] If we had started with the same theory and the same pool of items, but then devised a separate and *different* or *distinctive* scale of modernity for each of the six countries, the result might be interesting, but would not be compelling. Yet to find that in all six countries basically the *same set of items* both cohere psychologically and relate to external criterion variables in a strictly comparable fashion is, we believe, a finding of the first importance. It strongly suggests that men everywhere have the same structural mechanisms underlying their socio-psychic functioning, despite the enormous variability of the culture content which they embody. In our subsequent project publications we hope to elaborate on these connections, and through an analysis of the forces which make men modern to throw some light on the psychic unity of mankind—a unity which we can demonstrate is increasing.[39]

NOTES

1. This will, however, be done in the forthcoming full report on the project, to be titled *Becoming Modern*, by Alex Inkeles, David H. Smith, Howard Schuman and Edward Ryan. A brief review of the major themes may be found in Alex Inkeles, "The Modernization of Man," *Conspectus,* India International Center, New Delhi, Vol. 1, No. 4 (December, 1965), reprinted in Myron Weiner, ed., *Modernization: The Dynamics of Growth,* New York: Basic Books, 1966.

2. Items were taken directly or adapted from the questionnaires of the following studies, some of which were still in progress when we devised our measures: Gabriel A. Almond and Sidney Verba, *The Civic Culture: Political Attitudes and Democracy in Five Nations,* Princeton, New Jersey: Princeton University Press, 1963; Melvin Tumin and Arnold S. Feldman, *Social Class and Social Change in Puerto Rico,* Princeton, New Jersey: Princeton University Press, 1961; Alex Inkeles and Raymond A. Bauer, *The Soviet Citizen,* Cambridge, Mass.: Harvard University Press, 1959; Hadley Cantril, *The Pattern of Human Concerns,* New Brunswick, New Jersey: Rutgers University Press, 1965; J. A. Kahl, *The Measurement of Modernism: A Study of Values in Brazil and Mexico,* University of Texas Press, forthcoming; Julian L. Woodward and Elmo Roper, "Political Activity of American Citizens," in Heinz Eulau, et al., eds., *Political Behavior,* Glencoe, Illinois: The Free Press, 1956, pp. 133–137; Daniel Lerner, *The Passing of Traditional Society: Modernizing the Middle East,* New York: The Free Press, 1958; and Kalman H. Silvert, *Reaction and Revolution in Latin America,* New Orleans: Hauser Press, 1961.

3. The actual ranges were: Argentina, 1–15 yrs.; Chile, 2–11 yrs.; India, 0–11 yrs.; Israel, 2–14 yrs.; Nigeria, 4–13 yrs.; and Pakistan, 0–8 years. We also collected a sample of university students in each country, but since they have such special characteristics they are being studied apart from the main samples. They do not, therefore, figure in this analysis.

4. That is, for our sample, "Pakistan" should be read as "East Pakistan," "India" as "the State of Bihar," and "Nigeria" as "the large Nigerian Yoruba tribal area." For further details, see chapter 2, *Becoming Modern,* forthcoming.

5. In fact we have already applied the main body of our questions to a group of Protestant Americans in the Appalachian region of Kentucky. The men mostly had grade school education. The response to the interview was broadly comparable to its reception in developing countries. It was by no means considered an insult to anyone's intelligence. The structure of *individual* answers (as against the modal pattern or national average) was basically similar to the structure of attitudes encountered in other countries. For a brief report on this research see the unpublished Senior Honors Thesis of William W. Lawrence, "Occupations and Attitudes in Hazard, Kentucky," Department of Social Relations, Harvard College, June, 1965.

6. Indeed, as noted above, in several countries we administered our questionnaire to groups of university students. With modest adaptation is was completed by them without incident.

7. Most of the analysis reported here was done with the Harvard Data-Text System of Programs, created under the direction of Dr. Arthur Couch, Harvard University.

8. For a complete version of our questionnaire, and a list of the 159 items referred to here, order Document 9133 from the Chief, Photoduplication Service, Library of Congress, Washington 25, D.C., Auxiliary Publication Project, remitting $31.50 for microfilm (35mm) or $117.50 for photocopies.

9. There were many other items in the interview, but the large majority of these dealt with background data or else were only nominal (non-ordered) codes for open-ended items. In addition, there were some items excluded on theoretical or methodological grounds from the pool of 159 items: for example, items in the test of psychosomatic symptoms were excluded because theory and past results made us believe their relation to psychological modernity was complex or even unclear. Several work commitment and work satisfaction items, home and school experience items, and work experience items were excluded because we wished to use them as intervening and independent variables in our analysis, rather than as dependent variables. For further details, see *Becoming Modern,* forthcoming.

10. See *Becoming Modern,* forthcoming. One way to construct these more complex profiles is first to establish a set of distinctive specialized scales, and then to describe an individual in terms of the pattern of scale scores which characterizes him. Although this approach has many virtues, it is clearly not compatible with the objective we set for this [article]—to develop a *brief* and *easily scored,* simple measure of individual modernity.

11. Only in the forthcoming work of Joseph Kahl on Brazil and Mexico, *op. cit.,* is there a comparable breadth of coverage. Kahl attempted to test values in 14 different realms, with the scale for each area varying from a modern to a traditional pole. His scale areas included several, such as "activism" and "low integration with relatives," which are similar to ours. Tumin and Feldman, *op. cit.,* limited themselves to Puerto Rico. Although they used a wide variety of questions, they were mainly concerned with the single dependent variable area of educational and occupational aspirations. They presented an eight element theoretical model of the modern man (pp. 247–278), but did not systematically attempt to measure the qualities it delineated. Almond and Verba, *op cit.,* worked in six countries of which one, Mexico, qualifies as unambiguously underdeveloped; but they limited themselves to measures of political attitudes and relations. Lerner, *op. cit.,* dealt with six developing countries, all in the Middle East, but was restricted to attitudes and behavior in the realm of communications, using the individual's empathic ability as the key psychological attribute.

12. The average correlation of 5 (Israel missing) countries of the Long Form OM was: with education .434, with years of factory experience .179, and with rural/urban origin .142 (cultivators excluded). All the individual correlations (except for 2 in India) were at the .01 level of significance or better.

13. Although trichotomies might have been more effective for correlational analysis, some of the field directors used mainly two step, fixed alternative answers to questions. Accepting dichotomies made it possible to follow the same procedure in all countries. Because of the inherent variability of the response pattern in any country, however, we were obliged to make some divisions which

may not seem logical. For example, if 90 per cent of the sample said education was "good" or "very good," the 45 per cent saying it was only "good" (but not "very good") might be classified on the traditional side along with the 10 per cent who said it was "no good." Draconian as these procedures might seem, a case can be made for their logic on the grounds that we are judging not the *absolute* but the *relative* attitudinal modernity of an individual as compared to his peers and compatriots.

14. This means that the summary scale score cannot be used to compare individuals from different countries. This could be done only if the same absolute cutting point were used in all countries. When eventually we devise a short form on that basis it will be scored in a standard way for all countries, thus making the scores strictly comparable from individual to individual across national boundaries. To do so, however, will raise many thorny theoretical and methodological issues we are unable to take up at this time.

15. The classification was arrived at in accord with the general theory guiding the project, by the authors of this report. We consulted but were not bound by the opinion of those of the field directors who were in Cambridge and could be consulted. In case of disagreement, the opinion of David Smith, who had prime responsibility for this operation, generally prevailed. Inevitably, we made some mistakes, as indicated by the fact that some items had *negative* correlations with the summary score. Only 5 per cent of the items were thus incorrectly rated, whereas if chance alone operated, 50 per cent would have shown such minus correlations (see [note] 18, below, for further details).

16. When an individual had not answered a particular question the item was not considered in calculating his average score.

17. Happily, the chosen designation OM is the same as the Hindu mantra which expresses the triple constitution of the cosmos. In the Project's internal reference system, this Long Form OM is labelled OM–2. Use of that number here would be confusing, since the order in which the short forms are presented in this paper does not agree with the order of the Project's internal reference numbers. We cite these internal reference numbers, however, to facilitate responding to communications from our colleagues, concerning the various scale forms.

18. We use the term "reliability" here in a general sense. In a more technical sense, however, the Long Form used here (OM–2) does have the highest reliability coefficients, on the average, when compared to all six short forms. This is not to say it could not be improved. For example, hindsight could be used to eliminate, or alter, the assumed "modern" direction of items whose direction we misjudged. The project actually has in its battery another summary measure of modernity, designated OM–1 in our internal reference system, which was based more narrowly on items rated by 5 of 6 judges (Project directors and research associates) as unambiguously related to modernity. This procedure yielded a pool of not 119 but 79 items, and not 5 per cent of mistakes in judging direction, but only 2 per cent. It has higher reliabilities than OM–2.

19. A different way of selecting the items, which would still follow the logic of the item-analysis method, would be to do a factor analysis of the basic set of 119 items. We felt there was good reason to prefer a different approach, but plan later to conduct the factor analysis to permit the two methods to be compared.

20. We use formula 17.16, involving the average item-to-test correlations, from

p. 454 of Joy Paul Guilford, *Fundamental Statistics in Psychology and Education*, 3rd ed., N.Y.: McGraw-Hill, 1956.

21. For example, the average internal consistency of 11 scales from the Minnesota Multiphasic Personality Inventory is .69, and the median .75, with split half reliability coefficients ranging from −.05 to .96; see page 474 of W. Grant Dahlstrom and George Schlager Welsh: *An MMPI Handbook*, Minneapolis: The University of Minnesota Press, 1960.

22. Actually, we have not established that there is one and only one dimension underlying this item set, nor that all types of items enter equally, nor that the main underlying dimension is "modernity." But we have established *at least one* pervasive underlying dimension, and on prima facie grounds we can argue from the content of the items that this dimension is psychological modernity as we have conceptualized it. No other explanation, such as response set, will suffice.

23. For identification in documents internal to our project this scale (Short Form 1) is designated OM–6.

24. Table 1, of course, gives only a highly condensed version of each question. The full question wording may be identified by the alphabetical-numerical designation for each question in the copy of the full questionnaire on file as in the American Documentation Institute.

25. The theme list used, as given in Chart 1, is an expanded version of the list of code letter designations used in the Project's basic questionnaire. In making the list for Chart 1 we divided some of the more complex themes, such as *Efficacy* and *Women's Rights*, into sub-themes which are treated as separate units for present purposes. There is an inevitable element of arbitrariness in our selection and designation of both theme or sub-theme areas. We tried to be strictly "objective" about our decisions, but in the end appealed to a consensus of the field directors to settle difficult decisions regarding the final list of attitudinal themes for Chart 1.

26. We could have randomly split our own samples into two halves, and then derived a criterion group short form OM using one half and cross-validating it on the other random half in each country. We could also have used our countries in two sets of three, the second set testing the reliability of the first. The method we used is even more stringent, since, in effect, each of 4 countries is a reliability check for the others, in devising the criterion based short forms. But this does have the effect of precluding the use of those short forms in our own later analysis relating modernity to the independent variables.

27. The three variables are not completely independent. This is especially true for years of factory experience and years of urban experience, since most factories are located in cities. The average correlation of those two variables is .535. But our sampling procedure insured relatively low (Pearsonian) correlations between origin and education (average r=.271) and origin and years of factory experience (average r=.131) and education and factory experience (average r=.097). (All these averages are for five countries only, because the data for Israel were lacking here when "the r's" were computed.) Even though the variables are related, three such separate tests provide a more stringent and more broadly conceived criterion group test than would a single variable.

28. In the internal reference system of the Project, Short Form 3 is identified as OM–9.

29. Five out of the total 34 are EF-related items. There are also five items from the New Experience (NE) realm.

30. The maximum is defined by the attitude theme areas mentioned in Chart 1.

31. The Project's internal designation for this Short Form 4 is OM–8.

32. The internal project reference number of Short Form 5 is OM–11.

33. The internal project reference number for this Short Form 6 is OM–12.

34. This screening was done on the basis of the item-to-scale correlations in a pool of 159 items. This is different from the Long Form OM we are using in this paper, which had only 119 items. For internal reference in the project, this longer (159 item) summary measure is designated OM–4. In the item competition, we considered separately all information items as a sub-set, and all behavioral items as a sub-set, otherwise information items alone would have captured all the vacancies.

35. These correlations will not be found in Table 1. As indicated in the preceding note, the screening of behavioral and information items was on the basis of a Long Form (OM–4) which included them along with the attitude items. Since these information and behavior items were not included in the OM–2 version of the Long Form used in this report, there are blanks in column 1 of Chart 1 opposite the four relevant questions.

36. The project also collected measures of behavior other than those reported by the subject himself, such as those based on an individual's production record or the report of his foreman about his behavior on the job. These are being developed in a separate analysis, and will eventually be related both to general attitudes and self-reported behavior.

37. In the internal reference system of the Project, Short Form 6 is identified as OM–12.

38. In several of the countries studied there were fundamental ethnic subdivisions represented in our sample: In India, for example, we sampled tribal and often only nominally Hindu vs. well-established Hindu groups of classical Hindu culture. There were comparably important ethnic background distinctions in Israel and Nigeria and lesser but notable ethnic or sub-group differentiation in Argentina and Pakistan.

39. For earlier statements of this position and a different type of evidence see Alex Inkeles and Peter Rossi, "National Comparisons of Occupational Prestige," *American Journal of Sociology,* 61 (January, 1956), pp. 329–339; and Alex Inkeles, "Industrial Man: The Relation of Status to Experience, Perception, and Value," *American Journal of Sociology,* 66 (July, 1960), pp. 1–31.

QUESTIONS

1. To what type of case or unit do the authors apply the concept of "modernity"?
2. What are the sources of the items that the authors consider for use in their scale of modernity?
3. Describe the methods of sampling used in the several nations. Do they approach some form of random sampling? How do the authors defend their methods of sampling?

4. How do the authors handle the problem of item nonresponse?
5. Which of the several scales developed would you prefer? Defend your choice.

Is Everyone Going Modern?
A Critique and a Suggestion for
Measuring Modernism

JOHN B. STEPHENSON

Guttman scaling involves the selection of items that, when combined, provide information on a single universe of meaning. The idea is to choose items so that a favorable response to an item at one end of a continuum implies a favorable response to all items that are less extreme. The scaling process involves the selection of items, application of items to some sets of objects (people, or other units), and the analysis of responses in order to determine if they provide the patterns defined by Guttman as necessary to call the items an "ordinal scale." In the following article the several steps in a complete scaling procedure are clearly exemplified. In addition, the article presents a contrast to the preceding selection by Smith and Inkeles illustrating that the same concept may have very different operational and conceptual meanings when it is used by different researchers. (For further discussion on the issue of measuring modernity, see Inkeles and Stephenson's exchange in the *American Journal of Sociology* 75 [1969]:146–156.)

THE PROBLEM

A. CURRENT INTEREST IN SOCIAL CHANGE   The attention of social scientists has turned back again to the subject of change. Within the past fifteen years, neglect of the study of social dynamics has changed to active interest, as indicated by the increased number of articles in professional journals on the nature and consequences of change at various levels and in a variety of institutional areas—politics, economics, religion, for example—and of change in culture as well as social organization. In this growing body of literature different types of changes are given somewhat confusing and like-sounding labels, such as democratization, development, industrialization, urbanization, secularization, and modernization.[1] Agreement is not perfect, but it probably would be generally accepted that, whereas the terms "development" and "industrialization" are used to describe mainly economic growth, and "urbanization" is used to describe

Reprinted from *American Journal of Sociology* 74 (1968), 265–275, with permission of The University of Chicago Press.

shifts in population dispersion and concentration, the concept of modernization has to do with a transformation of culture and of personality insofar as it is influenced by culture, rather than of some aspect of social organization or of human ecology.[2] This paper is concerned with modernization in the cultural and personality sense, and more particularly with *measurements* of modernism.

B. MEASURES OF MODERNISM   It should be made clear that modern*ization* is not the same as modern*ism*. The idea of modern*ization* is that there is an alteration or a movement of something from a more traditional state to a more modern state from one point in time to another. The set of doctrines, values, or beliefs which makes up the "traditional" state is traditionism, while the comparable state at the other end of the continuum—the set of "modern" beliefs and values—is modernism. It is necessary to make this distinction because in discussing certain measures which purport to be indicators of "modernization," we shall find that it is not modernization itself that is measured, but the extent of modernism, or the extent to which individuals hold what are claimed to be modernist values. *Changes* in the proportion of people holding modern values, or changes in the extent to which individuals have "gone modern," constitute modernization. Thus, measuring modernism should be viewed as a means of assessing modernization. The latter, unlike the former, involves a temporal dimension.

The need for reliable and accurate indicators of modernism is thus obvious. Several such measures may be found in the literature, two of which will be reviewed briefly here.

In a recent article on culture change and stress in Peru, Kellert, Williams, Whyte, and Alberti look at the effects of "modernization" on symptoms of stress among a large sample of rural Peruvians.[3] We are here interested only in the three measures of modernism used by these investigators. In the first instance, "modernization" (Kellert's term for our "modernism") is measured by the degree to which individuals take sides with groups in the village representing "old custom" or "modern ideas."[4] A shortcoming of this indicator is that it does not specify the content of the old and the new ways. More serious problems in validity arise, however, with the other two indicators. One of these measures "modernization" by the amount of change in optimism or pessimism regarding the economic progress of the village.[5] The unstated assumption seems to be that the modern individual has the power of positive thinking and believes that everything is always getting better. The third indicator asks respondents whether they think the village is progressing slowly, not progressing, or going backward (no dimension of progress is specified).[6] Frankly, I need some assurance that the population under study adequately shared with the investigators the meaning of such a *yanqui* term as "progress." There is also a question regarding the relationship between perceived progress of local villages and modernism: Is this modernism to the researchers or to the respondents, or to both, or to neither?[7]

Another article, which outlines one of the most ambitious attempts yet to measure modernity, is one in which Smith and Inkeles report the cross-national application of 119-plus items which they conceptualize as relevant to individual modernity.[8] Their definition of "modern" and "modernity," with which this writer would basically agree, must be understood before describing the scales themselves.[9]

. . . "modern" generally means a national state characterized by a complex of traits including urbanization, high levels of education, industrialization, extensive mechanization, high rates of social mobility, and the like. When applied to individuals, it refers to a set of attitudes, values and ways of feeling and acting, presumably of the sort either generated by or required for effective participation in a modern society. In this report we deal only with *individual* modernity.[10]

They proceed to describe the development of the scale:

After reviewing the literature and defining our own theoretical position we identified some thirty topics, themes, areas, or issues which seemed relevant to a definition of modernity. . . . In this paper, unfortunately, we lack space either to define the content of any of these attitude and behavior realms or to indicate the reasons why we considered them relevant.[11]

This is indeed unfortunate, for, even though the authors promise that explanations will be given in a forthcoming book, one must read the remainder of the article having faith that the areas selected either have some logical connection with the definition of modernity offered or that these areas were found to be meaningfully associated with modernism in the minds of the people to whom the scale was applied.

Application of the scale and the resulting findings lead to the conclusion that "there is an underlying dimension of psychological modernity pervading our set of 119 attitude items."[12] Reliability appears quite high. The question of validity gnaws at me throughout, however. Perhaps it is not the validity of the scale in the minds of the investigators which is open to question so much as the validity of the scale for the various populations and subpopulations studied. Smith and Inkeles are indeed convinced that they have measured what they set out to measure: "We do not see how one could do better within the limits we imposed."[13] What is open to question is whether they set out to measure the right thing.[14]

Such studies as Smith and Inkeles' appear to share another assumption which this investigator feels is open to question: namely, that all modern cultures are basically similar in content and that all persons who can be said to be "going modern" share the same traits, regardless of what culture they are part of or out of what past they have moved. What is defined as modern for one population is assumed to be indicative of modernity for any other. It would appear that the search for change-universals (so that one can emerge from his studies with the conclusion that "Everything is changing in the direction of X") has biased measures in favor of this discovery. Whether all peoples in the world are indeed moving from one particular set of values toward another particular set should be left open for empirical proof or disconfirmation.[15]

We might pause to reconsider this position in the light of Lerner's argument, based on research evidence, that "the Western model of modernization exhibits certain components and sequences whose relevance is global."[16] He observes that "the same basic model reappears in virtually all modernizing societies on all continents of the world, regardless of variations in race, color, creed."[17] Lerner's conclusion seems to provide ample justification for the assumption that traits of the modern and the traditional must be shared worldwide. Yet he notes that not every society has accepted the message of modernity in the same way. Of the Middle East he says, "Wanted are modern institutions but not modern ideologies, modern power but not modern purposes, modern wealth but not modern wisdom, modern commodities but not modern cant."[18] While pointing out basic similarities, even Lerner recognizes that the nature of modernism varies according to the specific context.[19]

Hoselitz makes a similar point regarding variations in traditionism and modernism when he says that "culture change is not unilinear, but multilinear." He points out that "different varieties of belief and attitude systems, all of which may be lumped together under the general designation 'traditional,' do exist. Hence the processes of change in these contrasting situations begin from quite different starting points, would show considerable variation, and . . . the outcomes of these processes of change may vary considerably."[20]

C. AN ALTERNATIVE DEFINITION OF MODERNIZATION   A definition of modernization is needed which avoids the assumption that it is a universal process of unilinear change, and which avoids the assumption that the particular value contents of traditionism and modernism are everywhere the same, so that measures which follow from the definitions will not also be based on the same unfortunate assumptions. In this connection, the following definitions are suggested: *Modernization is the movement of persons or groups along a cultural dimension from what is defined by the cultural norms as traditional toward what is defined by the same culture as modern. Those values defined in the local culture as traditional comprise what may be called traditionalism; those defined as modern constitute modernism.* If no differentiation is made in the culture between traditionism and modernism, then movement along the dimension cannot be recognized by the participants, and study of modernization in this cultural setting is meaningless. If modernism and traditionism are seen by the population as different cultural entities, then measurement of change between the two becomes feasible through the measurement of changes in the extent of adherence to the particular value content of traditionism and modernism for that population.

AN ILLUSTRATION:
THE SHILOH STUDY

A case illustration may help demonstrate how such a definition can be put to use in actual measurement. It will be reasoned that although comparability across populations is lost, assertions about changes taking place in the population are given some empirical credibility, and assumptions about the universality of modernism and modernization need not be made. The illustration will revolve around the construction of an actual Guttman scale of modernism-traditionism for a particular population.

A. THE SETTING   The population under study is a small community (more precisely, a cluster of neighborhoods served in common by a school, churches, and stores) in the southern Appalachian Mountains. Approximately 200–250 households are located there. The community had been relatively (but never completely) isolated until the 1940's and 1950's, when roads, schools, and mass media effectively raised the "pine curtain" between it and the rest of the country. New occupations in industry have become available to members of the community, while at the same time older forms of work in agriculture, mining, and timber have grown less economically viable. As in most other parts of the Appalachians, the population of Shiloh is almost entirely white and native-born.[21]

B. THE INSTRUMENT   1. *Field Survey.* A four-month field study was conducted in Shiloh in the summer of 1965. Extensive notes were made of conversations, interviews, and observations. Among the varied statements made by the inhabitants of the community were many which indicated in local terms what it meant to be traditional and what it meant to be modern. Some informants referred, for example, to certain "old-timey ways," or commented that to believe so-and-so was "old-fashioned." Others made reference to things that were "newfangled," "new," or "outside" (a term used synonymously with "modern"—for instance, it was once noted that a certain individual had become "minded to outside ways," that is, he had become oriented to values from beyond the mountains). Thus it was possible later to catalogue over fifty statements taken directly from field notes in which the community itself defined traditionism and modernism.

Information from the field study also made it possible to conclude that it was meaningful to study moderni*zation* as a process occurring in Shiloh, since this kind of change was observed by many respondents. For example, one man noted that whereas some people stayed like their parents, others seemed to learn new ideas. Moreover, some informants marked with regret the fact that many young people were leaving the old ways; others ridiculed people who were old-fashioned and wouldn't, like themselves, become more up to date. Such statements are testimony to the existence of movement from traditionism to modernism in the community; it is a kind of change meaningful to the population under study.

2. *Use of Judges.*   In the winter of 1967 the fifty-odd statements referred to above were subjected to judgment by a panel of seven persons who were asked to sort them on the basis of their "traditional" or "modern" content. All the judges could be considered "expert" in the sense that they had had first-hand experience with Appalachian populations and were familiar with the notions of modernism and traditionism. Three of the judges were professors of sociology who can safely be said to be recognized authorities on the Appalachian region. Two judges were Ph.D. candidates in sociology who have lived and worked in southern Appalachia and who can claim personal as well as academic knowledge of the people of that area. The two remaining judges were not sociologists but

were individuals who had been exposed at length to the concepts of modernism and traditionism through me. They were called on for judgment primarily because of their lifelong residence among mountain people and their untrained natural capacity for analysis of those people.

The judges were required to sort statements into three piles: one which indicated a clearly "modern" attitude, one which clearly showed a "traditional" attitude, and one which showed neither and was therefore ambiguous. While systematic inquiries were not made into the criteria of classification held by the judges, comments occasionally were recorded which offer some insight into these standards. For example, one judge observed that the task of classifying statements was clouded by mental reference to particular individuals who had made such statements. Another noted that it was difficult to separate the traditional-modern dimension from a dimension of social class. One judge raised the possibility that there were several types of modernism rather than just one, a fact which raises doubts about the unidimensionality of the items in his mind. One of the non-sociologist judges admitted that he had been influenced by me in his conception of modernism and traditionism, but said also that his decisions were guided by "particular stereotypes" built from his own experience. Again, another of the sociologists said he was "confused because many items are multidimensional (indeed, modernism is multidimensional)." He also encountered frustration in attempting to keep modernism-traditionism distinct from social-class differences. By inference from these observations, it appears that among the criteria used for classification by these judges were reference to particular known individuals, value differences related to social class,[22] and conceptions obtained from me. (It appears, furthermore, that there was some discomfort among the judges when they were required to assume unidimensionality of modernism among an Appalachian population.)

Prior to the judging, each statement was coded to indicate which of seven "value areas" it represented: time, achievement, work, education, person-versus-object orientation, religion, sex role orientation. After the judging was complete, the two statements on which there was highest agreement were chosen from each value area to be placed in the final instrument.[23] With the addition of another last-minute insertion, the total battery of value statements included was fifteen[24] (see Table 1).

3. *The Larger Instrument.* The interview schedule of which the fifteen-item modernism-traditionism battery was a part was constructed for the primary purpose of collecting data in order to test hypotheses about modernism, marginality, and mental health. Interviews lasted between thirty and forty-five minutes on the average and were conducted for the most part in the homes of respondents.

4. *The Sample.* The sample consists of 130 respondents who are members of "whole" families with children living at home. The sample is almost coterminous with the number of people in this category who live in Shiloh, the remainder of the population being made up of older residents and couples who have retired here from "outside." The rate of refusals, most of them by females, was around 20 per cent. Where men and their wives were both interviewed, they were questioned simultaneously in different rooms by an interviewing assistant and myself. In

only a few instances were the couples interviewed sequentially by the same interviewer.

The sample includes seventy-one males and fifty-nine females. Occupations of heads of households ranged from professional, managerial, and white collar (20 respondents), through full-time blue collar, such as factory work (40 respondents), and seasonal blue collar, semiskilled, and unskilled work, such as farming, mining, and timber (59 respondents), to no significant gainful employment or dependence on agency support (11 respondents). Sixty respondents could be classified as upwardly mobile, in that their jobs were higher on the above fourfold occupational scale than the jobs of their fathers. Fifty-three could be labeled nonmobile by the same criterion, and twelve were downwardly mobile.[25] These figures reflect a change in the occupational structure affecting the people of Shiloh as the community becomes "industrialized."

C. CONSTRUCTION OF THE SCALE   A Guttman scale based on six of the original fifteen traditional-modern items was constructed with the use of the Gradgram instrument.

1. *Elimination of Items.*   The fifteen items were arranged in order from highest to lowest total score (traditional responses were scored "0"; modern responses, "3"; middle categories, "1" and "2," respectively). Answer categories for each item were then collapsed so that each item was dichotomized to produce more non-error than error in all categories, in accordance with usual scalogram procedure. This rule could not be met on three of the items (numbers 10, 1, and 2 in Table 1), and they were therefore discarded at this point.

Respondents were rearranged so as to minimize error with the new set of twelve items. It was clear that three more items would have to be discarded because they contributed so heavily to the over-all number of errors (numbers 15, 12, and 8 in Table 1). The remaining nine items and the respondents were rearranged again in line with scalogram procedure, with a resulting coefficient of reproducibility of .884. It was obvious from looking at the proportion of errors in each item that number 4 was contributing more than its share. With its elimination, the coefficient of reproducibility rose to .901.

One of the several criteria applied when assessing Guttman scales is that at least 5 per cent of the respondents must fall in each scale type. This is the same as requiring "spread" among the scale cut points. This requirement could be met better and the scale enhanced with the removal of item number 13, which, when accomplished, left seven items and a coefficient of reproducibility of .919.

It was noted that two of the seven items tapped virtually the same value area, education. If one of these two were removed from the scale, not only would cutting points between scale types be more evenly distributed, but the six remaining items would each tap a different value area and no two would tap the same one. (The only one of the original seven value areas included in the full battery which was *not* represented in the final scale was "work.") Therefore, item number 9 was eliminated from the scale.

2. *Data on Final Six-Item Scale.*   After items and respondents were

TABLE 1. Value Statements Initially Included in Instrument

Item No.	Statement*	"Modern" Response
1	A person should improve his living conditions even if he has to go into debt to do it.	Agreement
2	A person should stand up for his kin even when the law says they are in the wrong.	Disagreement
3	The old, small neighborhood school was better than the new consolidated schools.	Disagreement
4	There is a conflict between religion and science.	Disagreement
5	You can't make progress without change.	Agreement
6	I would rather be a person who tries to make do with what he has; being dissatisfied all the time just leads to problems.	Disagreement
7	I think the old ways are mostly best for me.	Disagreement
8	A person really shouldn't have to work any more than he has to to get by.	Disagreement
9	Consolidating the schools has improved educational opportunities for people like me and my children in almost every way.	Agreement
10	A person's job is so important that sometimes he has to turn his back on his family and friends.	Agreement
11	The old Bible (the King James version) is the only true word of God.	Disagreement
12	If a woman votes, she should probably vote the same way as her husband.	Disagreement
13	Planning a career is as important a responsibility as raising a family.	Agreement
14	Women should be allowed to "wear the britches" more (or have more say) than they have in the past.	Agreement
15	By and large, I am satisfied with my way of life.	Disagreement

* The answer categories used for all items were: Agree strongly, agree somewhat, disagree somewhat, disagree strongly.

rearranged for the final time, the coefficient of reproducibility was .916. The proportion of respondents in each scale type is about the same, as shown in Table 2, which indicates that cutting points are well distributed. Two of the cutting points are near the center of the scale, a feature regarded as desirable by some scalogram analysts.

Out of the 119 usable respondents scaled, 72 (60.5 per cent) were pure scale types, while 47 (39.5 per cent) were error types. The scale type with the largest proportion of error types was 7, which is the "most traditional" category. That there is patterned error here is suggested by the presence of six cases among the twelve error types in which the error was in the first column. Since the first item has to do with changing sex roles, it is a reasonable guess that these "errors" are made by females who are otherwise tradition-oriented. A large number of error types were found also in scale type 6. Only one of the errors is accounted for by item 1, but four are cases where there is an error in item 4, concerning orientation to the past. The only other instance of a large number of error types was in scale

TABLE 2. The Six-Item Modernism-Traditionism Scale

	Item Number (+ = "Modern" Response)						Distribution of Scale Types			
	1	2	3	4	5	6	Non-Scale Types	Perfect Scale Types	Total	% of Respondents
1*	+	+	+	+	+	+	4	12	16	13.4
2	−	+	+	+	+	+	5	10	15	12.6
3	−	−	+	+	+	+	8	7	15	12.6
4	−	−	−	+	+	+	4	17	21	17.7
5	−	−	−	−	+	+	5	14	19	16.0
6	−	−	−	−	−	+	9	7	16	13.4
7	−	−	−	−	−	−	12	5	17	14.3
Total							47	72	119	100.0

	Item Contents	Value Areas
1	"Women should be allowed to 'wear the britches' more (or have more say) than they have in the past."	Sex roles
2	"The old Bible (the King James version) is the only true word of God."	Religion
3	"I would rather be a person who tries to make do with what he has; being dissatisfied all the time just leads to problems."	Achievement/ satisfaction
4	"I think the old ways are mostly best for me."	Orientation to past
5	"The old, small neighborhood school was better than the new consolidated schools."	Education
6	"You can't make progress without change."	General value of change

* Scale runs from 1 (most modern) to 7 (most traditional).

3. Of the eight error types, four are ones in which an error occurs in the first item (changing sex roles), and four in which an error occurs in item 4 (orientation to the past). Thus, most of the scale impurities can be attributed to these two items. Patterned error in one of them (changing sex roles) suggests that the same dimension may not be appropriate for scaling both men and women.

The *error ratio* was computed by first computing the proportion of errors expected by chance[26] and then dividing that number into the proportion of actual errors. An acceptable error ratio is suggested by Riley to be anything less than .50. The error ratio for the present scale was .14.

The coefficient of scalability was computed at .621. Menzel suggests that the level of acceptance for this coefficient "may be somewhere between .60 and .65."[27]

Thus it appears that, by all the customary criteria, this set of six items and 119 respondents forms an acceptable Guttman scale. What does it mean?

3. *Interpretation of Scale.* It is said that although Guttman intended scalogram analysis to be a method whereby the unidimensionality of items could be demonstrated, scalability does not necessarily mean unidimensionality. There must be some theoretical or intuitive basis for asserting that items are selected from the same universe of content, in addition to meeting the more formal scalogram criteria. This raises an interesting question about the present scale, the six items of which are shown in Table 2. Are these from the same universe of content? Is this a unidimensional scale? Or is it simply an accidental artifact of the sampling of complex, unrelated cultural patterns? If there were no other evidence bearing on the matter, one would be tempted to dismiss this "scale of traditionism-modernism" as a mere artifact. There is, however, the knowledge that this particular set of items was chosen initially on the basis of its representativeness of a single universe or discourse. There is the further fact that these items were judged by seven knowledgeable persons to be the most accurate reflections of that dimension among the total pool of items. There was good reason, in short, to suspect that at least some of these value statements would belong on the same dimension, the dimension of traditionism-modernism.[28]

Even having a priori justification in addition to the confidence born of having met scalogram criteria of unidimensionality does not permit the conclusion that these value statements are linked consciously in the minds of the people of Shiloh in the fashion suggested by the scale. But whether conscious or not, the scale of items does suggest that there is a set of value "steps" which a person in Shiloh takes when leaving traditionism and entering modernism. First, he must agree that change in general is valuable, that "You cannot make progress without change." As a second step, he will probably note that older forms of education, while more comfortable, are not as effective as newer forms; he will not agree that "The old, small neighborhood school was better than the new consolidated schools." Next, he will give up his orientation to the past and will not agree that "the old ways are mostly best for me." Achievement orientation will probably change next, and the willingness to defer gratification, as expressed by disagreement with the statement, "I would rather be a person who tries to make do with what he has; being dissatisfied all the time just leads to problems." The next-to-last value area to change appears to be religion, at least as measured by disagreement with the statement that "the old Bible (the King James version) is the only true word of God." And last, one has become fully modern (by this set of items) when he accepts a more emancipated role for females: "Women should be allowed to 'wear the britches' more (or have more say) than they have in the past."

CONCLUSIONS

The traditionism-modernism scale from Shiloh illustrates the kind of measurement procedure which must be followed if we are not to assume what we set out to prove. Data from an earlier field survey indicated that modernization, as we have suggested that it be defined, is occurring in the community, and that study also provided a source from which to draw a pool of value statements comprising a single "universe of content." The use of judges gave even more assurance that the items used were valid indicators of traditionism and modernism. The fact that six of the fifteen original items form a Guttman scale makes more credible the contention that we are measuring something real "out there," and that that something is what we thought it was. We have not merely *imposed* a measure of modernism on the population under study, but have allowed the population to tell us whether modernism exists and what form it takes.[29]

To anticipate criticism, the heaviest argument against following this kind of procedure may also turn out to be an argument in favor of it. The greatest weakness of the present scale, it will probably be maintained, is that it obtains only for the population under study. Following the same procedure with any other population would probably yield a different set of value statements and hence a different scale. Therefore, with this type of measure of modernism, it becomes impossible to compare stages of modernization across cultural groups, something which would appear highly desirable. But is it realistic to expect that modernization *could* be comparable from one culture or society to another, or is it not at the very least an empirical question? For if we assume that modernism measures are comparable and valid cross-culturally, are we not forced to assume (1) that traditionism consists of the same set of values and beliefs wherever it is found,[30] (2) that the same path is followed from traditionism to modernism, via the same value "steps," and (3) that modernism consists of the same set of values and beliefs wherever it is found? How many would be willing to make those assumptions?

Therefore, it may not be proper, even if it appears possible, to compare the traditional-modern standing of one group with that of another. The technique illustrated here will permit such comparison when it is justified.

NOTES

1. For recent general discussions of these types of change, see, for example, Daniel Lerner, *The Passing of Traditional Society* (Glencoe, Ill.: Free Press, 1958); S. N. Eisenstadt, *Modernization: Protest and Change* (New York: Prentice-Hall, Inc., 1966); George M. Foster, *Traditional Cultures and the Impact of Technological Change* (New York: Harper & Row, 1962); Bert F. Hoselitz and Wilbert Moore (eds.), *Industrialization and Society* (Paris: UNESCO-Mouton, 1963); Ralph J. Braibanti and Joseph Spengler (eds.), *Tradition, Values, and Socio-Economic Development* (Durham, N.C.: Duke University Press, 1961); Myron Wiener (ed.), *Modernization: The Dynamics of Growth* (New York: Basic Books, 1966).

2. The term "secularization" and others of its order are seen as more specific classes of change within the larger category of cultural change.

3. Stephen Kellert, Lawrence K. Williams, William F. Whyte, and Giorgio Alberti, "Culture Change and Stress in Rural Peru: A Preliminary Report," *Milbank Memorial Fund Quarterly*, XLV, No. 4 (October, 1967), 391–415.

4. *Ibid.*, pp. 407–8.

5. *Ibid.,* p. 408.

6. *Ibid.,* p. 409.

7. Such criticisms are perhaps unduly harsh in view of the primary research interest of Kellert and his colleagues, who are more interested in the correlates of high rates of psychosomatic illness than in modernization. Still, the relevance of the particular indicators of modernism in the study has not been as fully demonstrated as one might desire.

8. David Horton Smith and Alex Inkeles, "The OM Scale: A Comparative Socio-Psychological Measure of Individual Modernity," *Sociometry,* XXIX, No. 4 (December, 1966), 353–77. Samples are drawn from six countries: Chile, Argentina, Pakistan, India, Nigeria, and Israel.

9. Actually, the authors present a long-form scale and several shorter forms consisting of subsets of items.

10. *Ibid.,* p. 353.

11. *Ibid.,* pp. 354–55.

12. *Ibid.,* p. 362. A footnote to this sentence, however, appears to contradict it: "Actually, we have not established that there is one and only one dimension underlying this item set, nor that all types of items enter equally, nor that the main underlying dimension is 'modernity.' But we have established *at least one* pervasive underlying dimension, and on prima facie grounds we can argue from the content of the items that this dimension is psychological modernity as we have conceptualized it. No other explanation, such as response set, will suffice."

13. *Ibid.,* p. 371.

14. There is no quarrel with the authors' conceptual definition of modernity; what is not clear is how they got from this abstract definition to the specific indicators of modernity that comprise their scale. Was it through intuition, or logic, or some empirically grounded linkage? Unfortunately, we will have to wait for the book to find out. But one suspects that members of populations later assessed by means of the scale may not have been permitted to suggest what traditionism and modernity meant to them, a shortcoming (and we cannot really be sure it is one in this case) which can have the unfortunate consequence of leaving the scientist with a well-constructed measuring stick which measures we know not what.

15. A closely related problem associated with measures of modernism which assume universality is that they do not allow for the possibility that traditional-to-modern changes are totally absent from a given population. One may find that he is able to classify personality types into "traditional" and "modern," but finding differentiation in a society does not offer anything but circumstantial evidence for change. The fact of change is assumed, not demonstrated; all we are offered is a static classification of cultural and personality types made by a professional observer.

16. Lerner, *op. cit.,* p. 46.

17. *Ibid.*

18. *Ibid.,* p. 47.

19. *Ibid.,* p. 47. Also see Eisenstadt, *op cit.,* p. 1.

20. Bert F. Hoselitz, "Economic Development and Change in Social Values and Thought Patterns," in George K. Zollschan and Walter Hirsch (eds.), *Explorations in Social Change* (Boston: Houghton Mifflin Co., 1964), p. 679.

21. A more complete description of the community and the changes it has undergone since 1940 may be found in my forthcoming (1968) book, *Shiloh: A Mountain Community* (Lexington, Ky.: University of Kentucky Press), especially chap. i.

22. The extent to which modernism is related to social class has never been made clear. Some have said that it *is* social class, while others have maintained that the two are separate dimensions. While I tend to hold the latter view, I know of no evidence which has direct bearing on the issue. This will be the subject of later study.

23. Placing an item into the "ambiguous" pile was considered an error and was scored "1." Placing of what was intended to be a modern or a traditional statement into the opposite pile was also considered an error and was scored "2" on the assumption that it is an even less clear indicator than had it been placed in the "ambiguous" pile. Total error scores for each statement range theoretically from 0 to 14. Two of the items used had error scores of 0, ten had error scores of 1, and five had error scores of 2.

24. A fifteenth statement was inserted in the instrument at the last minute without adequate justification. Interestingly, it was one of those discarded during construction of the scale.

25. Five individuals did not give sufficient information for mobility to be measured.

26. The coefficient of chance reproducibility itself was .407. It was computed by following the procedure described in Matilda White Riley, *Sociological Research: I. A Case Approach* (New York: Harcourt, Brace & World, 1963), pp. 476–77.

27. Herbert Menzel, "A New Coefficient of Scalogram Analysis," *Public Opinion Quarterly*, XVII, No. 2 (Summer, 1953), 279.

28. One would logically expect respondents of the more traditional scale type to be older, less educated, living farther from main roads, and in more traditional occupations which are seasonal or occasional and outdoor in nature. Fortunately, information on some of these variables was available. Looking only at extreme scale types 1 and 2 (most modern) and 6 and 7 (most traditional), it was found that 50.0 per cent of the 1's and 2's were over 39 years of age, while 40.6 per cent of 6's and 7's were over 39 years old. With regard to location of residence, 59.4 per cent of the 1's and 2's lived "on or near main highway," 31.3 per cent "off main highway but not isolated," and 9.4 per cent "relatively isolated or at end of road." Comparable percentages for 6's and 7's were 18.8, 53.1, and 28.1, respectively.

Occupations were classified into four categories: I. White collar or managerial. II. Full-time blue collar (such as factory work). III. Part-time or seasonal blue collar and unskilled (such as mining, timbering, small-time commercial farming). IV. Occasional or no employment, or agency support. When occupational categories I and II (more modern) and III and IV (more traditional) were combined, it was found that 71.0 per cent of scale types 1 and 2 were "more modern" in occupation, while 66.7 per cent of scale types 6 and 7 were "more traditional."

Thus, the scale appears validated with regard to location of residence and occupational type. No explanation can be offered for the lack of differentiation in ages (or even a slight reversal of expectations). Since the scale appears valid by other criteria, however, one might conclude that individuals in Shiloh do not become more traditional as they grow older.

29. At the risk of being unduly repetitive, it will be pointed out that I make a claim, not to have studied modernization, but to have devised a way of meaningfully measuring modernism which can later be used to gauge the extent of change over time. The present study (like most such research) is not a study of change because it omits the temporal dimension.

30. If this is true, then the most "traditionism" (or "modernism") can mean is "the belief in tradition (or modernity), whatever that may be." We have seen that modernism means more than that to at least a few students of the subject. It seems clear that either the terms must be defined so generally as to be useless or the specific content must be left to vary from culture to culture.

QUESTIONS

1. Contrast this article by Stephenson to the article by Smith and Inkeles (selection 11) in terms of their different treatments of the concept and measurement of "modernism."
2. How did Stephenson arrive at his original set of items? How did he narrow these down to a more limited set of items? What different criteria were invoked in settling down to the final six-item scale?
3. How does the author establish an interpretation for the scale? What kinds of evidence does he cite for an interpretation of the scale?

Replication of a Delinquency and Crime Index in French Canada

DOGAN D. AKMAN, ANDRÉ NORMANDEAU, and STANLEY TURNER

The scale forms illustrated in earlier articles, strictly speaking, permit only those operations appropriate to nominal and ordinal distinctions—difference, equality; less than, greater than. The tools of mathematics are most convincing when the scales are of the interval and ratio types—ones that include not only direction of difference and a statement of how many constant units of measurement separate two scale points, but a measure of how many times greater one scale point is compared to a second scale point. The following article illustrates the application of direct magnitude estimation to the replication of a ratio scale for the seriousness of criminal events. This article reports a repetition on a French Canadian group in Montreal of a basic set of research procedures (replication) used in a research study in Philadelphia. Because the findings in both settings are similar, we can have increased confidence in the utility of the research procedures in each setting. Once again, we have an article that is clear enough in its description of research procedures

Reprinted from The Canadian Journal of Corrections 8 (1966), 1–19, with permission of The Canadian Corrections Association.

essentially to permit the student to repeat the research with little further instruction.

I. INTRODUCTION

Criminal statistics are expected to serve two important functions. First, "as a management device to assist police administrators in delineating the nature, extent and seriousness of the crime and traffic problems facing the police departments, pinpointing these problems in time and space to provide the information required for the proper allocation of manpower."[1] Second, to provide the public and private bodies valid data on the changing incidence, frequency and character of both adult and juvenile crime to enable them to engage in the most meaningful, purposive, and effective action to control and reduce criminality.

The current criminal statistics compiled and published by the Dominion Bureau of Statistics can hardly be said to fulfill the above two functions in an adequate manner. While the rationale underlying the compilation methods of the Canadian criminal statistics based on the American Uniform Crime reports classification has many serious shortcomings, we shall mention here only four of these shortcomings which concern directly the topic of this [article]. They may be briefly described as follows:

1. The current system is wholly dependent upon the specific technical labels given to crime by the penal code and ignores the meaningful sociological dimensions of criminality.
2. The system assigns equal numerical value (weight) to offenses which are classified under the same legal definitions and consequently disregards the qualitative components of these offenses.
3. The system tabulates the composite type of criminal event (i.e., when more than one offense has been committed simultaneously) under the heading of the most serious one and thus fails to take into account the cumulative seriousness of a criminal event.
4. In view of the fact that the system now in use lumps together many different kinds of crimes, the resulting statistics do not permit comparison of the increase or decrease in the seriousness of the total volume of criminality registered during a given number of consecutive years.

If criminality is to be measured by an index constructed of data pertaining to a variety of offenses known to the police, the mere sum of these offenses, or a rate computed using that sum, would give no indication of the relative gravity of the offenses composing the rate. Suppose that, for example, in a given community the actual number of offenses remained unchanged during a decade and that the population base used in the computation of the rate of criminality also remained unchanged, the crime index would remain stabilized. But suppose that during that decade there were considerable changes in the relative proportions of the crimes committed, e.g., that offenses against the person decreased and offenses against property drastically increased. To illustrate this point suppose that, during year A, 15 homicides and 100 petty thefts occurred and, during the following year B, 5 homicides but 1,000 petty thefts are committed. Has the seriousness of crime increased, decreased, or has it remained unchanged? As Merton raises the question, "Is one homicide to be equated with 10 petty thefts? 100? 1,000?"[2] The Canadian Uniform Crime Reporting System, which simply counts the total in computing a rate, does not permit us to provide a logical answer. Thus, it may be affirmed that the currently available criminal statistics provide us only with an extremely crude counting system.

Any index of criminality must take into account and reflect qualitative as well as quantitative changes in criminal activity both in time and in space, and it is our contention that unless and until such a measurement of the amount and kinds of criminality and of the changing character of deviant acts is put into use, a community is not sufficiently informed to engage efficiently in crime control and prevention.

The foregoing considerations indicate the importance of constructing a crime index that will overcome the shortcomings of the current crime recording system (while still using—as the present system does—the information provided by the police) and reflect the "real" extent of the volume, degree, and nature of changes in a given time period, by taking into consideration the qualitative elements inherent in different criminal events and by quantifying these elements.

To accomplish these aims, a crime index should take into consideration not only the frequency of criminal acts but also a weighting system based on an empirically derived scale of relative seriousness which would reflect the sentiments of the community toward different types of crimes. A method of constructing such an index has been recently proposed by Thorsten Sellin and Marvin Wolfgang.[3]

In the following pages we shall briefly describe this index and report on the results of a partial replication of the original study which led to the construction of the index.[4]

II. SOME PERSPECTIVES

The shortcomings of the Canadian Uniform Crime Report Classification System are to be found in most criminal statistics compilation systems in the countries where such statistics exist. In fact, it can be said without any hesitation that these shortcomings present a perennial problem.

This problem has been attacked since the early part of the nineteenth century when criminal statistics first began to be collected on a uniform basis in some European countries by a great number of scholars. To name a few, Messedaglia,[5] von Mayr,[6] and Diego de Castro[7] attempted to construct an index of criminality similar to a price index. The differential weighting of these indexes was based on the possible and/or actual legal punishment provided for criminal acts. These indexes represented scales of the attitudes of the administrators of justice. In the field of juvenile delinquency construction of indexes was attempted by Clark,[8] Durea,[9] and Powers and Witmer.[10] The methods used by these authors, however, were rudimentary and the samples used in the construction of the indexes were too small to provide a reliable instrument.

III. THE SELLIN-WOLFGANG INDEX

The index developed by Sellin and Wolfgang were primarily focused on the measurement of juvenile delinquency. However, the index is not specifically an index of juvenile delinquency but also may be used to measure adult criminality.

The index is based on a scale that reflects community judgments of the relative seriousness of a selected number of offenses. The scale was arrived at by having nearly 800 policemen, university students in Philadelphia, and juvenile court judges in the state of Pennsylvania rate 141 different offense events on a magnitude-ratio estimation scale and a category interval scale of seriousness. Since their work gives a full report of the exacting and highly refined statistical procedures used in deriving the scores of seriousness for index purposes, we are taking the liberty of referring the reader to their work. We shall provide some of the methodological highlights of this work within the framework of the partial replication study conducted in Montreal as presented in the following pages.

IV. THE MONTREAL STUDY

The partial replication of the study of Sellin and Wolfgang for the purpose of assessing the reliability of their index in the French-Canadian milieu—as reflected by the University of Montreal social science students—is based on a replication model which may be called "a minimal replication model" since it assumes the validity and reliability of the basic procedures leading to the development of the original index. The assumption underlying the choice of this model was grounded on the strong, continuous demonstration by the authors of the original study of the logical, theoretical and empirical justification of each step of their research.

1. ASSUMPTIONS UNDERLYING THE MINIMAL MODEL   For purposes of constructing a minimal model for replication of Sellin's and Wolfgang's research, we have assumed:

a. That "judged seriousness" of violations of law is a single dimension along which all offenses can be measured from the most trivial to the most reprehensible. That is to say, this "measuring rod" is a single scale along which all criminal and/or delinquent acts can be examined and judged by large, theoretically significant social groups whose evaluations can be used as a basis for scoring quantitatively the differential qualitative elements of criminal acts. Consensus, obtained in this manner, will ascribe a series of weighted values to the acts along the continuum of seriousness. The graded seriousness of criminal acts can be measured by objective methods which have been borrowed from current techniques in psychophysics.[11]

b. That to devise a classification and a differential weighting of the seriousness of offenses that would be in some way independent of the specific technical labels given to crimes by the law, the index must take into account criminal "events" rather than legally defined discrete offenses. "An event refers to a *configuration* of objectively observable and describable elements of the law violation. It involves one or more violations of the criminal law." These events involve, separately or in combination, a personal injury, theft of property and property damage.[12] These violations of the criminal law to be judged by a group of sociologically meaningful subjects for index purposes are limited in kind and number. The focus must be placed on events which cause harm directly to a person (or persons), such as physical injury, property loss through theft and property damage. These events are assumed to have high reportability and the volume of these events does not depend upon changes in police activity.[13] When such offenses occur, the victim, or someone closely linked to him, under ordinary circumstances seeks the assistance of the police in finding and punishing the offender and possibly recovering the property. In view of their high reportability and their relative independence from the variations of the police activities, only such offenses are included in the index. Including these offenses will yield information concerning crimes such as criminal homicide, forcible rape, assault, larceny, auto theft, damage to city property, arson, malicious mischief, and some disorderly conduct offenses which cause property damage. Additional factors assumed to be important are the amount of money (in loss or damage), the degree of medical attention granted to the victim of an assault, forcible entry, and intimidation are sufficiently aggravating subsidiary components to require direct or indirect weighting. Seemingly important, subsidiary variables in a criminal act as, for example, the specific type of weapon used in assaults or the legal or illegal presence of the offender in property offenses, etc., do not increase the seriousness of an act and need not be weighted.

c. That the description of these offenses should always be presented as being committed by a male of unidentified age, because the majority of criminals and delinquents are males and because the age of the offender is a variable without significant influence on the ratings of the seriousness of the harm done. This empirically tested assumption permits wide applicability of the weighting system for all offenders, adults and juveniles alike.

d. That the choice of a magnitude estimation or ratio scale is the most appropriate for estimation of the seriousness of offenses. Theoretically, the ratio scale has no established or assigned upper limit, and the subject may select any number greater than zero to indicate the seriousness of offenses. Furthermore, the choice of scale can be justified by two reasons. First, the magnitude estimation scale values are a product of the rater rather than the experimenter and, as such, have an inherent validity that cannot be claimed for the imposition of a fixed range of category values by the experimenter on the rater's judgment. Second, an inherently greater nuance can be exhibited by the rater in his selection of responses. The freedom in the range of possible responses provides more information about the rater's judgments than the severely limited categories.

e. That the magnitude estimation along a unidimensional scale of seriousness permits, moreover, the isolation of certain items for special rating if additivity is assumed. For example, to a five-dollar theft a given increment of seriousness is added as the theft changes from a simple larceny to one following a forcible entry into a building. The score value of forcible entry can thus be rated indirectly in a burglary and the score of forcible entry is obtained by the subtraction of the score value of the larceny of five dollars from the score of the burglary of five dollars. Furthermore, a criminal homicide, for example, with a seriousness score of "218" can be said to be "really" 218 times as serious as a larceny of one dollar which has a score of "1" associated to it. Thus a question like "is one homicide to be equated with 10 petty thefts? 100? 1,000?" can now be answered. In the same perspective, an offense which involves a rape where the victim requires hospitalization and where the pocketbook containing twenty-five dollars is stolen can be considered a global act made up of the addition of the scores of rape, a high degree of medical attention, and a theft of twenty-five dollars.

f. That a group of university students represents an adequate sample as subjects for the scaling of seriousness. Practical, theoretical and empirical reasons underlie this assumption. The practical reasons—linked to considerations of time resources and availability—are that university students are easily accessible as a group and are traditionally captive for such experimental research. The theoretical reason is stated well by Sellin and Wolfgang:

The philosophy and the sociology of the criminal law suggest the principal culture themes of legal prescriptions and sanctions come from the middle-class value system. Representatives of this value system legislate and adjudicate. Thus the definition of crime and the administration of criminal justice are institutionalized expressions of the normative structure of the dominant middle class in American society. . . . Despite their occasional revolt against authority while part of the teen-age culture, university students, like their parents, generally hold the middle-class values embodied in the common law. Avoidance of physical aggression in the form of assaultive behavior, a quasi-sacred respect for property, the importance of using leisure time wholesomely and productively, emphasis upon ambition, etc., are components of the middle-class ethic and are values commonly shared by most university students. Although there is undoubtedly considerable diversity among some value orientations within any large student body, it seems safe to assume much homogeneity regarding attitudes toward crime and especially toward the offenses that logical inference and empirical reference point as index offenses.

As to the empirical reason, the original study has shown that the students tended to assign magnitude estimations to the seriousness of offenses similar to those assigned by police officers and judges. Students' sentiments and attitudes thus can be said to reflect those of a wider community.

2. RESEARCH PROCEDURES   a. Fifteen versions of the major offenses, derived from the second assumption, and similar to the offenses selected by Sellin and Wolfgang and rated by University of Pennsylvania students, were chosen for the replication. These offenses are described in Table 1.

Each offense was transcribed on a separate sheet and the resulting booklets consisting of a set of fifteen offenses were separately randomized

TABLE 1. List of Offense Versions Used to Obtain Discriminatory Score Values for Selected Offenses

A. *Without breaking into or entering* a building and with no one else present, an offender takes property worth $5.

B. *Without breaking into or entering* a building and with no one else present, an offender takes property worth $20.

C. *Without breaking into or entering* a building and with no one else present, an offender takes property worth $50.

D. *Without breaking into or entering* a building and with no one else present, an offender takes property worth $1,000.

E. *Without breaking into or entering* a building and with no one else present, an offender takes property worth $5,000.

F. An offender *breaks into* a building and with no one else present takes property worth $5.

G. An offender *without a weapon* threatens to harm a victim unless the victim gives him money. The offender takes the victim's money ($5) and leaves without harming the victim.

H. An offender *with a weapon* threatens to harm a victim unless the victim gives him money. The offender takes the victim's money ($5) and leaves without harming the victim.

I. An offender inflicts injury on a victim. The victim *dies* from the injury.

J. An offender inflicts injury on a victim. The victim is treated by a physician and his injuries require him to be hospitalized.

K. An offender inflicts injury on a victim. The victim is treated by a physician *but* his injuries do *not* require him to be hospitalized.

L1. An offender shoves (or pushes) a victim. The victim does *not* require any medical treatment.

L2. An offender beats a person with his fists. The victim is hurt but requires *no* medical treatment.

M. An offender forces a female to submit to sexual intercourse. No other physical injury is inflicted.

N. An offender takes an automobile which is recovered undamaged.

---

to avoid any specific bias which a particular ordering may have on the raters.

b. *The sample* consisted of male and female students enrolled in the course of introductory sociology at the University of Montreal. (Almost all the students of the social science faculty enroll in this course.) Of the 250 subjects, 18 were discarded because they were not French-Canadians. Of the remaining 232 subjects, 177 were males and 55 were females. At the University of Pennsylvania, 105 corresponding male subjects were used by Sellin and Wolfgang. No similar experiment was established with females in Philadelphia. The experiment took place in a single section to prevent communication between subject raters before the rating; no communication was allowed during the rating. Each rater was given a booklet with a set of instructions.

This booklet describes a series of violations of the law; each violation is different. Your task is to show how serious you think each violation is, not what the law says or how the courts might act.

You do this by writing down in a score box on each page a number which shows how serious each violation seems to you. The first violation has been done as an example. It shows a violation which is given a seriousness score of 10. Use this violation as a standard. Every other violation should be scored in relation to this standard violation. For example, if any violation seems twice as serious as the standard violation write in a score of 20. If any violation seems ten times as serious as the standard violation, write in a score of 100. If a violation seems half as serious as the standard, write in a score of 5. If a violation seems only a twentieth as serious as the standard, write in a score of ½ or .50. You may use *any* whole or fractional numbers that are greater than zero, no matter how small or large they are just so long as they represent how serious the violation is compared to the standard violation.

Take your time. Every page should have a number in the score box. Do not turn back once you have finished a page. Remember, this is not a test. The important thing is how *you* feel about each violation. Do not write your name on any of the sheets for you will not be identified.

(Of course, the instructions and all the offenses were presented in French.)

3. ANALYSIS OF THE RESULTS   Each offense in our study was judged by all subjects. To summarize these results each offense will be described by its *average* score. But which average should be chosen? The choice made was to use the *geometric* mean instead of the arithmetic mean, median, or any other type of average. This average is frequently used to average ratios and, since we have assumed that we have a ratio scale, the geometric mean seems appropriate. Furthermore, in situations like the present one, the geometric mean is probably more stable than other sorts of averages.*

Thus, when we refer to "raw magnitude scale scores" we mean the geometric mean of all subjects' scores. Table 2 presents the raw magnitude scale scores for all groups tested and also lists comparable scores of the Philadelphia study.

In order to compare our results to those of Sellin and Wolfgang, we plotted, in Figure 1, the raw magnitude scale scores of the fourteen offenses directly scored by both Montreal and Philadelphia subjects.** Figure 1 shows that there is, broadly speaking, a linear relation between the logs of the over-all Montreal scores and Philadelphia scores. Similarly, when Montreal is broken down into males and females, each of these

---

* The geometric mean (G) is the nth root of the product of n numbers. It is usually more convenient to use the following formula:

$$\log G = \frac{\Sigma \log X}{N}$$

This illustrates the fact that the geometric mean is the arithmetic mean of the logarithms of the scores. Several limitations of the geometric mean exist. Among them is the fact that if any of the scores is zero, the geometric mean is zero. Also, if any of the scores is negative, the geometric mean may be meaningless. For these reasons subjects were instructed to use only finite, positive numbers in judging offenses. For further information about the geometric mean and its relation to other measures of central tendency see a standard reference, for example, *Applied General Statistics*, Croxton and Cowden, Prentice-Hall, 1959.

** In fact, 15 offenses were directly scored, but offenses L1 and L2 have been pooled together under the label "minor assault."

TABLE 2. Geometric Means of 18 Offenses for Philadelphia and Montreal

Offense	Univ. of Pa.	Univ. of Montreal Males	Univ. of Montreal Females	Univ. of Montreal Males and Females
Larceny $5	22.09	3.63	2.11	3.18
Larceny $20	27.77	6.69	6.20	6.57
Larceny $50	32.31	7.74	9.63	8.15
Larceny $1,000	52.99	28.60	30.50	29.10
Larceny $5,000	69.13	42.70	48.30	43.95
Burglary $5	40.62	6.05	12.80	7.21
Robbery $5 (no weapon)	52.25	16.20	18.50	16.70
Robbery $5 (weapon)	86.33	36.10	32.80	35.30
Assault (death)	449.20	452.00	246.00	391.00
Assault (hospitalized)	115.60	45.70	54.90	47.70
Assault (treated and discharged)	69.20	17.10	40.70	21.00
Assault (minor)	22.50	5.50	14.28	6.89
Rape (forcible)	186.30	146.00	119.00	139.00
Auto Theft (recovered, no damage)	27.19	8.20	10.25	8.65
Larceny $1*	16.93	2.07	1.42	1.89
Forcible Entry*	18.53	2.41	10.69	4.03
Intimidation (verbal)*	30.15	12.57	16.39	13.52
Intimidation (weapon)*	64.24	32.47	30.69	32.12

*The last four offenses were used to scale complex acts, e.g., robbery *plus* intimidation by weapon.

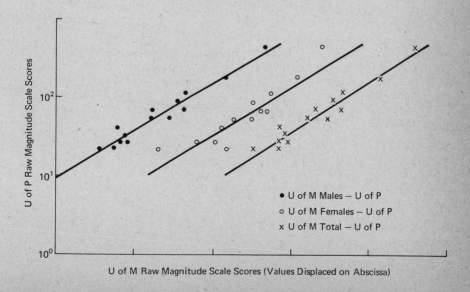

FIGURE 1: Comparison of 14 index offenses judged by U of P & U of M students. Raw magnitude scale scores plotted on log-log coordinates.

bears about the same relation to the Philadelphia scores. When Montreal males are compared with Montreal females, a similar linear relation appears.

The broad conclusion from Figure 1 is that there is evidence of a general agreement about the seriousness of offenses. It is not *merely* that Philadelphia and Montreal agree about what is serious and what is not; nor is it that Philadelphia and Montreal *merely* agree about that ranking of seriousness of offenses. What Figure 1 means is that there is a large amount of agreement about the *numerical* scoring of seriousness of offenses between both groups. Explicitly, one can say that, if the geometric means of offenses in both Philadelphia and Montreal are known, they are related by a power function of the form $Y = aX^b$ where a and b are constants estimated from the data.

And when two variables are related by a power function this means that as one changes by a given percentage the other changes by another fixed percentage.

The same conclusion holds through also for Montreal males versus Montreal females.

Sellin and Wolfgang explicitly state the relation between their own work and any future replication of it. They write:

It should be remembered that the ratios of score values, not necessarily the absolute numbers, have remained stable over the different rating groups used in the present study; and it is this ratio that would be important in further explorations. On the basis of our data, we would hypothesize that these relative offense score values would be preserved. To be more specific, we would hypothesize that in a replication of the magnitude and category scales, the scale values for offenses would be represented by (1) a slope not significantly different from those in our study, or minimally (2) a straight line when plotted on semilogarithmic paper. Over time and in quite different cultures, differences might occur; we are not suggesting that our final scale values or offense scores contain definitive features. But the offense items or delinquency events which we have scored are limited in number and character and represent fairly universal prescripts and prohibitions in Western culture so that we would not be surprised to find a high degree of consistent, stable responses over a wider range of subjects than was employed in this analysis.[15]

Let us consider the two major statements in the above paragraph in the light of our results.

a. *Similarity of slope.* The assertion was made that if the magnitude scale scores for index offenses were derived from a different population the slopes would be about the same. This means that if we plot the magnitude scale scores for the University of Pennsylvania against the magnitude scale scores for the University of Montreal we should expect a slope of 1 or thereabouts on log-log paper. This is not the case. Inspection of Figure 1 shows that the slopes for Montreal males, females and both of them combined differ from a slope of 1 by an appreciable amount. A rough interpretation would be that concern about seriousness grows at a faster rate in Montreal than in Philadelphia, at least for the subjects tested. In fact, as seriousness triples in Philadelphia, it increases by five times in

Montreal.* It is this difference that makes the slope different. If Philadelphia had concern about seriousness that grew at a faster rate than Montreal, the slope would have been greater than 1; if both were the same, the slope would have been 1; and if Montreal had grown more concerned about seriousness than Philadelphia, then the slope would have been less than 1. Clearly, the last is the best description of the data.

It is interesting to note, however, that the statement about similarity of slope does hold for comparisons *between* Montreal males and females. In this case, the slope is about 1 for the line drawn through the ratings of these two groups.** From what one can infer from the study of Sellin and Wolfgang, the slopes between Philadelphia judges, police, and students (on magnitude scale scores) are about 1 also. Thus, roughly, there have been no important differences discovered *within* cultures but there is a difference *between* cultures. The importance of this difference can be easily overrated. What is important is the fact that, although the slope is not 1, it is straight. This leads us to the analysis of the second statement made by Sellin and Wolfgang.

b. *Similarity of shape.* If magnitude scale scores are plotted against category scale scores, then a straight line will result on semi-log paper. Sellin and Wolfgang, however, recommend using the magnitude scale as the better indicator of changes in delinquency or criminality, and their recommendation appears to us to be well founded. In fact, we used this scale exclusively in our work. This means that we cannot test the above statement directly, but it is easy to test a slightly different version of their statement; namely, if the magnitude scale scores of Philadelphia are plotted on log-log paper against the magnitude scale scores of Montreal, then the result should be a straight line. This is apparently the case. Figure 1 shows that this relation is essentially a straight line. This implies, roughly, that a given ratio change in one is associated with a fixed ratio change in the other, e.g., if seriousness increases three times in Philadelphia, it increases five times in Montreal over the whole range of offenses. Similarly, if we knew the score for an offense in Philadelphia we could predict with considerable accuracy its score in Montreal and vice versa.

Apparently, then, the two statements made by Sellin and Wolfgang should be changed somewhat. We would suggest the following:

Minimum Claim:
If the magnitude scale scores of seriousness are derived for any two populations, the relation between them should be a power function of the form $Y = aX^b$ *(the points plotted should constitute a straight line on log-log paper), it being understood that this applies to offenses defined by Sellin and Wolfgang as "index offenses."*

---

* This conclusion is reached by the inspection of the power function relating Philadelphia and Montreal and more specifically of the numerical values of the relating slopes; (a) Philadelphia vs. Montreal (males) $Y = 0.985 \ X^{0.593}$, (b) Philadelphia vs. Montreal (females) $Y = 0.914 \ X^{0.611}$, and (c) Philadelphia vs. Montreal (males *and* females) $Y = 0.906 \ X^{0.647}$; the exponents of X being the relating slopes.
** The power function can be expressed as $Y = -0.103 \ X^{1.02}$ and slope is approximately 1.

Maximum Claim:

If the magnitude scale scores of seriousness are derived for any two populations *in the same culture*, the relation between them should be a power function of the form $Y = aX^b$ (the points plotted should constitute a straight line on log-log paper), and *where* $b = 1$. Again, this is taken to apply to index offenses only.

4. PROPOSED INDEX SCORES FOR MONTREAL   The process of transforming the offense geometric means to scale scores, for purposes of obtaining the simplification needed for index application, is a logical one. By dividing each value by the lowest mean among the offenses, namely, by using the estimated geometric mean for a theft of one dollar score values as weights can be obtained. Such a standardization preserves the ratios between offenses and permits a valid comparison between the results obtained by different indexes, as will be the case of Philadelphia and Montreal indexes.

The value for a theft of one dollar will be computed by using the regression equations of the geometric means of seriousness corresponding to the five money theft offense versions, namely ($5), ($20), ($50), ($1,000), and ($5,000): $Y = 0.317 \ X^{0.363}$ (in Montreal males), and $Y = 123 \ X^{0.165}$ (in Philadelphia). In the regression lines (not reproduced here) we used only the Montreal males' scores because, as we have seen above, Montreal males and females show equivalent ratings. The adjusted score of seriousness for a theft of one dollar in Montreal is 2.07 and 16.93 in Philadelphia.

The final scoring system can best be described by a form which contains all the elements that are scorable. The final system is presented in the form of a score sheet. Philadelphia males and Montreal males are compared on the same sheet, but it is obvious that one or the other of these two columns can be used in any given case. (See Table 3.)

The categories of dollars for property stolen, damaged, or destroyed and their related scores of seriousness were similarly derived from inter- and extrapolation along the regression lines mentioned above.

It must be remembered that what is scored is a *total* criminal "event." All constituents of the act, rather than its legal label and the actors committing it, are the important variables which have been considered.

As stated above, we have developed a ratio scale along a unidimensional "measuring rod" employing the notion of additivity. Three illustrations are provided at the bottom of the score sheet to show how this notion and that of an "event" described above can be combined and translated into practical usage.

To arrive at a final index, the sum total of the scores must be computed on a yearly basis, per thousand or ten thousand of the relevant population at risk. Sub-indexes for the three categories of bodily injury, loss of or damage to property could also be computed from this index.[16]

5. CONCLUSIONS   In the foregoing pages we have discussed the results of the Sellin and Wolfgang study and, in light of our replication study, made certain adjustments.

The use of the present index in French Canada may be valid but, in

TABLE 3. SCORE SHEET Effects of Event: Injury (Bodily), Theft (Loss of), Damage (Circle One or More as Required)

Elements Scored	Number X	Philadelphia Weight	Montreal Weight	Total
I. Number of victims of bodily harm				
a. receiving minor injuries		1	3	
b. treated and discharged		4	8	
c. hospitalized		7	22	
d. killed		26	218	
II. Number of victims of forcible sex intercourse		10	69	
a. number of such victims intimidated by weapon		2	10	
III. Intimidation (except II above)				
a. physical or verbal only		2	6	
b. by weapon		4	16	
IV. Number of premises forcibly entered		1	1	
V. Number of motor vehicles stolen		2	4	
VI. Value of property stolen, damaged, or destroyed (in dollars)				
a. under 10 dollars		1	2	
b. 10–250 dollars		2	7	
c. 251–2,000		3	16	
d. 2,001–9,000 dollars		4	27	
e. 9,001–30,000		5	42	
f. 30,001–80,000 dollars		6	61	
g. over 80,000 ($80,000 to $200,000)		7	84	

Illustration I. (The index Montreal score values are given in the parentheses.) Two girls are raped by a man $(2 \times 69 = 138)$; one requires hospitalization (22), the other is given medical treatment and discharged (8); one of them had been threatened with a knife (16). The rape occurred in a house to which the offender had secured entry by force (1) and upon leaving he took the pocketbooks of the girls, valued together with their contents at $25.00 (7). Total "new" score for event: 186.

Illustration II. A man breaks into a house (1), intimidates its occupants with a dangerous weapon (16), takes property from them and escapes in a car belonging to one of the victims (4). The car is recovered undamaged, but personal articles taken from it, together with the property taken during the holdup, are valued at $300.00 (16). Total score for event: 37.

Illustration III. A man breaks into a bulding (1), intimidates its occupants with a dangerous weapon (16), forces them to stand by while he sets fire to the premises causing damage to the extent of $3,000 (27). Total score for event: 44.

The Canadian Uniform Crime statistics would register and weigh the first event on two (2) rapes, the second one as one (1) robbery, and the third one as one (1) burglary.

view of limitations of the sample, this new index should be viewed and used with due caution.

Of course, before such an index may be recommended for usage on a provincial basis, and eventually on a national basis, it will be necessary to extend the scope of the replication to samples representative of the socio-economic and cultural areas which constitute French Canada in particular and Canada in general.

In view of the similarity of the results between the raters in Philadelphia and in Montreal, however, we feel that this initial adjusted index has adequate empirical value and could be put to use on a limited scale in a middle-sized community.

We hope that eventually we will be in a position to undertake a replication of the original study on a national basis.

6. SIGNIFICANCE AND CONTRIBUTIONS OF THE MONTREAL STUDY

We believe that this study has made possible the proposal of an index which will:

a. Provide an effective, valid, and more socially meaningful supplement (if not an alternative) to the current crime reporting system;
b. Constitute a significant contribution to any future analyses of the rates and changing character of crime and delinquency;
c. Provide specifically the means for testing the effectiveness of prevention and treatment programs designed to reduce the incidence of crime and delinquency;
d. In the long run, permit international comparisons which are today impossible because of the legal labels specific to each national system of criminal statistics.

With specific reference to the third point, as Wilkins stated, any index which makes our value systems more patent or facilitates rational decisions regarding crime and delinquency is to be welcomed.[17] This index has now been made possible by Sellin and Wolfgang and, on the basis of the results of the replication study presented above, we believe that we have at last solid ground on which to refine our current practices of recording crime and delinquency so that the agents of crime control and prevention and the community at large may be in a better position to examine realistically the problems of criminality and formulate the most appropriate policies in attempting to resolve them with the social and economic resources available at their disposal.

V. CURRENT USES OF THE INDEX

The index proposed by Sellin and Wolfgang has received wide and serious considerations. It has been adopted on a trial basis by the Juvenile Aid Division of the Philadelphia Police Department beginning January 1, 1964. The United States Children's Bureau has a current project of using a typical medium-sized city for an operationally demonstrated use of the index; this project is expected to begin shortly. The California Bureau of Criminal Statistics is enthusiastically interested in the index and is in a planning stage of utilization. In an international perspective, an interdepartmental committee on criminal statistics of the Home Office in England has the index under serious consideration and study. In the Netherlands, criminologists are preparing a proposal for testing the index. Finally, the index has been suggested to the Council of Europe for exploration as a means of developing international criminal statistics.

NOTES

1. Dominion Bureau of Statistics, *Uniform Crime Reporting Manual* (January 1962), p. 1.

2. Robert K. Merton, *Contemporary Social Problems: An Introduction to the Sociology of Deviant Behavior and Social Disorganization,* ed. Robert K. Merton and Robert A. Nisbet (New York: Harcourt, Brace & World, 1961), XIII, 754 pp., p. 703.

3. Thorsten Sellin and Marvin E. Wolfgang, *The Measurement of Delinquency* (New York: John Wiley & Sons, 1964), 423 pp.

4. Readers interested specifically in the construction of the index may refer to *Constructing an Index of Delinquency: A Manual* (Philadelphia: University of Pennsylvania, The Center of Criminological Research, 1963), 16 pp. (Available free on request.)

5. Angelo Messedaglia, "Esposizione critica delle statistiche criminali dell'Impero austriaco, con particolare riguardo al Lombardo-Veneto, secondo I Resoconti uffiziali del quadriennio 1856–1859 e col confronte dei dati posteriori" in *Atti dell'I. R. Istituto Veneto de Scienze, Letteri ed Arti,* vol. 11.

6. Georg Mayr (von), *Statistik der gerichtlichen Polizei im Königreichs bayern und in einigen anderen Landern* (200+187+10 pp. Munich 1867), *(Beitrage zur Statistik des Königreichs bayern,* heft XVI).

7. Diego de Castro, *Metodi per calcolare gli indici della criminalita* (119 pp. Turin: Istituto Giuridicho della R. Universita, 1934). (R. Univ. de Torino, *Memorie dell'Istituto Giuridicho.* ser. II, vol. 25).

8. William W. Clark, *Whittier Scale for Grading Juvenile Offenses* (State of California: Department of Institutions, Whittier State School, California Bureau of Juvenile Res. Bul. No. 11, April, 1922), 8 pp.

9. Mervin A. Durea, "An Experimental Study of Attitudes Toward Juvenile Delinquency," *J. Appl. Psychology,* 17: 522–524 (1933).

10. Edwin Powers and Helen Witmer, *An Experiment in the Prevention of Delinquency* (New York: Columbia University Press, 1951), 649 pp.

11. As stated by Sellin and Wolfgang, "it should, however, be made explicit that the truth claims made for the scales in psychophysical studies and for the scale in the present study are not necessarily identical. There are similarities and no contradictions, but there are some issues not examined by both sets of studies." *Op. cit.,* p. 271.

12. *Ibid.,* p. 15.

13. Two other categories of offenses which do not conform to these criteria have not been included. They are: (a) conspirational or consensual acts that may, by some means, become known to the police, and (b) offenses which may be regarded as causing the community to be the victim. "An index of delinquency (criminality)," write Sellin and Wolfgang, "should be based on offenses with assumed constant reportability, violating the criminal law, known to the police . . . and inflicting bodily harm on a victim and/or involving theft, damage or destruction of property." *Constructing an Index of Delinquency: A Manual, op. cit.,* p. 6.

14. Sellin and Wolfgang, *op. cit.,* pp. 249–250.

15. Sellin and Wolfgang, *op. cit.,* pp. 322–323.

Measurement

16. Sellin and Wolfgang have suggested a number of other specific formulas for computing index statistics. The reader may wish to refer to them. Cf. p. 306 and seq.

17. Leslie T. Wilkins, *Social Deviance: Social Policy, Action and Research* (Englewood Cliffs, N.J.: Prentice-Hall, Inc., 1965), 311 pp.

QUESTIONS

1. What are the shortcomings of the current crime recording systems? How do the authors think that their research will correct some of the shortcomings?
2. How do the results in Montreal differ from those in Philadelphia? In the Montreal research, how do the results differ between men and women?
3. Outline the research and statistical operations from selection of items to the conclusion that a ratio scale has been attained.

Marital Satisfaction over the Family Life Cycle

BOYD C. ROLLINS and HAROLD FELDMAN

In nominal measurement, the categories *cannot* be arranged along dimensions that are defined in terms of gradation of magnitude. For example, religious affiliation (Protestant, Catholic, Jewish, and so forth) does not involve any notion of magnitude; Protestants cannot be said to be higher than Catholics on the dimension of religious affiliation.

Examples of nominal measurement in sociology are numerous. In all likelihood the reader has encountered in the literature such simple and straightforward nominal measures as sex, race, religion, and political affiliation. However, at times the construction of nominal measures is neither simple nor straightforward. In the following study by Rollins and Feldman, the major independent variable, family life cycle, is one of those less "obvious" nominal measures.

■ The concept of developmental adjustment in marriage has recently stimulated concern for patterns of change in marital interaction over the family life cycle (Hill, 1951; Foote, 1956; Pineo, 1961; Farber, 1964:334–335; Rodgers, 1964; Magrabi and Marshall, 1965). This approach contrasts sharply with the earlier attempts to predict adjustment in the early stages of marriage (Terman, 1938; Burgess and Cottrell, 1939; Karlsson, 1951;

Reprinted from *Journal of Marriage and the Family* 32 (1970), 20–28, with permission of the National Council on Family Relations. (Editorial adaptation.)

Locke, 1951; Burgess and Wallin, 1953) under the assumption that personal readiness for marriage, compatible mate selection, and early adjustment were the keys to marital success. Dovetailing with the interest in developmental adjustment is the concept of stages of the family life cycle (Hill and Rodgers, 1964). Both Loomis (1936) and Lansing and Kish (1957) have demonstrated that stages of the family life cycle are more highly correlated with family economic behavior than either age of head of household or length of time a couple had been married. Lansing and Kish were so impressed with this concept that they called it an independent variable in family research and suggested that it provide a framework for the analysis of marital success. Impressed with the utility of the concept marital adjustment (marital success), Nye and MacDougall (1959) called it the dependent variable in family research. The issue of the meaning of marital success, its pattern over the family life cycle and its developmental antecedents and correlates is a primary issue in contemporary family sociology.

Burgess and Locke (1954) identified eight criteria of marital success that have been utilized in part in the evaluation of the strengths of marriages during the past three decades. These criteria are: (1) permanence, (2) social expectations, (3) personality development, (4) companionship, (5) happiness, (6) satisfaction, (7) adjustments and (8) integration. By 1964 about 400 articles or books on some aspect of marital success had been published (Aldous and Hill, 1967). About one half of these dealt with marital satisfaction or of somewhat similar criteria of success; namely, happiness, adjustment, integration, or companionship. However, only nine of them (Hamilton, 1929; Bernard, 1934; Terman, 1938:175–178; Burgess and Cottrell, 1939:246–247; Lang, 1953; Bossard and Boll, 1955; Blood and Wolfe, 1960:264–265; Gurin et al., 1960:84–116; Pineo, 1961) were empirical investigations of marital success over the family life cycle. Three additional studies published since 1964 (Luckey, 1966; Paris and Luckey, 1966; Marlowe, 1968) will complete the total of twelve studies on marital satisfaction over the family life cycle reviewed in this paper. Most of these studies included more than one of the Burgess and Locke criteria of marital success as did Nye and MacDougall (1959), but they all included marital satisfaction.

MARITAL SATISFACTION

According to Burgess and Locke (1945:439), "satisfaction appears to be a correspondence between the actual and the expected or a comparison of the actual relationship with the alternative, if the present relationship were terminated." Such a definition permits a focus on the total marital relationship or on specific aspects, on discrepancies between role expectations and perceived role performances, or between goals and perceived goal attainment, or between the personal qualities in one's conception of the ideal spouse and his perception of the actual personal qualities of his spouse. The meaning of such criteria is in the subjective evaluation of the individual participant from his particular point of view. Therefore, it is possible that psychological events such as perception of a values discrepancy with spouse when there is actually none, as well as the realities of married life circumstances over the family life cycle, influence the pattern of marital satisfaction or dissatisfaction. Also, the likelihood of such psychological events as well as their relationship to marital satisfaction might be very different for men than for women.

FAMILY LIFE CYCLE

As a descriptive device the family life cycle has been used to compare structures and functions of marital interaction in different stages of development. A fairly simple scheme and the one used in this study was to classify couples into eight stages of the family life cycle in terms of the age of the oldest child similar to what Duvall (1967:9) had done. The classification was as follows:

Stage I. Beginning Families (couples married 0 to 5 yrs. without children)

Stage II. Childbearing Families (oldest child, birth to 2 yrs. 11 mos.)

Stage III. Families with Preschool Children (oldest child, 3 yrs. to 5 yrs. 11 mos.)

Stage IV. Families with Schoolage Children (oldest child, 6 yrs. to 12 yrs. 11 mos.)

Stage V. Families with Teenagers (oldest child, 13 yrs. to 20 yrs. 11 mos.)

Stage VI. Families as Launching Centers (first child gone to last child's leaving home)

Stage VII. Families in the Middle Years (empty nest to retirement)

Stage VIII. Aging Families (retirement to death of first spouse)

A detailed rationale for family life cycle classification has been suggested by Rodgers (1962) and by Hill and Rodgers (1964). However, such a detailed scheme would require an extremely large sample size and was not feasible for this study. In fact, the review of literature required using extremely gross criteria such as the age of a married person or the length of time married as a rough estimate of stage of family life cycle.

LITERATURE REVIEW

The twelve studies reviewed are very consistent in showing a decline in marital satisfaction over the first ten years of marriage or to approximately the "schoolage" stage for wives. (See Table 1.) However, of the eight studies with data obtained and analyzed separately for husbands and wives, only four showed a decline through the early stages for husbands. Perhaps the studies using either couple scores or which do not differentiate the sexes in the data analysis find a decrease in marital satisfaction over time which should be attributed to wives only.

Dentler and Pineo (1960) found that the development of disenchantment in marriage was a common experience for only about 20 percent of the husbands in their study. Pineo (1961) suggested that disenchantment occurred sooner in marriage for husbands than for wives. Marlowe (1968) found males in "beginning families" to be much less satisfied than their

TABLE 1. A Summary of Twelve Studies of Marital Satisfaction over the Family Life Cycle

Study	FLC Stages Included*	Stage(s) Lowest in Satisfaction**	Number of Subjects			Pattern of Satisfaction Change Over the FLC		
			Males	Females	Total	Decrease	Decrease then Increase	No Change
Bernard	I–VIII	V–VI	109	122	231	—	♂♀	—
Blood	I–VIII	VIII	509	—	509	♀	—	—
Bossard	I–VII	IV–VII	225	215	440	♀	—	♂
Burgess	I–III	II–III	526	526	1,052	♂♀	—	—
Gurin	I–VIII	VII	—	—	1,867	♀	(♂♀)***	♂
Hamilton	I–IV	III–IV	100	100	200	♀	—	♂
Lang	I–V	IV–V	7,393	7,393	14,786	(♂♀)***	—	—
Luckey	II–V	IV–V	80	80	160	(♂♀)***	—	♂
Marlowe	I & III	III	60	60	120	♀	—	♂
Paris	IV–VI	V–VI	62	62	124	♀	—	♂
Pineo	II & V	V	400	400	800	♂♀	—	—
Terman	I–VII	III & V	792	792	1,584	—	♂♀	—

* Estimated from either age of subjects or length of time married. Definitions of the stages of the family life cycle are given in this paper under "Family Life Cycle."

** In every study marital satisfaction was highest at the beginning stages of the family life cycle.

*** It is not known whether the pattern of change is for husbands or wives or both.

173

wives with the marriage, while in the "preschool" stage they were at the same level of satisfaction. The wives decreased in satisfaction over time but the husbands did not. From analysis of within stage variations, Marlowe concluded that for the males disenchantment had already set in during the "beginning families" stage which would explain the lack of change for males between stages. Such an interpretation fits the suggestion of Pineo that disenchantment comes earlier for males than females. However, if it happens as early as during the first stage of the family life cycle this helps explain the lack of consistent evidence on between stage changes in marital satisfaction for males during the first ten years of marriage. Perhaps experiences before the arrival of children influence disenchantment for males while for females it begins with the arrival of children as suggested by Rossi (1968).

Only five of the 12 studies covered the whole life cycle of the family. The results are very confusing. Studying wives only, Blood and Wolfe (1960:265) found a continual decline in marital satisfaction throughout the family life cycle. Bossard and Boll (1955) found no further decline after the "schoolage" stage for wives and no decline at all for husbands. The other three studies (Bernard, 1934:57; Terman, 1938:178; Gurin et al., 1960:103) found a curvilinear trend with decreasing marital satisfaction during the early stages, a leveling off, and an increase during the later stages. However, the low point in Terman's study was at approximately the "preschool" stage while in Bernard's study it was closer to the "launching" stage and in the study by Gurin et al., closer to the "empty nest" stage, just before retirement. Gurin made no separate analysis for males and females which makes trend interpretations hazardous. The studies by Bernard, Blood, and Bossard all had very small samples at the "retirement" stage providing very limited evidence for a trend interpretation.

PURPOSE OF STUDY

The present study was done in an attempt to find answers to some of the discrepancies in the earlier studies, especially concerning the pattern of marital satisfaction following the "schoolage" stage of the family life cycle for wives and over the whole life cycle for husbands. The discrepancies in the previous studies were contaminated by extremely small samples in the later stages of the family life cycle or a failure to differentiate males and females in the data analyses. Also, it was hoped that a substantiated pattern of marital satisfaction would be described from this study and provide a basis for beginning attempts to construct a developmental theory of marital satisfaction.

METHOD

Data for this study were obtained through the use of an area survey sample of middle class residents of Syracuse, New York, in 1960. Dr. Charles Willie, a sociologist at the University of Syracuse, had previously classified all the census tracts in the city of Syracuse, New York, into one of six "social areas" in terms of (1) percent of single family dwellings, (2) average monthly rental, (3) average market value of owned homes, (4) median number of school years completed, and (5) percent of operatives, service workers, and laborers in the census tract. The census tracts in the top two social areas were considered to include a large proportion of upper middle class and upper class residents.

The nine census tracts in the top two socioeconomic categories of the city were sampled in this study. Each of these tracts was arbitrarily divided in half taking the half closest to the center of the city for one and the half furthest away for the next until a geographical area in each tract was selected. Every third housing unit in the selected area was a target dwelling. If either one or both spouses were to be absent from the household during the data gathering period, were unable to complete the questionnaire (illiterate in English, mental or serious illness), or the husband was a full-time student, the household was eliminated from the study.

Fieldworkers stopped at each selected housing unit, left a questionnaire for each husband and each wife and made an appointment to pick them up within a few days. The questionnaire asked for information on family of orientation and family of procreation, marital history, occupation, marital satisfaction, communication, decision making, methods of handling conflicts, values, frequency of integrative and disruptive experiences, and satisfaction with stages of the family life cycle from each individual. Only the data used to classify couples by stage of family life cycle and marital satisfaction are analyzed in this [article]. A high response rate of 85 percent useable questionnaires from both husbands and wives in the same households were collected from the target housing units. This provided data on a total of 852 married couples.

On religious preference 21 percent of the couples indicated Catholic, 35 percent Protestant, 27 percent Jewish, and 17 percent either mixed or none. Eighty-eight percent of the husbands were classified as white collar and only 12 percent as blue collar according to their occupation, and only 12 percent of the couples included a person who had been married previously to another person. Sixty-eight percent of the husbands had received some college education and 24 percent had received post graduate education. The sample was predominantly Caucasian, well-educated, middle and upper class persons in their first marriage with the wife not working outside the home.

Fifty-three of the initial 852 couples were married for more than five years and were still childless. They were eliminated from the analysis because they were considered atypical in terms of stages of the family life cycle. On the basis of length of time married, age of oldest child, and residence of children, the remaining 799 couples were classified into one of eight stages of the family life cycle. The distribution of these couples was as follows: 51 at Stage I ("Beginning"), 51 at Stage II ("Infant"), 82 at Stage III ("Preschool"), 244 at Stage IV ("Schoolage"), 227 at Stage V ("Teenage"), 64 at Stage VI ("Launching"), 30 at Stage VII ("Empty nest"), and 50 at Stage VIII ("Retirement").

The data on marital satisfaction were taken from four questions on the questionnaire as follows:

Measurement

1. General Marital Satisfaction—"In general, how often do you think that things between you and your wife are going well? —all the time, —most of the time, —more often than not, —occasionally, —rarely, —never."
2. Negative Feelings from Interaction with Spouse—"How often would you say that the following events occur between you and your husband (wife)? —never, —once or twice a year, —once or twice a month, —once or twice a week, —about once a day, —more than once a day." The combined responses of each individual in reply to "you feel resentful," "you feel not needed," and "you feel misunderstood" were used in the data analysis. In a factor analysis of the data these three events were equally highly loaded on a dominant factor.
3. Positive Companionship Experiences with Spouse—"How often would you say that the following events occur between you and your husband (wife)? —never, —once or twice a year, —once or twice a month, —once or twice a week, —about once a day, —more than once a day." The combined responses of each individual in reply to "laugh together," "calmly discuss something together," "have a stimulating exchange of ideas," and "work together on a project" were used in the data analysis. In a factor analysis of the data these four events were equally and highly loaded on a dominant factor.
4. Satisfaction with Present Stage of the Family Life Cycle—"Different stages of the family life cycle may be viewed as being more satisfying than others. How satisfying do you think the following stages are? —very satisfying, —quite satisfying, —somewhat satisfying, —not satisfying." Data on this question were used in reply to "before the children arrive" for individuals in Stage I, "first year with infant" for Stage II, "preschool children at home" for Stage III, "all children at school" for Stage IV, "having teenagers" for Stage V, "children gone from home" for Stages VI and VII, and "being grandparents" for Stage VIII.

The data analysis consisted of determining cross tabulation frequencies on the response categories for each of the four questions on marital satisfaction by stages of the family life cycle. This was done separately for each sex. Chi square was computed from the cross tabulation frequencies to test the null hypothesis that each stage of the family life cycle would have the same proportion of response frequencies for each of the response categories on marital satisfaction. Where necessary, marital satisfaction response categories were combined to meet the chi square assumptions (Blalock, 1960:220) of a minimal expected frequency of more than five in each cell of the cross tabulation. Also, the degree of association between stage of family life cycle and marital satisfaction was determined by the coefficient of contingency corrected for size of the contingency table (Blalock, 1960:230). The coefficiency of contingency rather than gamma was used because the relationships were not linear.

FINDINGS

The distribution of scores on "general marital satisfaction" was similar to that of many studies (cf. Hamilton, 1929; Bernard, 1934; Burgess and Cottrell, 1939; Burgess and Wallin, 1953; Lang, 1953; Bossard and Boll, 1955) using either a single item measurement or a composite index. The majority of subjects were on the high end of the scale. Eighty percent of the wives and 80 percent of the husbands indicated that things were going well in their marriage all of the time or most of the time. (See Tables 2 and 3.)

. . .

The pattern of "general marital satisfaction" for wives was a steady decline from the "beginning" to the "schoolage" stage; then a leveling off with a rapid increase from the "empty nest" to the "retired" stage of the family life cycle. (See Figure 1.) For the husbands there was a slight decline from the "beginning" to the "schoolage" stage, a slight increase to the "empty nest" stage and then a rapid increase to the "retired" stage. The amount of change for husbands, though statistically significant, was much less than that for the wives. However, this is accounted for in part by the fact that a greater percent of wives than husbands report their marriage to be "perfect" in Stage I of the family life cycle. The greatest fluctuation in marital satisfaction for husbands was the increase from Stage VII to Stage VIII. As indicated in Tables 2 and 3, the chi square and the contingency coefficient values were higher for wives than husbands.

Concerning a more specific aspect of marital satisfaction, "negative feelings resulting from interaction with spouse" were much more common for wives than husbands. Forty-seven percent of the wives gave responses of "once a month" or more often on the frequency of feelings of resentment, feelings of not being needed, and feelings of being misunderstood while only 37 percent of the husbands had such feelings. There was no statistically reliable family life cycle change for husbands $(.10 > P > .05)$.

For the wives there was a definite pattern. There was a sharp increase in the frequency of negative feelings with the arrival of the first child and then a leveling off until the "teenage" stage where a substantial decline

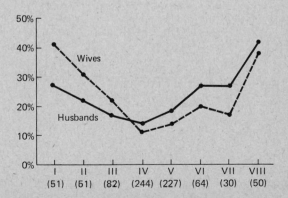

FIGURE 1: Percentage of individuals at each stage of the family life cycle (from Stage I, "beginning marriage," to Stage VIII, "retirement") reporting their marriage was going well "all the time." (Figures in parentheses indicate the number of husbands and also the number of wives in each stage. There was a total of 1598 cases.)

TABLE 2. Percentage Distribution of Wives by Stage of the Family Life Cycle and by Level of Marital Satisfaction for Four Measures of Marital Satisfaction

Measure and Level of Marital Satisfaction*	Stage of Family Life Cycle*								Total	Statistical Evaluation
	I N=51	II N=51	III N=82	IV N=244	V N=227	VI N=64	VII N=30	VIII N=50	N=799	
General Marital Satisfaction										
All the time	41%	31%	22%	11%	14%	20%	17%	38%	20%	x^2=55.8
Most of the time	47	51	58	63	55	56	43	50	56	df=14
Less often**	12	18	20	26	31	24	40	12	24	p < .001 C = .31
Negative Feelings										
Never	10%	4%	4%	8%	12%	25%	13%	28%	11%	x^2=61.9
Once-twice a year	41	37	40	36	49	42	54	44	42	df=21
Once-twice a month	35	41	45	39	26	20	30	18	33	p < .001
More often**	14	18	11	17	13	13	3	10	14	C = .31
Positive Companionship										
More than once a day	16%	10%	7%[a]	5%	5%	5%	10%	12%	7%[a]	x^2=46.0
About once a day	55	39	29	31	36	38	27	24	35	df=21
Once-twice a week	25	39	49	46	34	45	40	44	50	p < .001
Less often**	4	12	25	18	25	12	23	20	18	C = .27
Present FLC Stage										
Very satisfying	74%	76%	50%	35%	17%[a]	8%	17%	82%	45%	x^2=242.2
Quite satisfying	22	18	33	44	38	16	13	14	33	df=14
Less satisfying**	4	6	17	21	15	76	70	.4	22	p < .001 C = .59

* These indices and categories are explained in this paper under "Family Life Cycle" and "Research Methods."
** Two or more categories were combined for statistical analysis.
[a] Editors' note: These columns should, but do not, add to 100 percent.

TABLE 3. Percentage Distribution of Husbands by Stage of the Family Life Cycle and by Level of Marital Satisfaction for Four Measures of Marital Satisfaction

Measure and Level of Marital Satisfaction*	Stage of Family Life Cycle*								Total N=799	Statistical Evaluation
	I N=51	II N=51	III N=82	IV N=244	V N=227	VI N=64	VII N=30	VIII N=50		
General Marital Satisfaction										
All the time	27%	22%	17%	14%	18%	27%	27%	42%	20%	x^2=32.5
Most of the time	61	62	59	63	60	55	40	52	60	df=14
Less often**	12	16	24	23	22	18	33	6	20	$p < .01$
										C=.24
Negative Feelings										
Never	10%	10%	7%	15%	19%	12%	10%	32%	15%	x^2=32.4
Once-twice a year	41	47	54	50	44	63	43	40	48	df=21
Once-twice a month	31	31	28	25	28	17	37	22	27	$p > .05$
More often**	18	12	11	10	9	8	10	6	10	C=.23
Positive Companionship										
More than once a day	22%	8%	4%	6%	8%	10%	10%	6%	8%	x^2=42.2
About once a day	49	43	34	35	34	31	40	26	36	df=21
Once-twice a week	27	37	38	41	39	45	33	60	40	$p < .01$
Less often**	2	12	24	18	19	14	17	8	16	C=.26
Present FLC Stage										
Very satisfying	55%	69%	61%	39%	44%	9%	24%	66%	44%	x^2=184.7
Quite satisfying	39	23	31	45	41	25	13	30	37	df=14
Less satisfying**	6	8	8	16	15	66	63	4	19	$p < .001$
										C=.53

* These indices and categories are explained in this paper under "Family Life Cycle" and "Research Methods."
** Two or more categories were combined for statistical analysis.

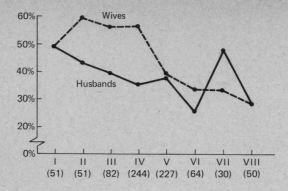

FIGURE 2: Percentage of individuals at each stage of the family life cycle (from Stage I, "beginning marriage," to Stage VIII, "retirement") reporting negative feelings "once or twice a month" or more often from interaction with their spouse. (Figures in parentheses indicate the number of husbands and also the number of wives in each stage. There was a total of 1598 cases.) Note—In this case, a decline in the curve indicates greater marital satisfaction.

in negative feelings began and continued to the "launching" stage leveling out through the "retirement" stage. The presence of dependent children in the home ("infant" through "schoolage" stages) appears to be related to a high level of negative feelings in the wife from her interaction with her husband. (See Figure 2.)

In the second area of specific marital satisfaction, "positive companionship experiences," husbands and wives were similar. Forty-two percent of the wives and 44 percent of the husbands gave responses of the frequencies of "once a day" or more often on laughing together, calmly discussing something together, having a stimulating exchange of ideas, and working together on a project. For both sexes there was a high frequency of positive companionship experiences at the beginning of marriage declining substantially to the "preschool" stage and then leveling off over the remaining stages. (See Figure 3.)

"Satisfaction with present stage of the family life cycle" was similar for husbands and wives. Forty-five percent of the wives and 44 percent of the husbands thought their present stage was "very satisfying." However, there was considerable variation between the sexes over the life cycle. (See Figure 4.) The majority of wives in the early stages were very satisfied. Then there was a gradual but extensive decline to the "teenage" stage, a leveling off to the "empty nest" stage, and an extensive increase during the "retirement" stage. However, the husbands indicated a relatively high satisfaction from the "beginning" through the "teenage" stage. Then there was an extensive decline to the "launching" stage and an increase to the "empty nest" and "retirement" stages.

Like general satisfaction with marriage, satisfaction with present stage did not vary as much over the family life cycle for husbands as it did for wives. Though a curvilinear pattern existed in the data on both general marital satisfaction and satisfaction with present stage, the low point on

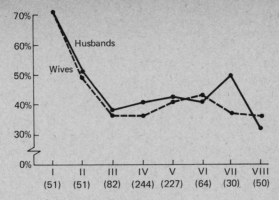

FIGURE 3: Percentage of individuals in each stage of the family life cycle (from Stage I, "beginning marriage" to Stage VIII, "retirement") reporting "positive companionship experiences with their spouse at least "once a day" or more often. (Figures in parentheses indicate the number of husbands and also the number of wives in each stage. There was a total of 1598 cases.)

general satisfaction was at the "schoolage" stage while the low point on satisfaction with present stage of the family life cycle was when children were being "launched" from the home.

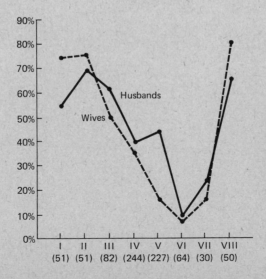

FIGURE 4: Percentage of individuals in each stage of the family life cycle (from Stage I, "beginning marriage," to Stage VIII, "retirement") reporting that their present stage of the family life cycle is very satisfying. (Figures in parentheses indicate the number of husbands and also the number of wives in each stage. There was a total of 1598 cases.)

181

SUMMARY AND CONCLUSIONS

On only two of the four indices of marital satisfaction is there a consistent pattern over the family life cycle for both husbands and wives. Concerning the frequency of positive companionship experience, they both reported a substantial decline from the beginning of marriage to the "preschool" stage and then a leveling off over the remainder of stages. The events used to form this scale, laughing together, calm discussions with each other, having a stimulating exchange of ideas with each other, and working together on a project are events to which they could both objectively report a frequency of occurrence. Since they were mutual events, we would expect a similar response from the husbands and wives in each couple, if they were objective in their evaluations. The pattern here seems to be very clear, that stimulating common activity in marriage decreases from the very beginning with no recovery. A similar result was found by Pineo (1961) from reports of both husbands and wives and by Blood and Wolfe (1960) from reports of wives only.

Concerning satisfaction with present stage of the family life cycle, both husband and wife rate highly the childbearing and early childrearing phases and are at a low point when launching the children from the home. Perhaps this is an indication of satisfaction with parenthood more than marriage.

The two indices of marital satisfaction in which husbands and wives follow different patterns over the family life cycle refer to the subjective affective state of each individual with reference to their marriage. In general, husbands seem to be much less affected by stage of the family life cycle in their subjective evaluations of marital satisfaction than are wives. The husbands vary little from the establishment through the childbearing and childrearing phases. However, the wives have a substantial decrease in general marital satisfaction and a high level of negative feelings from marital interaction during the childbearing and childrearing phases until the children are getting ready to leave home. After the childrearing phases both husbands and wives have a substantial increase in marital satisfaction through the "retirement" stage with an apparent temporary setback just before the husband retires.

These data suggest that experiences of childbearing and childrearing have a rather profound and negative effect on marital satisfaction for wives, even in their basic feelings of self-worth in relation to their marriage. Perhaps this is partly a consequence of the great reduction in positive companionship experiences with their husbands instigated by the pressures of childrearing responsibilities. On the other hand, the loss of companionship seems to occur for husbands without a decrease in marital satisfaction. The most devastating period of marriage for males appears to be when they are anticipating retirement. Marital satisfaction might be influenced more by occupational experiences for husbands than the event and developmental level of children in their families.

These data suggest that marriage has very different meanings for husbands than for wives and that very different events within or outside the marriage and/or family influence the developmental pattern of marital satisfaction in men and women. This might help explain the fact that some studies have found family life cycle differences for both men and women and some for women only. It seems that men are influenced more by events both before and after there are children in families while women are influenced more by the presence of children.

From a review of the literature and the data reported in this study it seems evident that marital satisfaction of husbands and wives is associated with stages of the family life cycle and a developmental theory of marital satisfaction is needed to explain this association. However, it is questionable that the same developmental theory would have utility for both husbands and wives. It is suggested that a developmental theory of marital satisfaction for wives would focus on the contingent role of parenthood while for husbands the contingent occupational role seems more relevant.

REFERENCES

ALDOUS, JOAN, and REUBEN HILL. 1967. *International Bibliography of Research in Marriage and the Family, 1900–1964.* Minneapolis: University of Minnesota Press.

BERNARD, JESSIE. 1934. "Factors in the distribution of success in marriage." *American Journal of Sociology* 40 (July):49–60.

BLALOCK, HUBERT M., Jr. 1960. *Social Statistics.* New York: McGraw-Hill.

BLOOD, ROBERT O., and DONALD M. WOLFE. 1960. *Husbands and Wives: The Dynamics of Married Living.* Glencoe, Illinois: Free Press.

BOSSARD, JAMES H. S., and ELEANORE S. BOLL. 1955. "Marital unhappiness in the life cycle of marriage." *Marriage and Family Living* 17 (February):10–14.

BURGESS, ERNEST W., and LEONARD S. COTTRELL, JR. 1939. *Predicting Success or Failure in Marriage.* New York: Prentice-Hall.

BURGESS, ERNEST W., and HARVEY J. LOCKE. 1945. *The Family: From Institution to Companionship.* New York: American Book Company.

BURGESS, ERNEST W., and PAUL WALLIN. 1953. *Engagement and Marriage.* Philadelphia: Lippincott.

COSTNER, HERBERT L. 1965. "Criteria for measures of association." *American Sociological Review* 30 (June):341–353.

DENTLER, ROBERT A., and PETER PINEO. 1960. "Sexual adjustment, marital adjustment and personality growth of husbands; a panel analysis." *Marriage and Family Living* 22 (February):45–48.

DUVALL, EVELYN M. 1967. *Family Development.* Philadelphia: Lippincott.

FARBER, BERNARD. 1964. *Family: Organization and Interaction.* San Francisco: Chandler Publishing Company.

FOOTE, NELSON N. 1956. "Matching of husband and wife in phases of development." *Transactions of the Third World Congress of Sociology* 4 (August):24–34.

GURIN, GERALD, JOSEPH VERHOFF, and SHEILA FELL. 1960. *Americans View Their Mental Health.* New York: Basic Books.

HAMILTON, GILBERT V. 1929. *A Research in Marriage.* New York: Boni.

HILL, REUBEN. 1951. "Marital success." Pp. 343–372 in Willard Waller and Reuben Hill (eds.), *The Family: A Dynamic Interpretation.* New York: Dryden Press.

HILL, REUBEN, and ROY H. RODGERS. 1964. "The developmental approach." Pp. 171–211 in Harold T. Christensen (ed.), *Handbook of Marriage and the Family.* Chicago: Rand McNally.

KARLSSON, GEORGE. 1951. *Adaptability and Communication in Marriage: A Swedish Predictive Study.* Uppsala: Almquist and Wiksells.

LANG, ROBERT O. 1953. "The rating of happiness in marriage." Pp. 536–539 in Ernest W. Burgess and Willard Waller (eds.), *Engagement and Marriage.* Philadelphia: Lippincott.

LANSING, JOHN J., and LESLIE KISH. 1957. "Family life cycle as an independent variable." *American Sociological Review* 22 (October):512–519.

LOCKE, HARVEY J. 1951. *Prediction Adjustment in Marriage: A Comparison of a Divorced and a Happily Married Group.* New York: Holt.

LOOMIS, CHARLES C. 1936. "The study of the life cycle of families." *Rural Sociology* 1 (June):180–199.

LUCKEY, ELEANORE B. 1966. "Number of years married as related to personality perception and marital satisfaction." *Journal of Marriage and the Family* 28 (February):44–48.

MAGRABI, FRANCES A., and WILLIAM H. MARSHALL. 1965. "Family development tasks: a research model." *Journal of Marriage and the Family* 27 (November):454–458.

MARLOWE, ROY H. 1968. "Development of marital dissatisfaction of Mormon college couples over the early stages of the family life cycle." Unpublished M.S. thesis, Brigham Young University.

NYE, F. IVAN, and EVELYN MacDOUGALL. 1959. "The dependent variable in marital research." *Pacific Sociological Review* 2 (Fall):67–70.

PARIS, BETHEL L., and ELEANORE B. LUCKEY. 1966. "A longitudinal study of marital satisfaction." *Sociology and Social Research* 50 (January):212–223.

PINEO, PETER C. 1961. "Disenchantment in the later years of marriage." *Marriage and Family Living* 23 (February):3–11.

RODGERS, ROY H. 1962. *Improvements in the Construction and Analysis of Family Life Cycle Categories.* Kalamazoo, Michigan: Western Michigan University.

———— 1964. "Toward a theory of family development." *Journal of Marriage and the Family* 26 (August):262–270.

ROSSI, ALICE S. 1968. "Transition to parenthood." *Journal of Marriage and the Family* 30 (February):26–39.

TERMAN, LEWIS M. 1938. *Psychological Factors in Marital Happiness.* New York: McGraw-Hill.

QUESTIONS

1. What different family characteristics go into defining the various stages of the family life cycle? What theoretical justification can be used to defend these variables as nominal and not ordinal, interval, or ratio?
2. It is possible to use as indicators of life cycle stage such measures as "age of household head" and "length of marriage." Both indicators employ "years" as the manifest measure—a measure that in some contexts is considered to be interval or ratio. How would you react if interval or ratio measures were to be used as indicators of life cycle stages?
3. Compare the tables and figures and describe the advantages and limitations of each of these presentation devices. Do the tables and figures agree with the descriptive statements in the text?
4. Carefully inspect Table 1 as a use of a systematic presentation device; how does it compare to a narrative presentation? What are the advantages and limitations of tabular versus textual presentation?
5. This article involves a "cross-sectional" analysis—that is, each family unit appears at only one stage of the family life cycle (contrasted to having measures of marital satisfaction on the same couple at several of the life cycle stages). Find where the authors are tempted to move into an interpretation of their cross-sectional data as though they were "processual" data (see article 21).
6. Why do the authors choose to use the statistic C instead of the rank order statistic gamma?

SUGGESTED READINGS

BONJEAN, CHARLES M., et al., *Sociological Measurement: An Inventory of Scales and Indices*. San Francisco: Chandler, 1967.

EDWARDS, ALLEN L. *Techniques of Attitude Scale Construction*. New York: Appleton-Century-Crofts, 1957.

HEMPEL, CARL G. "Fundamentals of Concept Formation in Empirical Science." In *International Encyclopedia of Unified Science*. Vol. 2, No. 7. Chicago: University of Chicago Press, 1952.

McKINNEY, JOHN C. *Constructive Typology and Social Theory*. New York: Appleton-Century-Crofts, 1966.

PARK, PETER. *Sociology Tomorrow: An Evaluation of Sociological Theories in Terms of Science*. New York: Pegasus, 1969.

SELLIN, THORSTEN, and WOLFGANG, MARVIN E. *The Measurement of Delinquency*. New York: Wiley, 1964.

STEVENS, S. SMITH. "Mathematics, Measurement, and Psychophysics." In S. S. Stevens (ed.), *Handbook of Experimental Psychology*. New York: Wiley, 1951.

TORGERSON, WARREN S. *Theory and Methods of Scaling*. New York: Wiley, 1958. Chapters 1 and 2.

■ The analysis of data involves the process by which the researcher moves from "observations" and measurement to a set of interpretable results. Analysis can vary in several important ways. For example, in univariate (one variable) analysis the principal function is to condense and to summarize a welter of data into a coherent and concise statement. This involves seeking ways of describing typicality in such terms as means, medians, and modes, as well as variability in terms of percent distributions, standard deviations, variance, and so forth. In situations involving two (bivariate analysis) or more (multivariate analysis) variables, the principal focus is placed on describing relationships between variables. Here one will encounter such things as percentage differences, correlation coefficients, and regression weights. Analysis can also vary from a qualitative approach (verbal descriptions, highlighting of illustrative cases) through simple quantitative techniques (frequency counts, percentages) to the very sophisticated and complex procedures (multiple correlation, path analysis, factor analysis, complex analysis of variance). As with other phases of the research process, there is no one *best* single technique of analysis. The researcher has many to choose from, and his decision should be governed by which techniques are best suited for his research purposes.

In the first article in this section, Jansyn provides us with a combination of "narrative" verbal analysis and quantitative procedures. Spady illustrates percentage analysis, a method of controlling for different frequencies of groups being compared. He also carries out percentage analysis within several subgroups as a form of controlling for effects of other variables. In comparing the zonal and sector hypotheses of urban patterning, Anderson and Egeland use census tract data in an "analysis of variance" design which tests for the separate and combined influences of sectors, zones, and specific cities. Walton's article is an example of a multivariate analysis aimed at testing causal relationships of a three variable system. Groves and Rossi display both percentage and regression methods of multivariate analysis, with controls not only for individual variables but for a "contextual" variable (e.g.,city) as well. This article is another example of causal analysis. Kasarda uses both cross-sectional and longitudinal data in a simple path analysis framework for distinguishing the impact of suburban population growth on central city functions.

Solidarity and Delinquency in a Street Corner Group

LEON R. JANSYN, JR.

Analysis of research findings often means the manipulation of numbers (frequency counts, percentages, correlation coefficients, and so forth); in other words, quantitative analysis. However, this is not always the case, for data analysis can be qualitative in nature as well. In the following article we see an example of qualitative analysis involving diary entries and narratives to assess such issues as organizational structures and types of leadership roles.

An interesting aspect of the Jansyn study is its use of both quantitative and qualitative procedures, especially in the way the same data (narratives) are subjected to both types of treatment. The article also illustrates a form of "participant observation"—the active involvement of the researcher in the social group being researched and the problems associated with this procedure (for example, the fact that the researcher can influence the very process that he is attempting to observe). We should also note that the research describes observations made over a period of a year or more and pertains to one group. As such it has all the limitations involved in generalizing from a single instance.

■ Questions have been raised as to whether gangs may be more usefully viewed as integrated groups, in the manner of Whyte's description of the Nortons[1] as mob-like assemblages under the leadership of disturbed persons,[2] or as loosely organized collectivities.[3, 4] The data presented here from the study of one group over a long period of time help in determining the relative merits of these perspectives.

This study reveals (1) that severely delinquent gangs can have a relatively high degree of organization and (2) that such a gang can go through phases of organization and disorganization and increases and decreases of solidarity. A realistic appreciation of the properties of the group can only be gained through extended, continuous observation.

The study is an attempt not to explain delinquency but to illuminate some of the ways in which variations in group activity are related to internal processes of the group and variations in group structure over time. Knowledge of such processes aids in the understanding of the episodic character of gang delinquency.[5]

Recent theories of gang delinquency are not explicit about the effects of the internal dynamics of the gang. There are many hypotheses about what goes on in gangs. Delinquency is learned; many personal needs are met; identities are formed; and techniques of neutralization, and rationalizations are developed and exercised. Perhaps most relevant to this study is the implication from Cohen's theory that the gang enhances the enthusiasm of the boys for delinquency, and Short's idea that participation in the gang affects aleatory elements, changing the probabilities of

Reprinted from *American Sociological Review* 31 (1966), 600–614, with permission of The American Sociological Association.

delinquency. For example, participation in the core group of a gang seems to have implications for the future illegitimate parenthood of the members. Status in the gang is as much a response to the changing structure of the group as it is an aspect of individual learning, needs or proclivities. The boys act with regard to the conditions within the gang. Here solidarity is evaluated as a dimension of the condition of the gang; knowledge of this dimension is necessary to understand the activity of the boys.[6]

The subjects were the Dons, an informal, autonomous, severely delinquent adolescent group.[7] This group was studied more or less systematically by direct observation over a period of five and one-half years. The author observed the group for slightly over two years. The data reported here cover fifteen months, during its fourth and fifth years. The data have been analyzed to show patterns of membership participation, changes in organization, and fluctuations in the frequency of the members' engagement in certain types of activity. The analysis leads to the recognition of an important relationship between organization and activity, and to a tentative general hypothesis: In corner groups deterioration of group solidarity is followed by an increase of group activity and a revival of solidarity.

METHOD AND SETTING OF STUDY

Two kinds of data are available for analysis, attendance records and daily narrative reports of group activities. The first are records of which boys participated with the group each day. These provide basic descriptions of the group. An index of solidarity is derived from the records of the daily number of man-hours which members of the group spent together during specified hours.

Social roles are revealed by the data. The attendance data are of particular interest in this respect; they permit the distinction of two role patterns of participation, core members and fringe members. Concentration of attention on role-specific patterns of attendance is believed to be warranted: the relationship of attendance to activity suggests that these patterns may be as significant to the outcome of behavior as the more usual forms of role behavior such as planning, leading or directing.

Written daily accounts of the group's activity make up a second body of data. From these data we derive descriptions of the level of group organization and a chronology of group activity. The description of changing levels of organization is used to validate man-hours as an index of solidarity. In the last section of the paper changes in group organization are shown to parallel roughly the solidarity index. In this section we also investigate the relationship between the index of solidarity (viewed as the independent variable) and variations in group activity (viewed as the dependent variable).

The observer resided in the Dons' neighborhood and associated with the group as a "detached worker."[8] Systematic recording of the participation of the members was begun after three months of close association with the boys.

The activities of the group were observed by staying with the boys at their current gathering-place for the entire evening. Usually they assembled on a particular street corner. They also spent much time in either of two restaurants and in a recreational agency clubroom. They participated in the recreational agency as an agency club; a number of girls were members. Most of these girls were close friends of the boys and associated with them nightly outside of recreational agency club meetings. The girls formed a street-corner group in their own right, with a name. It resembled what has been referred to in the literature as an "auxiliary."

The observations were recorded in a diary. Participation was recorded by notation of the persons who were gathered in the group on each of 197 days over a period of one year.[9] Notations were also made of the persons who were present during each hour of the period from 7:30 to 10:30 p.m. on 149 of these days. The days were selected essentially by chance.

The study was conducted in a neighborhood where groups such as the Dons are commonplace. It is an inner-city working-class neighborhood, one-half square mile in area, located two miles from the central business district. It ranks at the 85th percentile among the areas of the city according to the rates of official delinquency. For the past 25 years there has been extensive demolition of residential property in and adjacent to the neighborhood. This property has been replaced by a large public housing project and light industrial buildings. Further extensive slum clearance and redevelopment is planned for the area. It has been an area of first settlement of a series of immigrant groups, of which the Italians were the last major group; the ethnic composition is now mixed. From 1940 to 1957 the total population decreased from 27,145 to 24,074. However, there is a small but increasing number of Negro residents in the public housing projects.

A traditional, institutional form of association among male adolescents and young adults in the neighborhood is the social athletic club. Such clubs have been useful as mutual-aid societies and have assisted members in their aspirations toward occupational and social mobility. Though the use of this institutional form has declined, boys very often form autonomous groups with a view toward becoming such a club, hoping eventually to rent private premises for their gatherings.

The boys in the Dons were 14 to 16 years of age at the beginning of the study. Members of groups such as the Dons make up a large proportion of the very numerous official delinquents from this area. Of the 45 boys brought to the court from this area during the year of the study, 9 were members of the Dons. Fifteen were members of the two groups which preceded and succeeded the Dons on their corner. Twenty-six of the 60 members of the Dons were adjudged delinquent by the county court at some time.

The possession of private premises is an ideal. There were ten or fifteen adolescent groups in the neighborhood who had such. Most are not long in the boys' possession; a group may have three or four stores during its career. The Dons succeeded, with the author's help, in renting a store several months after the study. They were unable to maintain this after the author left the area. After a period of having no store, they again rented one. This, too, lasted only a few months.

The Dons also participated each year in the program of a recreational agency, and in this way obtained a clubroom. They were not all equally enthusiastic about this arrangement and there was constant division and contention, between those who were in favor of agency membership and those who were not. This contention divided the Dons into two overlapping and co-existing subgroups, the gang and the club. It was usual for the boys to assemble at a restaurant after the agency closed. The attendance at these two places reflected the division of the group.

ANALYSIS OF ATTENDANCE DATA

Membership, for the purpose of this study, is defined as the status of a boy who is observed to associate with the group with enough regularity to become familiar to the observer *and* who receives recognition as a member by at least two of the other boys.[10] Because attendance is often resumed after extended absences, all members were regarded as permanent during the year of observation.[11] Cumulative group membership increased during the year from 28 to 60 boys. Since the author associated with the boys for three months before this increase took place, he is fairly certain that almost all the additions were actually new members. Association with the group by some of these boys was infrequent and of short duration.

Attendance is defined as an observed appearance of a member with the group on any given evening during the hours of 7:30 to 10:30 p.m. The evening hours were chosen because this is the time most boys are present, and the time that external commitments to work, school, or family are least likely to intervene. Also, the attendance record is used to compare one day with another. It is more important then, that the criteria be permanent from day to day than that they result in a full representation of experience.

ATTENDANCE AND TIME SPENT TOGETHER There are two problems in the analysis of the attendance data: first, to observe change in the descriptive categories, and second, to use these attendance data to assess variables related to solidarity and role. The final assessment of solidarity is made by use of daily man-hours spent together by the group.[12] In regard to the first problem, which is essentially one of description, the variables were selected with a view toward practicality and the ability of the variables to reflect changes in the dynamics and structure of the group. The data are presented in a summary fashion in Table 1. The semi-monthly means of all variables are reported. The first half of October and the first half of September are not reported. There were only 2 observations in the first instance and none in the latter.

COMPOSITIONAL STABILITY Questions of solidarity obviously cannot be completely answered by means of daily man-hours. The attempt to use attendance data to assess solidarity, however, led to the assessment of compositional stability. Although this approach did not appear to result in a usable index of group solidarity, it provided interesting

Semi-Monthly Means of Daily Attendance Variables and Number of Group Activities

	Attendance			Daily Man-Hours			Hours per Boy			No. of Days	Activities*		
	Core	Fringe	Total	Core	Fringe	Total	Core	Fringe	Total		A.G.	D.G.	I.D.
Oct.	—	—	—	—	—	—	—	—	—	—	2	2	4
	6.6	7.0	13.6	15.0	11.3	26.3	2.3	1.6	2.0	7	4	2	4
Nov.	8.0	12.3	20.3	22.7	24.3	47.0	2.8	2.0	2.3	3	2	0	0
	6.9	9.7	16.6	16.1	18.3	34.4	2.2	1.9	2.0	9	1	0	1
Dec.	6.9	10.5	17.4	15.8	19.9	35.6	2.3	1.9	2.1	8	0	0	2
	5.3	7.8	13.0	12.8	18.8	31.5	2.4	2.5	2.4	4	2	0	4
Jan.	6.9	6.1	13.0	15.3	11.0	26.0	2.2	1.8	2.0	8	2	0	0
	7.0	10.3	17.3	16.6	18.6	35.3	2.4	1.8	2.0	8	1	0	1
Feb.	5.7	7.5	13.2	12.7	12.6	24.8	2.1	1.5	1.9	11	1	0	1
	5.4	8.3	13.7	12.7	17.4	30.1	2.3	2.1	2.2	7	1	1	1
Mar.	5.5	5.3	10.8	14.3	11.2	25.5	2.6	2.0	2.4	6	3	2	4
	6.9	6.7	13.6	17.6	13.6	31.1	2.5	1.8	2.3	7	0	0	0
Apr.	7.8	11.0	18.8	20.4	24.6	45.0	2.6	2.3	2.4	5	1	1	0
	6.5	11.8	18.3	15.3	19.5	34.8	2.4	1.7	1.9	6	1	0	0
May	7.6	11.0	18.6	15.2	21.2	36.4	2.0	1.9	1.9	5	1	0	2
	6.2	9.0	15.2	13.2	16.0	29.2	2.2	1.8	1.9	5	1	0	3
June	6.7	9.7	16.3	16.0	16.7	32.7	2.4	1.7	2.0	3	1	1	0
	6.0	8.8	14.8	15.0	15.8	30.8	2.5	1.8	2.1	4	1	0	1
July	7.3	8.0	15.3	15.7	13.7	26.4	2.2	1.7	1.9	7	0	0	3
	8.7	8.0	16.7	18.3	14.0	32.3	2.1	1.7	1.9	3	1	0	2
Aug.	6.6	4.6	11.2	14.8	8.8	23.6	2.0	1.4	2.0	5	0	0	1
	6.7	8.1	14.9	14.9	14.9	29.7	2.3	1.8	2.0	7	1	1	4
Sept.	—	—	—	—	—	—	—	—	—	—	2	2	0
	8.0	7.8	15.8	19.0	15.3	34.3	2.4	2.0	2.2	6	1	1	1
Mean	6.7	8.5	15.2	15.6	15.8	31.4	2.3	1.8	2.1	—	—	—	—
Standard Deviation	0.9	2.0	2.4	2.4	4.0	5.7	0.2	0.2	0.2	—	—	—	—
Totals	—	—	—	—	—	—	—	—	—	134	30	13	39

* A.G. = activity of the entire group.
D.G. = delinquencies of the entire group.
I.D. = delinquencies of individuals and cliques.

193

descriptive statistics concerning social roles in the group, and important corroboration for a number of the conclusions about roles, interpersonal relationships, and the structure of influence.

The assessment of compositional stability made it necessary to further limit the definition of the unit because a relatively constant interval between days to be compared is needed. Thus comparisons were made of all pairs of days in which the days were next to one another or separated by one day. For the entire study this procedure resulted in a reduction of the sample to one of 134 days, which is used in all presentations of attendance data.

The variable used to measure compositional stability is the duplication rate. The duplication rate for any pair of consecutive days is the ratio of the number of boys present on both days (counted twice) to the number of boys present on either day. The higher the rate, the more similar the composition of the group on those two days. The results of these calculations are presented in Table 2. The mean duplication rate for the group for the year was 0.63. This type of analysis is useful for questions of the extent to which the group is composed of the same persons from time to time.

TABLE 2. Semi-Monthly Means of Duplication Rates

	Core	Fringe	Total	N*
Oct.	—	—	—	—
	.76	.30	.58	6
Nov.	.90	.55	.68	3
	.75	.55	.65	10
Dec.	.81	.63	.69	8
	.78	.55	.64	3
Jan.	.77	.45	.62	12
	.81	.59	.68	9
Feb.	.65	.46	.55	15
	.45	.47	.49	5
Mar.	.74	.27	.53	5
	.73	.30	.55	7
Apr.	.89	.55	.70	6
	.76	.65	.70	6
May	.79	.69	.73	7
	.83	.31	.52	4
June	.85	.48	.63	3
	.86	.67	.75	4
July	.81	.50	.65	6
	.70	.63	.67	3
Aug.	.71	.62	.67	4
	.82	.41	.62	6
Sept.	—	—	—	—
	.91	.47	.69	5
Mean	.76	.51	.63	—
Standard Deviation	.18	.21	.14	—

*N refers to the number of pairs of days in which days were next to one another or separated by one day.

An attempt was made to compare attendance at times more widely separated. Ten pairs of days were selected randomly, each pair having one day in October and one day in the following September. The mean was 0.68; accordingly, two-thirds of the group was likely to be the same at times separated by a year. The same method was applied to samples between October and each other month. January and February were very low and March the lowest, when paired with October. It is noteworthy that in March the group participated in an episode of mob violence and attracted the attention and constant surveillance of the police. The first half of March shows some of the lowest values for the measures in Tables 1 and 2, but the very low fringe duplication rates reveal that even this low level of attendance was achieved by a large number of different boys rather than by one group. The core group showed different characteristics. Although it had an attendance and man-hours value in early March which were below the means for the year, its duplication rate was near the mean, indicating that the few boys who did participate early in March did so with greater regularity than did the fringe members. However, a word of caution needs to be added to this interpretation. The instability of the winter months as reflected in the duplication rate is partly due to low attendance because of cold weather.

CORE MEMBERS   Prior to analysis of the attendance data, and based on reported daily observations of group activity, nine boys were identified as core members. The criteria used were ability to influence the behavior of other boys, and ability to attract a following.[13] The same nine boys were later identified by means of the quantitative attendance data.

In analyzing the attendance data, the record of each boy was examined. It was found that these same nine boys had the highest frequency of attendance, ranging from 79 to 121 days in the sample of 134. The identification of this group on the basis of independent qualitative data, and the finding that the same boys were highest in attendance, suggests that the concept of a core group in a street-corner group is valid, precisely definable and significant to the behavior of the group.[14]

These considerations, added to the discussion of the duplication rate in the preceding section, provide evidence that the core group is much more than a statistical construct. Additionally, although the data are not discussed in detail here, records were made each evening of several instances of companionship choice. That is, notice was taken of subgroups of boys who were associating in some activity apart from the rest of the group, either talking together, engaged in some activity together, or just standing apart. Also, the changing composition of the group as boys came and went was recorded. The total instances of companionship choice for each month (75 to 100) were then arranged in a matrix, and by manipulation of rows and columns, three subgroups became apparent.[15] The core members distributed themselves among all of these subgroups in each month except March, in which they were all in one subgroup. This example of cohesiveness is believed to be a reaction to the crisis brought on by the riot, and further evidence of the greater solidarity of the core group in comparison to the fringe members. It is also a further indication of the ability of attendance data to reflect the operation of group dynamics.

Analysis

DIFFERENTIAL ATTENDANCE OF CORE AND FRINGE MEMBERS
The hours per boy for the group, while related to total daily man-hours for the group, appears mainly to amplify the fluctuations determined by attendance. Attendance for the fringe group is closely related to group attendance and total daily man-hours, while attendance for the core group and hours per boy for both core and fringe are relatively stable. It appears then, that the behavior which causes greatest fluctuations in total daily man-hours for the group (the solidarity index) is the attendance of fringe members. This, incidentally, is consistent with the common conclusion that a corner group is made up of a nucleus of core members, and an extremely variable number of fringe members.

The specific hypothesis that the amount of time the group spends together is related to its activity is examined in the final section of this paper, in the discussion of solidarity and activity. However, if the proposition is tenable, these patterns of attendance become related to variations in activity and may be seen as part of the mechanism by which the group responds to its changing situation, and by which its activity is regulated.

ANALYSIS OF THE NARRATIVE DATA

LEADERSHIP AND INFLUENCE AS CHARACTERISTICS OF ORGANIZATION
The analysis of the activity reports is used in this section to describe the organization of the group. Organization, as used here imples a status structure of influence and the presence of implcit or explicit group goals. The readiness with which the observer can find evidence of the existence of these, in the boys' reported behavior, is a positive indicator of the level of organization. When little evidence appears in the reports, organization is presumed to be low. Influence is seen in such actions as expressing approval or disapproval, or instructing someone as to proper behavior. Status is judged by the amount of such behavior on the part of a member. Goals are defined as the apparent object of group activity at any given time.

In October there was ready evidence of both a group goal and a structure of influence. The observer reported on October 14, "The Dons have arranged to get a clubroom in the agency . . . It appears that Paul has been the one who has pushed for this arrangement." The boys organized themselves around Paul, identified in this study as the club-segment leader, and directed their behavior toward the goal of becoming an agency club.

One of my earliest conversations with the boys occurred in July, two months before the agency club program started. In it, Paul expressed his persistent concern to involve the boys in this program. He continued to promote the idea among the boys, and apparently tried to recruit into the group boys who would be favorable.

Bobby, the gang-segment leader, was usually opposed to the idea; this gives an insight into the structure of leadership in the group. Another long-enduring interest on the part of many of the boys was to purchase uniform club jackets. Bobby was in favor of this idea but Paul was not. Nonetheless the group made the purchase.

The two leaders often supported each other's conflicting intentions.

Each of them had their own following, but neither could consistently control the entire group. As observed below, the two leaders conferred on group problems, spoke for the group, and even acted as emissaries. Paul was more willing to act in the latter role.

The following excerpt, like the others, is included to illustrate the kinds of records that were kept, as well as to describe these particular situations. It relates an incident in which Paul exercised his influence by introducing, supporting, and encouraging a new boy into membership in the group:

Later, Paul and his group returned in John's car, John drove across the park without any lights on, and then drove around it again, this time with the lights on. When he stopped the riders came over and the boys talked about how they narrowly missed the trees. The other boys did not seem too impressed by this display, at least not as impressed as they were with an earlier fist fight. Some of them seemed somewhat critical, saying that the riders would have been sorry if they had hit an open sewer. . . .

We stayed around talking for a while when Bill, who had been refused admission to the club Wednesday night, said that he would like to break a window. He picked up a rock and after a few comments about where he should throw it he broke a window on the first floor of the project. The boys all ran, some got into John's car, and the others left on foot.

(*Daily Report,* October 10.)

The usual routine for introducing new members like Bill and John was to allow the candidate to "hang around" until the others either rejected him or became accustomed to him. In the latter case, explicit recognition followed, usually in the form of some kind of vote. The outcome of the vote was only rarely negative, and when it was the boys would usually vote again later on. The real issue was whether to have a vote and when it was to occur. Paul was trying to induct the new members without the preliminaries. In the case of John this was not contrary to the boys' desires, but Bill was not generally welcome. No one else, including Bobby, ever attempted this; Paul succeeded.[16] On November 18, Bill was elected into the club.

In contrast to this, a friend of Bobby's spent the whole summer in the process of induction.[17] It is significant, however, that he was much better socialized to the ways of the group when he finally was accepted. There follow a few excerpts about his career. At first the boys tended to be quite critical of Jim and ridicule everything he did. One time he was quite aggressive toward a smaller boy, completely in keeping with ordinarily acceptable and desirable behavior according to the norms of this group:

A young boy who appeared to be ten or eleven approached on the sidewalk and wanted to pass between the stand and the building. Jim was in his way, and the boy stood and waited and looked at Jim. Jim asked him what he wanted and he said to go through. Jim looked at him as if the boy was being impertinent and told the kid he could go around the stand in the street. Then Jim threatened to beat up the boy and approached him menacingly. The boy stood up to him and offered to fight. Meanwhile, the others were commenting and antagonizing the boy. Finally they let the boy past and everyone started commenting and criticizing Jim for picking on such a little kid. . . . The boys knew the kid's sister and informed Jim that the boy had six sisters and five bigger brothers. . . .

(*Daily Report,* July 17.)

This had occurred more than a month after Jim had begun to associate with the group. The following excerpts reveal how the other members acted toward him even after he was in association with the group for some time:

Earlier Jim said he was owed money by Jack and he intended to get it that night. Before he went to the shack Paul told Johnny that Jim wanted his money and that he hadn't better come around if he didn't have it. But he didn't seem to care. Apparently he was correct in not caring because Jim didn't say anything to him.

(*Daily Report,* July 25.)

The same day I discussed the organization of the Dons with another one of the "detached workers":

Andy and I spoke a little of the organization of the Dons. He feels that it is very loose at present and I agree; there are two leaders now, Bobby who is top man and Paul who is second. They are also divided into at least two cliques, and a group of unattached members. *There are a number of boys hanging around who are not considered members; Jim and Phil are such.* In Andy's view, Bobby is well respected and the boys turn to him for leadership because of his good sense, while Paul is feared for his strength and aggressiveness.

(*Daily Report,* July 25.)

Jim went on to gain more and more status and to become an important, well-accepted member. Bill became quite prominent during the critical period of February, March and April, but soon after ceased his association with the group, never having gained much respect from the members.

Further discussion of the process of induction and the dynamics of status in the group is reported elsewhere.[18] We are concerned here with illustrating the kind of leadership and organization which existed. The ability to act successfully without general support of the group, and even to deviate, and still have the acceptance of the group is one mark of leadership. It is not the same kind of leadership as the kind wherein one influences and guides a consensus, but it is still leadership.

CHANGES IN ORGANIZATION AND LEVEL OF ORGANIZATION   As seen in well-attended meetings, parties, and socials, and in organization around various tasks and projects of the club, the group showed a continually increasing level of organization. Late in November, however, the boys began more frequently to raise questions about Paul's leadership. One report indicates that several higher-status members interfered with Paul's selection of a clubroom. Another states that, on November 25, the members elected one of the girls to the presidency of the club and made Paul the vice-president. Also, in November, Bobby, the leader of the gang, began to absent himself from the club, to attract a small group into association with him, and to demonstrate his influence in other ways. To understand the shifts of group organization, it is necessary to understand that the boys' interests alternated between club and gang goals. This duality is seen in the division of feeling toward the gang leaders and in a marked difference in the behavior of the leaders.

Under Bobby's leadership, the boys started having meetings of the Dons separate from those of the recreational agency club. These began late in November. Bobby, who was never enthusiastic about or active in club affairs, or Gene, one of the core members, presided over these meetings. Paul attended most, but never presided. He had always presided over the agency club meetings along with the president. Bobby was able to initiate these meetings and not care whether they were well conducted, or even, at first, well attended, partly because of the characteristics of his role as gang leader.

The gang goals include little that requires efficient performance of tasks. The gang leader can therefore be casual about developing his following, relate himself to the members in a more personal manner, and try to win loyalties of the more popular members. The club leader, however, is concerned about the performance of tasks and must choose followers from among those willing to work. These are not always the boys he likes, nor the most popular, nor the most solidly entrenched members. Also, unlike the gang leader, he must often relate himself to the members in a formal, instrumental way which is uncomfortable, at least for members of the Dons and apparently for many corner boys.

The fact that there is concern with both fighting and club activities at the same time is further evidence of duality of interest. This fact also enables the observer to make a useful distinction between "main interests" from time to time, by determining the degree to which members just talk about fighting as opposed to placing themselves in a position where fighting is imminent. Such a distinction is useful as an aid in assessing the level of organization. If lower-status members, for example, rather than leaders, place the group in a position of imminent conflict, it may be taken as evidence of disorganization in the group.[19]

Interest in club activities fell in December and many of the members began to gather in a nearby restaurant under Bobby's leadership. Some lower-status members who had been recruited by Paul in October (Bill among them), participated in this change of loyalties, and a conflict between Paul and Bobby became apparent when some of the very-high-status boys also changed loyalties (after a Christmas party). One interesting expression of this change was the fact that Paul was the only member who said he was satisfied with the Christmas party. One other core member went so far as to say that the food was good. All others said nothing or were critical.

The fact that the boys left the club in the process of changing loyalties and that low-status members became influential in the group indicates that Bobby did not just usurp Paul's position but started a basic structural realignment. This implies a prior disorganization. The apparent disorganization of the preceding month was therefore real.

Interest in gang activities became more prominent. Apparently as an attempt to enhance their own position, several of the lower-status members actively participated in a growing conflict with another group. The boys again changed the location of their gatherings. The new gathering-place was three miles from the Dons' neighborhood and in the neighborhood of the group with which the conflict was developing. Paul had made unsuccessful attempts to arbitrate this conflict, even going on January 5 as emissary to discuss the dispute with members of the other group. It appeared however that Bobby encouraged the boys in their conflict, as in the following report:

. . . On the way back, Tommy told how a couple of the Circles had come into the restaurant and were very nice to him. He said they talked to Bobby about stopping the Dons from fighting them but Bobby told them there was no stopping them now, as supposedly a number of other clubs from Thompson Street have joined the Dons. . . .

Earl repeated a theme that he has put forth in the past, namely that the reason people are getting smart with the Dons is because they have been inactive for so long. . . .

When Paul came into the place the boys told him about the fight they were going to have. They also told him that some of the Circles had phoned them this evening to try and get out of the fight. Paul seemed to think that this would be reason not to go but the boys told him they were not going to let the Circles cop a plea again. Paul then said, "Well, lots of luck to you," and told me that "If the guys think this is going to be a pushover, they've got another thought coming."

(*Daily Report,* February 13.)

A few days later many of the members were arrested while watching a fight between one of the Dons (a member of low status) and one of the boys from the other group. This incident is an example of placing the group in a position of imminent conflict, characteristic of the gang orientation. The fact that it was uncontrollable, and led by lower-status members, indicated the degree of disorganization. Early in March the boys participated in a riot originally intended as an attack on some Negro boys with whom another conflict had started. This conflict also was initiated by lower-status members. This riot, as mentioned above, received considerable attention from the police and newspapers. There were banner headlines, front page pictures and feature articles for several days. A number of the Dons and many strangers assembled and milled on the street near the corner. Suddenly someone threw a rock through a window and the mob dispersed, running in all directions and breaking windows in the process. Although considerable damage was done, the police prevented the activity from reaching serious proportions, as it might have done had there been a re-assembly, by arresting several of the boys.

Several events in the two months following the riot suggest that the group was experiencing an increase in organization as well as continuation of interest in gang activities. They participated in formal meetings with representatives of the group of Negro boys who were objects of the hostility expressed in the riot. Bobby refused to participate in these meetings but encouraged Paul to do so. Paul reported to Bobby on the proceedings of each meeting. Bobby teased him one time, saying that Paul would some day be famous as a great peacemaker, and then added that he, Bobby, would paint his face red, yellow and brown and be King of Brotherhood. The satire appeared to reflect the attitude of most of the boys and reflects Bobby's ascendance as leader during the period.

Second, there were more frequent expressions among the boys of the "proper" form of interpersonal relationships in the group. In contrast with the recruiting done by Paul in October, the group was "polled" before the introduction of a recruit at this time. Third, the conflict with the Circles continued, but no individual fights were held and an older group was called upon to help resolve the issues and suppress the conflict by a show of support for the Dons. The show of support was done in a way that made fighting appear to be out of the question, as each of the older boys was accompanied by his girl-friend. Other disputes were initiated with other groups, but this time by high-status members, and all the disputes were very highly controlled.

At least twice, early in April, it was noted that Tommy, one of the core members, severely criticized and insulted two of the lower-status members who were prominent in the Circles' conflict and threatened them with beatings if they caused any more trouble. Also, the group resisted attempts on the part of a Mexican clique to involve them in affairs and conflicts in the Mexican neighborhood. The Mexican clique then discontinued participation with the Dons. Paul also made overt demonstration of his subordination to Bobby.

The gang orientation continued and became firmly established in April. The boys in one instance adopted a uniform front of deception of the authorities in regard to the breaking of some school building windows. This deception was diffused even among non-members to the point where a non-member, on being arrested, tried to assume the blame for shooting at the windows. Open and obvious violative behavior, particularly vandalism, became quite common. This performance was by lower-status members. In May the two leaders withdrew from frequent participation with the group for approximately a month. From May through August, the group took on a segmented appearance. The leaders' return in July was followed by attempts to organize the group by getting the "segments" to gather in one place, and by re-entering the group in the recreational agency program. Neither of these attempts succeeded immediately. In August, with the group still quite segmented, the boys commenced a series of assaults and fights with Negro boys in the neighborhood. Outsiders frequently participated in these incidents. Also, at this time some of the members participated in several fights at a bathing beach.

The boys oriented themselves toward gang goals at times when the group was organized and at times when it was relatively disorganized. The same is true of club goals. The degree of organization in the group varies widely and does not appear to depend on the content, violative or not, of the boys' behavior. However, during disorganized times, the likelihood increases that more erratic persons, who are not highly regarded by the boys, will exert influence. It may be this aspect of group life which results in the gang appearing, as it does at times, to be a mob led by disturbed people who assume leadership for their own purposes. This kind of leadership does not imply much control over the group, since the group at these times appears to be very deficient in any kind of control. Leadership, in the sense of continuing influence over the members, appears to go to boys who are held in high regard by the members and who possess many of the qualities ordinarily associated with leadership.[20] Thus, the fact that disorganization occurs does not indicate that the gang is completely outside the scope of explanation by the usual theories of group dynamics, and does indicate that it is necessary to combine ideas of collective behavior and ideas of group dynamics to understand what many gangs do.

VARIABILITY IN MEANING OF MEMBERSHIP   Membership is defined as it is in this study so that attendance can be counted. Such a conception of membership might tend to give the group a more organized appearance than is warranted. However, the definition has a basic similarity to the boys' own conceptions, based on participation as evidence of membership.

Among the boys there was little agreement as to size of group or definition of membership at any given time. The reason for this disparity was not ignorance of who was and who was not a member. Consensus was high whenever the status of a particular person was at question. The fact of participation was at all times the final criterion. It was the abstract ideas of definition of membership and size of group which varied from boy to boy and in relation to varying purposes. Discrepancies in size and composition appeared when the boys were considering membership as related to different goals or to certain projects. Thus one must be clear, when considering membership, about the situation to which the use of the idea of membership is relevant. Also, the fact that the boys' conceptions vary while the researcher's remains the same emphasizes the need to be specific about the definition of membership when generalizing about gangs.

A CHRONOLOGY OF GROUP ACTIVITY   In order to examine the proposition that group activity is related to changes in unity as reflected in the index it is necessary to abstract categories of action from the daily narrative reports. These categories are intended to comprise a behavioristic index of changes in the frequency of group action in general and differences in the content of this action as well. The diary was examined in detail and all activity meeting the definitions of the following categories was noted.

The first, of most general significance, is "actions of the entire group" (A.G.). Then, because of a particular interest in delinquent activities as a special type of group activity, a subcategory of "delinquencies of the entire group" (D.G.) was defined. These are considered separately because delinquency was expected to show fluctuations similar to activity in general. The high frequency of delinquencies by the Dons adds to the interest and utility of delinquency as a class of activity. Since there is a similar interest in other delinquent acts of members, another category is defined as "delinquencies of individuals and cliques" (I.D.).

The following is a part of the chronology of group activities:

Feb. 15   The group decided to buy sweaters. (A.G.)
Feb. 17   A member had a fight with a member of Circles; those watching were arrested. (D.G.)

Feb. 28   A member was driving a stolen car. (I.D.)

Mar. 1   Two members tried to steal a car battery. (I.D.)

Mar. 2   A member fired a gun at a group of Negro boys and members chased the Negro boys. (D.G.)

Mar. 2   A member started a fight with some Negro boys. (I.D.)
          (The participation of the entire group was not apparent in this particular incident.)

Mar. 3   Many of the members participated in a riot. (D.G.)

Actions of the entire group are defined as those either involving the total membership at any given time, or planned, or supported, or anticipated and tolerated by the entire membership. Unless the participation of the entire group was obvious, the act was not so classified. A delinquent act is one which would be so judged by the police at the time and place it occurred if called to their attention.[21] Finally, all those delinquencies which are not actions of the entire group were considered to be delinquencies of individuals and cliques.

A list of the activities, both group and individual which are included in the Daily Reports, and which meet these definitions, amounts to 30 actions of the entire group (including 13 delinquent actions), and 39 delinquencies of individuals and cliques. The reliability of this procedure is obviously questionable. However, the list was made for analysis of another index of solidarity sometime before the present analysis was conceived. One reason the excerpts and part of the chronology are provided, is so that the reader may know the nature of the qualitative data used. It is the rate of occurrence of these activities which is to be related to the variations in group solidarity.

LEVEL OF ORGANIZATION, MAN-HOURS, AND ACTIVITY

First, the relation between the rise and fall in degree of organization and the rise and fall of total daily man-hours is examined, and then the relation between daily man-hours and changes in frequency of group action.

The narrative material, related above, indicates that the group underwent a process of increasing organization in the fall. Late in December and throughout January and February the withdrawal from the club by the gang leader, and the restructuring of the group under his leadership, marked a period of disorganization. Leadership conflict and attempts by low-status members to increase their status became prominent as this disorganization progressed. After the riot, throughout March and April until another withdrawal by the leadership in May, signs of increasing organization were again observed. Stability of the gang orientation and segmentation of the group are aspects of a period of slow decline which ended in August, and was in turn followed by reinvolvement of active leadership. A rough parallel to this rise and decline exists in the curve of daily man-hours.[22] (See Figure 1.)

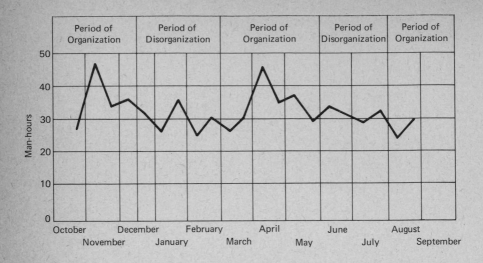

FIGURE 1: Semi-monthly means of the total daily man-hours spent together for the entire group, divided into periods of organization and disorganization as described in the analysis of the narrative reports.

The periods where the high points occur are also periods of a high level of organization. The periods where the low points occur are the periods described above as relatively disorganized. The parallel is by no means exact. One interesting difference between man-hours and the division by analysis of the qualitative reports is that the decline in man-hours starts in both instances of disorganization long before the disorganization is apparent in the narrative. The rise in solidarity takes place briefly, during the early part of the organized periods. The rise is precipitous, while the decline is gradual. This is consistent with the theory underlying this paper. Solidarity, it appears, has a tendency to decline. It reaches a level where it becomes threatening to the boys. There is a spurt of group activity which generates interest and increases attendance and solidarity.

In order to test the relationship between the rate of occurrence of activities, and the trends in man-hours, it is necessary to divide the curve into periods of rise and decline. It is difficult to determine valid division points by looking at the curve by itself. We will consider a period of rise to be marked by the beginning of the precipitous rise occurring early in the organized periods, and consider that they end when the rise reaches its highest point. The results of this analysis are presented in Table 3.

From this analysis it appears that group activity in general, including group delinquencies, increases after low points in man-hours. The rate of activity then decreases after a high point is reached, only to increase again following the next low point.

There are many obvious problems in this analysis. The curve can be divided in many ways. It can be divided to dissipate the relationships. This is more true of activity in general than of the subset of delinquent

TABLE 3. Trends of Change in the Number of Man-Hours and Trends in Frequency of Activities

Period	Direction of Change	Number of Semi-Monthly Periods	Number of Activities per Semi-Monthly Period	
			A.G.*	D.G.*
October to mid-November	Rising	3	2.67	1.33
Mid-November through February	Declining	7	1.14	0.14
March through mid-April	Rising	3	1.33	1.00
Mid-April through July	Declining	7	0.86	0.14
August through September	Rising	4	1.00	1.00
Totals		24	1.25	0.54

* A.G. = activities of the entire group; D.G. = delinquencies of the entire group.

activities. (The relationship is stronger for group delinquencies.) It appears that these boys found it easier to act as a group in a delinquent manner than in a conventional manner. The fact that the author helped the boys in carrying out conventional group activities and not with their delinquent ones adds to the importance of the relation between activity and group delinquency. In fact he worked against the hypothesis presented here by encouraging them in activities while solidarity was high.

Although the curve of solidarity can be divided in a way which eliminates the appearance of the relationship found here, no way has been found to divide it to show the opposite relationship. Because of these problems, sufficient data have been included that the reader may investigate alternative arrangements himself. It is also possible that other combinations of the data will produce better indices of solidarity. In spite of these difficulties, however, considerable leverage is gained on these problems by the use of the kind of data presented here. At least one can approach the problems in relatively objective terms.

INTERPRETATION OF FINDINGS

These findings are interpreted on the basis of the proposition that the solidarity of the group is important to the boys and its decline beyond a certain level is threatening to them. They respond to this threat by group action which arouses interest, and attracts and reinvolves members.[23] The content of their action is quite often delinquent. This is a result of the orientation the boys have developed, making delinquency easier for the group than conventional activity. This orientation arises from the tradition of the neighborhood, the response of the conventional community to their action, and the history of the group. Also the boys are quite delinquent individually. They have problems of being rejected at school and in other areas of contact with conventional society. They often express considerable animosity toward teachers, police, certain ethnic groups (especially Negroes and Puerto Ricans), people from other neighborhoods and even some from their own neighborhood. In many ways the Dons were not well integrated into the life of the neighborhood. They "hung around" the public housing project and many lived in the project. This is not to say that they were not a part of the life of the neighborhood, but that they were a marginal group.

The boys saw many of the people whom they considered enemies to be a threat to them, to the group, to the neighborhood, and even to their way of life. It is partly in regard to these threats that the group is important to them. They see the group as a defense. There are many other threats, particularly from other adolescent groups. Altercations frequently arise between them and Negro and Puerto Rican groups, and groups from other locations or neighborhoods. Many of these arise out of interaction in school and other places where adolescents are brought together. Thus the group is important as a matter of self-defense. Finally, in the existing situation, there was a likelihood that a boy who did not belong to a group was always eligible for harassment by any of the numerous groups in the area.

It is also clear that these boys were comfortable in interaction with each other and desired such interaction. They are socialized to depend heavily on the response of their peers for the organization of their own life. Gans' discussion of peer-group society is especially relevant in this regard. Although he is not concerned with describing delinquent groups, his remarks seem to apply rather well to some aspects of the Dons' life when he discusses the West Ender's dependence on his group:

The West End adolescent, as noted before, is alive only with his peer group; outside it, he exists as a quiet and almost passive individual. With adults, he is likely to be lethargic and sullen, seeking always to minimize contact with them. In the peer group, however, the style of life is one of action-seeking. Much of the conflict between adolescent and adult therefore is that between the action-seeking and the routine-seeking patterns.

In the adolescent peer group, manifesting the episodic search for action in an almost pure, ideal-typical form, life alternates between killing time and searching for action. Some of it takes place right within the group, in a dialectic of conformity and competitiveness through which the individual realizes himself.[24]

The development of their own conception of their legitimate social roles may depend on experiences in an all-male peer group. Inability to participate successfully in such a group may be a threat to their own self conception. Miller found that the all-male adolescent group is a necessity in lower-class life:

The "hanging" peer group is a unit of particular importance for the adolescent male. In many cases it is the most stable and solidary primary group he has ever belonged to; for boys reared in female-based households the corner group provides the first real opportunity to learn essential aspects of the male role in the context of peers facing similar problems of sex-role identification.[25]

Opportunities for occupation in the conventional world did not seem to be a great concern of these boys. They felt a heavy dependence on relatives, and on friends with "connections" to get jobs later on. As stated above in regard to integration, they were a marginal group. Perhaps this marginality accounts for the mixture of fighting and stealing in their activities. At any rate, they could not be seen as clearly participating in either a criminal or a conflict culture, but in a mixture.

Rather than the causes of delinquency, our main concern has been group solidarity and the influence of its changes on group activity. Though at times the group acts like a mob, these same boys make up a more or less well-organized group. In fact it appears that, unless the group is disorganized, mob-like behavior is unlikely.

The behavior of the boys may be understood as arising in part from experiences in activities which they pursue in response to concern aroused by instability in their peer group. The content of their behavior is to some extent culturally delimited; standards, definitions, and values are learned in association with their peers in the street corner group. But when they act, and how often, are controlled in part by variation in the solidarity of the group.

NOTES

1. William F. Whyte, *Street Corner Society*, Chicago: University of Chicago Press, 1943.

2. Lewis Yablonsky, "The Delinquent Gang as a Near Group," *Social Problems*, 7 (Fall, 1959), pp. 108–117.

3. Harold W. Pfautz, "Near Group Theory and Collective Behavior," *Social Problems*, 9 (Fall, 1961), pp. 167–174.

4. James F. Short, "Street Corner Groups and Patterns of Delinquency: A Progress Report," *American Catholic Sociological Review*, 24 (Spring, 1963), pp. 13–32.

5. James F. Short, and Fred L. Strodtbeck, "The Response of Gang Leaders to Status Threats: An Observation on Group Process and Delinquent Behavior," *American Journal of Sociology*, 68 (March, 1963), pp. 571–579.

6. Examination of group factors in delinquency, especially those factors having to do with processes in the group, has been closely restricted to observation in an institutional setting; the observation of such a group process in the natural setting is quite uncommon. See Short and Strodtbeck, *op. cit.*, p. 592.

7. Yablonsky, *op. cit.*, in his discussion of "near groups" points out that a gang may be the product of the attention of "detached workers": "Approaching the gang as a group, when it is not, tends to project onto it a structure which formerly did not exist." This is especially likely to happen in studies which do not make detailed observations over a long period of time. But even informal observation can establish the validity of a conception of a number of boys as a group. For example, in the case presented here, the group persisted for a number of years before and after the study was done and it was recognized as a group with a name by numerous adolescents, adults of the community, social workers, and the police and courts. The group, including a conception of who were members and some idea of a structure, existed several years before the author arrived. These conceptions were contained in written records of former observations of

the group, and it was in terms of these conceptions that he was introduced to the group. The author's informal experiences with the group and all the above mentioned people confirmed the existence of this consensus as to the identity and reality of the group.

8. The observer was employed by a civic group of local residents, whose sanction was invaluable to the research. This group had employed, over the years, a number of young men to associate with and, hopefully to influence some of the more troublesome boys in the area. Records of this work, including daily accounts of the activity of the Dons, the preceding and succeeding groups on their corner, and other similar groups, were valuable in understanding the boys' activity. The civic group has been working in varying degrees of intensity with groups and persons in this neighborhood for over twenty years in efforts to prevent delinquency. Much of the work has been conducted in cooperation with a state welfare agency. The detached worker program was coordinated with similar activities in a city-wide program. The wealth of information and experience represented by these efforts has been a source as well as a test for some of the ideas presented here.

9. These days were scattered throughout the year. The author deliberately made his work week irregular, and varied days off from week to week. Occasionally other duties would keep him from meeting the group. Sundays are somewhat underrepresented in the observations. When the author arrived after 7:30 P.M. or left before 10:30 P.M., it was not possible to observe the man-hours. Therefore a number of days had to be left out of the sample. There was no indication that the days observed differ in any systematic way from those not observed.

10. In no case was a boy's attendance as a member recorded until one week after his first observed appearance. Membership in a gang is a vague status and has not been precisely defined in the literature. For example, in Short's and Strodtbeck's researches in Chicago, the identification of members was largely a matter of the judgment of the "detached worker," it was not operationally defined, and the worker's criteria were not specified in detail. This is due to both the condition of field work and the diffuseness of gang membership itself. Objectivity was maintained by means of weekly interviews of the "detached workers" and by field observations by the research staff. See Short, "Street Corner Groups and Patterns of Delinquency," op. cit., p. 17.

11. The purpose of this was to avoid the possibility of failing to record the attendance of any boy who, though absent for an extended period, for example by being in jail, was still important to the group. If such an absent member never returned, nothing would be lost, because the data refer only to boys whose presence with the group was actually observed.

12. Numerous indices of solidarity were attempted, some of which are described below. This one was chosen because of its concreteness. direct observability, objectivity and simplicity.

13. The identification of core members by any method which is demonstrably objective is difficult in this kind of field operation. Attendance records are useful; in this case they support the judgment of the author. There is, however, the need to assess characteristics like status and influence. For example, the boy who makes no suggestions or whose suggestions are often rejected is presumed to be of low status. Attracting a following is seen especially well in changes of meeting places, as described below.

This problem recurs in the literature; explicit definitions of status, and the criteria observed are not always stated operationally. See Whyte, *op. cit.*, pp. 11–14, 326–327, and Short and Strodtbeck, "The Response of Gang Leaders to Status Threats," *loc. cit.*, pp. 577–579. Short and Strodtbeck discuss the complexity of (often deliberately concealed) status in the gang. An operational definition is obviously difficult; Short and Strodtbeck offer no such definition in this article. In the present research it is extremely important that the author's judgment of status be supported, at least in the case of "core" status by the attendance data, and the companionship choice data discussed below.

14. Such calculations do not preclude the possibility of change in the core group over a longer period of time, as well as the possibility of identifying a different core group if a different time period were observed. This consideration re-emphasizes the necessity, in any study of corner groups, of taking into account the extent and continuity of time of observations.

15. An illustration of the method is to be found in George C. Homans, *The Human Group*, New York: Harcourt Brace, 1950, p. 83.

16. Before the author came in contact with the group, Bobby had supported a friend of his in gaining membership. However, Bobby kept this boy in a personal friendship relationship. Paul wanted Bill brought into membership in his own right. This difference in approaches has to do with the instrumental-expressive difference between the two leaders. Paul as the task leader was not able to continue to lend personal support to an unpopular boy for a very long period of time because this might alienate the other boys from whom he wished to demand task performance. He needed the additional support of the new members but could not continue to be responsible for their actions. Bobby, in contrast, made no task demands and could stay aligned with his not-so-popular friend, and depend on his personal attraction to maintain the loyalty of his followers. It made no difference to him if he alienated someone this week; he would come back next week. Paul, however, when he needed task performance, needed it at a particular time; next week might be too late.

17. Neither of these inductees were strangers. They had known the members of the Dons for years, had attended school with them and probably had associated closely with them at times in the past. Neither however was a member of the group.

18. Leon R. Jansyn, "Group Structure and Ceremony in a Street Corner Group" (unpublished manuscript), 1962.

19. It is also difficult to determine whether this group is properly called a fighting gang. Though they conceived of themselves as such, and received considerable publicity as a warring gang from the metropolitan press, they were never observed in anything which might be called a "gang fight." There were legends of gang fights when they were younger, but their notoriety seems to be based on participation in a riot and numerous episodic assaults. This is not to minimize the harm done, but it may help to specify what is and is not a "gang war."

20. A similar conclusion was drawn from data concerning later research by Short and Strodtbeck, discussed by Short in "Street Corner Groups and Patterns of Delinquency: A Progress Report," *American Catholic Sociological Review*, 24 (Spring, 1963), pp. 29–32.

21. The problem of making a useful definition of delinquency is widely recog-

nized, but not yet solved. For example, see the discussion by Herbert A. Bloch and Frank T. Flynn, *Delinquency*, New York: Random House, 1956.

22. In a previous report on these data, a different index was used. See Leon R. Jansyn, "Solidarity and Delinquency in a Street Corner Group: A Study of the Relationship Between Changes in Specified Aspects of Group Structure and Variations in the Frequency of Delinquent Activity" (unpublished M.A. thesis, University of Chicago, 1960). The former index, however, did not parallel any observed development of the group. On the contrary the social process of the group was divided according to divisions in the purely empirical trends of the index of solidarity. The present index has a different configuration of trends and, upon analysis of the activity reports from the point of view of "degree of organization," was found (as noted here) to conform to trends in organization. The present index was therefore considered more useful. Further relationships, such as role differentiation and identification of core members, confirmed the greater utility of the simple measure of daily man-hours.

23. There are alternative interpretations, and the data are not conclusive. One might see increasing activity merely as a probable result of the influx of fringe members. The organizational change, however, would still be a phenomenon of interest as an intervening variable if this were the case. That the influx of fringe members is due solely to some extragroup cause is unlikely, however, in view of the precipitous increases in fringe and entire group attendance and man-hours, as opposed to the gradualness of decline which follows each of the increases.

24. Herbert J. Gans, *The Urban Villagers*, Glencoe: The Free Press, 1962, p. 65, and generally pp. 64–83.

25. Walter B. Miller, "Lower Class Culture as a Generating Milieu of Gang Delinquency," *Journal of Social Issues*, 14 (1958), p. 14.

QUESTIONS

1. What are the two distinct bodies of data used in this research? What "variables" are derived from each body of data?
2. What problems of "sampling" of observational periods are involved in research, such as this, which is extended over a long period of time?
3. The author refers to "many obvious problems in this analysis." What are some of these problems?
4. Use the data in Table 1 to practice the computation of means and standard deviations, and to check the author's work.
5. See if you can derive the results in the last two columns of Table 3 from the equivalent A.G. and D.G. columns of Table 1.

Educational Mobility and Access: Growth and Paradoxes

WILLIAM G. SPADY

Once the decision is made to use quantitative techniques to analyze research findings, the researcher is faced with a wide variety of analytical techniques and procedures. Which alternative or alternatives are chosen depends on many considerations: for example, the number of variables, level of measurement, degree of precision desired, overall research design (experimental-nonexperimental, sampling techniques employed), types of theoretical issues being pursued, researcher's awareness or knowledge of available techniques, and access to computation resources (computers, desk calculators, graduate students). The most commonly used and perhaps the simplest procedures are tabular and percentage analyses.

Constructing a table that speaks to questions raised by a theoretical issue or by an earlier step in the analysis is not always an obvious or simple task. The same can be said of the interpretation of the resulting tables. Tables differ in the number of variables involved, the reference of the cell entry, and the kind of statistic (frequency, proportion, percentage) that appears in a cell. The reader should carefully inspect each table and note, among other things, the base numbers, if the cell entries add to the marginal entries, and if not, why not. If you do not understand how conclusions result from the tables, you do not understand the meaning of the table in the analysis.

In the following article by Spady, tabular and percentage analyses are used as the principle modes of analysis. Spady makes use of several different types of tables, which can introduce some difficulty for the superficial reader. Pay careful attention to the interchange between text and tables, because in that interchange lies the worth of the tables.

■ One of the truisms of American sociology is the marked increase since the turn of the century in median years of schooling among successive cohorts of young people. Since formal education has traditionally been viewed as a means to occupational and social mobility, the expansion of secondary and college enrollment rates is often interpreted as a sign of increasing equality of educational and social opportunity. We propose to show, however, that utilization of higher education has spread much more slowly among young men with poorly educated fathers than among those with well-educated fathers. The conditional probabilities of attending and completing college (given that one completed high school and entered college respectively) have in fact decreased over time for the sons of poorly educated men. The educational attainments of Negroes, moreover, are consistently lower than those of whites holding father's education constant.

It is necessary, therefore, that we distinguish between the aggregate and distributional trends in education. It is important to recognize also that in

Reprinted from *American Journal of Sociology* 73 (1967), 273–286, with permission of The University of Chicago Press.

a population with a rising median schooling, a youth can receive more schooling than his father without advancing educationally relative to his age peers. Unless we examine how aggregate increases in school attainment are distributed among youth from different social origins, there is no way of knowing to what extent children from any given social stratum may have benefited from these improvements. Therefore, patterns of upward educational mobility may operate quite independently of rates of access to given levels of education. The children of men who failed to finish elementary school experience upward educational mobility merely by reaching high school, whereas the sons of college graduates must themselves finish college just to "inherit" their father's educational status. It is entirely possible, therefore, that expanding proportions of children with poorly educated fathers may be upwardly mobile in schooling without improvement in their chances of college attendance.

The reason for concerning ourselves with this topic extends beyond an interest in "democratization" of educational opportunities. According to findings by James A. Davis, a son must obtain more schooling than his father to achieve the same level of occupation.[1] In addition, the proportion of white-collar workers with less than a high school diploma is diminishing, and college graduates are becoming more "professionalized." Stipulated levels of schooling become progressively more necessary, if not sufficient, for obtaining the more preferred jobs. These wider issues of mobility are not explored in this paper, but an exploration of the patterns of educational mobility can contribute to a more adequate determination of the schooling-mobility matrix. For example, has completing high school and college improved for children with poorly educated fathers as much as for the children of college graduates? Have the rates of college attendance and graduation improved for high school graduates of all social backgrounds? Has completion of high school and college improved as much for non-whites as for whites with similar backgrounds?[2]

The dependent variable in this report is the highest level of education obtained by the respondent. The three independent variables we shall consider are the respondent's age, race, and father's educational background. The latter is broken into four categories (less than eight years,[3] eight through eleven years, high school graduation, and one year of college or more) and serves as a rough index of family socioeconomic status. Respondents' ages are also classified into four categories: 25–34, 35–44, 45–54, and 55–64. (Given these categories, we should keep in mind that the youngest group would have moved from high school to college in the postwar years, the second group during the late thirties and World War II, the third during the late twenties and the Depression, and the oldest after World War I.) The data are also divided by race: white and non-white.

FINDINGS

The proportion of sons with more schooling than their fathers has increased over time from about half of the 55–64 age group to two-thirds of the 25–34-year-olds (Table 1).[4] Both educational "inheritance"

TABLE 1. Intergenerational Educational Mobility* of Respondent by Age

	Educational Mobility			Total	
Age	Upward	Stable	Downward	%	N†
25–34	63.5	29.8	6.6	99.9	(10,612)
35–44	62.4	30.6	7.0	100.0	(11,608)
45–54	54.5	37.7	7.8	100.0	(10,161)
55–64	47.0	42.4	10.6	100.0	(7,585)

* The term "intergenerational educational mobility" refers to a comparison of son's educational attainment with that of his parents, in this case his father.
† Base N for the percentage expressed in thousands.

and downward mobility have decreased. The chances of being upwardly mobile educationally have improved despite steady improvements in paternal levels of schooling.

Although upward educational mobility historically has facilitated upward social mobility, the Davis findings suggest that whether sons have more education than their fathers is less important in explaining social stratification or mobility than is the actual amount of education a son received (irrespective of his father's educational or occupational status). We must take into account not only aggregate rates of educational mobility but differential rates of attainment of levels of education that serve as criteria in employment. This brings us to the question: has completion of high school (or college) improved equally for children from all social strata? By using father's education as a measure of son's status of origin, we find that it has not (Table 2).

In this table we are considering access to four different levels of education: (a) reaching high school,[5] (b) high school graduation, (c) at least one year of college, and (d) college graduation. Each cell within one section of the table reports the proportion of men with a particular family background and age who had completed a specified level of education. A cursory scanning of the table reveals that completion of successively higher levels of education has risen steadily over time for sons from each stratum of origin. However, we find for each age cohort that a son's chances of completing any given level of schooling are also associated positively with his father's education.

For example, the upper-left-hand cell of each section represents the (3,969,000) men aged 25–34 whose fathers had less than eight years of schooling. By tracing this group from Section A through Section D of Table 2, we find that 83 per cent completed grade school, 45 per cent graduated from high school, 14 per cent had at least a year of college, and over 6 per cent received a bachelor's degree. Among sons of the same age cohort having college-educated fathers, however, 99 percent reached high school, 93 per cent finished high school, 78 per cent had at least a year of college, and 52 per cent completed college. There are persisting and marked disparities in educational opportunities.[6]

Since for most status categories rates of completion improve consistently across age cohorts,[7] however (the partial Gammas between age and education range from −.180 to −.278 among the four status groups),

TABLE 2. Percentage of Sons Obtaining a Given Level of Education by Age and
Father's Education

	Father's Education				
Son's Age	Less than Eight (%) (1)	Some High School (2)	High School Graduate (3)	Some College or More (4)	Attainment Gap (%) (col. 4 − col. 1)
	A. Reaching High School				
25–34	82.9 (3,969)*	94.6 (4,012)	97.4 (1,518)	99.6 (1,113)	+16.7
35–44	78.7 (5,598)	92.7 (3,803)	97.7 (1,278)	98.8 (929)	+20.1
45–54	70.1 (5,320)	90.9 (3,142)	96.4 (993)	97.6 (706)	+27.5
55–64	60.4 (4,318)	85.8 (2,188)	88.4 (662)	93.0 (417)	+32.6
	B. Graduating from High School				
25–34	44.6	69.4	84.2	92.8	+48.2
35–44	41.2	59.5	79.6	92.8	+51.6
45–54	32.1	46.9	76.0	78.4	+46.3
55–64	19.6	34.3	58.9	73.9	+54.3
	C. Obtaining at Least One Year of College				
25–34	14.2	27.8	44.1	78.0	+63.8
35–44	14.4	22.0	44.9	70.4	+56.0
45–54	11.0	19.1	33.2	62.3	+51.3
55–64	8.4	15.0	31.4	47.3	+39.8
	D. Graduating from College				
25–34	6.5	16.6	24.9	51.7	+45.2
35–44	5.8	11.0	27.5	53.1	+46.3
45–54	5.4	8.9	14.5	37.7	+32.3
55–64	5.4	8.5	16.9	27.6	+22.2
Partial Gammas: son's ed. × age/ father's ed.†	−.203	−.278	−.180	−.251	

* Projected base N for the percentage expressed in thousands.
† Son's Ed. × F. Ed./Age: 25–34, +.513; 35–44, +.482; 45–54, +.470; 55–64, +.507.

one can estimate how much this educational "attainment gap" between
children from the top and bottom strata of our society appears to have
increased or decreased over time. For each age group we subtract the proportion of sons with grade-school–educated fathers who reach a given
level of education from the proportion of their cohorts with college-
educated fathers who complete that level of schooling (Table 2, col. 5).[8]

As we move from Section A to Section D of the table, the pattern of change in this "opportunity gap" definitely reverses. We can see in Section A, for example, that status differences in high school attendance diminish from 33 per cent for the 55–64-year-olds to only 17 per cent for those aged 25–34; that is the diffusion of norms for some high school attendance has become almost universal.

Let us next consider differences in graduation from high school (Section B, col. 5). Except for an irregularity among 45–54-year-olds,[9] there is a small decline in status disparities over time which will probably continue to close as the percentage of graduates among sons having college-educated fathers approaches 100 per cent, and state attendance requirements are enforced. Yet we cannot overlook the fact that more than half of the youngest men in this low social group lack a high school diploma. For college attendance, by contrast, the gap widens over time. In Section C, the difference between the two extreme status categories increases from 40 to 64 per cent. Although the proportion of sons from the top stratum who reached college increased by over 30 percentage points between the twenties and the fifties, the corresponding percentage among sons from low-status homes rose less than 6 points. The gap in college graduation also widened, from 22 to 45 per cent (Section D). The proportion of sons from low-status homes who finished college has risen imperceptibly while that for sons of college alumni doubled in a period of forty years.

This reversal can also be viewed as a process of shifting educational norms across both social strata and time. As certain levels of education become defined as "basic" to any sort of non-menial employment, the gap in attainment rates between high- and low-status sons diminishes. Simultaneously, however, new and more restrictive sets of criteria become established which also become recognized in time as meaningful alternatives by increasing segments of the population. The rapid rise in college attendance and graduation rates among the sons of college-educated men can be viewed not only as a new momentum in the process of educational diffusion but as the gradual formation of a new educational norm. The extent to which this college gap may level off and even diminish over time depends on the diffusion of this norm throughout all strata of the population.

The discussion of educational attainment has relied up to this point on one method of contrasting the school attainment of children from the "extremes" of American society. Using alternative strategies of analysis would not change the findings or interpretations greatly. If we were to assume that fathers who did not finish grade school have become an atypical[10] group and therefore distort the measurement of "attainment gap," the sons of men who at least reached high school could be set as the "bottom" of the scale instead. Although the size of this new "gap" is always smaller than that shown in Table 2, the patterns of change remain basically the same: The gap decreases over time for high school entrance (7 to 5 per cent) and high school graduation (40 to 23 per cent) but increases over time for college entrance (32 to 50 per cent) and college graduation (19 to 35 per cent).[11]

A closer look at the relative sizes of the original attainment gaps also reveals, however, that the status effects on school completion are less marked at the two extremes of the educational attainment scale (some high school and college graduation) than in the middle completion range. This may be related to ability segregation at the extremes of the scale. Failing to reach high school when high school attendance is viewed as a norm may stem from a definite lack of mental ability. Graduating from college may require very high intelligence irrespective of one's social background. At the intermediate levels of schooling, however, environmental influences operate across an intellectually more heterogeneous population.

This also raises issues concerning the operation of other social influences on educational attainment for which we lack data. We do not know, for example, to what extent the apparent influence of father's education is a proxy for rural-urban differences in the educational composition of the population and in the quality of educational facilities. If limited education is becoming a preponderantly rural (and Southern) phenomenon, then having a poorly educated father may increasingly have meant attending a small town or country school.[12]

Another question of relevance is to what extent not finishing grade school has come to reflect a genuine lack of innate mental ability. Since a substantial part of what we know as intelligence is inherited, being the son of a poorly educated man in an educationally expanding society may have come to mean being the son of a man who lacked the mental ability to go very far in school. Inheriting such low ability is in turn bound to handicap a son's chances of completing his schooling, particularly in the absence of positive family attitudes toward education.[13]

CONDITIONAL PROBABILITIES

If we think of the educational system as, in part, a selection process, sorting out people lacking adequate ability, motivation, and opportunity at various points, large-scale attrition affects children from the lower classes earlier. Since our data show that this selection eventually affects children from all social strata, we might find that low-status sons who have demonstrated the ability and motivation to survive the initial stages have a better chance of surviving the final stages than their high-status cohorts whose mettle has yet to be tested. In light of the expansion of secondary and college enrollments, we would also expect these conditional probabilities to increase over time. The validity of this interpretation can be tested by the data in Table 3.

Unlike the percentages in Table 2, the interpretation of these figures changes for different sections of the table. Each cell in Section A of Table 3 shows what percentage of the men in each age and status cohort who got past grade school eventually graduated from high school. Section B shows what percentage of high school graduates had one to three years of college, and Section C shows what percentage of these college entrants received a degree. For example, among the youngest sons with poorly educated fathers, 54 per cent of those who entered high school eventually finished. Of these graduates (Section B), 31 per cent entered college, and 46 per cent of those who entered received a degree (Section C). Once again we see, however, that the conditional probabilities for sons with college-educated fathers are considerably higher at every stage of education: 93, 84, and 67 per cent respectively. Close inspection of the data in all three sections clearly demonstrates in fact that the hypothesis stated in the preceding paragraph is not valid, since in every row of Sections A and B (and for the two youngest cohorts in Section C) the conditional probabilities increase by at least 20 percentage points as father's education improves. The relatively stable percentages in the bottom two rows of Section C suggest that a leveling of life chances during the college years may have occurred prior to World War II but disappeared again recently.

That social background has had an increasing impact on college attendance and graduation over time is suggested by the magnitude and direction of increase in the partial Gammas between sons' and fathers' education across age cohorts Table 3, col. 6. Since the Gammas in Section B are higher than those in Section C for each age cohort, we can conclude that father's status affects the chances of going from high school to college more than the chances of completing college once you are there. However, in three of the four age cohorts the Gammas in Section A are higher than those in either Sections B or C. This suggests that low family status has been more of a handicap in finishing high school once you got there than in either entering or finishing college.

Although we expect that these conditional probabilities would improve over time for all status groups at each level of education, that is true only for high school graduation. The only status group whose conditional probabilities definitely improve over time for both college entry and graduation is sons of college-educated fathers. The percentage of high school graduates from the top stratum who went on to college increased from 64 to 84 per cent, while the percentage of those college entrants who ultimately received a degree rose from 59 to 76 per cent (for the 35–44-year-olds) but dropped again to 66 per cent for the youngest group.[14] On the other hand, the percentage of high school graduates in the lowest status group who have gone on to college has almost steadily *decreased*.

The opposing attainment trends of the two extreme status categories result in a widening in the college-attendance and college-graduation attainment gaps over time. This again supports our earlier conclusion that college aspirations and attainments are becoming mass phenomena very gradually as high-status norms become diffused and assimilated by successively lower strata of the society. The widening of the gap over time for Sections B and C is reflected in the Gammas between son's education and age across status groups. High-status boys have plus Gammas over time (.217 and .017) while their low-status cohorts have reversed (−.088 and −.145).

While boys with low social origins are slowly catching up with their more fortunate counterparts in terms of basic and intermediate levels of education, they are falling relatively farther behind the latter's rapid increase in college attendance and graduation. It appears, then, that, if anything, boys with uneducated fathers have continued to have only limited chances of obtaining the educational credentials necessary for "getting to the top," particularly in comparison to boys whose fathers had already arrived there.

TABLE 3. Conditional Probabilities of Respondents Obtaining a Given Level of Education by Age and Father's Education

| | Father's Education | | | | Attainment Gap (%) (col. 4 − col. 1) (5) | Partial Gammas: Son's Ed.×Father's Ed./Age |
Son's Age	Less than Eight (%) (1)	Some High School (2)	High School Graduate (3)	Some College or More (4)		
A. Proportion Graduating from High School Among Those Reaching High School						
25–34	53.9 (3,287)*	73.2 (3,795)	86.5 (1,480)	93.0 (1,110)	+39.1	+.530
35–44	52.4 (5,408)	64.2 (3,525)	81.5 (1,247)	93.9 (919)	+41.5	+.317
45–54	45.6 (3,737)	51.8 (2,853)	79.1 (957)	80.2 (690)	+34.6	+.362
55–64	32.5 (2,611)	39.9 (1,879)	66.6 (585)	79.2 (389)	+46.7	+.407
Partial Gammas: Son's Ed.×Age/F. Ed.	+.236	+.361	+.269	+.391		
B. Proportion with at Least One Year of College Among Those Finishing High School						
25–34	30.9 (1,767)†	39.8 (2,784)	52.4 (2,178)	84.2 (1,032)	+53.3	+.456
35–44	35.0 (3,307)	37.0 (2,262)	56.3 (1,016)	75.9 (862)	+40.9	+.374
45–54	34.1 (1,711)	40.9 (1,474)	43.7 (755)	75.9 (554)	+41.8	+.335
55–64	42.8 (850)	43.6 (750)	53.4 (390)	63.9 (308)	+21.1	+.192
Partial Gammas: Son's Ed.×Age/F. Ed.	−.088	−.024	+.003	+.217		

C. Proportion Graduating from College Among Those with at Least One Year of College

25–34	45.7	59.7	56.5	66.3	+20.6	+.714
	(562)‡	(1,115)	(669)	(867)		
35–44	47.2	50.0	55.1	75.6	+28.4	+.313
	(807)	(936)	(573)	(654)		
45–54	49.5	46.4	43.5	60.6	+11.1	+.094
	(589)	(601)	(330)	(440)		
55–64	64.3	56.6	53.9	58.9	−5.4	−.094
	(366)	(328)	(208)	(197)		

Partial Gammas: Son's
Ed.×Age/F. Ed.   −.145   +.115   +.088   +.071

* Projected number of respondents entering high school expressed in thousands.
† Projected number of respondents graduating from high school expressed in thousands.
‡ Projected number of respondents with at least one year of college expressed in thousands.

EDUCATIONAL ACHIEVEMENT AND RACE

In view of widespread concern about the plight of the American Negro, it is natural to ask whether the foregoing findings characterize both whites and non-whites. Do non-white sons go as far in school as white sons when their fathers' education is taken into account?[15] The Bowman data cited earlier tell us that the occupational and economic statuses of men in these education categories differ according to both region and race. Being white and living in the North both improve one's occupational and economic circumstances, given the same number of years of schooling. It follows, then, that the objective circumstances faced by Negro sons in each of these educational status categories tend to be poorer than those of whites.

TABLE 4. Percentage of Sons Obtaining a Given Level of Education by Age, Race, and Father's Education

| | Father's Education | | | |
| | Less than Eight (%) | | Some High School or More (%) | |
Son's Age	Non-White	White	Non-White	White
	A. Reaching High School			
25–34	71.6	85.2	89.9	96.5
	(684)*	(3,285)	(462)	(6,183)
35–44	60.7	82.0	72.0	95.9
	(848)	(4,751)	(326)	(5,684)
45–54	42.3	74.8	71.3	93.9
	(752)	(4,568)	(215)	(4,627)
55–64	31.2	65.0	61.0	88.1
	(586)	(3,732)	(100)	(3,166)
	B. Graduating from High School			
25–34	24.2	48.8	58.2	78.0
35–44	25.1	44.2	46.7	70.1
45–54	18.1	34.4	28.2	58.9
55–64	6.2	21.9	14.0	45.0
	C. With Some College			
25–34	6.0	15.7	25.6	41.0
35–44	10.1	15.3	17.8	35.3
45–54	4.7	12.0	17.9	28.7
55–64	2.1	9.5	4.0	22.8
	D. Graduating from College			
25–34	1.0	7.7	11.5	25.3
35–44	4.0	7.4	8.9	21.7
45–54	1.9	5.9	5.2	14.6
55–64	1.1	6.2	3.0	12.8

*Projected base N for the percentage expressed in thousands.

It is, therefore, not surprising that the data in Table 4 reveal that both race and social status influence educational attainment in all four age cohorts. Since being white and having a better-educated father are both advantages in reaching all levels of schooling, it follows that the sons of white, better-educated fathers have the highest attainment rates. In addition, attainment increases over time (except for four cases, three of which involve the youngest group of non-whites with poorly educated fathers). In an era when high school graduation is almost taken for granted and a bachelor's degree is by no means an exceptional achievement, less than three-fourths of all low-status Negroes reach high school, less than a quarter finish, only 6 per cent enter college, and a mere 1 per cent complete the work necessary for their degrees. This college completion rate is one twenty-fifth that of their white age cohorts with better-educated fathers.

Although these data clearly reflect the social and educational deprivation which Negroes and other racial minorities have endured, during the past two generations social status has come to be a more important determinant of educational achievement than race. Section B of Table 4 shows, for example, that until World War II whites were more likely to finish high school than non-whites, regardless of paternal education. After World War II, having a better-educated father was a clearer advantage than being white, although differences between white and non-whites continued to persist within each education category. During the thirties, the same patterns of stronger status influences became true of entering college, but the stronger impact of race on college graduation persisted into the forties. The influence of paternal education and race on rates of educational attainment is compared in Table 5.

The data in Section A of Table 5 show that the gap between high- and low-status categories has increased for both races over time for all levels of son's educational attainment except high school entrance. At this latter level of schooling initially large status differences have diminished generally over time within both races, although the differences among non-whites are generally larger than among whites. In terms of high school graduation and beyond, however, status differences are greater among whites than non-whites. Although this suggests that having a well-educated father is more of an advantage in obtaining a college education if one is white than if he is not, the advantage may be due to the greater percentage of college-educated fathers among whites in the High School or More category than among non-whites.

Nonetheless, these data continue to reflect a pattern of shifting educational norms and opportunities across both racial and status lines that is clearly dominated by the upper strata of white society. Although the realization of norms to attend high school and college has gradually crossed the color line, Negroes from families who have moved into the middle educational strata of American society have apparently not reaped the same occupational and financial benefits from their schooling as their white counterparts have. This may have resulted in a self- as well as socially imposed ceiling on educational aspirations and attainments, particularly in the South. Although the Bowman data also show that having more education has a clear economic payoff for both Negroes and whites

TABLE 5. Summary of Differences in Attainment due to Father's Education and Race

A. Percentage Difference Between Sons with High School or More-Educated Fathers and Sons with Fathers Who Did Not Complete Grade School by Son's Age, Race, and Level of Education (from Table 4)*

Son's Education	Some High School		High School Graduation		Some College		College Graduation	
Age	Non-White	White	Non-White	White	Non-White	White	Non-White	White
25–34	18.3	11.3	34.0	30.0	19.6	25.3	10.5	17.6
35–44	11.3	13.9	21.6	25.9	7.7	20.0	4.9	14.7
45–54	29.0	19.1	10.1	24.4	13.2	16.7	3.3	8.8
55–64	29.8	23.1	7.8	23.1	1.9	13.3	1.9	6.6

B. Percentage Difference Between White and Non-White Sons by Age, Level of Education, and Father's Education (from Table 4)†

Son's Education	Some High School		High School Graduation		Some College		College Graduation	
	Father's Education		Father's Education		Father's Education		Father's Education	
Age	Less Than Eight	Some H.S. or More	Less Than Eight	Some H.S. or More	Less Than Eight	Some H.S. or More	Less Than Eight	Some H.S. or More
25–34	13.6	6.6	24.6	19.8	9.7	15.4	6.7	13.8
35–44	21.3	23.9	19.1	23.4	5.2	17.4	3.4	12.8
45–54	32.5	22.6	16.3	30.7	7.3	10.8	4.0	9.4
55–64	33.8	27.1	15.7	31.0	7.4	18.8	5.1	9.8

* A positive percentage difference indicates that sons with high school or more-educated fathers have the advantage.
† A positive percentage difference indicates that whites have the advantage.

222

in both North and South, the financial advantage that accrues to whites vis-à-vis Negroes appears to increase with education in most age groups. In addition, if we assume that family income has some bearing on son's chances of finishing high school or going to college irrespective of paternal education, the comparatively lower income of moderately well-educated Negroes would itself inhibit the likelihood of son's advancing his schooling, relative occupational and economic returns notwithstanding.

There is also some support for this interpretation in the data pertaining to racial differences within status groups (see Table 5, Section B). There we find that while racial differences in reaching high school are generally higher among low-status sons, the superior educational attainments of whites beyond high school are most evident among high-status boys. This also suggests that race affects attainment at different points in the education cycle for different status groups. Low-status boys have been affected primarily at the fundamental levels, while higher-status non-white boys have labored under what we have called an "aspiration ceiling," even through their college years. The data do show, however, that race has had its largest effect at the early and most basic stages of education, a phenomenon apparently linked primarily to the rural South.

Since we have seen that both race and social status independently affect access to all levels of education, we would probably not be surprised to find that both affect the conditional probabilities of going from one level to another in similar fashion. Because the data are too extensive to present in table form and resemble those in Table 3, we shall mention only salient findings. First, in nearly every case the conditional probabilities for whites are larger than for non-whites. Second, in most cases the probabilities for higher-status respondents exceed those for men from lower origins. Third, for the two youngest age groups the conditional probabilities increase with paternal education at all but the highest education level of sons (as in Table 4); status differences have more effect on school attainment within racial groups than has race within status groups. Fourth, the probabilities of entering and completing high school increase for all four status groups over time (as in Table 3), but (aside from one exception) with entering and finishing college they decrease over time for low-status men of *both* races. This, too, parallels our previous findings. Although the conditional probabilities of entering and completing college remain fairly stable over time for high-status whites, the influence of status on attainment at all three levels for whites definitely increases over time. Because of the irregular pattern of conditional probabilities among older, high-status non-whites, the overall pattern of differences due to status is similar but not as consistent.

SUMMARY AND CONCLUSIONS

The data in this report have provided an empirical basis for examining a series of issues concerning the patterns of educational mobility and attainment among American males over the past forty years. Contrary to the assumption that the observed increases in high school and college graduation rates during this time have particularly benefited boys from the lower social strata, we found that the *relative* chances of such boys having reached and completed college compared with the sons of college-educated fathers have diminished over time. Paradoxically, while completion rates have continued to rise for all men, the probabilities of going to college, given that you finished high school, and finishing college once you entered, have decreased over time for low-status sons. Basically the same findings appear for each race separately. For nearly every status and age group both the objective and conditional probabilities of reaching given educational levels are higher for whites than for non-whites. There is also considerable evidence that status differences have had an increasingly important effect on post–high school attendance even when race is taken into account. One illustration of these racial and status differences among the youngest age cohort is that 63 per cent of the sons of white college graduates completed college compared with 1 per cent of the non-whites with grade school–educated fathers.

Since these data do not provide controls for either region urbanization, or intelligence of the respondent, it is likely that the patterns we have examined would vary as we introduced additional explanatory variables. Bowman's data help us to suggest (but not demonstrate) that a large part of the depressed attainments of low-status sons (both Negro and white) can be traced to their Southern and/or rural origins. As migration has removed many of the better educated and able from the farm to the city and from the South to the North, restricted educational attainments have tended to center upon those who remain.

At the same time educational upgrading in the advanced sectors of the scale has moved much more rapidly for men from strata in which large amounts of schooling have provided distinctive occupational and economic advantages. As these advantages are perceived as realistic and desirable by members of a given stratum, school completion norms develop. As norms for given attainment levels diffuse throughout the status hierarchy, attainment gaps close. This is apparent from our data in terms of high school attendance and, to some extent, to high school graduation. Accompanying this closure at the high school level, however, is an increasingly large gap in college attendance and completion. Only when the symbolic and utilitarian values of college are recognized by members of the lower strata will their aspirations and rates of attendance rise and the initial gap begin to close. Although the marked expansion of community college facilities may provide one institutional means for closing this gap, the shift from a widening to a diminishing college attendance gap is not likely until high school completion rates for low-status youth increase substantially. While this principle of establishing and diffusing educational attainment norms from the upper strata appears to be valid in terms of high school attendance and graduation, its complete applicability in relation to college graduation at present seems quite uncertain. Whether the creation or realization of college aspirations in more than token proportions will someday reach what begins to look like the "perpetual poor" may seem unlikely on the basis of the increasing attainment gaps evident in these data.

Nonetheless, Davis reminds us that occupational destinations and formal education appear to be more closely linked today than forty years ago. To what extent these educational trends may affect subsequent patterns of occupational mobility is not yet certain. What seems likely, however, is that there are apt to be few cases of sharp upward occupational mobility among present-day sons with poorly educated fathers and a possible increase in "status inheritance" within the highest and lowest strata of society. Unless a more concerted effort is made to create and stimulate more meaningful opportunities for the people caught in the bottom strata, however, what now seems like a paradox is likely to evolve into a social dilemma which neither indifference, hostility, nor legislative reaction will be able to ameliorate. The urban riots and destruction of recent summers strongly indicate, in fact, that this dilemma may already be upon us.

NOTES

1. James A. Davis, "Higher Education: Selection and Opportunity," *School Review*, LXXI, No. 3 (Autumn, 1963), 249–65.

2. The data we shall use in an attempt to answer these questions were derived from the *Current Population Reports* of the U.S. Bureau of the Census, Ser. P-20, No. 132, September 22, 1964. They were originally compiled as a supplement to the March, 1962, *Current Population Survey* on which Peter M. Blau and Otis Dudley Duncan based their analysis of occupational mobility. Although the case bases presented in our tables are only projected estimates of actual population parameters, they are based on a representative probability sample of the non-institutionalized male population of the United States in the spring of 1962. See Peter M. Blau, "The Flow of Occupational Supply and Recruitment," *American Sociological Review*, XXX, No. 4 (August, 1965), 475–90; and Otis Dudley Duncan, "Occupational Mobility in the United States," *American Sociological Review*, XXX, No. 4 (August, 1965), 491–98. For a different analysis based on these same data, see Charles B. Nam, "Family Patterns of Educational Attainment," *Sociology of Education*, XXXVIII, No. 5 (Fall, 1965), 393–403.

3. Included in the less than eight years category are respondents who did not report their father's education. This decision was made in order to include all of the respondents interviewed in our tabulations, thereby eliminating gaps in the data which might have impaired if not distorted the detail of the findings reported here. The decision was based on two empirical reasons. First, of the respondents who reported their father's education, those in the less than eight years category had the lowest achievement profiles in all four age groups, yet the profiles of the "No Response" group were either very similar to or even lower than this bottom group. Second, not knowing the education of one's father seemed most likely to occur either in families in which education was of such little relevance that it was never discussed or mentioned (i.e., father had so little schooling that education was never a viable reference point in family affairs), or in cases in which the son never knew or knew little of his actual father. Either case represents a phenomenon strongly associated with what is known today as the "poverty syndrome"; the lack of a skilled and productive male identity figure in the household.

4. The mobility data in Table 1 were derived for each age group by cross-tabu-

lating the four categories of father's education with similar categories of respondent's education. The total number of cases falling on the major diagonal of each resulting 4 × 4 table was divided by the total number of respondents in the table, thereby giving the percentage who are educationally "stable." The respondents in the six cells of the table "above" the diagonal are upwardly mobile, and those in the six cells below the diagonal are downwardly mobile.

5. This category includes an undetermined number of respondents who completed eight years of schooling but did not go on to high school. The category in the original report ranges from eight to eleven years. We are, therefore, unable to distinguish men with only eight years of schooling from men who also went on to high school.

6. Although this point hardly requires further substantiation, the partial Gammas between father's and son's education only fluctuate from .470 to .513 among the four age cohorts. For an interpretation of Gamma, see James A. Davis, "A Partial Coefficient for Goodman and Kruskal's Gamma," *Journal of the American Statistical Association*, LXII, No. 317 (March, 1967), 189–93.

7. The notable exceptions to this rule nearly all involve the youngest age group, and most of them concern college graduation. Although this drop in graduation may reflect a genuine reversal in the assumed trend toward increasing proportions of college graduates in the United States, it is more likely the result of two processes: completion of undergraduate degrees by many men after the age of 25, and extended tours of military duty for college graduates in the officer ranks, thereby excluding them from our sample.

8. It can be argued, of course, that the meaning and occupational implications of a less than grade school education have changed over time. As Davis shows, a lack of formal education qualifications did not necessarily imply low social status forty years ago, but it clearly does today. Hence, some might argue that using this criterion to define the low end of the social scale for all four age groups is misleading. Since our concern is with relative as well as absolute differences, however, it is just as easy to argue that a college-educated father was by far a more unique figure forty years ago than he is today. As a result, the social realities associated to these two terms may have changed somewhat over the past forty years, but the relative difference between them has shifted less. Ideally, of course, we would like to break each cohort of sons into quintiles (for example) on the basis of their father's educational attainments and use these rather than father's absolute level of schooling as our control measure. We could then examine for each age cohort the percentage of sons in the upper (or lower) quintile of fathers' education that fell into some specified quintile of sons' attainments. Although this strategy would eliminate possible biases arising out of the shifting meanings of educational levels over generations, it would obscure the relevance of attainment levels that have had fairly clear implications over time. For an example that uses both analytic strategies, see C. Arnold Anderson, "Social Class Differentials in the Schooling of Youth Within the Regions and Community-Size Groups of the United States," *Social Forces*, XXV, No. 4 (May, 1947), 434–40.

9. The exceptional case can, in fact, be accounted for by the marked improvement in high school graduation among the sons of grade school dropouts during the Depression, a time when staying in school was often a wiser decision than entering the labor market.

10. Although these men may be "atypical" according to current middle-class educational standards, over a third of the sons in the yougest age group have fathers with less than eight years of schooling.

11. Another method of estimating percentage differences which minimizes the spurious "floor and ceiling" effects of extreme marginals and emphasizes "relative" rates of change is to compute the percentage of possible increase according to the formula:

$$(pT2 - pT1)/(100.0\% - pT1)$$

where $pT1$ is the percentage "successful" at time 1, and $pT2$ is the percentage "successful" at time 2. The formula shows the percentage of possible improvement that occurred between times 1 and 2. If we were to apply this method to Section A of Table 2, for example, we would find that the sons of men with less than eight years of schooling increased 22.5 out of a possible 39.6 per cent (56.8%), while the sons of college graduates increased 6.6 out of a possible 7.0 per cent (94.3%). Computed on this basis, the rate of improvement increases with father's education in all four sections of this table.

12. Support for this suggestion can be found in Mary Jean Bowman's "Human Inequalities and Southern Underdevelopment," *Southern Economic Journal*, XXXII, No. 1 (July, 1965), Part II, 73–102; and C. Arnold Anderson's "Inequalities in Schooling in the South," *American Journal of Sociology*, LX, No. 6 (May, 1955), 547–61. Professor Bowman shows that men with less than eight years of schooling are disproportionately from the South and (within region) from farms. Although her data trace complex generational changes in the educational distribution of males (controlling for region and urbanization), they do not, however, provide controls for father's educational or occupational status at the same time.

13. Although Eckland's study of over 1,300 college freshmen shows that the correlation between social class background and intelligence is virtually nil, Sewell and Armer's findings on all high school seniors in Wisconsin in 1957 demonstrate that there is some relationship between intelligence and the relative socioeconomic status of one's neighborhood. (See Bruce K. Eckland, "Academic Ability, Higher Education, and Occupational Mobility," *American Sociological Review*, XXX, No. 5 [October, 1965], 735–46; and William H. Sewell and J. Michael Armer, "Neighborhood Context and College Plans," *American Sociological Review*, XXXI, No. 2 [April, 1966], 159–68.) Presumably the intelligence–family status correlation would increase as the cohort under study becomes less determined by intellectual selectivity. Although Sewell and Armer do show that the percentage of high-ability boys from low SES neighborhoods with college plans exceeds that of low-ability boys in high SES neighborhoods, the latter are over twice as likely to have college plans as their low SES counterparts.

14. This drop might be explained by two somewhat related phenomena. The first is that attending college has been so widely accepted as "the thing to do" by members of the upper middle class that nearly everyone "goes" somewhere regardless of his academic ability, motivation, or desire to finish. The second is that many of these boys have the financial resources necessary to prolong their undergraduate careers by taking years off to travel abroad or even work in the family business.

15. Since the number of non-white fathers with either high school or college

diplomas was so small that reliable cross-tabulations were impossible, it was necessary to collapse the parental status categories: less than 8 years of schooling, and "some high school or more."

QUESTIONS

1. Name the three variables utilized in Table 2. Which one is the dependent variable? Is the dependent variable being used as the numerator or denominator of the computed percentages? For the same relative cell entries, what does the difference between the entries in section A and B represent?
2. How is Table 4 different from Table 2? How does Table 5 relate to Table 4? For Table 5, how do parts A and B differ from each other?
3. What tactic is used to treat the situation where there is a nonresponse on the item "father's education"?
4. Practice phrasing out the interpretation of some of the percentage differences (for example, out of each 100 sons aged 25–34, 16 more reached high school if their fathers had some college than if their fathers had fewer than eight years of schooling).
5. For what purpose did Spady use a measure of association (gamma) in addition to percentage differences applied to the same data? In other words, what added information, if any, would a gamma add that was not forthcoming from a percentage analysis?
6. Using the same data, can you suggest different analytic techniques that might be more efficient in answering the theoretical questions posed by Spady?

Spatial Aspects of Social Area Analysis

THEODORE R. ANDERSON and JANICE A. EGELAND

Multivariate analysis is somewhat simplified if the independent variables are truly independent of each other—that is, knowledge of the outcome on one independent variable for a unit does not help in predicting the outcome on another independent variable. Typically, this condition is exemplified by having the same number of observations in each combination of outcomes of the set of independent variables. Yet specific combinations of the independent variables can have influences on the dependent variable not simply predictable from knowledge of the influences of the independent variables treated separately. This type of complex outcome is known as a "statistical interaction." Anderson

Reprinted from *American Sociological Review* 26 (1961), 392–398, with permission of The American Sociological Association.

and Egeland's research illustrates how the steps of analysis can be influenced by a statistical interaction and then can lead to a sensible interpretation of the data.

INTRODUCTION

A classic problem in urban ecology has been the succinct description of the location of residential areas by type. Hurd,[1] as early as 1903, developed the conception that urban growth proceeded according to two patterns: central growth and axial growth. By these terms he meant to convey the idea that growth tends to occur in all directions outward from the center of the city, and that it occurs most rapidly along major transportation routes. In consequence, at any one time the total structure of the city forms a roughly star-shaped pattern. While Hurd discussed the location of residential areas by type (especially by income or rental value), he did not systematically use the principles of central and axial growth to generate overall, concise descriptive generalizations.

Burgess,[2] during the 1920s, emphasized the importance of central (or concentric growth and used this pattern to generate the now-famous concentric zone hypothesis of the distribution of residential areas by type. Residential areas were classified both according to the density characteristics of dwelling units and according to the typical socio-economic status of the residents. According to his hypothesis, these two classifications were inversely related to each other (i.e. high status persons lived in low dwelling unit density areas and vice versa). Residential areas were then classed into four types, each forming a concentric band about the center of the city—which was, itself, called Zone 1. Zone 2, immediately adjacent to the center, was characterized by rooming houses, tenements, and other forms of structures in which dwelling unit densities are very high and also by a population of low socio-economic status and usually of recent immigrant stock. Moving outward, the zones became progressively less dense in dwelling unit patterns (out of the single-family, large-lawn suburban or commuters zone) and characterized by residents of increasingly high socio-economic status.

Burgess' hypothesis formed the basis for a vast amount of research during the ensuing years. In these researches the concept of four distinct zones (or five counting the central business district) was dropped rather early and replaced by an indefinite number of concentric zones arbitrarily located at half-mile or mile intervals around the central business district. The typical method used to "test" the hypothesis was to aggregate relevant information within each zone, express the aggregated information in the form of an average for the zone, and note the variation in this average from zone to zone. If the average or aggregate measure declined regularly (or increased regularly) with increasing distance from the center, then the Burgess zonal hypothesis was held to be confirmed, but if the measure went down and then up, or varied in some other irregular manner, then the hypothesis was held suspect for that characteristic.[3] This methodology is important for two reasons. First, it in effect transforms the Burgess hypothesis into the hypothesis that regular gradients will be found by distance from the center of the city in characteristics such as average dwelling unit density and average socio-economic status. Second, it tests this hypothesis by examining the regression line and its regularity alone, without considering the variation of local areas within a zone about the zonal average or regression. By ignoring the variation of individual tracts about the regression line it is (a) impossible to bring the relatively powerful, modern statistical procedures to bear upon the tests, since unexplained, or residual, or random variation is not estimated, except very indirectly through variation in the zonal means about the regression line. It is also (b) essentially impossible to compare the effectiveness of the Burgess hypothesis with that of any competing hypothesis, since one cannot estimate the proportion of the total variance that is accounted for by the hypothesis in question.

In one important related area, however, a major advance has occurred. Obviously, before the concentric zone and sector hypotheses can be meaningfully compared, a characteristic of local areas must be selected for analysis. Should the rental value of dwelling units be used? Or the proportion of dwelling units which are in single-family structures? Or the proportion of dwelling units occupied by non-whites? Or what? The census alone reports on a very large number of characteristics both of dwellings and of residents for local areas (census tracts) within many large cities. Earlier research on the concentric zone hypothesis suggests that some of these characteristics will manifest a zonal pattern and that others will not. To compare the hypotheses on all of the characteristics for which data are available would be tedious to say the least. Furthermore, the results would almost certainly be ambiguous.

Fortunately, such a laborious procedure is no longer necessary. Shevky and Bell[7] have developed three indices of urban neighborhoods which have considerable promise and which they call urbanization (or family status), social rank, and segregation. A recent study by Van Arsdol, Camilleri, and Schmid[8] has shown that these indices possess a rather stable structure from one city to another within the United States. There is also some reason to believe (though it is a more speculative point at the present) that these indices effectively summarize the bulk of the common information contained in the characteristics reported for census tracts by the census. As more evidence accumulates, it will probably be shown that these indices should be modified somewhat, but in their present form they appear to be sound first approximations. Thus, it is possible today to compare the zonal and sector hypotheses in terms of the Shevky-Bell indices with considerable confidence that the results will have general significance.

One conceptual modification of the Shevky-Bell system will, however, be incorporated in this paper. Anderson and Bean,[9] in a factor analysis of Toledo data, have shown that the social rank index might better be considered as a measure of the prestige value of a neighborhood. These two concepts (i.e. social rank and prestige value) are superficially very similar. However, recent studies of socio-economic status have indicated that socio-economic status is not simply a unidimensional phenomenon.[10] In particular, measures based on occupation and education are not closely correlated to measures based on income. The term prestige has come to be identified with the invidious ranking of occupations and of educational categories. Since the Shevky-Bell social rank index is based almost entirely upon the occupational and educational composition of the tract's population, the term prestige value seems more appropriate than social rank. This index will be called a measure of the prestige value of a neighborhood (rather than its social rank) throughout the remainder of this paper.

PROBLEM

This paper reports a statistical comparison of the concentric zone and sector hypotheses of urban residential structure, where residential structure is measured by the prestige value (social rank) and the urbanization indices proposed and developed by Shevky and Bell. The third index (segregation) was not included primarily because the distribution of Negroes within the large U.S. city is known not to fit either of these patterns well. The index components used in this study are the same as those used by Van Arsdol, Camilleri, and Schmid. Equal weight was assigned to each component when it was expressed in standard score form. Thus, the prestige value index consisted of the percentage of employed persons not classified as craftsmen, operatives, and laborers, added to the percentage of persons twenty-five years old and over who have completed at least one to three years of high school. The urbanization index consisted of the fertility ratio (reflected), plus the percentage of all females fourteen years of age and over who are in the labor force, plus the percentage of all dwelling units that are multi-family. In each case the unit of observation was a census tract.

The basic statistical tool used in the study was the analysis of variance, since sectors are qualitative, and distances from the center of the city were only ranked in this study. Four cities (Akron and Dayton, Ohio, Indianapolis, Indiana, and Syracuse, New York) were selected for study on the basis of their having populations between 200,000 and 500,000 in 1950 (thus rendering them roughly comparable as to size), because their outlying territory was also tracted, and on the basis of their having roughly circular over-all shapes. This last criterion was invoked as a means of eliminating the dominant impact of major geographic disturbances that might destroy the possibility of filling each cell in the variance analysis data matrix. Thus, a city located on a large body of water (and hence not circular) will not extend as far in some sectors as in others, tending to confound sectors and distances. To achieve independent estimates of the main effects, it was necessary to consider only reasonably circular cities.

Within each city, sectors were identified in the following manner. First, the center of the city was located, using a detailed map showing the location of major buildings (and transportation routes). Then the direction, due east, was labelled direction O, and sectors were marked off at successive thirty-degree angles from this direction. Thus, each city was divided into 12 sectors, each 30 degrees wide. One of these sectors was selected randomly, and each third sector from this one was included in the sample. Hence, in each city four sectors were studied. The sectors studied in each

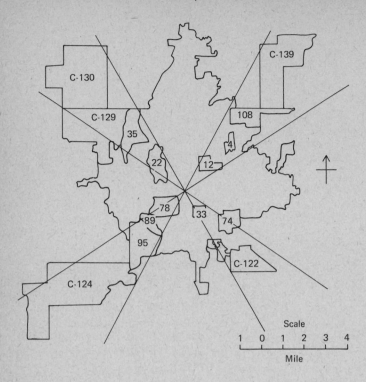

FIGURE 1: Map of Indianapolis and suburbs showing sectors and tracts used in the analysis.

city had the same orientation as those in each other city. In particular, the Northeast, Northwest, Southwest, and Southeast sectors were used in each city. This structure permitted a three-way analysis of variance designed to be used, including cities, distances, and oriented sectors. Within each selected sector, four census tracts were selected in such a way as to secure one as near as possible to the center, one as far from the center as possible, and two located one-third and two-thirds of the way between these. Essentially no random selection of individual tracts was involved since rarely did more than four tracts effectively meet the selection criteria. Indeed, the usual problem was to find four appropriate tracts, not to select from among some larger number.

In this manner, 64 census tracts were selected, one each from the 64 cells formed by all possible combinations of four cities, four oriented sectors, and four ranked distances. Thus, a "one observation per cell" analysis of variance design was used, which means that the triple interaction of cities by sectors by distances was indistinguishable from the within cell variance. Two-way interactions can, however, be tested with this design. For each census tract selected, two measurements were computed: the urbanization index and the prestige value index. The results of the analyses of these two measures will be presented separately.

RESULTS: URBANIZATION

The urbanization index contrasts areas characterized by many apartments, families with few young children, and families in which the wife works (high urbanization) with areas characterized by many single-family dwellings, families with many young children, and families in which the wife does not work (low urbanization). Where are such areas located within the city? Table 1 provides at least a

TABLE 1. Analysis of Variance for the Urbanization Index

Source	Sum of Squares	df	Variance Estimates	F	Decision on H_o
Total	49,639.0	63	—	—	—
Between cities	4,816.3	3	1,605.4	5.68*	Reject
Between sectors	948.4	3	316.1	1.12*	Accept
Between distances	28,418.6	3	9,472.8	33.49*	Reject
Cities × sectors	3,864.0	9	429.3	1.62	Accept
Cities × distances	1,692.2	9	188.0	.71	Accept
Sectors × distances	2,756.6	9	306.3	1.16	Accept
Residual	7,142.9	27	264.6		
Pooled error	15,275.8	54	282.9		

* Since the interactions were not significant, the main effects were tested from the pooled error estimate (residual plus the interactions).

partial answer. None of the interactions is significant. Cities differ somewhat in urbanization, sectors within cities do not differ, and distances differ a great deal. An examination of the Variance Estimates column of Table 1 shows clearly that the variation between distances is by far the largest in the entire table. Clearly, urbanization within a city is a concentric phenomenon and not a sectorial phenomenon.

Locating the high and low average scores for cities and distances reveals, first, that Syracuse has the highest average score on urbanization (113.7) while the other cities are about equal. (The norm for the entire sample is 100.) This finding suggests that eastern cities may be more urbanized than are midwestern cities, a fact which has long been recognized at least with respect to multi-family dwelling units. Second, these comparisons reveal that, as expected, tracts located nearest the city center are most highly urbanized (129.6) while tracts furthest from the center are least urbanized (73.4). This finding suggests that the principal impact of the urbanization index is to differentiate between near-center and far-from-center areas, between central and peripheral areas.

Analysis

RESULTS: PRESTIGE VALUE

The prestige value (or social rank) index contrasts areas characterized by a resident population with a high proportion of persons with at least a high school education and a high proportion of persons with non-manual occupations (high prestige) with areas characterized by many laborer residents and many persons with relatively little education (low prestige). Where are areas of high prestige found within the city? Table 2 presents the analysis of variance results

TABLE 2. Analysis of Variance for the Prestige Value Index

Source	Sum of Squares	df	Variance Estimates	F	Decision on H_0
Total	32,154.24	63	—	—	—
Between cities	1,810.77	3	603.59	—	—
Between sectors	1,835.76	3	611.92	—	—
Between distances	1,907.26	3	635.75	—	—
Cities × sectors	19,224.79	9	2,136.09	12.16	Reject
Cities × distances	1,775.02	9	197.22	1.12	Accept
Sectors × distances	858.92	9	95.44	.54	Accept
Residual	4,741.73	27	175.62	—	—

for prestige value using the same design as in the case of urbanization. Only the interaction F values have been presented in this table for a reason that will become clear in a moment.

An examination of the interaction F values indicates that only the cities by sectors interaction is significant and that its significance is essentially beyond doubt. Cities and sectors do interact. What this interaction means, in particular, is that the sector that manifests a high prestige in one city is not oriented in the same direction from the center as the high prestige sector in another city. For example, the sector with the highest prestige (among those studied) was the southeast sector in Akron, the northwest sector in Dayton, the southeast one in Indianapolis, and the northeast one in Syracuse. Thus the interaction here indicates that cities are not uniformly structured with respect to prestige value. This should surprise no one. The interaction between cities and sectors is so great, however, with about 60 per cent of the total sum of squares contained in it, as to completely dominate the main effects. The implication to be drawn from the size of this interaction is that cities should not be combined in comparing sectors and distances on prestige variations. Therefore, main effects were not tested from this table, but rather were tested separately for each city, producing four separate two-way analyses of variance.

The results as shown in Table 3 are clear. In each city tested, the null hypothesis must be rejected with respect to sectors. In three of the four cities, the null hypothesis is accepted with respect to distances. Prestige is primarily distributed within sectors rather than within distance bands.

TABLE 3. Analysis of Variance of Prestige Value by Distance and Sectors Within Each City

Source	Sum of Squares	df	Variance Estimates	F	Decision on H_o
Akron					
Total	7,698.8	15	—	—	—
Between distances	897.9	3	299.3	1.93	Accept
Between sectors	5,407.6	3	1,802.5	11.64	Reject
Remainder	1,393.4	9	154.8	—	—
Dayton					
Total	4,816.4	15	—	—	—
Between distances	607.8	3	202.6	2.88	Accept
Between sectors	3,576.4	3	1,192.1	16.97	Reject
Remainder	632.1	9	70.2	—	—
Indianapolis					
Total	5,011.3	15	—	—	—
Between distances	1,694.9	3	565.0	5.77	Reject
Between sectors	2,435.0	3	811.7	8.29	Reject
Remainder	881.4	9	97.9	—	—
Syracuse					
Total	12,817.0	15	—	—	—
Between distances	481.7	3	160.6	.54	Accept
Between sectors	9,641.6	3	3,213.9	10.74	Reject
Remainder	2,693.8	9	299.3	—	—

Only in Indianapolis was a significant secondary pattern found with respect to distance. Hoyt's sector hypothesis may be considered confirmed with respect to prestige value.

DISCUSSION

        In sum, the principal findings of this study are that urbanization (at the tract level) varies primarily concentrically or by distance from the center of the city, while prestige value (or social rank) varies primarily sectorially, with very little distance variation. These conclusions, of course, are restricted to American cities whose total spatial aspect is roughly circular and which have between 200,000 and 500,000 population. The impact of major geographic disturbances and larger city size on these conclusions remains as a problem for future research. In this connection, it should be noted that it is somewhat surprising to find that prestige value does not vary concentrically. It is common to visualize the suburban sections of a city as having residents of higher average socio-economic status than are found in the central sections of the city. The findings reported here apparently do not support this contention. However, recent evidence indicates that the Shevky-Bell social rank index is not a general measure of the average socio-economic status of local residents. In particular, an article by Anderson and Bean[11] indicates that in Toledo, average family income is more highly loaded on urbanization than on social rank. The apparently higher average socio-economic status of suburban families may be manifest largely in higher average incomes. If so, then this effect is incorporated primarily in the urbanization index in the Shevky-Bell system rather than in the social rank index. This fact further suggests the desirability of substituting the phrase prestige value for social rank. It is also possible that the absence of any marked concentric pattern with respect to prestige value (or social rank) is limited to smaller and medium-sized metropolitan areas. Some very slight evidence in favor of this hypothesis is indicated in this study by the fact that Indianapolis, the largest of the four cities studied here, did show a significant variation in prestige by distance from the center of the city. Despite these qualifications, however, the major impact of the findings reported here is that Burgess' concentric zone hypothesis (as modified) is supported with respect to urbanization but not prestige value, while Hoyt's sector hypothesis is supported with respect to prestige value but not urbanization.

NOTES

1. Richard M. Hurd, *Principles of City Land Values*, New York: The Record and Guide, 1903. "A continual contest exists between axial growth pushing out from the centre along transportation lines and central growth, constantly following and obliterating it, while new projections are being made further out the various axes" (p. 59).

2. Ernest W. Burgess, "The Growth of the City," in Robert E. Park, editor, *The City*, Chicago: University of Chicago Press, 1925.

3. See, for example, Ralph C. Fletcher, Harry L. Hornback, and Stuart A. Queen, *Social Statistics of St. Louis by Census Tracts, 1935*, for the use of this general method in connection with many characteristics of residents and dwelling units.

4. Homer Hoyt, *The Structure and Growth of Residential Neighborhoods in American Cities*, Washington, D.C.: United States Government Printing Office, 1939.

5. *Ibid.*, p. 75.

6. *Ibid.*, p. 76.

7. For a recent discussion of these indices, and an extensive bibliography of work already done using them, see Wendell Bell, "Social Areas: Typology of Urban Neighborhoods," in Marvin B. Sussman, editor, *Community Structure and Analysis*, New York: Thomas Y. Crowell Company, 1959, pp. 61–92.

8. Maurice D. Van Arsdol, Jr., Santo F. Camilleri, and Calvin F. Schmid, "The Generality of Urban Social Area Indexes," *American Sociological Review*, 23 (June, 1958), pp. 277–284.

9. Theodore R. Anderson and Lee L. Bean, "The Shevky-Bell Social Areas: Confirmation of Results and a Reinterpretation," paper presented at the annual meeting of the Eastern Sociological Society, April 23–24, 1960.

10. See, for instance, Joseph A. Kahl and James A. Davis, "A Comparison of Indexes of Socio-Economic Status," *American Sociological Review*, 20 (June, 1955), pp. 317–325.

11. Anderson and Bean, *op. cit.*

QUESTIONS

1. What are the two different levels of case or unit involved in this research? Which level of unit is the one about which the conceptualization is concerned? Which level of unit is the primary unit of statistical analysis?
2. How did previous research in another conceptual area influence the definition, specification, and measurement of the dependent variables?
3. For the conceptually important unit of analysis, how many units are actually studied? How were these units selected or sampled?
4. How were the data used in this study collected?
5. The statistics in this article are used for inferential purposes. What justification is there for using inferential statistics in this research? What would be appropriate descriptive statistics for describing the findings? From the analysis of variance tables, it is possible for you to compute "correlation ratios" to describe the amount of association between the independent variables and the dependent variables. Does their magnitude influence your impression of the findings?
6. How does the analysis illustrated in this article compare to "causal analysis or inference" in terms of its goals and procedures?
7. Are the two formulations guiding this research mutually exclusive or complementary?

Discipline, Method, and Community Power: A Note on the Sociology of Knowledge

JOHN WALTON

Bivariate analysis, the consideration of two variables at a time, constitutes a large part of sociological research. However, if sociology is to make any significant advancement in prediction and understanding of social phenomena, it must sooner or later invest a good part of its energies in multivariate analysis (the consideration of more than two variables at a time).

In the following study a very simple type of multivariate analysis is carried out with three variables, each dichotomized. The analysis consists primarily of a small number of 2 × 2 tables; three for bivariate analysis and four for the three-variable analysis. It should be easy to visualize the increase in complexity if a fourth variable were to be introduced.

Another important aspect of this study is its attempt at a causal analysis,

Reprinted from *American Sociological Review* 31 (1966), 684–689, with permission of The American Sociological Association.

and as such it illustrates a simple and basic approach that is available to the social scientist in making causal inferences in nonexperimental research.

■ The principal thesis of the sociology of knowledge—"that there are modes of thought which cannot be adequately understood as long as their social origins are obscured"[1]—has been widely accepted and employed by social scientists in research on various social groups, classes, and cultures. Seldom, however, have social scientists examined their own knowledge in this light, the assumption being that scientific rigor tends to eliminate the influence of group-determined perspectives. We will be concerned with an investigation of the credibility of this assumption.

Important differences exist between the intellectual worlds of the political scientist and the sociologist. The former is socialized in the tradition of Locke, Jefferson, Bentley, Dahl, and Easton, while the latter is more apt to encounter Durkheim, Weber, Pareto, Parsons, and C. Wright Mills. A cursory glance at the professional journals of the two disciplines reveals divergent perspectives. Sociologists tend to be concerned with theoretical and methodological considerations, political scientists with descriptive studies. Evidence is also available pointing to differences in political attitudes, with sociologists tending to be somewhat more liberal.[2]

In recent years, a distinct interdisciplinary field has developed that provides a setting for a systematic comparison between the findings of the two disciplines. The study of community power structure has been actively undertaken by both sociologists and political scientists. Their investigations have led to disparate conclusions, and ensuing debate has concerned the relative merits of an elitist[3] versus a pluralist[4] interpretation of local politics, as well as appropriate research methods. Political scientists have stressed the analysis of participation in actual community decisions[5] while certain sociologists have opted for the virtues of the reputational method.[6]

In a recent analysis of community power research, thirty-three studies dealing with fifty-five communities were classified with respect to a number of variables.[7] It was demonstrated that there are certain correlates of power structure types and possible biases associated with particular research methods. An extension of this analysis, introducing the disciplinary background of the investigator as a variable, provides an opportunity to examine the relevance of the sociology of knowledge to social research.

PROCEDURE

Attention is focused on three variables: the disciplinary background of the researcher, the research method used, and the type of power structure identified.

The selection of studies was intended to be exhaustive of the published literature in social science devoted to the study of community power structure. Thus, the thirty-three studies are regarded as a universe rather than a sample.[8] The universe was defined by three criteria. First, by dealing with the published literature some unpublished studies were excluded, especially dissertations. Second, confining the analysis to the social science literature excluded journalistic reports.[9] Third, the criterion that the research be specifically concerned with community power excluded a number of community studies dealing with stratification, local government, and related aspects of social and political life.[10] These criteria were employed in a screening of the literature, and the resulting list of studies was checked against several lengthy bibliographies to insure its inclusiveness.[11]

Research methods used in identifying leadership groups have been classified by various schemes.[12] In the area of community power, four types of method adequately encompass the variety of procedures encountered in the literature.[13]

1. *The Reputational Method.* Informants are asked to identify the most influential people in the community. Leaders may be nominated directly, in a one-step procedure, or nominees of informants may be interviewed and leaders designated by this second panel.
2. *The Decision-Making Method.* Historical reconstructions of community decision are made using documents; active participants are defined as leaders.
3. *The Case Study Method.* Includes less explicit approaches based on general observation.
4. *Combined Methods.* Simultaneous use of 1 and 2.

The studies provide considerable variation with regard to the types of power structure identified. The terms "elitism" and "pluralism" did not adequately distinguish a number of cases and the following scheme was adopted to accomplish that end.[14]

1. *Pyramidal.* A monolithic, monopolistic, or single cohesive leadership group.
2. *Factional.* At least two durable factions that compete for advantage.
3. *Coalitional.* Leadership varies with issues and is made up of fluid coalitions of interested persons and groups.
4. *Amorphous.* The absence of any persistent pattern of leadership or power exercised on the local level.

Employing these classifications, a coding guide was developed and applied to each of the studies.

RESULTS

Table 1[15] summarizes the thirty-three studies dealing with fifty-five communities in terms of the three variables.[16] Tables 2, 3, and 4 indicate the zero-order association between each of these variables.[17] Inspection of the tables[18] demonstrates that (1) sociologists have more frequently employed the reputational technique while political scientists tend to prefer the decision-making and closely related methods; (2) political scientists compared to sociologists tend to find less monolithic power structures, and (3) use of the reputational method tends to be associated with identification of a monolithic power structure.

Analysis

TABLE 1. List of Community Power Studies by Discipline of Investigator, Research Method, and Type of Power Structure Identified

Discipline and Investigator	Method	Type of Power	Discipline and Investigator	Method	Type of Power
Sociologists			Political Scientists		
1. Hunter	R	P	21. Scoble	RD	F
2. McKee	CS	F	22. Gore, Peabody	CS	C
3. Olmstead	R	F	23. Dahl	D	C
4. Pellegrin, Coates	CS	A	24. Sofen, Wood[a]	CS	A
5. Belknap, Smuckler	R	P	25. Martin *et al.*	D	C
6. Fanelli	R	P	26. McClain, Highsaw[a]	D	C
7. Miller	R	P	27. Booth, Adrian	R	F
	R	C	28. Kammerer[a]	CS	P
8. Schulze	R	F		CS	F
9. Vidich, Bensman	CS	P		CS	F
10. Form, D'Antonio	R	C		CS	P
	R	F		CS	P
11. Klapp, Padgett	R	A		CS	F
12. Smith	R	P		CS	F
13. Barth	R	P		CS	F
	R	P	29. Presthus	RD	C
	R	F		RD	F
	R	F	30. Kimbrough[a]	RD	F
	R	A		R	C
	R	A		R	P
14. Stone	CS	C		R	P
15. Freeman *et al.*	RD	C	31. Jennings	RD	C
16. Miller	R	C	32. Agger *et al.*	RD	P
17. Bonjean	R	P		RD	C
18. Belknap, Steinle	R	P		RD	C
	R	P		RD	P
19. Thometz	R	P	33. Wildavsky	D	C
20. Clelland, Form	R	F			

[a] These researchers are not political scientists; see note 16.
Note: Labels are as follows: Research method: R—reputational, D—decision-making, CS—case study, and RD—combined. Type of power structure: P—pyramidal, F—factional, C—coalitional, and A—amorphous.

TABLE 2. Classification of Community Power Studies by Discipline of Investigator and Research Method Used

	Discipline of Investigator		
Research Method Used	Sociology	Political Science	Total
Reputational	23	4	27
Other	5	23	28
Total	28	27	55

Note: Q = +0.93; chi-square = 24.91, p < .0005 (one-tailed).

TABLE 3. Classification of Community Power Studies by Discipline of Investigator and Type of Power Structure Identified

	Discipline of Investigator		
Type of Power Structure Found	Sociology	Political Science	Total
Pyramidal	12	7	19
Other	16	20	36
Total	28	27	55

Note: Q= +0.36; chi-square=1.75, p<.10 (one-tailed).

TABLE 4. Classification of Community Power Studies by Research Method Used and Type of Power Structure Found

	Research Method Used		
Type of Power Structure Found	Reputational	Other	Total
Pyramidal	13	6	19
Other	14	22	36
Total	27	28	55

Note: Q= +0.55; chi-square=4.33, p<.025 (one-tailed).

Given the fact that the time-order of the variables is clear [discipline→ method (independent variables)→power structure (dependent variable)], one of three interpretations is possible: (1) the association between method and results is spurious and can be accounted for by the antecedent variable, discipline of the investigator; (2) the associations represent a developmental of causal sequence[19] (an "interpretation" in Hyman's terms);[20] (3) there is interaction among the three.

Controlling for academic discipline, shown in Table 5, rules out the

TABLE 5. Classification of Community Power Studies by Research Method Used and Type of Power Structure Found, for Sociologists and Political Scientists

	Research Method Used		
Discipline and Type of Power Stucture Found	Reputational	Other	Total
Sociologists			
Pyramidal	11	1	12
Other	12	4	16
Total	23	5	28
Political Scientists			
Pyramidal	2	5	7
Other	2	18	20
Total	4	23	27

Note: For sociologists, Q= +0.57; for political scientists, Q= +0.57.

first possibility, for the association between method employed and results obtained remains substantially unchanged.[21] Table 6 indicates no associa-

TABLE 6. Classification of Community Power Studies by Type of Power Structure Identified and Discipline of Investigator, for Reputational and All Other Research Methods

Research Method Used and Type of Power Stucture Found	Discipline of Investigator		
	Sociology	Political Science	Total
Reputational			
Pyramidal	11	2	13
Other	12	2	14
Total	23	4	27
Other Methods			
Pyramidal	1	5	6
Other	4	18	22
Total	5	23	28

Note: For the reputational method, $Q = -0.04$; for the other methods combined, $Q = -0.05$.

tion between academic discipline and type of power structure identified after controlling for type of method used. Since "in general, the association between two variables in a developmental or causal sequence will tend to disappear when an intervening variable is held constant,"[22] the existence of a developmental sequence has been demonstrated: the disciplinary background of the investigator tends to determine the method of investigation he will adopt which, in turn, tends to determine the image of the power structure that results from the investigation.

DISCUSSION

These results illustrate the influence of ideological perspectives within one area of social research. This finding, however, has implications for a wide variety of social research. If it can be shown that similar perspectives operate in other areas,[23] social scientists will have to begin a reappraisal of their knowledge. In so doing, however, it is essential that the import of these applications of the sociology of knowledge be recognized. Commenting on a paper which parallels the present discussion in many respects,[24] one sociologist observed:

What I do deny is that the findings of a Wissensoziologie (sic) of sociology demonstrate the inherent unreliability in the scientifically controlled investigations of sociological research.[25]

The point is that to demonstrate the influence of ideological perspectives is not to demonstrate "inherent unreliability."[26] Mannheim was most explicit about this:

We cannot emphasize too much that the social equation does not always constitute a source of error but more frequently than not brings into view certain interrelations which would not otherwise be apparent. . . . In every situation, it is, therefore, indispensable to have a total perspective which embraces all points of view.[27]

Once we recognize the influence of our own perspectives on the research process we are in a position to control them and, perhaps, move a bit closer to Mannheim's "total perspective."

CONCLUSION

Studies of local power structure will benefit from use of a combination of research methods as protection against this source of bias.

Comparative studies provide another avenue for the elimination of bias and the development of generalizations about community power. As one writer has put it:

So long as community power studies remain on the level of case studies of individual communities, the constraint of data upon interpretation will be minimal.[28]

The development of comparative research methods is one of the principal tasks facing students of community power. Progress in this direction will not only serve to temper biases, but should also lead to a better understanding of the exercise of power on the local level.

In more general terms, this analysis documents the significance of the sociology of knowledge as a perspective for interpreting social research. Mannheim has commented on the significance in the following way:

Perhaps it is when the hitherto concealed dependence of thought on group existence and its rootedness in action becomes visible that it becomes possible for the first time, through becoming aware of them, to obtain a new mode of control over previously uncontrolled factors in thought.[29]

NOTES

1. Karl Mannheim, *Ideology and Utopia: An Introduction to the Sociology of Knowledge,* New York: Harcourt, Brace and World, 1961, p. 2.

2. Henry A. Turner, Charles B. Spaulding, and Charles G. McClintock, "Political Orientations of Academically Affiliated Sociologists," *Sociology and Social Research,* 47 (April, 1963), pp. 273–289, and "The Political Party Affiliation of American Political Scientists," *Western Political Quarterly,* 16 (September, 1963), pp. 650–665.

3. Floyd Hunter, *Community Power Structure: A Study of Decision Makers,* Chapel Hill: University of North Carolina Press, 1953, and Hunter's review of Dahl's *Who Governs?, Administrative Science Quarterly,* 6 (March, 1962), pp. 517–519.

4. Robert A. Dahl, *Who Governs?: Power and Democracy in an American City,* New Haven: Yale University Press, 1961; Nelson W. Polsby, *Community Power and Political Theory,* New Haven: Yale University Press, 1963.

Analysis

5. Robert A. Dahl, "A Critique of the Ruling Elite Model," *American Political Science Review*, 52 (June, 1958), pp. 463–469; Nelson W. Polsby, "How to Study Power: The Pluralist Alternative," *Journal of Politics*, 22 (August, 1960), pp. 474–484; Raymond E. Wolfinger, "Reputation and Reality in the Study of Community Power," *American Sociological Review*, 25 (October, 1960), pp. 636–644.

6. William V. D'Antonio and Eugene Erickson, "The Reputational Technique as a Measure of Community Power: An Evaluation Based on Comparative and Longitudinal Studies," *American Sociological Review*, 27 (June, 1962), pp. 362–376; Howard J. Ehrlich, "The Reputational Approach to the Study of Community Power," *American Sociological Review*, 26 (December, 1961), pp. 926–927; Baha Abu-Laban, "The Reputational Approach in the Study of Community Power: A Critical Evaluation," *Pacific Sociological Review*, 8 (Spring, 1965), pp. 35–42. In recent studies, these methods have been combined by representatives of both fields. See, for example, Robert Presthus, *Men at the Top: A Study in Community Power*, New York: Oxford University Press, 1964; William V. D'Antonio and William H. Form, *Influentials in Two Border Cities: A Study in Community Decision-Making*, Notre Dame, Ind.: University of Notre Dame Press, 1965.

7. John Walton, "Substance and Artifact: The Current Status of Research on Community Power Structure," *American Journal of Sociology*, 71 (January, 1966), pp. 430–438.

8. Any claim to exhaustiveness is, of course, impossible to support. While an effort was made to accomplish this, it was subject to limitations of knowledge and accuracy of decisions made with respect to the criteria defining the universe. Following the completion of this [article], the literature was re-surveyed and six additional studies were found that met the criteria. A replication of this analysis, using the larger universe, produced nearly identical results. The studies added include: Floyd Hunter, Ruth C. Schaffer, and Cecil G. Sheps, *Community Organization: Action and Inaction*, Chapel Hill: University of North Carolina Press, 1956; Edward C. Banfield, *Political Influence: A New Theory of Urban Politics*, New York: The Free Press, 1961; Benjamin Walter, "Political Decision Making in Arcadia," in F. Stuart Chapin, Jr., and Shirley F. Weiss (eds.), *Urban Growth Dynamics*, New York: John Wiley, 1962, pp. 141–186; Floyd Hunter, *Housing Discrimination in Oakland, California*, a study prepared for the Mayor's Committee on Full Employment and the Council of Social Planning of Alameda County, 1964, and *The Big Rich and the Little Rich*, Garden City, N.Y.: Doubleday and Co., 1965; Francis M. Carney, "The Decentralized Politics of Los Angeles," *The Annals*, 353 (May, 1964), pp. 107–121; Ritchie P. Lowrey, *Who's Running This Town?*, New York: Harper, Row, 1965.

9. No implication of the inferiority of these reports is intended; the criterion was adopted for the sake of practicality.

10. It was in connection with this criterion that the most difficult decisions arose. Several excellent studies were excluded from consideration because they dealt primarily with the more formal workings of local government. See, for example, Wallace Sayre and Herbert Kaufman, *Governing New York City*, New York: Russell Sage Foundation, 1960, and Oliver P. Williams and Charles Adrian, *Four Cities*, Philadelphia: University of Pennsylvania Press, 1963.

11. For their assistance in providing bibliographies I am indebted to Michael T. Aiken, Terry N. Clark, and Claire W. Gilbert. Other sources employed include Wendell Bell, Richard J. Hill, and Charles R. Wright, *Public Leadership*, San

Francisco: Chandler Publishing Co., 1961, and Charles Press, *Main Street Politics: Policy-Making at the Local Level,* East Lansing: Michigan State University, 1962.

12. Bell, Hill, and Wright, *op. cit.;* Peter H. Rossi, "Community Decision Making," *Administrative Science Quarterly,* 1 (March, 1957), pp. 415–443; Charles M. Bonjean and David M. Olsen, "Community Leadership: Directions of Research," *Administrative Science Quarterly,* 9 (December, 1964), pp. 278–300.

13. The "positional" method, in which leaders are taken to be those persons occupying important positions in formal and/or informal organizations, is frequently used in these studies but always in conjunction with one of the four listed.

14. Except for some differences in emphasis in types 2 and 3, this typology closely resembles one proposed by Peter H. Rossi, "Power and Community Structure," *Midwest Journal of Political Science,* 4 (November, 1960), pp. 390–401.

15. The identification of each study can be found in Walton, *op. cit.,* footnote 5.

16. No difficulty was encountered in classifying sociologists. In the case of political scientists, however, several researchers did not fit precisely into that category. These are indicated by superscripts in Table 1. In the order of their appearance these investigators belong to the field of government, the next two from public administration, and finally, education. In the first three instances, I had no hesitancy in grouping them with the political scientists. The educator was included with the political scientists in order to provide a constrast between sociologists and others. If the four communities listed under #30 are dropped from the analysis, the Q measures in Tables 5 and 6 are somewhat altered (due to the small N's) but the patterns within the tables remain the same.

17. The rationale for the dichotomies employed on the method and power structure variables is provided in Walton, *op. cit.,* footnoes 15 and 16. Following the procedure outlined there, the case study and combined methods are grouped with the decision-making category in order to contrast the reputational method with others.

18. It should be noted that the cell frequencies represent communities, not studies. The chi-square test is employed in the Tables 2, 3, and 4 with the recognition that the assumption of independent cell frequencies is not fully met, since over half of the communities were studied in conjunction with at least one other. With respect to the Q measures, this assumption does not apply.

19. David Gold, "Independent Causation in Multivariate Analysis: The Case of Political Alienation and Attitude Toward a School Bond Issues," *American Sociological Review,* 27 (February, 1962), pp. 85–87.

20. Herbert Hyman, *Survey Design and Analysis,* Glencoe, Ill.: The Free Press, 1955, ch. 7.

21. Table 5 is presented to make this point explicit though obviously Table 6 implies that the association in Table 5 will not change, i.e. "within a system of three variables, all of which are related at the zero-order level, if the association between any two disappears with the third held constant, then the association between any other two will not change with the third constant and, in particular, cannot become zero," Gold, *op. cit.,* footnote 5.

22. Gold, *op. cit.,* p. 85.

23. For a suggestive discussion of that possibility see John Horton, "Order and Conflict Theories of Social Problems as Competing Ideologies," *American Journal of Sociology*, 71 (May, 1966), pp. 701–713, and "The Dehumanization of Anomie and Alienation: A Problem in the Ideology of Sociology," *British Journal of Sociology*, 15 (December, 1964), pp. 283–300.

24. Horton, *op. cit.*

25. Robin M. Williams, Jr., "Some Further Comments on Chronic Controversies," *American Journal of Sociology*, 71 (May, 1966), p. 720.

26. Mannheim recognized two usages of the "theory of ideology," the first referring to intentional falsifications or incorrect observations (Marx' meaning) and the second referring to "total mental structure." Realizing the need for a distinction, he termed the first type "particular" conceptions and the second "total" conceptions or perspectives. It is this second type that interested Mannheim and was the subject of his sociology of knowledge or *Wissenssoziologie*. Mannheim, *op. cit.*, pp. 265–266.

27. Mannheim, *op. cit.*, p. 172.

28. Peter H. Rossi in a review of M. Kent Jennings, *Community Influentials: The Elites of Atlanta*, *American Journal of Sociology*, 71 (May, 1966), p. 725.

29. Mannheim, *op. cit.*, p. 5.

QUESTIONS

1. What are the three variables, and how are they linked to a causal sequence?
2. Do the assumption of the causal sequence and the evidence of the research rule out the interpretation that researchers are attracted to, or selected into, a particular discipline according to prevailing methods of the discipline?
3. Notice that Table 1 is actually a "data table," in which for each research case you have its outcomes on each of the variables. Construct your own 2×2 analysis tables and check for their agreement with those of the author. You can also check the author's statement that the findings are not significantly changed by using the researcher rather than the researched community as the basic research case. How will you handle the fact that some researchers are associated with more than one researched community?
4. Using this article as an empirical observation, describe both the explicit and implicit rules of causal analysis.
5. Causal analysis has been discussed within a context of using Pearson correlation coefficients (r) (see H. Blalock, *Causal Inferences in Nonexperimental Research*, University of North Carolina Press, 1963). The author in this study uses the coefficient Q, which is not a 2×2 equivalent of r. Reanalyze these tables, using ϕ (phi) which is an equivalent of r and see if the conclusions remain unchanged.

Police Perceptions of a Hostile
Ghetto: Realism or Projection

W. EUGENE GROVES and PETER H. ROSSI

In the previous article the author used a fairly simple multivariate technique
employing three variables in a series of 2×2 tables. This approach has
the obvious limitation of being too cumbersome when more than three variables
are considered. In such situations we must turn to more sophisticated, and
usually more difficult, procedures, among which are multiple and partial
correlation, factor analysis, configurational analysis, cluster analysis, and path
analysis. All these techniques are capable of handling many variables but
because of their computational complexity usually require a computer for
their application to social research.

Of the sophisticated multivariate techniques, multiple and partial correlation
and regression are perhaps the most widely used in sociology. The authors of
the following article employ these techniques to analyze as many as six
variables at one time. (In the multiple correlation analysis the sixth variable
is city but is considered as twelve variables in the analysis, one variable for
each city in the sample.) Pay close attention to how the authors move back and
forth between analysis and interpretation, and to the kinds of theoretical
statements that could not be made without the multivariate procedures. Another
important aspect of this paper is the use of different levels of analysis,
especially percentage analysis and multiple correlation.

■ Self-fulfilling prophecies create a larger share of the results of social
interaction than we sometimes care to admit. So it may be with the police
and some of the local communities in which they are charged with maintaining "law and order." In the last few years, there have been a number
of instances where police departments, anticipating disorders either from
black populations or white protestors, have acted in such a manner as to
ensure that the anticipated disorders actually occurred. The Walker
Report (1968) to the National Commission on the Causes and Prevention
of Violence assails the Chicago police for acting with such unrestrained
violence and vindictiveness toward the protestors during the Democratic
National Convention in 1968 that formerly peaceful demonstrators were
led to more militant actions.

Perhaps the clearest case of police expectations leading to the outbreak
of a civil disorder was described by an unpublished staff report of the
National Advisory Commission on Civil Disorders (the Kerner Commission)[1] on the 1967 civil disorders in Cambridge, Maryland. The scheduling
of a speech in that city by H. Rap Brown led to police to anticipate that
civil disorders would break out, to mobilize their reserves, and to place
the Maryland National Guard on an alert status. The speech itself appeared
to have added to the police perception of immediate threat to the point
that when Brown was walking with the remnants of his audience down

Reprinted from *American Behavioral Scientist* 13 (1970), 727–743, with permission of
Sage Publications.

the street in the general direction of the downtown area of Cambridge, the local police began firing on the group. Soon after that, several carloads of local whites drove through the black residential section firing guns out of the windows. Blacks and whites quickly hardened into positions of hostility and the result was a minor civil disorder in which a local school and a local motel (both used by blacks) were burnt down. The conflict was brought under control after the State Police and National Guard with cooler heads intervened to de-escalate the conflict.

In other disorders, particularly Newark, Detroit, and Plainfield, New Jersey, there is considerable evidence that violent police overreaction to relatively slight hostile acts led what might have been minor incidents into major disorders with heavy tolls of life and property.

Although not as well documented because the actors in collective disorders rarely leave behind records, it is probably the case that black populations have also overreacted to specific actions of police. Thus in the 1967 Detroit riot, the raiding of a "blind pig" by a very large task force of Detroit policemen dressed in a new type of uniform led the local populace to believe that the raid in question was an unusual and especially harsh intervention into local privileges. During the riots which ensued photographs were circulated in the black ghetto of a badly mutilated black man allegedly tortured to death by the police.[2] Many blacks had come to expect through past experience that they would not be treated fairly and humanely by the police, so that any rumor, especially one originating in a situation where police were essentially unrestrained, seemed credible.

The dramatic instances of overreaction on the part of police or their clients occur in connection with major civil disturbances. But what is the day-to-day manifestation of these attitudes? On the beat, policemen and blacks meet, interpret each other's behavior in terms of the meanings each imputed to the actions of the other, and act on those bases. In situation after situation, an officer has to make a judgement whether or not a particular person is hostile, friendly, or indifferent—and act accordingly. Conversely, the civilian black encountering an officer has to judge how the latter is going to behave in the encounter and judge how to act accordingly. These are the judgements and actions which are more difficult to study and assess, yet are the stuff out of which police-community relations are formed.

The relationships between police departments and the black populations of our cities are made up cumulatively out of the day-to-day actions and reactions of the two groups. In this [article], we wish to examine some of the conditions under which police view the residents of the black ghetto as hostile, whether police perceptions are primarily a response to the actual expressed antagonism of blacks, or whether they arise more from causes independent of the black community. It is a critical issue, if we assume, as has been shown in so many cases, that perceptions of others tend to strongly influence one's own actions toward others. And it is particularly important, since police are the primary representative of white power with which blacks continuously come into potentially threatening personal contact.

Of course, to look at police perceptions of blacks is to look at only one of the two major self-fulfilling prophecy mechanisms that may be at work in police-black relationships. There is also the question of how blacks view the police, an issue into which we will not go in this [article]. But, in a real sense, the attitudes of the police are more critical. In theory, at least, police are supposed to serve the communities where they patrol, and be accountable to political authority. And from a practical policy viewpoint, one can do more to affect the views of policemen than to affect the views of ghetto blacks. Police are organized into a para-military organization, making them more accessible (at least from within the police organization) and more likely to respond to organizational efforts to change their practices and behavior.

CONTACT, PREJUDICE, AND THE PERCEPTION OF HOSTILITY

Unlike some other public services which are delivered to local neighborhoods in an impersonal way, the services of a police department are essentially activities conducted in face-to-face encounters between local neighborhood residents and police personnel. One might, therefore, expect that the officers on daily patrol in a neighborhood would have ample opportunity to build an empirical base underneath their perceptions of how their services are viewed by local residents, assuming, of course, that they make an effort to understand and be informed about the community. In particular, we would expect that officers on daily patrol in black neighborhoods would have a very good chance to form assessments of the general tone of the community that might easily reflect the level of hostility that black citizens generally direct toward police officers. In addition, the interchange among police colleagues concerning their individual experiences should provide policemen in any particular city with some common assessment of the support and approval they can expect, and the dangers they face, in their patrol neighborhoods.

On the other hand, most of what we know from studies in the psychology of perception would lead us to expect that prior definitions of the situation, generalized expectations, and pressure from peers often will override the content of specific experiences, so that generalized social assessments will not reflect simply the content of a myriad of specific encounters. Furthermore, such prior definitions may affect the extent to which a policeman will penetrate a neighborhood—in the sense of developing a wide network of acquaintances and reliable sources of information. In short, a policeman may be in a neighborhood but penetrate it only superficially. He may be out of touch with the residents either because he does not make efforts to become acquainted or because his personal antagonism toward the residents prevents such acquaintances from developing.

Under such conditions, minor incidents, or even harmless street corner gatherings, may be blown out of proportion, and interpreted as exceptionally hostile in confirmation of the policeman's preexisting mental set. The policeman may then assault a person who used incautious phrases, or may summarily order a group to disperse, thus engendering the actual hostility he initially imagined. This self-fulfilling prophecy may be at work early enough in the cycle of police-community interaction to prevent the development of (or perhaps to partially create) a realistic basis for local neighborhood assessments or prevent what is actually the first model.

Thus we pose two models to characterize an aspect of police-community relations in the black community. One model suggests that a policeman's assessment of the hostility of local black neighborhoods is based largely on the actual level of friendliness or hostility toward the police. The other model suggests that these assessments are generated by processes that have little to do with the black community, but may arise from prior attitudes, from definitions of the situation shared by certain police subcultures, or from unique experiences the policeman himself generates by his own friendly or hostile actions toward residents. Of course, models set up in opposition to each other have a distressing tendency not to be clearly separable when applied to empirical data. Hence, we have to consider that both sets of processes may be going on at the same time: the actual level of community hostility toward the police, and the perceptual screens of the individual may both bear a significant relationship to the policeman's final assessments.

THE SAMPLE

To examine which of these models is more plausible, we have drawn upon the results of interviews with five hundred and twenty-two policemen drawn from thirteen major central cities. These interviews were part of a study conducted for the Kerner Commission[3] concerned with the attitudes toward blacks displayed by persons who occupy positions on the interfaces between local institutions and residents of the ghettos. The interviews were conducted in the Spring of 1968; most were completed before the round of civil disorders broke out following the assassination of Martin Luther King. The study design was based upon drawing a sample of fifteen cities, five of which had major riots or widespread civil disorders in 1967 (Detroit, Newark, Milwaukee, Boston, and Cincinnati), five of which had riots in previous years or only a low level of disorder in 1967 (Brooklyn, Cleveland, Chicago, Philadelphia, and San Francisco), and five which had had no major disorders in 1967 or earlier (Washington, D.C., Pittsburgh, Gary, Baltimore, and St. Louis).[4]

About forty policemen were quota sampled in each city, quotas being set to obtain twenty-four white patrolmen, six white supervisors, eight black patrolmen and two black supervisors. To qualify for interviews, the policemen had to be working in police districts which were predominantly black and, hence, hopefully representative of the policemen black ghetto residents encounter.

Respondents were in most cases chosen by local police officials and, hence, can be expected to be biased toward the kinds of policemen officials felt might present their cities in the best light. The interview contained questions about local community problems, items concerning their perceptions of civil disorders, about their patrol practices, about their own attitudes toward blacks, and about their backgrounds.

Samples were obtained from only thirteen of the fifteen cities in the sample. The police departments of Milwaukee and Boston not only refused official participation but also forbade their policemen from granting interviews on their own. The analysis which follows is based on the five hundred fifteen usable interviews obtained in the thirteen cooperating cities.

If police assessments of black hostility are sensitive to actual experiences in patrolling the ghetto, then we would expect that there would be significant variation from city to city. After all, at the time of our interviews some of the cities (notably Detroit and Newark) had recently experienced widespread civil disorders, and other cities (notably Baltimore, Gary, and St. Louis) had not even experienced minor disorders. The salience of police behavior as an issue in the civil rights agitation also varied considerably. In New York and Baltimore, for example, local public officials had instituted policies stressing police restraint in the ghettos of those cities, while in other cities, like Chicago, Milwaukee, and Newark, police departments had notorious reputations among blacks for mistreatment and brutality. Qualitative interviews with public officials in each of these cities demonstrated considerable variation in the control which mayors exercised over their police departments, and similar interviews with black leaders showed differences from place to place in the extent to which police behavior was a local issue in the struggle for black parity.

RESULTS

Overall, the police perceived a large proportion of the residents as hostile. Thirty-one percent felt that "most Negroes regard police as enemies," another 31% felt that "most Negroes regard police as on their side," and 36% felt that "most Negroes are indifferent toward the police." When asked about young adults, 42% felt that young blacks considered police as enemies, while only 16% thought they considered police as friends. From these two questions and three others ("How much respect does the average resident of this precinct have for the police?" and "How do people *in general* in this precinct regard the police?" and "How satisfied are you with the respect you get from citizens?"), all of which were related to all others with gamma (γ) greater than .47, we constructed an index of perceived hostility. (Responses to each question were given a -1, 0, or $+1$ for perception of friendliness, neutrality, and hostility, respectively, and the responses to the five questions added together.)

The resulting index gave scores from -5 to $+5$, with a mean of -0.28 (as shown in Table 1) and a population standard deviation of 2.91, indicating that, on the average, police perceived the residents of these largely black precincts as indifferent toward the police. As we would expect, black police perceive the population as less hostile than do white police. (The difference is significant at $p \leqslant .001$, two-tailed test.)

When we examine the average (of all black and white policemen) perceived hostility in each of the thirteen cities, differences do emerge. Baltimore is the lowest with an average index score of -1.83, while Detroit is the highest with a score of $+0.92$. An analysis of variance of city differences shows that 8.7% of the total variance among policemen is accounted for by differences in city means[5] (see Table 2). We can, therefore, reject the hypothesis that cities do not differ at a level of significance beyond p = .001. Separate analyses for white and black policemen lead to interesting findings: among blacks, the intercity differences account for 19.3% of the total variance among individuals, while among whites only 7.4% of the variance can be "explained" (see Table 5).

TABLE 1. Scores on Perceived Hostility Index

	Mean	Standard Error of Mean
All respondents (n=515)	−.28	.13
White respondents (n=391)	−.04	.15
Black respondents (n=124)	−1.09	.24

TABLE 2. Contribution to Variance of Independent Variables in Linear Model (n=515) (Perceived Hostility Is Dependent Variable)

	R^2	Unique[a] Contribution to R^2	F Ratio for Unique Contribution	Significance Level[b]
City differences (12 variables)	.087[c]	.078[c]	4.26	.001
Individual attributes (5 variables)	.158[c]	.150[c]	19.10	.001
Race	.024	.0002	0.15	n.s.
Rank	.027	.0011	0.72	n.s.
Age	.071	.0352	22.95	.001
Prejudice	.092	.0521	34.00	.001
Acquaintance	.031	.0075	4.91	.05
City + individual attributes (17 variables)	.236[a]	—	9.05	.001

[a] "Unique contribution" indicates the amount that is subtracted from multiple R^2 when the variable (or set of variables) is removed from the model. Thus the unique contribution may be less than the R^2 from that variable by itself, since that variable may be correlated with other independent variables in the model.
[b] Significance with which we can reject the hypothesis that the attribute(s) has no effect independent of the other variables in the model.
[c] Multiple R^2.

In terms of the two basic models posed earlier, this result suggests that black policemen have an assessment of residents' hostility that may be more closely related to the actual differences in city characteristics. We should normally expect black policemen to be more closely in touch than white policemen with residents of the black community, and therefore, that their perceptions of residents would more accurately reflect the actual attitudes they confront in daily encounters—as suggested in our first model.

In order to more adequately determine whether intercity differences in perceived hostility do, in fact, reflect real differences in the level of hostility, we would need to develop some measure that accurately characterized the antipolice hostility among blacks in each city. In this paper we will not attempt to employ such a measure. Therefore we can only observe that the differences between cities in the way police perceive black residents may be due not only to differences in actual hostility, but also to such factors as police hiring and assignment practices, variations in city sampling biases, or aggregation or compositional effects in different police departments. It will not be possible, therefore, to examine the exact extent to which our first model describes the source of police perceptions about residents.

However, it is clear that once we control for city differences, 91.3% of the variance among police (black and white combined) remains to be explained. Obviously there are individual characteristics of each policeman that make—in total—ten times as much difference in his perception of hostility as do city characteristics. Put another way, the variation within city among individuals is ten times as great as the variation across cities. The important determinants of police perceptions, therefore, do not depend upon the characteristics (including the black communities) of the cities themselves. The most interesting problem to explore, then, is whether we can find measurable characteristics of individuals that are at least as important as city differences and which can clarify exactly how our second model operates.

To carry out this analysis we examined the residuals after removing city means from a number of variables, in order to find relationships between perceived hostility and other attributes that would be unconfounded with intercity variation. We conjectured that a number of attributes might be related to individual variation in perceived hostility: education, human relations training, prejudice against blacks,[6] acquaintance with residents of the community,[7] age, rank, participation in community affairs, assignment to interracial patrol, and race. Since we were not certain of the accuracy of representation of a quota sample, especially in establishing generalizable zero-order relationships, we selected for further analysis only those variables which showed a zero-order correlation to perceived hostility at a level of significance greater than $p = .001$ (two-tailed test). A correlation coefficient of at least .15 met this criterion.

Five variables achieved at least this level of significance in their relationship to perceived hostility. They are listed in Table 2, along with the variance they "explain" alone, and the unique addition to variance "explained" which they account for in a linear model of individual attributes and city effects. The five individual attributes together account for almost twice as much variance as do city differences. At least 15% of the variation among individuals (both before and after city effects are controlled) can be "explained" by race, rank, age, prejudice, and acquaintance. To illustrate the magnitude of the effects of individual attributes, we have dichotomized individuals into those who scored higher and lower than the median in each city on appropriate variables. The zero-order effects are illustrated in Table 3.

Two of these five individual attributes, race and rank, do not have a

Analysis

TABLE 3. Effects of Individual Attributes on Perceived Hostility

Variable	Value	% Who Are Above City Median in Perceived Hostility
Race	White	.53
	Black	.34
Prejudice[a]	Low	.37
	High	.61
Acquaintance[a]	Low	.53
	High	.43
Age[b]	Young	.59
	Old	.37
Rank	Patrolman	.52
	Supervisor	.31

[a] "High," "low" mean above or below city median, respectively.
[b] "Young," "old" mean above or below city median, respectively.

significant relationship to perceived hostility, when we control for the other variables. To clarify why race and rank have no independent direct effect, we can first examine the correlation matrix of these five variables and perceived hostility (Table 4).

TABLE 4. Intercorrelations of Variables Determining Perceived Hostility (Based on Variables as Deviations from City Means)

	Rank	Age	Prejudice	Acquaintance	Perceived Hostility
Race	−.027	+.000	−.560	.161	−.157
Rank		.434	−.056	.098	−.161
Age			.017	.198	−.262
Prejudice				−.129	.297
Acquaintance					−.176

There are two pairs of fairly highly related variables: age and rank, and race and prejudice. The nature of the causal relationships in these two sets can be seen more clearly by setting out reasonable causal hypotheses and examining partial correlation coefficients. With race and prejudice, for example, the reasonable alternative hypotheses are (1) race affects both prejudice and perceived hostility, or (2) only prejudice affects perceived hostility directly, while race acts entirely through its effect upon prejudice (see Figure 1).

Which hypothesis is more supported by the data can best be seen by comparing the partial correlation coefficient of race and perceived hostility with prejudice controlled. In hypothesis one we would expect some, but not substantial reduction in the partial compared to the zero order correlation coefficient. In hypothesis two we would expect the partial correlation to approach zero. The partial is .018, compared to a zero order correlation of −.157, indicating that hypothesis two is the better repre-

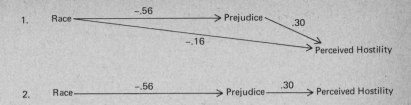

FIGURE 1: Alternative hypothetical causal models relating race, prejudice, and perceived hostility (zero order correlations are listed for each relationship).

sentation of the data, i.e. race has little effect upon perception once we have accounted for the effect of the policeman's prejudice, but it does explain a sizeable fraction of the variation in prejudice.

This suggests that black and white policemen with similar levels of prejudice react similarly to actions by people in their precincts. Furthermore, since for obvious reasons the average level of "prejudice" among black police (if the index can even be appropriately interpreted for blacks) is much lower than the average level for whites (mean of 2.07, compared to 5.84 for whites, in a 12-point index), and the population variance on the prejudice index is about one-third as high for blacks as for whites (2.53 compared to 7.18 for whites), it is clear that most of the variation in hostility that is related to prejudice comes from the variation in white prejudice. To further substantiate this claim, we have separated black from white policemen, and analyzed separately the variance explained for each by the remaining four independent variables, viz. rank, age, prejudice, and acquaintance. The results are shown in Table 5.

The hypothesis that the effects of these four variables are nil for blacks cannot be rejected even at a level of $p = .10$. The hypothesis of no effect is clearly rejected for whites (at a level of $p \leqslant .001$). This result rather strongly indicates that the background variables we earlier suggested

TABLE 5. Importance of Two Sets of Variables in "Explaining" White and Black Perceived Hostility

		Multiple R^2 for Set	F Ratio	Unique Contribution to R^2	F Ratio	Level of Significance of Unique Contribution
(n = 391)	City differences	.074	2.54	.074	3.07	$p = .005$
	Four individual variables	.167	19.40	.167	28.22	$p = .001$
Black	City + individual	.242	7.47	—	—	$p = .001$[a]
(n = 124)	City differences	.193	2.21	.169	1.92	$p = .05$
	Four individual variables	.043	1.33	.019	0.95	n.s.
White	City + individual	.212	1.80	—	—	$p = .05$[a]

[a] Refers to multiple R^2 for full model.

Analysis

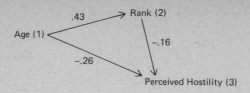

FIGURE 2: Hypothetical relationship among age, rank, and perceived hostility (zero order correlations are listed for each relationship).

might be related to the ascription of hostility are *only* important for white policemen. The significance of the individual attributes of whites, versus presumably more objective city attributes affecting blacks, is more clearly exemplified when we recall the much greater importance that city differences played in determining black perceptions of hostility. We can see in Table 5 that for whites the individual attributes are more than twice as important as intercity differences, while for blacks, the individual differences are quite small compared to intercity differences.

We can dispense with another attribute in the analysis. Rank does not contribute a significant unique amount to the variance "explained." The only reasonable causal chain connecting age, rank, and perceived hostility is shown in Figure 2. The two partial correlation coefficients (age by perceived hostility controlling for rank, and rank by perceived hostility controlling for age) can clarify what the predominant relationship is. If $r_{13.2} = 0$, then age acts entirely through its effect on a person's rank. But if $r_{23.1} = 0$, then the correlation between rank and perceived hostility is spurious, arising from the effect that age has upon both. We find that

$$r_{13.2} = .22 \qquad r_{23.1} = .055$$

indicating that the age is the important determinant, with rank largely related spuriously to perceived hostility due to older people occupying higher ranks.

HOW INDIVIDUAL ATTRIBUTES WORK

We have concluded that for *white* police, three individual attributes have a significant independent relationship to perceived hostility: age, prejudice, and acquaintance. Of these the unique contribution to variance "explained" by prejudice is most significant, that by acquaintance least significant (see Table 2). Table 6 shows the relationships between these three variables and perceived hostility, with individuals dichotomized at the city medians on all variables (thus the effects are not confounded with the actual level of hostility in each city, unless, of course, there is an interaction between level of hostility and the operation of these variables—which we have not yet examined). The fraction of police who are above city medians in perceived hostility ranges from 23% of the old, low prejudice, low acquaint-

TABLE 6. Perception of Hostility by White Policemen (Proportion Higher than City Median in Perceived Hostility)

	Young	Old	All Ages
Low Prejudice			
Low acquaintance	.51	.23	.39
	(49)	(39)	(88)
High acquaintance	.60	.29	.41
	(25)	(41)	(66)
High Prejudice			
Low acquaintance	.75	.63	.71
	(88)	(52)	(140)
High acquaintance	.63	.37	.49
	(51)	(46)	(97)

ance group, to 75% of the young, high prejudice, low acquaintance group. Both higher prejudice and younger age increase the perceived hostility under all combinations of the other attributes (though the magnitude of the effects is not uniform). Acquaintance, however, does not change perceptions in the same direction in all cases. The apparent interactions bear closer examination.

A higher level of acquaintance may conceivably either raise or lower the perception of others as hostile, depending upon what other factors are at work. Initial strong antagonism toward blacks could be an important enough screen through which a policeman would view his interaction with the residents that increased contact might add to his perceptions of hostility, as each encounter reinforces his own preconceptions. Or, on the other hand, the necessity that a good policeman make peace with the residents and have a friendly working relationship in order to more adequately perform his duties might constitute enough of an overriding imperative that a latently hostile policeman would be forced to look more fairly upon the black residents he is supposed to serve. The latter suggestion seems more plausible from our data. Table 6 indicates that for the high prejudice policemen, a higher level of acquaintance implies a lower level of perceived hostility (chi square is significant at $p \leqslant .001$). On the other hand, for those with low prejudice, acquaintance makes little difference in perceived hostility—if anything, the trend suggests that the more acquainted, but less prejudiced individuals might perceive more hostility, perhaps from a realization that some of the residents are, in fact, hostile, even though the policeman may be sympathetic with their complaints.

It is clearly the highly prejudiced, out of touch, white policeman— regardless of his age—who believes the residents to be antagonistic. Or put another way, most white policemen, like most other white Americans, tend to project their own prejudices and fears upon blacks, ascribing to them a level of hostility that more adequately reflects the hostility of the perceiver. Fortunately, however, it appears that a great deal of "reality testing" can somewhat temper these projections.

The significant difference between age groups is a little more difficult to interpret. A number of observers have suggested that older policemen are typically more prejudiced and also more accustomed to the "old days" before civil rights protests had gained significant strength—when police were much freer to act the way they wanted toward black citizens. One of the problems police departments often claim they face is that human relations training may have little impact on a recruit after he has spent some time on the beat being socialized by older policemen into the way "it is really done." But to counter this influence, most police departments have taken steps in the last decade to recruit more highly educated, less prejudiced, and more psychologically stable cadets.

If these measures have been at all successful in fulfilling their claims, we should expect to find the younger policemen less prejudiced, and would hope to discover that they had developed a more realistic perception of the residents. There was no significant relationship between age and prejudice in our sample. But we did discover a significant difference in the perception of hostility depending upon age—the younger police viewed the residents as more hostile. From Table 6 it is clear that age makes a striking difference in perception for all except those who are highly prejudiced and not well acquainted with the community.

The greater amount of hostility perceived by the younger policemen may have to remain an interesting but unexplained finding. Given the trends in the general society and the trends in recruitment, training, and the like, in police departments over the past decade one would expect to find the younger policemen more receptive to an unstereotyped approach to the black ghetto. One may speculate that these younger policemen are given different—perhaps more difficult and dangerous—tasks in patrolling the ghetto, that they may be self-selected from among the more apprehensive young whites and so on. It also may be the case that young white policemen are more the target of black hostility than their older colleagues. Whatever the ultimate explanations, these differences do not bode well for the future of relationships between police departments and the black communities they serve.

CONCLUSIONS

A large proportion of the police who serve in the black communities of our major cities see themselves as pursuing their tasks in, at worst, a hostile, and, at best, an indifferent environment. Less than one in three sees his clients as friendly. Urban police find themselves to a large extent in the position of troops who are sent to occupy conquered enemy territory.

Our attempt to discern how much of this view depended upon the hard characteristics of the ghetto reaction to the police, and how much was due to the perceptual screens which the policemen brought with them to their task was made difficult by the absence of hard data on black perceptions and actions toward the police. However, we can judge that not more than 8.7% of the variance among individual policemen—and probably much less—can be accounted for by variation from city to city. This is much less than we might expect from the known variation in militancy among black communities in major cities. Particularly, we have noted that black policemen, presumably more in tune with ghetto reality than are whites, do have perceptions which differ much more from city to city.

By far most of what a white policeman anticipates from black citizens is determined by factors other than the actual level of hostility in a city. A good deal of the perceived antagonism appears to be a projection of the policeman's own fears and prejudices—although a high level of acquaintance with community residents, leaders, and other individuals tends somewhat to mitigate a highly prejudiced policeman's projection of his hostility. It is not completely clear from the analysis presented whether the perception of hostility by the more prejudiced policeman is a result only of his own interpretations, or a result of actual experiences that he may generate day to day by his own overreactions—though both processes presumably would go hand in hand.

What we should be particularly disturbed about are those policemen who are both highly prejudiced and out of touch with the community. They are most like an occupying army, and are most likely to generate increased antagonisms through their overreaction to, and lack of realistic differentiation among, black residents. Particularly alarming was the finding that among the policemen interviewed, 31% reported that they did not even know one important teenage or youth leader in their precincts well enough to speak with whenever they saw him. It would be difficult to imagine how these policemen could formulate realistic judgements about the actions of ghetto youth—the source of the most militant actions.

We have presented what is only one side of an interactive system. The behavior of blacks and their perceptions of the hostility of policemen are also parts of a system which interact with the characteristics of policemen, the structure of police departments, and the nature of public opinion to produce what we experience as police-ghetto relationships. The end result, in any case, is a tangle of mutual suspicion and hostility.

We might extend the findings based upon variation within police departments to argue that decreasing the prejudice of policemen, and increasing their acquaintance and experience, might somewhat reduce the apprehensions of the otherwise more insensitive police. But this is valid only to a certain point. There is no assurance that reducing the average prejudice level, for example, will substantially change the nature of police-black relations, as the source of conflict extends far beyond the personalities of those involved. It arises from the general discriminatory treatment in unemployment, in education, in legal norms, in housing, and in most other aspects of daily life that blacks face. And police are stuck, regardless of their level of prejudice, with a most difficult task of maintaining social control in the face of blacks reacting to continuous substantive injustice. Even if the police, and the blacks, were realistic about their perceptions of each other, we would have little reason to believe that the general level of tension would be reduced as long as there is a substantial conflict of goals and norms between the black community and the police departments. This is especially true when police are asked to maintain order for city governments which lack sufficient funds, and will power, to eradicate the economic and social causes of black protest.

Analysis

NOTES

1. The report was uncovered and summarized by Robert Walters in the *Washington Star,* March 4, 1968.

2. Fact and fancy are close together in situations of this sort. At the same time that this photograph was being circulated from hand to hand, an authentic police atrocity was being committed in the Algiers Motel. See Hersey (1968).

3. Interviews with policemen were part of a larger study in which surveys were made of frontline personnel in major community institutions which dealt with their black ghettos, including educators, social workers, ghetto merchants, political party workers, and personnel managers of large employers. The major findings of the study relating to differences among these groups are reported by the National Advisory Commission on Civil Disorders (1968).

4. Note that in three of the five "nonriot" cases, riots soon broke out in Spring 1968, shortly after most of our interviewing was completed. Pittsburgh, Washington, and Baltimore suffered major riots in response to King's assassination.

5. For the analysis we used a linear model in which the thirteen cities were coded into twelve "dummy" variables. See Bottenberg and Ward (1963) for a good explanation of the use of a general linear model.

6. "Prejudice" in this case was a measure of how apprehensive the individual was about blacks gaining ground in areas not directly related to police work. The index is the sum of answers (coded 2, 1, and 0) to five items: One question about whether Negroes have tried to move too fast in gaining what they feel to be equality, and four items about whether "you are very disturbed, slightly disturbed, or not disturbed at all about": "Negroes draining resources through welfare payments," "Negroes taking over political power," "Negroes moving into areas that, until recently, were occupied only by whites," and "Negroes socializing with whites." These items were interrelated with gammas (γ) at least .45. Thus our index does not entail negative stereotypes of blacks held by whites, but reflects a general antagonism toward or fear of blacks getting "out of place."

7. The level of acquaintance is measured by the sum of the number of persons in six categories whom the policeman reported he knew well enough to "speak with whenever you see them." The categories were: shop owners, managers, clerks; important adult leaders in the neighborhoods; residents in general; important teenage and youth leaders; people from various government and private agencies who work in the neighborhoods; and the continual troublemakers. This index gave us a generalized level of community acquaintance for each patrolman.

REFERENCES

BOTTENBERG, R. A., and J. H. WARD, Jr. (1963) *Applied Multiple Linear Regression.* Technical Documentary Report PRL-TDR-63-6. Springfield, Va.: U.S. Department of Commerce.

HERSEY, J. (1968) *The Algiers Motel Incident.* New York: Bantam Books.

National Advisory Commission on Civil Disorders (1968) *Supplemental Studies.* Washington, D.C.: U.S. Government Printing Office.

WALKER, D. (1968) *Rights in Conflict*. Report Submitted to the National Commission on the Causes and Prevention of Violence. New York: Bantam Books.

QUESTIONS

1. The authors "stratify" cities according to a variable that is not directly involved in their conceptualization about perceptions of public hostility. What is this variable, and what importance does it assume in the analysis and interpretation of the data?
2. The authors stress the finding that black policemen's perception of public hostility varies with city, whereas the perceptions of white policemen do not. Of what importance is this finding for the authors' argument about the source and validity of policemen's perception of the hostility of blacks?
3. How was the dependent variable generated from the data?
4. Which of the analyses tables already have city differences "taken out"? What is the reason for "taking out" the effects of cities?
5. Compare the "causal inference" analysis in this article to that of article 18. Do both articles seem to follow the same "rules" of causal inference?

The Impact of Suburban Population Growth on Central City Service Functions
JOHN D. KASARDA

What an analysis reveals depends upon what we put into it—the skill of the researcher, the quality of the data, the number and types of controls, the variables we explicitly include and our assumptions about them, and the assumptions about the variables not included in the analysis.

Thinking only of the variables included in analysis, we can treat variables symmetrically (equal in priority) or asymmetrically (some unequal in priority). An asymmetric treatment is found most simply in the distinction of independent and dependent; more elaborately, there can be shifting statuses of independence-dependence. As a simple illustration, say variable A has priority to variable B, which in turn has priority to variable C; then B can be treated as both a dependent (to A) and an independent (to C) variable. Further, we can think of A as being both directly linked to C without any reference to B and indirectly linked to C through B. Then the effect of A on C would have two components—a direct effect and an indirect effect mediated through B.

Reprinted from *American Journal of Sociology* 77 (1972), 1111–1124, with permission of The University of Chicago Press.

Analysis

As the number of variables in analysis increases one by one, the number of different ways in which we might conceive of their being linked increases exponentially. Path analysis is one approach being used in sociology to provide a set of explicit conventions for analyzing a set of variables into their direct and indirect effects. Typically, we assume one-way connections between variables, with the possibility that the correlation between two variables is not analyzed (conventionally represented by a curved two-headed arrow). As for the variables in the analysis, assumptions must be made about influences of unmeasured variables—typically that they are independent of each other and of other variables in the analysis. Under these circumstances, a path coefficient is a type of regression coefficient, that is, a numerical statement of how much change in the dependent variable can be expected to be associated with a unit change in the independent variable, the differences being that other prior variables in the analysis have been statistically held constant and that the unit of change is a standardized one such that the dependent variable can change (either increase or decrease) no more than one whole standard unit.

In the following article, Kasarda uses a path analysis as a method for delineating the magnitude of direct effects upon the dependent variable, central city expenditures. Note that expenditures are expressed as dollars per inhabitant, not as total dollars spent.

■ Since World War II, dynamic yet disproportionate growth has been occurring in our metropolitan areas. Between 1950 and 1970, the standard metropolitan statistical areas (SMSAs) accounted for approximately 80% of the national increase in population. Almost all the metropolitan growth, however, has occurred in the suburban rings surrounding the central cities, while most central cities have grown very little and many have experienced a decline in population. As a result, for SMSAs as a whole, more people are now residing in the suburban rings than in the central cities.

Concurrent with this population redistribution has been a significant alteration in the social morphology of our urban areas. The compact urban community of nineteenth-century America has been replaced by the diffuse metropolitan area as entire communities have become territorially specialized and dependent on one another. This new entity consists of a large central city nucleus and a plethora of politically autonomous but functionally dependent suburban populations serviced by the central city. As a specialized service center, the city's facilities are utilized intensely by a large part of the suburban population for employment, shopping, recreation, professional services, and other needs.

This study examines the central city as a service center for the suburban population. More specifically, it addresses two issues: (1) does the size of the suburban population have a significant impact on service functions performed in the central city, and (2) what effect, if any, have recent increases in the suburban population had on public services provided by central city governments? Primary attention is given to the latter issue and its implications for central city planning and metropolitan reorganization.

DATA AND METHOD

The metropolitan communities to be examined are all SMSAs as of 1950 ($N = 168$). Data representing four broad, but distinct, categories of service functions performed in central cities were obtained from the 1948, 1958, and 1967 Censuses of Business and the 1950, 1960, and 1968–69 Compendia of City Government Finances (U.S. Bureau of the Census). The categories are: (1) retail trade, (2) wholesale trade, (3) business and repair services, and (4) public services provided by central city governments. Sales and receipts for central city retail trade, wholesale trade, and business and repair services are used as indicators of the magnitude of these three categories of service functions, whereas annual operating expenditures for noneducational services provided by central city governments are used as indicators of the magnitude of the public service functions. For cross-sectional analysis, the sales, receipts, and operating expenditures are expressed in terms of "amount per central city resident"; for longitudinal analysis, these data are converted to constant dollars and expressed in terms of first differences.

Demographic data were obtained from the 1950, 1960, and 1970 Censuses of Population. The suburban population is defined as all population residing outside the central city but within the metropolitan area for those SMSAs that contain a single central city, and as all population residing outside the largest central city but within the metropolitan area of SMSAs that contain more than one central city.[1]

The primary method used is path analysis, which provides an algorithm for decomposing the total correlation between the dependent and independent variables so that the direct effects of each independent variable on the dependent variables may be ascertained. For example, if central city service functions vary with both the size of the central city population and the size of the suburban population, then a path model mapping the relationship appears as shown in Figure 1.

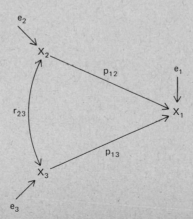

FIGURE 1: X_1, central city service variable; X_2, central city population size; X_3, suburban population size; p_{12} and p_{13}, path coefficients; r_{23}, zero-order correlation coefficient; e_1, e_2, and e_3, error terms.

263

Analysis

In a multivariate path model such as this, the zero-order correlation between an independent variable and the dependent variable is the sum of its direct effect via the path from that independent variable to the dependent variable and its *indirect effect*[2] through its correlation with the other independent variable (Land 1969, pp. 12–15). In terms of the coefficients,

$$r_{12} = p_{12} + r_{23}\, p_{13}$$
$$r_{13} = p_{13} + r_{23}\, p_{12}$$

The path coefficients (p_{12} and p_{13}) measure the variants in X_1 for which each independent variable (X_2 or X_3) is *directly* responsible, while the other independent variable is held constant.[3] Therefore, by computing path coefficients, we will be able to determine the direct effect of variation (or change) in both the central city and suburban populations on each central city service function as well as the direct effects of other independent variables.

FINDINGS

Does the size of the suburban population have any bearing on service functions performed in the central city? Table 1 presents the path

TABLE 1. Path Coefficients Between per Capita Measures of Central City Service Functions and Population Size (Log) of Central Cities and Suburban Areas, 1960 and 1970

Population Size	Central City Service Functions			
	Retail Trade (1958)	Wholesale Trade (1958)	Business and Repair Services (1958)	Public Services (1960)
1960				
Central city	−.76*	.33*	.11	.01
Suburban area	.83*	.27*	.54*	.39*
	Retail Trade (1967)	Wholesale Trade (1967)	Business and Repair Services (1967)	Public Services (1969)
1970				
Central city	−.83*	.16	.04	.06
Suburban area	.61*	.36*	.53*	.41*

* Significant at .001.

coefficients between each of the four general categories of central city service functions and the population sizes of the central city and suburban areas.[4]

Looking first at the direct effects of central city size on the central city service functions, we observe that only central city wholesale trade in 1958 exhibits a significant positive relationship with central city size. Business and repair services along with public services show little relationship with central city size. Also interesting is that, when suburban population size is held constant, a strong inverse relationship emerges between retail trade per capita in the central city and the population size of the central city.[5]

On the other hand, all four categories of central city service functions exhibit highly significant positive relationships with the size of the suburban population, both in 1960 and 1970. Moreover, with the exception of wholesale trade at the former point in time, suburban population has a larger direct (positive) effect on every category of central city service functions than does central city population.

Having noticed the close association cross-sectionally between central city service functions and population size of the suburban areas, the question now becomes, To what extent are changes over time in these service functions influenced by, or related to, changes in the suburban population size? This is determined in Table 2 which shows the path coefficients between changes in the four categories of central city service functions and changes in the population of central cities and suburban areas during the two most recent decades.

The longitudinal results indicate that changes in the size of the suburban population have had highly significant direct effects on all four categories of central city service functions. The proportion of variants in the four service categories for which changes in the suburban population

TABLE 2. Path Coefficients Between Changes in Central City Service Functions and Changes in the Population Size of Central Cities and Suburban Areas, 1950–60 and 1960–70

	Central City Service Functions			
Population Change	Retail Trade (1948–58)	Wholesale Trade (1948–58)	Business and Repair Services (1948–58)	Public Services (1950–60)
1950–60				
Central city	.54**	.41**	−.15	−.18
Suburban area	.47**	.71**	.69**	.65**
	Retail Trade (1958–67)	Wholesale Trade (1958–67)	Business and Repair Services (1958–67)	Public Services (1960–69)
1960–70				
Central city	.74**	.27**	.22*	.11
Suburban area	.31**	.62**	.51**	.45**

* Significant at .01.
** Significant at .001.

were directly responsible ranged from 22% to 51% during the 1950–60 decade, and from 10% to 38% during the 1960–70 decade.[6] It is again important to observe that changes in the suburban population exerted much larger direct effects on every central city service category, with the exception of retail trade, than did changes in the central city population.

The path coefficients presented in Tables 1 and 2 clearly indicate that the suburban population has a strong influence on central city service functions. Perhaps the most notable finding is that virtually no relationship exists between noneducational public services provided by the central city government and its population, either cross-sectionally or longitudinally, while positive and strong relationships exist both cross-sectionally and longitudinally between increases in the suburban population and central city public services. The obvious and important inference suggested by this finding is that the suburban population has at least as great an impact on public services provided by central city governments as does the central city population itself. The remainder of the study will examine this issue in more detail.

THE PUBLIC SERVICE ISSUE

One of the most serious problems facing our central cities in recent years has been the growing service-resource gap that has developed from a disproportional increase in public services provided by central city governments over that of their resources. Either explicit or implicit in most discussions addressing this problem has been the suggestion that the major force behind the increasing demand for public services is the changing composition of the central city population. Much less emphasis has been given to the increased demand for public services in the central cities created by the rapidly expanding suburban populations.

It would be difficult to deny that the changing composition of the central city population has increased the need for certain municipal services, such as public welfare and housing. However, we should not overlook the fact that increases in suburban populations have created a large demand for many other central city services. For example, the suburban population makes regular use of central city streets, parks, zoos, museums, and other public facilities; its routine presence in the central city increases problems of the sanitation department and contributes to the costs of fire protection; the daily movement in and out of the central city of the large commuting population requires services that constitute a large portion of the operating budget of both the police and highway departments (Hawley 1957, p. 773). These are only some of the costs experienced by central city governments as a result of services they provide to their suburban neighbors. Just what has been the relationship between growth of suburban populations and services commonly provided by the central city?

In Table 3 are presented the path coefficients between the sizes of the central city and suburban populations and the annual per capita expenditures for six common central city service functions.[7] We see that the suburban population exhibits a higher positive relationship with every cen-

TABLE 3. Path Coefficients Between per Capita Expenditures for Common Central City Service Functions and Population Size (Log) of Central Cities and Suburbs, 1960 and 1970

	Population, 1960		Population, 1970[a]	
Central City Service Function	Central City	Suburb	Central City	Suburb
Police	.15	.56**	.09	.61**
Fire	−.22*	.43**	−.35**	.57**
Highway	−.19*	.11	−.28**	.25**
Sanitation	−.01	.31**	−.15	.56**
Recreation	−.12	.24**	−.03	.37**
General control	.06	.33**	−.02	.41**

[a] Central city service data for 1969.
* Significant at .01.
** Significant at .001.

tral city service function than does the central city population. Moreover, while the direct effects of the suburban population are significant at the .001 level on every central city service function, except highway services in 1960, not a single significant positive relationship exists between the central city population and the central city service functions when suburban population size is held constant. These data provide support, in the cross-sectional case, to the contention that increases in the size of the suburban population are a major contributor to increased expenditures for common service functions performed by central city governments.

The next step is to examine the direct effects of changes (over time) in the size of the central city and suburban populations on changes in expenditures (in constant dollars) for the six central city services. Table 4 lists the path coefficients between changes in each service service function and

TABLE 4. Path Coefficients Between Change in Expenditures (in Constant Dollars) for Common Central City Service Functions and Change in the Central City and Suburban Populations, 1950–60 and 1960–70

	1950–60		1960–70[a]	
Central City Service Function	Central City	Suburb	Central City	Suburb
Police	−.12	.74**	.13	.56**
Fire	.01	.79**	.17	.54**
Highway	−.13	.61**	.17	.51**
Sanitation	−.03	.72**	.18	.62**
Recreation	−.10	.80**	.23*	.54**
General control	−.10	.51**	.20*	.58**

[a] Central city service function change 1960–69.
* Significant at .01.
** Significant at .001.

changes in the central city and suburban populations during the 1950–60 interval and during the 1960–70 interval.

We observe that the impact of the suburban population on the six central city service functions is even larger longitudinally than was true cross-sectionally. The percentage of change in these service functions for which changes in the suburban population are directly responsible range from 26% to 64% during the 1950–60 interval and from 26% to 38% during the 1960–70 interval. Only during the 1960–70 interval do we find changes in central city population size exhibiting consistent positive relationships with changes in the city services. Even during this time period, however, the direct effects of changes in the suburban population were much larger than the effects of changes in the central city population.[8]

OTHER CAUSAL FACTORS

Having demonstrated through both static and dynamic analyses that the growth of common central city service functions is strongly related to population increases in suburban areas, we now test for the possibility that some third variable or combination of variables are responsible for the strong relationships between suburban populations and central city public services. First, we must account for the effects of the age of the city. We know that suburban populations in the older SMSAs are generally larger than those in younger SMSAs. It has also been found that "older cities bearing the stamps of obsolescence, high density, high industrialization, and aging inhabitants, generate higher expenses than their size alone might have led one to suspect" (Vernon 1960, p. 172).

Another important variable is personal income of central city residents. Cities whose residents have higher personal incomes are usually able to provide more and better quality services than those whose population has lower personal incomes. It has also been long known that city-to-suburb migration is closely related to personal income of central city residents. Residents with higher incomes have a much larger choice of residential locations than do low income residents who are often economically and socially confined to the inner city.

Finally, we must control for the racial composition of the central city. One may suspect that certain municipal expenditures are either directly or indirectly related to the racial composition of the central city population. At the same time, the "flight to the suburbs" has been greatest in those cities that have experienced the largest influx of nonwhite migrants in the past 25 years.

To discover if each of the above three variables were positively related to both per capita operating expenditures for services provided by central city governments and population size of suburban areas, zero-order correlations were computed.[9] As may be observed in Table 5, all relationships are positive. Per capita operating expenditures for central city services were found to be positively related at the .001 level of significance to the age of the central city, but positively related at only the .05 level of significance to per capita income of central city residents and percentage nonwhite in the central city population. Similarly, the size of the suburban

TABLE 5. Zero-Order Correlation Coefficients Between Selected Characteristics of Central Cities and per Capita Operating Expenditures of Central City Governments and Size of Suburban Population, 1960

	Central City Characteristics		
	Age	Per Capita Income	Non-White %
Per capita operating expenditures in central city (all services)	.43*	.14	.17
Size of suburban population (log)	.65*	.16	.28*

* Significant at .001.

population was found to be positively related at the .001 level of significance to both the age of the central city and the percentage nonwhite in the central city population, but less so (p = .05) to per capita income of central city residents.

These results raise an important question: what is the relationship between suburban population size and per capita operating expenditures for central city public services when we control, not only for central city size, but also for age of the central city, per capita income of the central city residents, and the percentage nonwhite in the central city population? In addition, we might ask: what is the relationship between per capita expenditures for central city services and each of the three central city variables (age, income, percentage nonwhite) when the remaining two central city variables, as well as central city size and suburban size, are held constant? Table 6 answers these questions.

TABLE 6. Path Coefficients Between per Capita Expenditures for Central City Services and Selected Variables, 1960

	Central City Population (log)	Suburban Population (log)	Age	Per Capita Income	Nonwhite (%)
All services	−.24**	.38**	.34**	.10	.09
Police	−.04	.60**	.02	.15	.16
Fire	−.51**	.45**	.30**	.20*	−.03
Highway	−.29**	.08	.19*	.19*	−.04
Sanitation	.05	.28**	−.19*	.14	.27**
Recreation	−.19*	.27**	.04	.10	.12
General control	−.22*	.33**	.23*	.18	.22*

* Significant at .01.
** Significant at .001.

The crucial finding in Table 6 is that the impact of the suburban population remains strong and in the hypothesized direction when controls are introduced for central city size, age, per capita income, and percentage nonwhite. With these variables held constant, the direct effects of the size of the suburban population on the central city service functions are all positive, with significance at the .001 level for every service function except highway services.

Central city size exhibits a negative relationship to all service functions except sanitation services when the other variables are held constant. The significant negative relationships found between central city size and a number of the services indicate that economies of scale may operate in the provision of these services.

Examining the direct effects of central city age, per capita income, and percentage nonwhite on the service functions, we observe that age has a substantial direct effect on the total operating expenditures and on expenditures for fire and highway services, as well as on general control. Also as expected, personal income of the central city residents exerts a positive effect on all services, with significant direct effects on fire and highway services. Percentage nonwhite exerts significant direct effects on sanitation services and general control but, in contrast to the effects of age and personal income, exhibits essentially no relationship with fire and highway services.

In sum, Table 6 indicates that size of the suburban population, rather than size or composition of the central city population, is the most important determinant of central city expenditures for public services. It may also be inferred from Table 6 that, *ceteris paribus*, the overall per capita operating expenditures for central city services increase with the age of the central city and decline with increases in its size.

THE COMMUTING POPULATION

In an effort to refine the above analysis and determine the impact on central city public services of suburban residents who utilize central city services daily, data were obtained from the journey to work reports of the 1960 Census of Population on the total number of people in each SMSA who reside in the suburbs and commute to work in the central city. Path coefficients were again computed, substituting the number of commuters for suburban population size in the least-squares equations. The results are presented in Table 7.

TABLE 7. Path Coefficients Between per Capita Expenditures for Central City Services and Selected Variables, 1960

	Central City Population (log)	Commuters (log)	Age	Per Capita Income	Nonwhite (%)
All services	−.23*	.35**	.35**	.11	.08
Police	−.02	.52**	.06	.17	.16
Fire	−.52**	.44**	.32**	.21*	−.04
Highway	−.40**	.28**	.14	.18	−.08
Sanitation	.02	.31**	−.18	.14	.26**
Recreation	−.18	.24**	.03	.11	.12
General control	−.21*	.28**	.25**	.20*	.22*

* Significant at .01.
** Significant at .001.

We observe that the number of suburbanites who commute to work in the central city has a direct impact at the .001 level of significance on the total per capita operating expenditures for central city services as well as on per capita expenditures for each individual central city service. Recalling that highway services was the only central city function to which size of the suburban population was not significantly related (Table 6), it is noteworthy that, when number of commuters is used as the independent variable, a highly significant positive relationship emerges.

The fact that the overall results in Table 7 are so similar to those in Table 6 indicates that the number of suburban residents who commute to work in the central city corresponds closely with the size of the suburban population. When the zero-order correlation between size of the suburban population and the number of suburban residents who commute to the central city was computed, it was found to be .95. Regression analysis showed the unstandardized slope between suburban size and number of commuters to be .105. In other words, an almost perfect linear relationship exists between suburban population size and the number of suburban residents who commute daily to the central city, with each increase of 1,000 suburban residents leading to an additional 105 commuters. Furthermore, the ratio of suburban residents who work in the central city to the central city resident population increases with the size of the suburban population. A correlation coefficient of .46 exists between suburban population size (log) and the ratio of commuters to central city residents. Thus, as the size of the suburban population increases, not only do larger numbers of suburban residents daily utilize central city public services, but, more important, the proportion of suburban residents relative to central city residents who utilize city services also increases. On the average, there are 132 commuters using central city services per 1,000 central city residents. These findings along with the results provided in Tables 3 through 7 offer empirical support to the argument that the rapid growth of suburban populations has contributed greatly to the increased demand and, hence, increased expenditures for common central city public services.

SUMMARY AND IMPLICATIONS

This study examined the relationship between suburban population growth and service functions performed in central cities of 168 SMSAs. While most sociologists acknowledge that the suburban population influences the service structure of central cities, the degree of that influence has often been underestimated. Both cross-sectional and longitudinal analysis demonstrate that the suburban population has a large impact on central city retail trade, wholesale trade, business and repair services, and public services provided by central city governments. More detailed examination of the public sector shows that the suburban population in general, and the commuting population in particular, exerts strong effects on police, fire, highway, sanitation, recreation, and general administrative functions performed in the central cities. The impact of the suburban population remains strong when controls are introduced for central city size and age, annexation, per capita income of central city residents, and percentage of the central city population that is nonwhite.

What implications do these results have for the present and future planning of the metropolitan community? First, the findings indicate that central city officials and planners should be particularly attentive to trends in the population growth of their outlying areas when projecting future demands for central city services. As long as areal specialization continues to increase within the metropolitan community, we can expect the impact of the suburban population on central city facilities and services to grow.

A second implication is that the suburban population, by its daily use of central city facilities, substantially raises the costs of municipal services. While suburban residents do partially reimburse central cities in some SMSAs through employment and sales taxes, it is not likely that these "user charges" generate sufficient revenue to cover the additional costs.[10] A strong case can therefore be made for consolidating the politically autonomous suburban units with the central city in the form of a metropolitan-wide government. With a single jurisdiction controlling the services and resources, not only would the tax load for the provision of municipal services be spread in a more equitable fashion throughout the metropolitan area, but economies of scale might also be realized. Heavy resistance from suburban populations to political reorganization, however, makes the outlook for consolidation in the near future quite pessimistic. For the time being, then, the only recourse open to the central city is increased financial assistance for the provision of municipal services. Perhaps suburban resistance to consolidation will only recede when the circuitous flow of taxes from suburb to Washington to central city increases to an extent that the service-resource gap begins to favor the central city.

NOTES

1. Since much of the detailed data analyzed in this study were available for only the largest central city of those SMSAs that contain two or more central cities, the largest city was considered the nucleus, and the other cities were treated as suburban to that nucleus. There are two exceptions to this rule. Both the twin cities of Minneapolis–Saint Paul and San Francisco–Oakland, because of their size and the availability of data for all four cities, were taken as single centers by summing the data for each respective pair.

2. Blalock (1971) provides a convincing argument that, whenever the direction of causation between exogenous (independent) variables is ambiguous, we cannot reliably estimate indirect effects through those variables. This being the case with our models, we shall restrict our analysis to the direct effects of each independent variable on the dependent variables.

3. In simple recursive models such as ours, the path coefficients are equivalent to standardized-partial regression coefficients.

4. For cross-sectional analysis, the logs of the size of the central city and suburban populations were regressed on the per capita service measures, since a

preliminary plotting of these per capita measures with central city size and suburban size showed a slight bending effect at the upper ends of the distributions.

5. This, of course, does not mean that central city retail trade declines with increases in central city size but rather that, controlling for the effects of the suburban population, increments in central city population are associated with less than proportionate increases in central city retail trade.

6. The squared path coefficients measure the proportion of variance (or change) in the dependent variable for which the determining variable is directly responsible (Land 1969, p. 10). The zero-order correlations between changes in central city and suburban populations were .11 during the 1950–60 time period and −.27 during the 1960–70 time period.

7. Police service includes police patrols and communications, crime-prevention activities, detention and custody of persons awaiting trial, traffic safety, vehicular inspection, and the like. Fire-prevention services include inspection for fire hazards, maintaining firefighting facilities such as fire hydrants, and other fire-prevention activities. Highway services include maintenance of streets, highways, and structures necessary for their use, snow and ice removal, toll highways and bridge facilities, and ferries. Sanitation services include street cleaning, collection and disposal of garbage and other waste, sanitary engineering, smoke regulation, and other health activities. Recreation facilities and services include museums and art galleries, playgrounds, play fields, stadiums, swimming pools and bathing beaches, municipal parks, auditoriums, auto camps, recreation piers, and boat harbors. General control includes central staff services and agencies concerned with personnel administration, law, recording, planning and zoning, municipal officials, agencies concerned with tax assessment and collection, accounting, auditing, budgeting, purchasing, and other central finance activities (source: U.S. Bureau of the Census 1970, pp. 64–67).

8. Cross-sectional and longitudinal analysis was also carried out, controlling for suburban population annexed by central cities between 1950 and 1960. With this control instituted, the direct effects of the suburban population on all service functions remained positive and strong cross-sectionally and actually increased in the longitudinal analysis.

9. The correlation and path coefficients presented in Tables 5, 6, and 7 apply to 157 SMSAs in 1960 for which complete data were available on central city age (operationalized as the number of decades since the central city first attained a population size of 50,000 or more), per capita income of central city residents, percentage nonwhite in the central city, and the number of suburban residents who commute to work in the central city.

10. A recent study (Neenan 1970) of benefit and revenue flows between Detroit and six of its suburban municipalities, representing both residential and industrial suburbs, shows that the suburban communities enjoy a considerable net gain from the public sector of Detroit. Neenan's analysis indicates that the net subsidy from Detroit ranges from $1.73 per capita for the low income industrial suburb (Highland Park) to $12.58 per capita for the high income residential and commercial suburb (Birmingham). Although not specifically analyzed in the present study it should also be noted that many central cities indirectly subsidize their suburban areas by having to pay an unfair share of the metropolitan area's welfare services. Through zoning restrictions and discriminatory practices,

Analysis

the suburban populations have been able to insure that most of the low income, poorly educated, and chronically unemployed people in the metropolitan area are confined in the central cities. Suburban residents are therefore able to avoid the costs of public housing, public health, and other welfare services, which often impose a heavy burden on the operating budget of central cities.

REFERENCES

BLALOCK, HUBERT M. 1971. "Path Analysis Revisited: The Decomposition of Unstandardized Coefficients." Unpublished research note. Department of Sociology, University of Washington, Seattle.

HAWLEY, AMOS H. 1957. "Metropolitan Population and Municipal Government Expenditures in Central Cities." In *Cities and Society,* edited by Paul K. Hatt and Albert J. Reiss. New York: Free Press.

LAND, KENNETH. 1969. "Principles of Path Analysis." In *Sociological Methodology 1969,* edited by Edgar Borgatta. San Francisco: Jossey-Bass.

NEENAN, WILLIAM. 1970. "The Suburban–Central City Exploitation Thesis: One City's Tale." *National Tax Journal* 23 (June):117–39.

U.S. Bureau of the Census. 1970. *City Government Finances in 1968–69.* Washington, D.C.: Government Printing Office.

VERNON, RAYMOND. 1960. *Metropolis 1985.* Cambridge, Mass.: Harvard University Press.

QUESTIONS

1. List the data sources used in this research and note which variables come from which sources.
2. How do the results from the cross-sectional analyses compare to those from the longitudinal analyses?
3. Which types of central city expenditure are most influenced by suburban population? By central city population?
4. Carefully state your interpretation of finding that the path coefficient between central city population and per capita retail trade is −.76; between suburban population and per capita retail trade is +.83.
5. This article and the two preceding ones (by Walton and by Groves and Rossi) all use arrow diagrams; compare how they are used similarly and differently in the analyses and interpretations of the three articles.

SUGGESTED READINGS

BLALOCK, HUBERT M., JR. *Causal Inferences in Nonexperimental Research.* Chapel Hill: University of North Carolina Press, 1964.

HIRSCHI, TRAVIS, and SELVIN, HANNAN C. *Delinquency Research: An Appraisal of Analytical Methods.* New York: Free Press, 1967.

LOFLAND, JOHN. *Analyzing Social Settings: A Guide to Qualitative Observation and Analysis.* Belmont, Calif.: Wadsworth Publishing Co., 1971. Chapters 2, 3, and 6.

ROSENBERG, MORRIS. *The Logic of Survey Analysis.* New York: Basic Books, 1968.

SCHUESSLER, KARL. *Analyzing Social Data: A Statistical Orientation.* Boston: Houghton Mifflin, 1971.

YOUNG, PAULINE V. *Scientific Social Surveys and Research.* 4th ed. Englewood Cliffs, N.J.: Prentice-Hall, 1966. Chapter 10, "The Use of Case Data in Social Research."

ZEISEL, HANS. *Say It with Figures.* 5th ed. New York: Harper & Row, 1968.

■ "Research design" is a term that is easy to use but difficult, short of a complete textbook in research methods, to explicate. As a working and rough approximation, we shall use "research design" to refer to the plan of operations by which one moves from a set of research objectives or goals to the empirical results that speak to those goals. In short it is a plan of operations to allow empirical findings to speak to the research problem. Operationally, this means trying to assure that appropriate sets of variables are either permitted to vary, held constant, or randomized, with regard to the level of explanation being sought. Hence, for example, if the intent is to be exposed to the "richness" of a natural situation and the discovery of which variables are important to the participants, we are likely to choose either participant observation or "open-ended" interviewing. Either method seeks to assure variation in a large number of dimensions. At the other extreme, in which the concern is with the existence of a cause and effect relationship, the attempt is to assure: (1) that the "causal" variable varies in a precise manner; (2) that the effect variable is not constrained and is reliably measured; and (3) that all other variables are taken into account by being either held constant, randomized, or reliably measured so that they can be controlled through statistical analysis.

One useful way to analyze research design is to determine to what extent the design allows the researcher to "rule out" or discredit plausible alternative explanations of the findings (or what Campbell calls "threats to validity"). In the first article in this part, Campbell introduces this perspective and applies it to several "quasi-experiments." The Bandura, Ross, and Ross study illustrates a "well-controlled" experiment, and it is instructive to compare their design with those discussed in the Campbell article. The "panel" technique employed by Colombotos enables the direct study of change but differs from a "true" experimental technique because of the inability of the researcher to manipulate the independent variables and to control the assignment of "subjects" to treatments. Another approach to studying changes over time, especially large periods of time, is exemplified in article 24 by Dornbusch and Hickman. One "threat to validity" that often proves troublesome to "eliminate" is the respondent's reacting to or being affected by his awareness of being a research subject; in article 25 Milgram, Mann, and Harter describe a technique that attempts to avoid this particular problem.

Omitted from this section is a study employing the most commonly used research design in sociology—a "cross-sectional" survey. This design basically involves the questioning of a sample of subjects at a single point in time, and in most instances the researcher is unable to manipulate directly any of the independent variables of interest. Several of the other papers in this book utilize this design; hence there is no difficulty in finding examples. However, of special interest are article 16 by Spady and article 14 by Rollins and Feldman because of their attempts to handle the variable of time within the context of a "cross-sectional" survey design. Finally, an example of participant observation can be found in the Jansyn study (article 15).

Reforms as Experiments
DONALD T. CAMPBELL

It is often tempting in the social sciences to lament the fact that the reality
that we study is not easily researched in the laboratory. However, when
working in the "field" we are often torn between either ignoring our realization
of "complexity" by making the simplistic interpretation or giving up any hope
of being able to draw inferences with confidence from "natural" social
phenomena. But we need not always anticipate or fear by overwhelming
complexity; for many opportunities in the field approach true experiments in
important ways. Campbell calls these alternatives to experiments
"quasi-experiments."

In the provocative paper by Campbell several "quasi-experimental" designs
are discussed and illustrated by different "programs of social amelioration."
The issues discussed by Campbell not only are important to the social
researcher, but also have enormous relevance to those interested in "rational"
social change.

■ The United States and other modern nations should be ready for an
experimental approach to social reform, an approach in which we try out
new programs designed to cure specific social problems, in which we
learn whether or not these programs are effective, and in which we retain,
imitate, modify, or discard them on the basis of apparent effectiveness on
the multiple imperfect criteria available. Our readiness for this stage is
indicated by the inclusion of specific provisions for program evaluation in
the first wave of the "Great Society" legislation, and by the current congressional proposals for establishing "social indicators" and socially relevant "data banks." So long have we had good intentions in this regard
that many may feel we are already at this stage, that we already are continuing or discontinuing programs on the basis of assessed effectiveness.
It is a theme of this article that this is not at all so, that most ameliorative
programs end up with no interpretable evaluation (Etzioni, 1968; Hyman
and Wright, 1967; Schwartz, 1961). We must look hard at the sources of
this condition, and design ways of overcoming the difficulties. This article
is a preliminary effort in this regard.

Many of the difficulties lie in the intransigencies of the research setting
and in the presence of recurrent seductive pitfalls of interpretation. The
bulk of this article will be devoted to these problems. But the few available solutions turn out to depend upon correct administrative decisions in
the initiation and execution of the program. These decisions are made in
a political arena, and involve political jeopardies that are often sufficient
to explain the lack of hard-headed evaluation of effects. Removing reform
administrators from the political spotlight seems both highly unlikely, and
undesirable even if it were possible. What is instead essential is that the
social scientist research advisor understand the political realities of the

Reprinted from *The American Psychologist* 24 (1969), 409–429, with permission of the
American Psychological Association. (Revised by the author.)

situation, and that he aid by helping create a public demand for hard-headed evaluation, by contributing to those political inventions that reduce the liability of honest evaluation, and by educating future administrators to the problems and possibilities.

For this reason, there is also an attempt in this article to consider the political setting of program evaluation, and to offer suggestions as to political postures that might further a truly experimental approach to social reform. Although such considerations will be distributed as a minor theme throughout this article, it seems convenient to begin with some general points of this political nature.

POLITICAL VULNERABILITY FROM KNOWING OUTCOMES

It is one of the most characteristic aspects of the present situation that *specific reforms are advocated as though they were certain to be successful.* For this reason, knowing outcomes has immediate political implications. Given the inherent difficulty of making significant improvements by the means usually provided and given the discrepancy between promise and possibility, most administrators wisely prefer to limit the evaluations to those the outcomes of which they can control, particularly insofar as published outcomes or press releases are concerned. Ambiguity, lack of truly comparable comparison bases, and lack of concrete evidence all work to increase the administrator's control over what gets said, or at least to reduce the bite of criticism in the case of actual failure. There is safety under the cloak of ignorance. Over and above this tie-in of advocacy and administration, there is another source of vulnerability in that the facts relevant to experimental program evaluation are also available to argue the general efficiency and honesty of administrators. The public availability of such facts reduces the privacy and security of at least some administrators.

Even where there are ideological commitments to a hard-headed evaluation of organizational efficiency, or to a scientific organization of society, these two jeopardies lead to the failure to evaluate organizational experiments realistically. If the political and administrative system has committed itself in advance to the correctness and efficacy of its reforms, it cannot tolerate learning of failure. To be truly scientific we must be able to experiment. We must be able to advocate without that excess of commitment that blinds us to reality testing.

This predicament, abetted by public apathy and by deliberate corruption, may prove in the long run to permanently preclude a truly experimental approach to social amelioration. But our needs and our hopes for a better society demand we make the effort. There are a few signs of hope. In the United States we have been able to achieve cost-of-living and unemployment indices that, however imperfect, have embarrassed the administrations that published them. We are able to conduct censuses that reduce the number of representatives a state has in Congress. These are grounds for optimism, although the corrupt tardiness of state governments in following their own constitutions in revising legislative districts illustrates the problem.

One simple shift in political posture which would reduce the problem is the shift from the advocacy of a specific reform to the advocacy of the seriousness of the problem, and hence to the advocacy of persistence in alternative reform efforts should the first one fail. The political stance would become: "This is a serious problem. We propose to initiate Policy A on an experimental basis. If after five years there has been no significant improvement, we will shift to Policy B." By making explicit that a given problem solution was only one of several that the administrator or party could in good conscience advocate, and by having ready a plausible alternative, the administrator could afford honest evaluation of outcomes. Negative results, a failure of the first program, would not jeopardize his job, for his job would be to keep after the problem until something was found that worked.

Coupled with this should be a general moratorium on ad hominem evaluative research, that is, on research designed to evaluate specific administrators rather than alternative policies. If we worry about the invasion-of-privacy problem in the data banks and social indicators of the future (e.g., Sawyer and Schechter, 1968), the touchiest point is the privacy of administrators. If we threaten this, the measurement system will surely be sabotaged in the innumerable ways possible. While this may sound unduly pessimistic, the recurrent anecdotes of administrators attempting to squelch unwanted research findings convince me of its accuracy. But we should be able to evaluate those alternative policies that a given administrator has the option of implementing.

FIELD EXPERIMENTS AND QUASI-EXPERIMENTAL DESIGNS

In efforts to extend the logic of laboratory experimentation into the "field," and into settings not fully experimental, an inventory of threats to experimental validity has been assembled, in terms of which some 15 or 20 experimental and quasi-experimental designs have been evaluated (Campbell, 1957, 1963; Campbell and Stanley, 1963). In the present article only three or four designs will be examined, and therefore not all of the validity threats will be relevant, but it will provide useful background to look briefly at them all. Following are nine threats to internal validity.[1]

1. *History:* events, other than the experimental treatment, occurring between pretest and posttest and thus providing alternate explanations of effects.
2. *Maturation:* processes within the respondents or observed social units producing changes as a function of the passage of time per se, such as growth, fatigue, secular trends, etc.
3. *Instability:* unreliability of measures, fluctuations in sampling persons or components, autonomous instability of repeated or "equivalent" measures. (This is the only threat to which statistical tests of significance are relevant.)

4. *Testing:* the effect of taking a test upon the scores of a second testing. The effect of publication of a social indicator upon subsequent readings of that indicator.
5. *Instrumentation:* in which changes in the calibration of a measuring instrument or changes in the observers or scores used may produce changes in the obtained measurements.
6. *Regression artifacts:* pseudo-shifts occurring when persons or treatment units have been selected upon the basis of their extreme scores.
7. *Selection:* biases resulting from differential recruitment of comparison groups, producing different mean levels on the measure of effects.
8. *Experimental mortality:* the differential loss of respondents from comparison groups.
9. *Selection-maturation interaction:* selection biases resulting in differential rates of "maturation" or autonomous change.

If a change or difference occurs, these are rival explanations that could be used to explain away an effect and thus to deny that in this specific experiment any genuine effect of the experimental treatment had been demonstrated. These are faults that true experiments avoid, primarily through the use of randomization and control groups. In the approach here advocated, this checklist is used to evaluate specific quasi-experimental designs. This is evaluation, not rejection, for it often turns out that for a specific design in a specific setting the threat is implausible, or that there are supplementary data that can help rule it out even where randomization is impossible. The general ethic, here advocated for public administrators as well as social scientists, is to use the very best method possible, aiming at "true experiments" with random control groups. But where randomized treatments are not possible, a self-critical use of quasi-experimental designs is advocated. We must do the best we can with what is available to us.

Our posture vis-à-vis perfectionist critics from laboratory experimentation is more militant than this: The only threats to validity that we will allow to invalidate an experiment are those that admit of the status of empirical laws more dependable and more plausible than the law involving the treatment. The mere possibility of some alternative explanation is not enough—it is only the *plausible* rival hypotheses that are invalidating. Vis-à-vis correlational studies and common-sense descriptive studies, on the other hand, our stance is one of greater conservatism. For example, because of the specific methodological trap of regression artifacts, the sociological tradition of "ex post facto" designs (Chapin, 1947; Greenwood, 1945) is totally rejected (Campbell and Stanley, 1963, pp. 240–241; 1966, pp. 70–71).

Threats to external validity, which follow, cover the validity problems involved in interpreting experimental results, the threats to valid generalization of the results to other settings, to other versions of the treatment, or to other measures of the effect:[2]

1. *Interaction effects of testing:* the effect of a pretest in increasing or decreasing the respondent's sensitivity or responsiveness to the experimental variable, thus making the results obtained for a pretested population unrepresentative of the effects of the experimental variable for

the unpretested universe from which the experimental respondents were selected.

2. *Interaction of selection and experimental treatment:* unrepresentative responsiveness of the treated population.

3. *Reactive effects of experimental arrangements:* "artificiality"; conditions making the experimental setting atypical of conditions of regular application of the treatment: "Hawthorne effects."

4. *Multiple-treatment interference:* where multiple treatments are jointly applied, effects atypical of the separate application of the treatments.

5. *Irrelevant responsiveness of measures:* all measures are complex, and all include irrelevant components that may produce apparent effects.

6. *Irrelevant replicability of treatments:* treatments are complex, and replications of them may fail to include those components actually responsible for the effects.

These threats apply equally to true experiments and quasi-experiments. They are particularly relevant to applied experimentation. In the cumulative history of our methodology, this class of threats was first noted as a critique of true experiments involving pretests (Schanck and Goodman, 1939; Solomon, 1949). Such experiments provided a sound basis for generalizing to other *pretested* populations, but the reactions of unpretested populations to the treatment might well be quite different. As a result, there has been an advocacy of true experimental designs obviating the pretest (Campbell, 1957; Schanck and Goodman, 1939; Solomon, 1949) and a search for nonreactive measures (Webb, Campbell, Schwartz, and Sechrest, 1966).

These threats to validity will serve as a background against which we will discuss several research designs particularly appropriate for evaluating specific programs of social amelioration. These are the "interrupted time-series design," the "control series design," "regression discontinuity design," and various "true experiments." The order is from a weak but generally available design to stronger ones that require more administrative foresight and determination.

INTERRUPTED TIME-SERIES DESIGN

By and large, when a political unit initiates a reform it is put into effect across the board, with the total unit being affected. In this setting the only comparison base is the record of previous years. The usual mode of utilization is a casual version of a very weak quasi-experimental design, the one-group pretest-posttest design.

A convenient illustration comes from the 1955 Connecticut crackdown on speeding, which sociologist H. Laurence Ross and I have been analyzing as a methodological illustration (Campbell and Ross, 1968; Glass, 1968; Ross and Campbell, 1968). After a record high of traffic fatalities in 1955, Governor Abraham Ribicoff instituted an unprecedentedly severe crackdown on speeding. At the end of a year of such enforcement there had been but 284 traffic deaths as compared with 324 the year before. In announcing this the Governor stated, "With the saving of 40 lives in 1956, a reduction of 12.3% from the 1955 motor vehicle death toll, we can say

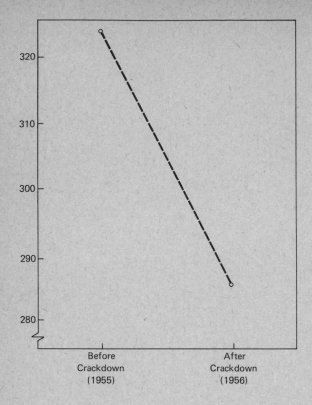

FIGURE 1: Connecticut traffic fatalities.

that the program is definitely worthwhile." These results are graphed in Figure 1, with a deliberate effort to make them look impressive.

In what follows, while we in the end decide that the crackdown had some beneficial effects, we criticize Ribicoff's interpretation of his results, from the point of view of the social scientist's proper standards of evidence. Were the now Senator Ribicoff not the man of stature that he is, this would be most unpolitic, because we could be alienating one of the strongest proponents of social experimentation in our nation. Given his character, however, we may feel sure that he shares our interests both in a progressive program of experimental social amelioration, and in making the most hard-headed evaluation possible of these experiments. Indeed, it was his integrity in using every available means at his disposal as Governor to make sure that the unpopular speeding crackdown was indeed enforced that make these data worth examining at all. But the potentials of this one illustration and our political temptation to substitute for it a less touchy one, point to the political problems that must be faced in experimenting with social reform.

Keeping Figure 1 and Ribicoff's statement in mind, let us look at the same data presented as a part of an extended time series in Figure 2 and

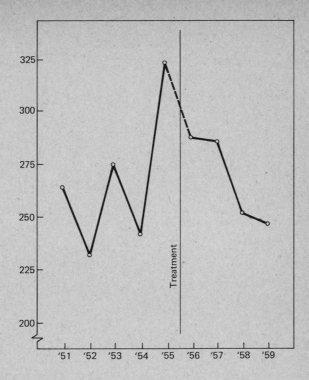

FIGURE 2: Connecticut traffic fatalities. (Same data as in Figure 1 presented as part of an extended time series.)

go over the relevant threats to internal validity. First, *History.* Both presentations fail to control for the effects of other potential change agents. For instance, 1956 might have been a particularly dry year, with fewer accidents due to rain or snow. Or there might have been a dramatic increase in use of seat belts, or other safety features. The advocated strategy in quasi-experimentation is not to throw up one's hands and refuse to use the evidence because of this lack of control, but rather to generate by informed criticism appropriate to this specific setting as many *plausible* rival hypotheses as possible, and then to do the supplementary research, as into weather records and safety-belts sales, for example, which would reflect on these rival hypotheses.

Maturation. This is a term coming from criticisms of training studies of children. Applied here to the simple pretest-posttest data of Figure 1, it could be the plausible rival hypothesis that death rates were steadily going down year after year (as indeed they are, relative to miles driven or population of automobiles). Here the extended time series has a strong methodological advantage, and rules out this threat to validity. The general trend is inconsistently up prior to the crackdown, and steadily down thereafter.

Instability. Seemingly implicit in the public pronouncement was the assumption that all of the change from 1955 to 1956 was due to the crackdown. There was no recognition of the fact that all time series are unstable even when no treatments are being applied. The degree of this normal instability is the crucial issue, and one of the main advantages of the extended time series is that it samples this instability. The great pretreatment instability now makes the treatment effect look relatively trivial. The 1955–56 shift is less than the gains of both 1954–55 and 1952–53. It is the largest drop in the series, but it exceeds the drops of 1951–52, 1953–54, and 1957–58 by trivial amounts. Thus the unexplained instabilities of the series are such as to make the 1955–56 drop understandable as more of the same. On the other hand, it is noteworthy that after the crackdown there are no year-to-year gains, and in this respect the character of the time series seems definitely to have changed.

The threat of instability is the only threat to which tests of significance are relevant. Box and Tiao (1965) have an elegant Bayesian model for the interrupted time series. Applied by Glass (1968) to our monthly data, with seasonal trends removed, it shows a statistically significant downward shift in the series after the crackdown. But as we shall see, an alternative explanation of at least part of this significant effect exists.

Regression. In true experiments the treatment is applied independently of the prior state of the units. In natural experiments exposure to treatment is often a cosymptom of the treated group's condition. The treatment is apt to be an *effect* rather than, or in addition to being, a cause. Psychotherapy is such a cosymptom treatment, as is any other in which the treated group is self-selected or assigned on the basis of need. These all present special problems of interpretation, of which the present illustration provides one type.

The selection-regression plausible rival hypothesis works this way: Given that the fatality rate has some degree of unreliability, then a subsample selected for its extremity in 1955 would on the average, merely as a reflection of that unreliability, be less extreme in 1956. Has there been selection for extremity in applying this treatment? Probably yes. Of all Connecticut fatality years, the most likely time for a crackdown would be after an exceptionally high year. If the time series showed instability, the subsequent year would on the average be less, *purely as a function of that instability.* Regression artifacts are probably the most recurrent form of self-deception in the experimental social reform literature. It is hard to make them intuitively obvious. Let us try again. Take any time series with variability, including one generated of pure error. Move along it as in a time dimension. Pick a point that is the "highest so far." Look then at the next point. On the average this next point will be lower, or nearer the general trend.

In our present setting the most striking shift in the whole series is the upward shift just prior to the crackdown. It is highly probable that this caused the crackdown, rather than, or in addition to, the crackdown causing the 1956 drop. At least part of the 1956 drop is an artifact of the 1955 extremity. While in principle the degree of expected regression can be computed from the autocorrelation of the series, we lack here an extended-enough body of data to do this with any confidence.

Advice to administrators who want to do genuine reality testing must include attention to this problem, and it will be a very hard problem to surmount. The most general advice would be to work on chronic problems of a persistent urgency or extremity, rather than reacting to momentary extremes. The administrator should look at the pretreatment time series to judge whether or not instability plus momentary extremity will explain away his program gains. If it will, he should schedule the treatment for a year or two later, so that his decision is more independent of the one year's extremity. (The selection biases remaining under such a procedure need further examination.)

In giving advice to the *experimental* administrator, one is also inevitably giving advice to those *trapped* administrators whose political predicament requires a favorable outcome whether valid or not. To such trapped administrators the advice is pick the very worst year, and the very worst social unit. If there is inherent instability, there is no where to go but up, for the average case at least.

Two other threats to internal validity need discussion in regard to this design. By *testing* we typically have in mind the condition under which a test of attitude, ability, or personality is itself a change agent, persuading, informing, practicing, or otherwise setting processes of change in action. No artificially introduced testing procedures are involved here. However, for the simple before-and-after design of Figure 1, if the pretest were the first data collection of its kind ever publicized, this publicity in itself might produce a reduction in traffic deaths which would have taken place even without a speeding crackdown. Many traffic safety programs assume this. The longer time-series evidence reassures us on this only to the extent that we can assume that the figures had been published each year with equivalent emphasis.[3]

Instrumentation changes are not a likely flaw in this instance, but would be if recording practices and institutional responsibility had shifted simultaneously with the crackdown. Probably in a case like this it is better to use raw frequencies rather than indices whose correction parameters are subject to periodic revision. Thus per capita rates are subject to periodic jumps as new census figures become available correcting old extrapolations. Analogously, a change in the miles per gallon assumed in estimating traffic mileage for mileage-based mortality rates might explain a shift. Such biases can of course work to disguise a true effect. Almost certainly, Ribicoff's crackdown reduced traffic speed (Campbell and Ross, 1968). Such a decrease in speed increases the miles per gallon actually obtained, producing a concomitant drop in the estimate of miles driven, which would appear as an inflation of the estimate of mileage-based traffic fatalities if the same fixed approximation to actual miles per gallon were used, as it undoubtedly would be.

The "new broom" that introduces abrupt changes of policy is apt to reform the record keeping too, and thus confound reform treatments with instrumentation change. The ideal experimental administrator will, if possible, avoid doing this. He will prefer to keep comparable a partially imperfect measuring system rather than lose comparability altogether. The politics of the situation do not always make this possible, however. Consider, as an experimental reform, Orlando Wilson's reorganization of the police system in Chicago. Figure 3 shows his impact on petty larceny in Chicago—a striking *increase!* Wilson, of course, called this shot in

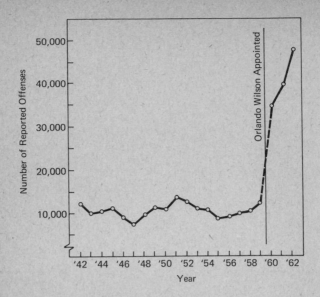

FIGURE 3: Number of reported larcenies under $50 in Chicago, Illinois, from 1942 to 1962 (data from *Uniform Crime Reports for the United States,* 1942–62).

advance, one aspect of his reform being a reform in the bookkeeping. (Note in the pre-Wilson records the suspicious absence of the expected upward secular trend.) In this situation Wilson had no choice. Had he left the record keeping as it was, for the purposes of better experimental design, his resentful patrolmen would have clobbered him with a crime wave by deliberately starting to record the many complaints that had not been getting into the books.[4]

Those who advocate the use of archival measures as social indicators (Bauer, 1966; Gross, 1966, 1967; Kaysen, 1967; Webb et al., 1966) must face up not only to their high degree of chaotic error and systematic bias, but also to the politically motivated changes in record keeping that will follow upon their public use as social indicators (Etzioni and Lehman, 1967). Not all measures are equally susceptible. In Figure 4, Orlando Wilson's effect on homicides seems negligible one way or the other.

Of the threats to external validity, the one most relevant to social experimentation is *irrelevant responsiveness of measures.* This seems best discussed in terms of the problem of generalizing from indicator to indicator or in terms of the imperfect validity of all measures that is only to be overcome by the use of multiple measures of independent imperfection (Campbell and Fiske, 1959; Webb et al., 1966).

For treatments on any given problem within any given governmental or business subunit, there will usually be something of a governmental monopoly on reform. Even though different divisions may optimally be trying different reforms, within each division there will usually be only one reform on a given problem going on at a time. But for measures of

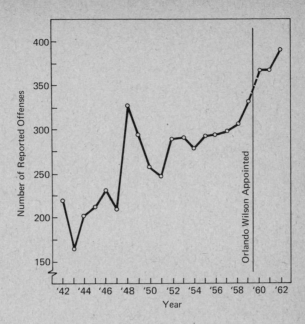

FIGURE 4: Number of reported murders and nonnegligent manslaughters in Chicago, Illinois, from 1942 to 1962 (data from *Uniform Crime Reports for the United States*, 1942–62).

effect this need not and should not be the case. The administrative machinery should itself make multiple measures of potential benefits and of unwanted side effects. In addition, the loyal opposition should be allowed to add still other indicators, with the political process and adversary argument challenging both validity and relative importance, with social science methodologists testifying for both parties, and with the basic records kept public and under bipartisan audit (as are voting records under optimal conditions). This competitive scrutiny is indeed the main source of objectivity in sciences (Polanyi, 1966, 1967; Popper, 1963) and epitomizes an ideal of democratic practice in both judicial and legislative procedures.

The next few figures return again to the Connecticut crackdown on speeding and look to some other measures of effect. They are relevant to the confirming that there was indeed a crackdown, and to the issue of side effects. They also provide the methodological comfort of assuring us that in some cases the interrupted time-series design can provide clear-cut evidence of effect. Figure 5 shows the jump in suspensions of licenses for speeding—evidence that severe punishment was abruptly instituted. Again a note to experimental administrators: with this weak design, *it is only abrupt and decisive changes that we have any chance of evaluating*. A gradually introduced reform will be indistinguishable from the background of secular change, from the net effect of the innumerable change agents continually impinging.

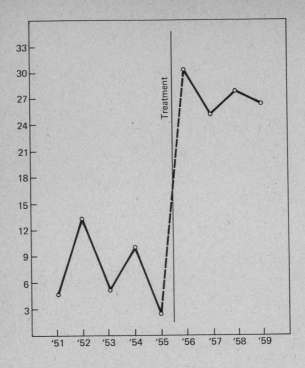

FIGURE 5: Suspensions of licenses for speeding, as a percentage of all suspensions.

We would want intermediate evidence that traffic speed was modified. A sampling each year of a few hundred five-minute highway movies (random as to location and time) could have provided this at a moderate cost, but they were not collected. Of the public records available, perhaps the data of Figure 6, showing a reduction in speeding violations, indicate a reduction in traffic speed. But the effects on the legal system were complex, and in part undesirable. Driving with a suspended license markedly increased (Figure 7), at least in the biased sample of those arrested. Presumably because of the harshness of the punishment if guilty, judges may have become more lenient (Figure 8) although this effect is of marginal significance.

The relevance of indicators for the social problems we wish to cure must be kept continually in focus. The social indicators approach will tend to make the indicators themselves the goal of social action, rather than the social problems they but imperfectly indicate. There are apt to be tendencies to legislate changes in the indicators per se rather than changes in the social problems.

To illustrate the problem of the irrelevant responsiveness of measures, Figure 9 shows a result of the 1900 change in divorce law in Germany. In a recent reanalysis of the data with the Box and Tiao (1965) statistic, Glass

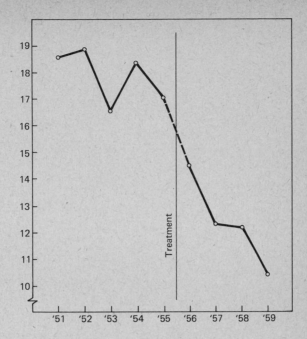

FIGURE 6: Speeding violations, as a percentage of all traffic violations.

(Glass, Tiao, and Maguire, 1969) has found the change highly significant, in contrast to earlier statistical analyses (Rheinstein, 1959; Wolf, Lüke, and Hax, 1959). But Rheinstein's emphasis would still be relevant: This indicator change indicates no likely improvement in marital harmony, or even in marital stability. Rather than reducing them, the legal change has made the divorce rate a less valid indicator of marital discord and separation than it had been earlier (see also Etzioni and Lehman, 1967).

CONTROL SERIES DESIGN

The interrupted time-series design as discussed so far is available for those settings in which no control group is possible, in which the total governmental unit has received the experimental treatment, the social reform measure. In the general program of quasi-experimental design, we argue the great advantage of untreated comparison groups even where these cannot be assigned at random. The most common of such designs is the nonequivalent control-group pretest-posttest design, in which for each of two natural groups, one of which receives the treatment, a pretest and posttest measure is taken. If the traditional mistaken practice is avoided of matching on pretest scores (with resultant regression artifacts), this design provides a useful control over those aspects of history, maturation, and test-retest effects shared by both groups. But it does not control for the plausible rival hypothesis of

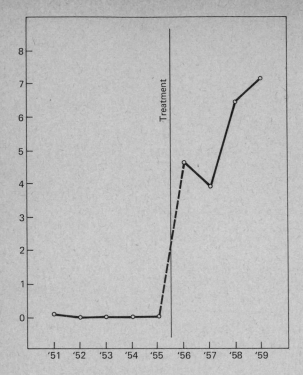

FIGURE 7: Arrested while driving with a suspended license, as a percentage of suspensions.

selection-maturation interaction—that is, the hypothesis that the selection differences in the natural aggregations involve not only differences in mean level, but differences in maturation rate.

This point can be illustrated in terms of the traditional quasi-experimental design problem of the effects of Latin on English vocabulary (Campbell, 1963). In the hypothetical data of Figure 10b, two alternative interpretations remain open. Latin may have had effect, for those taking Latin gained more than those not. But, on the other hand, those students taking Latin may have a greater annual rate of vocabulary growth that would manifest itself whether or not they took Latin. Extending this common design into two time series provides relevant evidence, as comparison of the two alternative outcomes of Figures 10c and 10d shows. Thus approaching quasi-experimental design from either improving the non-equivalent control-group design or from improving the interrupted time-series design, we arrive at the control series design. Figure 11 shows this for the Connecticut speeding crackdown, adding evidence from the fatality rates of neighboring states. Here the data are presented as population-based fatality rates so as to make the two series of comparable magnitude.

The control series design of Figure 11 shows that downward trends were available in the other states for 1955–56 as due to history and

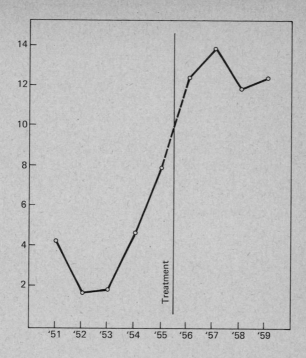

FIGURE 8: Percentage of speeding violations judged not guilty.

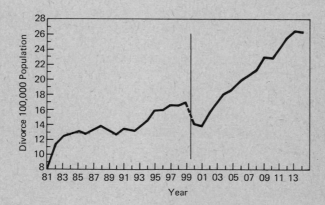

FIGURE 9: Divorce rate for German Empire, 1881–1914.

maturation, that is, due to shared secular trends, weather, automotive safety features, etc. But the data also show a general trend for Connecticut to rise relatively closer to the other states prior to 1955, and to steadily drop more rapidly than other states from 1956 on. Glass (1968) has used our monthly data for Connecticut and the control states to generate a monthly difference score, and this too shows a significant shift in trend

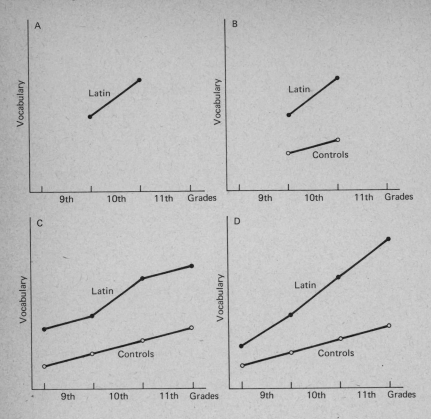

FIGURE 10: Forms of quasi-experimental analysis for the effect of specific course work, including control series design.

in the Box and Tiao (1965) statistic. Impressed particularly by the 1957, 1958, and 1959 trend, we are willing to conclude that the crackdown had some effect, over and above the undeniable pseudo-effects of regression (Campbell and Ross, 1968).

The advantages of the control series design point to the advantages for social experimentation of a social system allowing subunit diversity. Our ability to estimate the effects of the speeding crackdown, Rose's (1952) and Stieber's (1949) ability to estimate the effects on strikes of compulsory arbitration laws, and Simon's (1966) ability to estimate the price elasticity of liquor were made possible because the changes were not being put into effect in all states simultaneously, because they were matters of state legislation rather than national. I do not want to appear to justify on these grounds the wasteful and unjust diversity of laws and enforcement practices from state to state. But I would strongly advocate that social engineers make use of this diversity while it remains available, and plan cooperatively their changes in administrative policy and in record keeping so as to provide optimal experimental inference. More

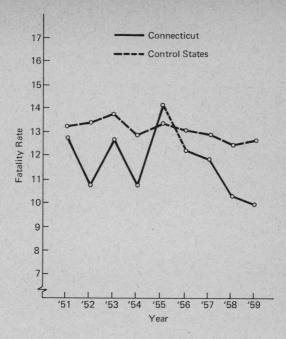

FIGURE 11: Control series design comparing Connecticut fatalities with those of four comparable states.

important is the recommendation that, for those aspects of social reform handled by the central government, a purposeful diversity of implementation be envisaged so that experimental and control groups be available for analysis. Properly planned, these can approach true experiments, better than the casual and ad hoc comparison groups now available. But without such fundamental planning, uniform central control can reduce the present possibilities of reality testing, that is, of true social experimentation. In the same spirit, decentralization of decision making, both within large government and within private monopolies, can provide a useful competition for both efficiency and innovation, reflected in a multiplicity of indicators.

THE BRITISH BREATHALYSER CRACKDOWN

One further illustration of the interrupted time series and the control series will be provided. The variety of illustrations so far have each illustrated some methodological point, and have thus ended up as "bad examples." To provide a "good example," an instance which survives methodological critique as a valid illustration of a successful reform, data from the British Road Safety Act of 1967 are provided in Figure 11a (Ross, Campbell, and Glass, 1970).

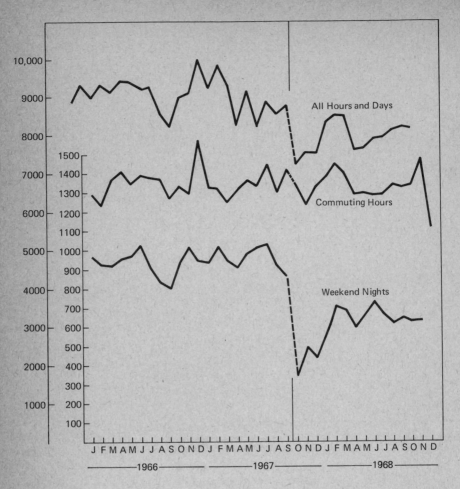

FIGURE 11a: British traffic fatalities plus serious injuries, before and after the Breathalyser crackdown of October 1967 (seasonally adjusted).

The data on a weekly hours basis are only available for a composite category of fatalities plus serious injuries, and Figure 11a therefore uses this composite for all three bodies of data. The Weekend Nights comprises Friday and Saturday nights from 10:00 p.m. to 4:00 a.m. Here, as expected, the crackdown is most dramatically effective, producing initially more than a 40% drop, leveling off at perhaps 30%, although this involves dubious extrapolations in the absence of some control comparison to indicate what the trend over the years might have been without the crackdown. In this British case, no comparison state with comparable traffic conditions or drinking laws was available. But controls need not always be separate groups of persons, they may also be separate samples of times or stimulus materials (Campbell and Stanley, 1966, pp. 43–47). A cigarette company may use the sales of its main competitor as a control comparison to evaluate a new advertising campaign. One should search around for the most nearly appropriate control comparison. For the Breathalyser crackdown, commuting hours when pubs had been long closed seemed ideal. (The Commuting Hours figures come from 7:00 a.m. to 10:00 a.m. and 4:00 p.m. to 5:00 p.m. Pubs are open for lunch from 12:00 to 2:00 or 2:30, and open again at 5:00 p.m.)

These commuting hours data convincingly show no effect, but are too unstable to help much with estimating the long-term effects. They show a different annual cycle than do the weekend nights or the overall figures, and do not go back far enough to provide an adequate base for estimating this annual cycle with precision.

The use of a highly judgmental category such as "serious injuries" provides an opportunity for pseudo-effects due to a shift in the classifiers' standards. The overall figures are available separately for fatalities, and these show a highly significant effect as strong as that found for the serious injury category or the composite shown in Figure 11a.

More details and the methodological problems are considered in our fuller presentation (Ross, Campbell, and Glass, 1970). One further rule for the use of this design needs emphasizing. The interrupted time series can only provide clear evidence of effect where the reform is introduced with a vigorous abruptness. A gradually introduced reform has little chance of being distinguished from shifts in secular trends or from the cumulative effect of the many other influences impinging during a prolonged period of introduction. In the Breathalyser crackdown, an intense publicity campaign naming the specific starting date preceded the actual crackdown. Although the impact seems primarily due to publicity and fear rather than an actual increase of arrests, an abrupt initiation date was achieved. Had the enforcement effort changed at the moment the act had passed, with public awareness being built up by subsequent publicity, the resulting data series would have been essentially uninterpretable.

REGRESSION DISCONTINUITY DESIGN

We shift now to social ameliorations that are in short supply, and that therefore cannot be given to all individuals. Such scarcity is inevitable under many circumstances, and can make possible an evaluation of effects that would otherwise be impossible. Consider the heroic Salk poliomyelitis vaccine trials in which some children were given the vaccine while others were given an inert saline placebo injection—and in which many more of these placebo controls would die than would have if they had been given the vaccine. Creation of these placebo controls would have been morally, psychologically, and socially impossible had there been enough vaccine for all. As it was, due to the scarcity, most children that year had to go without the vaccine anyway. The creation of experimental and control groups was the highly moral allocation of that scarcity so as to enable us to learn the true efficacy of the supposed good. The usual medical practice of introducing new cures on a so-called trial basis in general medical practice makes evaluation impossible by confounding prior status with treatment, that is, giving the drug to the most needy or most hopeless. It has the further social bias

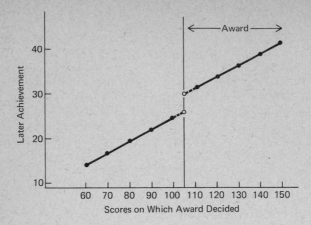

FIGURE 12: Tie-breaking experiment and regression discontinuity analysis.

of giving the supposed benefit to those most assiduous in keeping their medical needs in the attention of the medical profession, that is, the upper and upper-middle classes. The political stance furthering social experimentation here is the recognition of randomization as the most democratic and moral means of allocating scarce resources (and scarce hazardous duties), plus the moral imperative to further utilize the randomization so that society may indeed learn true value of the supposed boon. This is the ideology that makes possible "true experiments" in a large class of social reforms.

But if randomization is not politically feasible or morally justifiable in a given setting, there is a powerful quasi-experimental design available that allows the scarce good to be given to the most needy or the most deserving. This is the regression discontinuity design. All it requires is strict and orderly attention to the priority dimension. The design originated through an advocacy of a tie-breaking experiment to measure the effects of receiving a fellowship (Thistlethwaite and Campbell, 1960), and it seems easiest to explain it in that light. Consider as in Figure 12, pre-award ability-and-merit dimension, which would have some relation to later success in life (finishing college, earnings 10 years later, etc.). Those higher on the premeasure are most deserving and receive the award. They do better in later life, but does the award have an effect? It is normally impossible to say because they would have done better in later life anyway. Full randomization of the award was impossible given the stated intention to reward merit and ability. But it might be possible to take a narrow band of ability at the cutting point, to regard all of these persons as tied, and to assign half of them to awards, half to no awards, by means of a tie-breaking randomization.

The tie-breaking rationale is still worth doing, but in considering that design it became obvious that, if the regression of premeasure on later effects were reasonably orderly, one should be able to extrapolate to the results of the tie-breaking experiment by plotting the regression of post-test on pretest separately for those in the award and nonaward regions. If there is no significant difference for these at the decision-point intercept, then the tie-breaking experiment should show no difference. In cases where the tie breakers would show an effect, there should be an abrupt discontinuity in the regression line. Such a discontinuity cannot be explained away by the normal regression of the posttest on pretest, for this normal regression, as extensively sampled within the nonaward area and within the award area, provides no such expectation.

Figure 12 presents, in terms of column means, an instance in which higher pretest scores would have led to higher posttest scores even without the treatment, and in which there is in addition a substantial treatment effect. Figure 13 shows a series of paired outcomes, those on the left to be interpreted as no effect, those in the center and on the right as effect. Note some particular cases. In instances of granting opportunity on the basis of merit, like 13a and b (and Figure 12), neglect of the background regression of pretest on posttest leads to optimistic pseudo-effects: in Figure 13a, those receiving the award do do better in later life, though not really because of the award. But in social ameliorative efforts, the setting is more apt to be like Figures 13d and e, where neglect of the background regression is apt to make the program look deleterious if no effect, or ineffective if there is a real effect.

The design will of course work just as well or better if the award dimension and the decision base, the pretest measure, are unrelated to the posttest dimension, if it is irrelevant or unfair, as instanced in Figures 13g, h, and i. In such cases the decision base is the functional equivalent of randomization. Negative background relationships are obviously possible, as in Figures 13j, k, and l. In Figure 13, m, n, and o are included to emphasize that it is a jump in intercept at the cutting point that shows effect, and that differences in slope without differences at the cutting point are not acceptable as evidences of effect. This becomes more obvious if we remember that in cases like m, a tie-breaking randomization experiment would have shown no difference. Curvilinear background relationships, as in Figures 13p, q, and r, will provide added obstacles to clear inference in many instances, where sampling error could make Figure 13p look like 13b.

As further illustration, Figure 14 provides computer-simulated data, showing individual observations and fitted regression lines, in a fuller version of the no-effect outcome of Figure 13a. Figure 15 shows an outcome with effect. These have been generated[5] by assigning to each individual a weighted normal random number as a "true score," to which is added a weighted independent "error" to generate the "pretest." The "true score" plus another independent "error" produces the "posttest" in no-effect cases such as Figure 14. In treatment-effect simulations, as in Figure 15, there are added into the posttest "effects points" for all "treated" cases, that is, those above the cutting point on the pretest score.

This design could be used in a number of settings. Consider Job Training Corps applicants, in larger number than the program can accommodate, with eligibility determined by need. The setting would be as in Figures 13d and e. The base-line decision dimension could be per capita

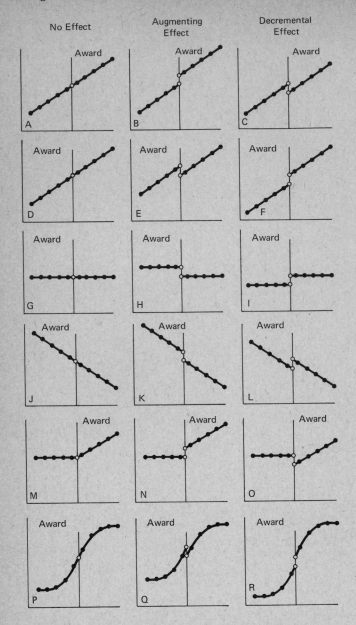

FIGURE 13: Illustrative outcomes of regression discontinuity analyses.

family income, with those at below the cutoff getting training. The outcome dimension could be the amount of withholding tax withheld two years later, or the percentage drawing unemployment insurance, these follow-up figures being provided from the National Data Bank in response to categorized social security numbers fed in, without individual ano-

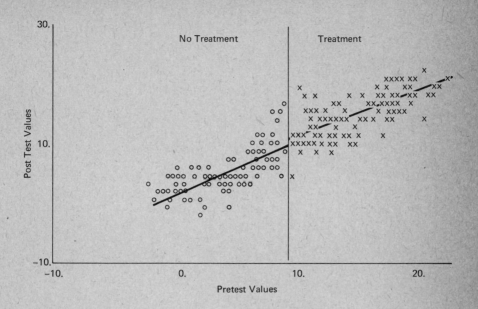

FIGURE 14: Regression discontinuity design: No effect.

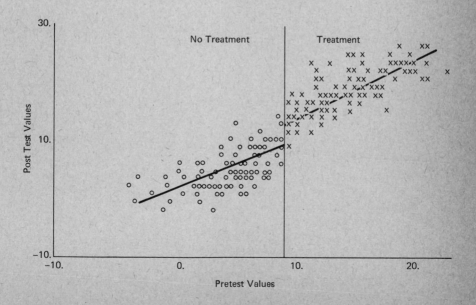

FIGURE 15: Regression discontinuity design: Genuine effect.

nymity being breached, without any real invasion of privacy by the technique of mutually insulated data banks. While the plotted points could be named, there is no need that they be named. In a classic field experiment on tax compliance, Richard Schwartz and the Bureau of Internal Revenue have managed to put together sets of personally identified interviews and tax-return data so that statistical analyses such as these could be done, without the separate custodians of either interview or tax returns learning the corresponding data for specific persons (Schwartz and Orleans, 1967; see also Schwartz and Skolnick, 1963).

Applied to the Job Corps illustration, it would work as follows: Separate lists of Job Corps applicants (with social security numbers) would be prepared for every class interval on per capita family income. To each of these lists an alphabetical designation would be assigned at random. (Thus the $10.00 per week list might be labeled M; $11.00, C; $12.00, Z; $13.00, Q; $14.00, N; etc.) These lists would be sent to Internal Revenue, without the Internal Revenue personnel being able to learn anything interpretable about their traineeship status or family income. The Internal Revenue statisticians would locate the withholding tax collected for each person on each list, but would not return the data in that form. Instead, for each list, only the withholding tax amounts would be listed, and these in a newly randomized order. These would be returned to Job Corps research, who could use them to plot a graph like Figures 10 and 11, and do the appropriate statistical analyses by retranslating the alphabetical symbols into meaningful base-line values. But within any list, they would be unable to learn which value belonged to which person. (To ensure this effective anonymity, it could be specified that no lists shorter than 100 persons be used, the base-line intervals being expanded if necessary to achieve this.) Manniche and Hayes (1957) have spelled out how a broker can be used in a two-staged matching of doubly coded data. Kaysen (1967) and Sawyer and Schechter (1968) have wise discussions of the more general problem.

What is required of the administrator of a scarce ameliorative commodity to use this design? Most essential is a sharp cutoff point on a decision-criterion dimension, on which several other qualitatively similar analytic cutoffs can be made both above and below the award cut. Let me explain this better by explaining why National Merit scholarships were unable to use the design for their actual fellowship decision (although it has been used for their Certificate of Merit). In their operation, diverse committees make small numbers of award decisions by considering a group of candidates and then picking from them the N best to which to award the N fellowships allocated them. This provides one cutting point on an unspecified pooled decision base, but fails to provide analogous potential cutting points above and below. What could be done is for each committee to collectively rank its group of 20 or so candidates. The top N would then receive the award. Pooling cases across committees, cases could be classified according to number of ranks above and below the cutting point, these other ranks being analogous to the award-non-award cutting point as far as regression onto posttreatment measures was concerned. Such group ranking would be costly of committee time. An equally good procedure, if committees agreed, would be to have each member, after full discussion and freedom to revise, give each candidate a grade, A+, A, A−, B+, B, etc., and to award the fellowships to the N candidates averaging best on these ratings, with no revisions allowed after the averaging process. These ranking or rating units, even if not comparable from committee to committee in range of talent, in number of persons ranked, or in cutting point, could be pooled without bias as far as a regression discontinuity is concerned, for that range of units above and below the cutting point in which all committees were represented.

It is the dimensionality and sharpness of the decision criterion that is at issue, not its components or validity. The ratings could be based upon nepotism, whimsey, and superstition and still serve. As has been stated, if the decision criterion is utterly invalid we approach the pure randomness of a true experiment. Thus the weakness of subjective committee decisions is not their subjectivity, but the fact that they provide only the one cutting point on their net subjective dimension. Even in the form of average ratings the recommended procedures probably represent some slight increase in committee work load. But this could be justified to the decision committees by the fact that through refusals, etc., it cannot be known at the time of the committee meeting the exact number to whom the fellowship can be offered. Other costs at the planning time are likewise minimal. The primary additional burden is in keeping as good records on the nonawardees as on the awardees. Thus at a low cost, an experimental administrator can lay the groundwork for later scientific follow-ups, the budgets for which need not yet be in sight.

Our present situation is more apt to be one where our pretreatment measures, aptitude measures, reference ratings, etc., can be combined via multiple correlation into an index that correlates highly but not perfectly with the award decision. For this dimension there is a fuzzy cutoff point. Can the design be used in this case? Probably not. Figure 16 shows the pseudo-effect possible if the award decision contributes any valid variance to the quantified pretest evidence, as it usually will. The award regression rides above the nonaward regression just because of that valid variance in this simulated case, there being no true award effect at all. (In simulating this case, the award decision has been based upon a composite of true score plus an independent award error.) Figure 17 shows a fuzzy cutting point plus a genuine award effect.[6] The recommendation to the administrator is clear: aim for a sharp cutting point on a quantified decision criterion. If there are complex rules for eligibility, only one of which is quantified, seek out for follow-up that subset of persons for whom the quantitative dimension was determinate. If political patronage necessitates some decisions inconsistent with a sharp cutoff, record these cases under the heading "qualitative decision rule" and keep them out of your experimental analysis.

Almost all of our ameliorative programs designed for the disadvantaged could be studied via this design, and so too some major governmental actions affecting the lives of citizens in ways we do not think of as experimental. For example, for a considerable period, quantitative test scores have been used to call up for military service or reject as unfit at the lower ability range. If these cutting points, test scores, names, and social security

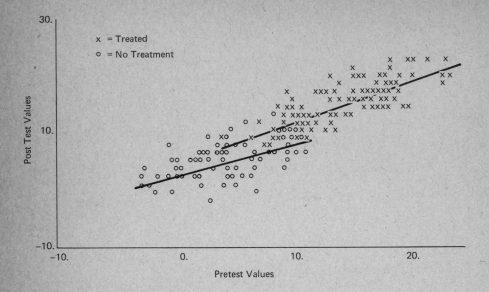

FIGURE 16: Regression discontinuity design: Fuzzy cutting point, pseudo treatment effect only.

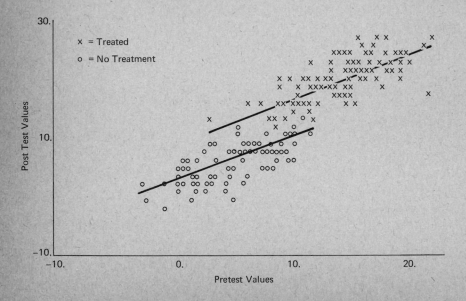

FIGURE 17: Regression discontinuity design: Fuzzy cutting point, with real treatment plus pseudo treatment effects.

numbers have been recorded for a number of steps both above and below the cutting point, we could make elegant studies of the effect of military service on later withholding taxes, mortality, number of dependents, etc.

This illustration points to one of the threats to external validity of this design, or of the tie-breaking experiment. The effect of the treatment has only been studied for that narrow range of talent near the cutting point, and generalization of the effects of military service, for example, from this low ability level to the careers of the most able would be hazardous in the extreme. But in the draft laws and the requirements of the military services there may be other sharp cutting points on a quantitative criterion that could also be used. For example, those over 6 feet 6 inches are excluded from service. Imagine a five-year-later follow-up of draftees grouped by inch in the 6 feet 1 inch to 6 feet 5 inches range, and a group of their counterparts who would have been drafted except for their heights, 6 feet 6 inches to 6 feet 10 inches. (The fact that the other grounds of deferment might not have been examined by the draft board would be a problem here, but probably not insurmountable.) That we should not expect height in this range to have any relation to later-life variables is not at all a weakness of this design, and if we have indeed a subpopulation for which there is a sharp numerical cutting point, an internally valid measure of effects would result. Deferment under the present system is an unquantified committee decision. But just as the sense of justice of United States soldiers was quantified through paired comparisons of cases into an acceptable Demobilization Points system at the end of World War II (Guttman, 1946; Stouffer, 1949), so a quantified composite index of deferment priority could be achieved and applied as uniform justice across the nation, providing another numerical cutting point.

In addition to the National Data Bank type of indicators, there will be occasions in which new data collections as by interview or questionnaire are needed. For these there is the special problem of uneven cooperation that would be classified as instrumentation error. In our traditional mode of thinking, completeness of description is valued more highly than comparability. Thus if, in a fellowship study, a follow-up mailed out from the fellowship office would bring a higher return from past winners, this might seem desirable even if the nonawardees' rate of response was much lower. From the point of view of quasi-experimentation, however, it would be better to use an independent survey agency and a disguised purpose, achieving equally low response rates from both awardees and nonawardees, and avoiding a regression discontinuity in cooperation rate that might be misinterpreted as a discontinuity in more important effects.

RANDOMIZED CONTROL GROUP EXPERIMENTS

Experiments with randomization tend to be limited to the laboratory and agricultural experiment station. But this certainly need not be so. The randomization unit may be persons, families, precincts, or larger administrative units. For statistical purposes the randomization units should be numerous, and hence ideally small. But for reasons of external validity, including reactive arrangements, the randomization units should be selected on the basis of the units of administrative access. Where policies are administered through individual client contacts, randomization at the person level may be often inconspicuously achieved, with the clients unaware that different ones of them are getting different treatments. But for most social reforms, larger administrative units will be involved, such as classrooms, schools, cities, counties, or states. We need to develop the political postures and ideologies that make randomization at these levels possible.

"Pilot project" is a useful term already in our political vocabulary. It designates a trial program that, if it works, will be spread to other areas. By modifying actual practice in this regard, without going outside of the popular understanding of the term, a valuable experimental ideology could be developed. How are areas selected for pilot projects? If the public worries about this, it probably assumes a lobbying process in which the greater needs of some areas are only one consideration, political power and expediency being others. Without violating the public tolerance or intent, one could probably devise a system in which the usual lobbying decided upon the areas eligible for a formal public lottery that would make final choices between matched pairs. Such decision procedures as the drawing of lots have had a justly esteemed position since time immemorial (e.g., Aubert, 1959). At the present time, record keeping for pilot projects tends to be limited to the experimental group only. In the experimental ideology, comparable data would be collected on designated controls. (There are of course exceptions, as in the heroic Public Health Service fluoridation experiments, in which the teeth of Oak Park children were examined year after year as controls for the Evanston experimentals [Blayney and Hill, 1967].)

Another general political stance making possible experimental social amelioration is that of *staged innovation*. Even though by intent a new reform is to be put into effect in all units, the logistics of the situation usually dictate that simultaneous introduction is not possible. What results is a haphazard sequence of convenience. Under the program of staged innovation, the introduction of the program would be deliberately spread out, and those units selected to be first and last would be randomly assigned (perhaps randomization from matched pairs), so that during the transition period the first recipients could be analyzed as experimental units, the last recipients as controls. A third ideology making possible true experiments has already been discussed: randomization as the democratic means of allocating scarce resources.

This article will not give true experimentation equal space with quasi-experimentation only because excellent discussions of, and statistical consultation on, true experimentation are readily available. True experiments should almost always be preferred to quasi-experiments where both are available. Only occasionally are the threats to external validity so much greater for the true experiment that one would prefer a quasi-experiment. The uneven allocation of space here should not be read as indicating otherwise.

MORE ADVICE FOR TRAPPED ADMINISTRATORS

But the competition is not really between the fairly interpretable quasi-experiments here reviewed and "true" experiments. Both stand together as rare excellencies in contrast with a morass of obfuscation and self-deception. Both to emphasize this contrast, and again as guidelines for the benefit of those trapped administrators whose political predicament will not allow the risk of failure, some of these alternatives should be mentioned.

GRATEFUL TESTIMONIALS   Human courtesy and gratitude being what it is, the most dependable means of assuring a favorable evaluation is to use voluntary testimonials from those who have had the treatment. If the spontaneously produced testimonials are in short supply, these should be solicited from the recipients with whom the program is still in contact. The rosy glow resulting is analogous to the professor's impression of his teaching success when it is based solely upon the comments of those students who come up and talk with him after class. In many programs, as in psychotherapy, the recipient, as well as the agency, has devoted much time and effort to the program and it is dissonance reducing for himself, as well as common courtesy to his therapist, to report improvement. These grateful testimonials can come in the language of letters and conversation, or be framed as answers to multiple-item "tests" in which a recurrent theme of "I am sick," "I am well," "I am happy," "I am sad" recurs. Probably the testimonials will be more favorable as: (a) the more the evaluative meaning of the response measure is clear to the recipient—it is completely clear in most personality, adjustment, morale, and attitude tests; (b) the more directly the recipient is identified by name with his answer; (c) the more the recipient gives the answer directly to the therapist or agent of reform; (d) the more the agent will continue to be influential in the recipient's life in the future; (e) the more the answers deal with feelings and evaluations rather than with verifiable facts; and (f) the more the recipients participating in the evaluation are a small and self-selected or agent-selected subset of all recipients. Properly designed, the grateful testimonial method can involve pretests as well as posttests, and randomized control groups as well as experimentals, for there are usually no placebo treatments, and the recipients know when they have had the boon.

CONFOUNDING SELECTION AND TREATMENT   Another dependable tactic bound to give favorable outcomes is to confound selection and treatment, so that in the published comparison those receiving the treatment are also the more able and well placed. The often-cited evidence of the dollar value of a college education is of this nature—all careful studies show that most of the effect, and of the superior effect of superior colleges, is explainable in terms of superior talents and family connections, rather than in terms of what is learned or even the prestige of the degree. Matching techniques and statistical partialings generally undermatch and do not fully control for the selection differences—they introduce regression artifacts confusable as treatment effects.

There are two types of situations that must be distinguished. First, there are those treatments that are given to the most promising, treatments like a college education which are regularly given to those who need it least. For these, the later concomitants of the grounds of selection operate in the same direction as the treatment: those most likely to achieve anyway get into the college most likely to produce later achievement. For these settings, the trapped administrator should use the pooled mean of all those treated, comparing it with the mean of all untreated, although in this setting almost any comparison an administrator might hit upon would be biased in his favor.

At the other end of the talent continuum are those remedial treatments given to those who need it most. Here the later concomitants of the grounds of selection are poorer success. In the Job Training Corps example, casual comparisons of the later unemployment rate of those who received the training with those who did not are in general biased against showing an advantage to the training. This seems to have been the case in the major Head Start evaluation (Campbell and Erlebacher, 1970). Here the trapped administrator must be careful to seek out those few special comparisons biasing selection in his favor. For training programs such as Operation Head Start and tutoring programs, a useful solution is to compare the later success of those who completed the training program with those who were invited but never showed plus those who came a few times and dropped out. By regarding only those who complete the program as "trained" and using the others as controls, one is selecting for conscientiousness, stable and supporting family backgrounds, enjoyment of the training activity, ability, determination to get ahead in the world—all factors promising well for future achievement even if the remedial program is valueless. To apply this tactic effectively in the Job Training Corps, one might have to eliminate from the so-called control group all those who quit the training program because they had found a job—but this would seem a reasonable practice and would not blemish the reception of a glowing progress report.

These are but two more samples of well-tried modes of analysis for the trapped administrator who cannot afford an honest evaluation of the social reform he directs. They remind us again that we must help create a political climate that demands more rigorous and less self-deceptive reality testing. We must provide political stances that permit true experiments, or good quasi-experiments. Of the several suggestions toward this end that are contained in this article, the most important is probably the initial theme: Administrators and parties must advocate the importance of the problem rather than the importance of the answer. They must advocate experimental sequences of reforms, rather than one certain cure-all, advocating Reform A with Alternative B available to try next should an honest evaluation of A prove it worthless or harmful.

MULTIPLE REPLICATION IN ENACTMENT

Too many social scientists expect single experiments to settle issues once and for all. This may be a mistaken generalization from the history of great crucial experiments in physics and chemistry. In actuality the significant experiments in the physical sciences are replicated thousands of times, not only in deliberate replication efforts, but also as inevitable incidentals in successive experimentation and in utilizations of those many measurement devices (such as the galvanometer) that in their own operation embody the principles of classic experiments. Because we social scientists have less ability to achieve "experimental isolation," because we have good reason to expect our treatment effects to interact significantly with a wide variety of social factors many of which we have not yet mapped, we have much greater needs for replication experiments than do the physical sciences.

The implications are clear. We should not only do hard-headed reality testing in the initial pilot testing and choosing of which reform to make general law; but once it has been decided that the reform is to be adopted as standard practice in all administrative units, we should experimentally evaluate it in each of its implementations (Campbell, 1967).

CONCLUSIONS

Trapped administrators have so committed themselves in advance to the efficacy of the reform that they cannot afford honest evaluation. For them, favorably biased analyses are recommended, including capitalizing on regression, grateful testimonials, and confounding selection and treatment. *Experimental administrators* have justified the reform on the basis of the importance of the problem, not the certainty of their answer, and are committed to going on to other potential solutions if the one first tried fails. They are therefore not threatened by a hard-headed analysis of the reform. For such, proper administrative decisions can lay the base for useful experimental or quasi-experimental analyses. Through the ideology of allocating scarce resources by lottery, through the use of staged innovation, and through the pilot project, true experiments with randomly assigned control groups can be achieved. If the reform must be introduced across the board, the interrupted time-series design is available. If there are similar units under independent administration, a control series design adds strength. If a scarce boon must be given to the most needy or to the most deserving, quantifying this need or merit makes possible the regression discontinuity analysis.

NOTES

1. This list has been expanded from the major previous presentations by the addition of *Instability* (but see Campbell, 1968; Campbell and Ross, 1968). This has been done in reaction to the sociological discussion of the use of tests of significance in nonexperimental or quasi-experimental research (e.g., Selvin, 1957; and as reviewed by Galtung, 1967, pp. 358–389). On the one hand, I join with the critics in criticizing the exaggerated status of "statistically significant differences" in establishing convictions of validity. Statistical tests are relevant to at best 1 out of 15 or so threats to validity. On the other hand, I join with those who defend their use in situations where randomization has not been

employed. Even in those situations, it is relevant to say or to deny, "This is a trivial difference. It is of the order that would have occurred frequently *had* these measures been assigned to these classes solely by chance." Tests of significance, making use of random reassignments of the actual scores, are particularly useful in communicating this point.

2. This list has been lengthened from previous presentations to make more salient Threats 5 and 6 which are particularly relevant to social experimentation. Discussion in previous presentations (Campbell, 1957, pp. 309–310; Campbell and Stanley, 1963, pp. 203–204) had covered these points, but they had not been included in the checklist.

3. No doubt the public and press shared the Governor's special alarm over the 1955 death toll. This differential reaction could be seen as a negative feedback servosystem in which the dampening effect was proportional to the degree of upward deviation from the prior trend. Insofar as such alarm reduces traffic fatalities, it adds a negative component to the autocorrelation, increasing the regression effect. This component should probably be regarded as a rival cause or treatment rather than as artifact. (The regression effect is less as the positive autocorrelation is higher, and will be present to some degree insofar as this correlation is less than positive unity. Negative correlation in a time series would represent regression beyond the mean, in a way not quite analogous to negative correlation across persons. For an autocorrelation of Lag 1, high negative correlation would be represented by a series that oscillated maximally from one extreme to the other.)

4. Wilson's inconsistency in utilization of records and the political problem of relevant records are ably documented in Kamisar (1964). Etzioni (1968) reports that in New York City in 1965 a crime wave was proclaimed that turned out to be due to an unpublicized improvement in record keeping.

5. J. Sween and D. T. Campbell, Computer programs for simulating and analyzing sharp and fuzzy regression-discontinuity experiments. In preparation.

6. There are some subtle statistical clues that might distinguish these two instances if one had enough cases. There should be increased pooled column variance in the mixed columns for a true effects case. If the data are arbitrarily treated as though there had been a sharp cutting point located in the middle of the overlap area, then there should be no discontinuity in the no-effect case, and some discontinuity in the case of a real effect, albeit and underestimated discontinuity, since there are untreated cases above the cutting point and treated ones below, dampening the apparent effect. The degree of such dampening should be estimable, and correctable, perhaps by iterative procedures. But these are hopes for the future.

REFERENCES

AUBERT, V. Chance in social affairs. *Inquiry,* 1959, 2, 1–24.

BAUER, R. M. *Social indicators.* Cambridge, Mass.: M.I.T. Press, 1966.

BLAYNEY, J. R., and HILL, I. N. Fluorine and dental caries. *The Journal of the American Dental Association* (Special Issue), 1967, 74, 233–302.

BOX, G. E. P., and TIAO, G. C. A change in level of a nonstationary time series. *Biometrika,* 1965, 52, 181–192.

CAMPBELL, D. T. Factors relevant to the validity of experiments in social settings. *Psychological Bulletin*, 1957, 54, 297–312.

CAMPBELL, D. T. From description to experimentation: Interpreting trends as quasi-experiments. In C. W. Harris (Ed.), *Problems in measuring change*. Madison: University of Wisconsin Press, 1963.

CAMPBELL, D. T. Administrative experimentation, institutional records, and nonreactive measures. In J. C. Stanley (Ed.), *Improving experimental design and statistical analysis*. Chicago: Rand McNally, 1967.

CAMPBELL, D. T. Quasi-experimental design. In D. L. Sills (Ed.), *International encyclopedia of the social sciences*. New York: Macmillan and Free Press, 1968, Vol. 5, 259–263.

CAMPBELL, D. T., and ERLEBACHER, A. How regression artifacts in quasi-experimental evaluations can mistakenly make compensatory education look harmful. In J. Hellmuth (Ed.), *Compensatory education: A national debate*. Vol. 3, *The disadvantaged child*. New York: Brunner/Mazel, 1970, 455–463.

CAMPBELL, D. T., and FISKE, D. W. Convergent and discriminant validation by the multitrait-multimethod matrix. *Psychological Bulletin*, 1959, 56, 81–105.

CAMPBELL, D. T., and ROSS, H. L. The Connecticut crackdown on speeding: Time-series data in quasi-experimental analysis. *Law and Society Review*, 1968, 3(1), 33–53.

CAMPBELL, D. T., and STANLEY, J. C. Experimental and quasi-experimental designs for research on teaching. In N. L. Gage (Ed.), *Handbook of research on teaching*. Chicago: Rand McNally, 1963. (Reprinted as *Experimental and quasi-experimental design for research*. Chicago: Rand McNally, 1966.)

CHAPIN, F. S. *Experimental design in sociological research*. New York: Harper, 1947.

ETZIONI, A. "Shortcuts" to social change? *The Public Interest*, 1968, 12, 40–51.

ETZIONI, A., and LEHMAN, E. W. Some dangers in "valid" social measurement. *Annals of the American Academy of Political and Social Science*, 1967, 373, 1–15.

GALTUNG, J. *Theory and methods of social research*. Oslo: Universitetsforloget; London: Allen & Unwin; New York: Columbia University Press, 1967.

GLASS, G. V. Analysis of data on the Connecticut speeding crackdown as a time-series quasi-experiment. *Law and Society Review*, 1968, 3(1), 55–76.

GLASS, G. V., TIAO, G. C., and MAGUIRE, T. O. The 1900 Revision of German Divorce Laws: Analysis of Data as a Time-Series Quasi-Experiment. *Law and Society Review*, 1971, 5 (4), 539–562.

GREENWOOD, E. *Experimental sociology: A study in method*. New York: King's Crown Press, 1945.

GROSS, B. M. *The state of the nation: Social system accounting*. London: Tavistock Publications, 1966. (Also in R. M. Bauer, *Social indicators*. Cambridge, Mass.: M.I.T. Press, 1966.)

GROSS, B. M. [Ed.], Social goals and indicators. *Annals of the American Academy of Political and Social Science*, 1967, 371, Part 1, May, pp. i–iii and 1–177; Part 2, September, pp. i–iii and 1–218.

GUTTMAN, L., An approach for quantifying paired comparisons and rank order. *Annals of Mathematical Statistics*, 1946, 17, 144–163.

HYMAN, H. H., and WRIGHT, C. R. Evaluating social action programs. In P. F. Lazarsfeld, W. H. Sewell, and H. L. Wilensky (Eds.), The uses of sociology. New York: Basic Books, 1967.

KAMISAR, Y. The tactics of police-persecution oriented critics of the courts. Cornell Law Quarterly, 1964, 49, 458–471.

KAYSEN, C. Data banks and dossiers. The Public Interest, 1967, 7, 52–60.

MANNICHE, E., and HAYES, D. P. Respondent anonymity and data matching. Public Opinion Quarterly, 1957, 21(3), 384–388.

POLANYI, M. A society of explorers. In, The tacit dimension. (Ch. 3) New York: Doubleday, 1966.

POLANYI, M. The growth of science in society. Minerva, 1967, 5, 533–545.

POPPER, K. R. Conjectures and refutations. London: Routledge and Kegan Paul; New York: Basic Books, 1963.

RHEINSTEIN, M. Divorce and the law in Germany: A review. American Journal of Sociology, 1959, 65, 489–498.

ROSE, A. M. Needed research on the mediation of labor disputes. Personnel Psychology, 1952, 5, 187–200.

ROSS, H. L., and CAMPBELL, D. T. The Connecticut speed crackdown: A study of the effects of legal change. In H. L. Ross (Ed.), Perspectives on the social order: Readings in sociology. New York: McGraw-Hill, 1968.

ROSS, H. L., CAMPBELL, D. T., and GLASS, G. V. Determining the social effects of a legal reform: The British "Breathalyser" crackdown of 1967. American Behavioral Scientist, 1970, 13(4), 493–509.

SAWYER, J., and SCHECHTER, H. Computers, privacy, and the National Data Center: The responsibility of social scientists. American Psychologist, 1968, 23, 810–818.

SCHANCK, R. L., and GOODMAN, C. Reactions to propaganda on both sides of a controversial issue. Public Opinion Quarterly, 1939, 3, 107–112.

SCHWARTZ, R. D. Field experimentation in sociological research. Journal of Legal Education, 1961, 13, 401–410.

SCHWARTZ, R. D., and ORLEANS, S. On legal sanctions. University of Chicago Law Review, 1967, 34, 274–300.

SCHWARTZ, R. D., and SKOLNICK, J. H. Televised communication and income tax compliance. In L. Arons and M. May (Eds.), Television and human behavior. New York: Appleton-Century-Crofts, 1963.

SELVIN, H. A critique of tests of significance in survey research. American Sociological Review, 1957, 22, 519–527.

SIMON, J. L. The price elasticity of liquor in the U. S. and a simple method of determination. Econometrica, 1966, 34, 193–205.

SOLOMON, R. W. An extension of control group design. Psychological Bulletin, 1949, 46, 137–150.

STIEBER, J. W. Ten years of the Minnesota Labor Relations Act. Minneapolis: Industrial Relations Center, University of Minnesota, 1949.

STOUFFER, S. A. The point system for redeployment and discharge. In S. A. Stouffer et al., The American soldier. Vol. 2, Combat and its aftermath. Princeton: Princeton University Press, 1949.

SUCHMAN, E. A. *Evaluative research: Principles and practice in public service and social action programs.* New York: Russell Sage, 1967.

SWEEN, J., and CAMPBELL, D. T. A study of the effect of proximally auto-correlated error on tests of significance for the interrupted time-series quasi-experimental design. Available from author, 1965. (Multilith)

THISTLETHWAITE, D. L., and CAMPBELL, D. T. Regression-discontinuity analysis: An alternative to the ex post factor experiment. *Journal of Educational Psychology,* 1960, 51, 309–317.

WALKER, H. M., and LEV, J. *Statistical inference.* New York: Holt, 1953.

WEBB, E. J., CAMPBELL, D. T., SCHWARTZ, R. D., and SECHREST, L. B. *Unobtrusive measures: Nonreactive research in the social sciences.* Chicago: Rand McNally, 1966.

WOLF, E., LÜKE, G., and HAX, H. *Scheidung und Scheidungsrecht: Grundfrägen der Ehescheidung in Deutschland.* Tübigen: J. C. B. Mohr, 1959.

QUESTIONS

1. Where do tests of significance fit into the set of threats that Campbell lists?
2. Choose some other articles in this reader and determine if the research design eliminates or reduces the "threats to validity" listed by Campbell. In addition note carefully if the authors are aware of any plausible alternative hypotheses for their findings.
3. For the Connecticut "speeding crackdown" example, list the different data sources referred to and indicate the use made of each one in supporting the interpretation about the effectiveness of the crackdown.

A Comparative Test of the Status Envy, Social Power, and Secondary Reinforcement Theories of Identificatory Learning

ALBERT BANDURA, DOROTHEA ROSS, and SHEILA A. ROSS

Although in many ways "true" experimental procedures—where the researcher has control over the assignment of subject to control and experimental groups and at least one independent variable—can be considered to be the "best" way of achieving valid cause and effect generalizations, their use in the social sciences has been fairly rare. The reasons for this have been many.

Reprinted from *Journal of Abnormal and Social Psychology* 67 (1963), 527–534, with permission of the American Psychological Association.

Consideration of ethics, difficulty in manipulating experimental variables, and the inability to control the assignment of research units to control and treatment groups are a few of the major factors making experiments either impossible or too costly to carry out. Despite the many barriers, a few notable attempts in the social science have employed "true" experimental designs.

In the following article, the authors describe one such attempt at experimentation. Although the design is an unusually complex one, it illustrates the kind of innovative thinking that is often required to execute experiments testing social theories.

■ Although it is generally assumed that social behavior is learned and modified through direct reward and punishment of instrumental responses, informal observation and laboratory study of the social learning process reveal that new responses may be rapidly acquired and existing behavioral repertoires may be considerably changed as a function of observing the behavior and attitudes exhibited by models (Bandura, 1962).

The latter type of learning is generally labeled "imitation" in behavior theory, and "identification" in most theories of personality. These concepts, however, are treated in the present [article] as synonymous since both encompass the same behavioral phenomenon, i.e., the tendency for a person to match the behavior, attitudes, or emotional reactions as exhibited by actual or symbolized models. While the defining properties of identification are essentially the same in different personality theories, a host of divergent learning conditions have been proposed as the necessary antecedent variables for matching or identificatory behavior (Bronfenbrenner, 1960; Freud, 1946; Freud, 1924, 1948; Kagan, 1958; Klein, 1949; Maccoby, 1959; Mowrer, 1950; Parsons, 1955; Sears, 1957; Whiting, 1960).

In the experiment reported in this [article] predictions were derived from three of the more prominent theories of learning by identification, and tested in three-person groups representing prototypes of the nuclear family. In one condition of the experiment an adult assumed the role of controller of resources and positive reinforcers. Another adult was the consumer or recipient of these resources, while the child, a participant observer in the triad, was essentially ignored. In a second treatment condition, one adult controlled the resources; the child, however, was the recipient of the positive reinforcers and the other adult was assigned a subordinate and powerless role. An adult male and female served as models in each of the triads. For half the boys and girls in each condition the male model controlled and dispensed the rewarding resources, simulating the husband dominant family; for the remaining children, the female model mediated the positive resources as in the wife dominant home. Following the experimental social interactions the two adult models exhibited divergent patterns of behavior in the presence of the child, and a measure was obtained of the degree to which the child subsequently patterned his behavior after that of the models.

According to the *status envy theory* of identification recently proposed by Whiting (1959, 1960), where a child competes unsuccessfully with an adult for affection, attention, food, and care, the child will envy the consumer adult and consequently identify with him. Whiting's theory represents an extension of the Freudian defensive identification hypothesis that identificatory behavior is the outcome of rivalrous interaction between the child and the parent who occupies an envied consumer status. While Freud presents the child as in competition with the father primarily for the mother's sexual and affectional attention, Whiting regards any forms of reward, material and social, as valued resources around which rivalry may develop. The status envy theory thus predicts that the highest degree of imitation by the child will occur in the experimental condition in which the rivalrous adult consumes the resources desired by the child, with the consumer adult serving as the primary object of imitation.

In contrast to the envy theory, other writers (Maccoby, 1959; Mussen and Distler, 1959; Parsons, 1955) assume that the controller, rather than the consumer, of resources is the main source of imitative behavior. The *power theory* of social influence has received considerable attention in experimental social psychology, though not generally in the context of identification theories.

Social power is typically defined as the ability of a person to influence the behavior of others by controlling or mediating their positive and negative reinforcements. French and Raven (1959) have distinguished five types of power based on expertness, attractiveness, legitimacy, coerciveness, and rewarding power, each of which is believed to have somewhat differential effects on the social influence process. For example, the use of threat or coercion, in which the controller derives power from his ability to administer punishments, not only develops avoidance behavior toward the controller but also decreases his attractiveness and hence his effectiveness in altering the behavior of others beyond the immediate social influence setting (French, Morrison, and Levinger, 1960; Zipf, 1960). The use of reward power, in contrast, both fosters approach responses toward the power figure and increases his attractiveness or secondary reward value through the repeated association of his attributes with positive reinforcement. Attractiveness is assumed to extend the controller's power over a wide range of behavior (French and Raven, 1959).

In the present investigation power based upon the ability to dispense rewards was manipulated experimentally. In accordance with the social power theory of identification, but contrasting with the status envy hypothesis, one would predict that children will reproduce more of the behavior of the adult who controls positive reinforcers, than that of the powerless adult model, and that power inversions on the part of the male and female models will produce cross-sex imitation.

The *secondary reinforcement theory* of identification, which has been alluded to in the discussion of social power through attractiveness, has been elaborated in greatest detail by Mowrer (1950, 1958). According to this view, as a model mediates the child's biological and social rewards, the behavioral attributes of the model are paired repeatedly with positive reinforcement and thus acquire secondary reward value. On the basis of stimulus generalization, responses which match those of the model attain reinforcing value for the child in proportion to their similarity to those made by the model. Consequently, the child can administer positively conditioned reinforcers to himself simply by reproducing as closely as possible the model's positively valenced behavior. This theory predicts that the experimental condition in which the child was the recipient of positive reinforcements will yield the highest imitation scores with the model who dispensed the rewards serving as the primary source of imitative behavior.

METHOD

SUBJECTS   The subjects were 36 boys and 36 girls enrolled in the Stanford University Nursery School. They ranged in age from 33 to 65 months, although the variability was relatively small with most of the ages falling around the mean of 51 months.

An adult male and female served as models in the triads so as to reproduce possible power structures encountered in different types of family constellations. A female experimenter conducted the study for all 72 children.

DESIGN AND PROCEDURE   The subjects were assigned randomly to two experimental groups and one control group of 24 subjects each. Half the subjects in each group were males, and half were females.

High rewarding power was induced experimentally through the manipulation of material and social reinforcements, and the use of verbal structuring techniques. While accompanying the child to the experimental room, for example, the experimenter informed the child that the adult who assumed the role of controller owned the nursery school "surprise room," as well as a fabulous collection of play materials. After introducing the child to the controller, the experimenter asked whether the child may play in the surprise room. The controller explained that he was on his way to his car to fetch some of his most attractive toys, but the experimenter and the child could proceed to the room where he would join them shortly. As the controller left, the experimenter commented on how lucky they were to have access to the controller's play materials.

On the way to the experimental room they met the other adult who insisted on joining them but the experimenter informed her that she would have to obtain permission from the controller since he owned the room, and it was doubtful whether sufficient play materials were available for both the adult and the child. This brief encounter with the other adult was designed primarily to create the set that rewards were available to one person only and thereby to induce rivalrous feelings over the controller's resources.

As soon as the experimenter and the child arrived in the experimental room, they sat down at a small table and played with the few Lincoln Logs and two small cars that were provided. A short time later the other adult appeared and announced that the controller also granted her permission to play in the room.

The controller then entered carrying two large toy boxes containing a variety of highly attractive masculine and feminine toys, a colorful juice dispensing fountain, and an ample supply of cookies. As soon as the controller appeared on the scene, the experimenter departed.

316

For children in the Adult Consumer condition, the adult who assumed the role of consumer requested permission to play with the articles and the controller replied that, since the child appeared to be occupied at his table, the consumer was free to use the play materials. This monopolistic move by the consumer adult left the child stranded at a table with two relatively uninteresting toys.

During the 20-minute play session, the controller offered the consumer, among other things, miniature pinball machines, mechanical sparkling toys, kaleidoscopes, dolls, and actively participated with the consumer in dart games and other activities. To add to the credibility of the situation, both the controller and consumer devoted most of their attention to articles, such as the pinball machine and dart game, which could be used in adult appropriate activities. Throughout the interaction the controller was most helpful, supportive, and generous in dispensing social reinforcers in the form of praise, approval, and positive attention. The consumer, in turn, commented frequently on the controller's highly attractive resources so as to further enhance the controller's rewarding status. The consumer also verbalized considerable positive affect characteristic of a person experiencing positive reinforcements.

Approximately half way through the session, the controller remarked, "Say, you look hungry. I have just the thing for you." He then brought forth the soda fountain dispenser, poured colorful fruit juices into paper cups and served them to the consumer along with a generous supply of cookies. While the consumer was enjoying his snack, the controller turned on a "TV-radio" that played a nursery melody while a revolving dial displayed a series of storybook scenes.

Toward the end of the session, the controller informed the consumer that he will be leaving on a shopping trip to San Francisco that afternoon, and asked the consumer if there was anything special she would like him to buy for her. The consumer requested a super two-wheel bicycle, a high status object among the nursery school children. The controller promised to purchase the bicycle along with any other items the consumer might think of before the controller departed for the city.

The procedure for the Child Consumer condition was identical with that described above except the child was the recipient of the material rewards and the social reinforcement. During the session the other adult sat at the opposite end of the room engrossed in a book, and was totally ignored by the controller. In discussing the prospective San Francisco shopping trip, the controller mentioned to the child that he was planning to visit some toy stores in the city that afternoon, and asked for suggestions of attractive toys he might purchase for future play sessions with children.

For half the boys and girls in each treatment condition the male model controlled and dispensed the resources, simulating the husband dominant family; for the remaining children the female model mediated the positive resources as in the wife dominant home.

At the completion of the social interaction session the controller announced that he had a surprise game in his car that the three of them could play together. The controller then asked the other adult to fetch the experimenter to assist them with the game, and as soon as the adult departed, the controller removed the toys and assembled the imitation task apparatus.

IMITATION TASK The imitation task was essentially the same two-choice discrimination problem utilized in an earlier experiment (Bandura and Huston, 1961), except the response repertoires exhibited by the models were considerably extended, and the procedure used in the acquisition trials was somewhat modified.

The apparatus consisted of two small boxes with hinged lids, identical in color and size. The boxes were placed on stools approximately 4 feet apart and 8 feet from the starting point. On the lid of each box was a rubber doll.

As soon as the other adult returned with the experimenter, the controller asked both the child and the experimenter to be seated in the chairs along the side of the room, and the other adult to stand at the starting point, while the controller described the game they were about to play. The controller then explained that the experimenter would hide a picture sticker in one of the two boxes and the object of the game was to guess which box contained the sticker. The adults would have the first set of turns, following which the child would play the guessing game.

The discrimination problem was employed simply as a cover task that occupied the children's attention while at the same time permitted observation of the models as they performed divergent patterns of behavior during the discrimination trials in the absence of any set to attend to or learn the responses exhibited by the models.

Before commencing the trials, the controller invited the other participants to join him in selecting a "thinking cap" from hat racks containing two identical sets of four sailor caps, each of which had a different colored feather. The controller selected the green feathered hat, remarked, "Feather in the front," and wore the hat with the feather facing forward. The other model selected the yellow feathered hat, commented, "Feather in the back," and placed the hat on her head with the feather facing backward. The child then made his choice from the four hats in the lower rack and it was noted whether he matched the color preference, hat placement, and the verbal responses of the one or the other model.

The models then went to the starting point, the child returned to his seat, and the experimenter loaded both boxes with sticker pictures for the models' trials.

During the execution of each trial, each model exhibited a different set of relatively novel verbal and motor responses that were totally irrelevant to the discrimination problem to which the child's attention was directed. At the starting point the controller stood with his arms crossed, but at the experimenter's warning not to look, the controller placed his hands over his eyes, faced sideways, and asked, "Ready?" The other model stood with his arms on his hips, then squatted with his back turned to the boxes, and asked, "Now?"

As soon as the experimenter gave the signal for the first trial, the controller remarked, "Forward march," and began marching slowly toward the designated box repeating, "March, march, march." When he reached the box he said, "Sock him," hit the doll aggressively off the box, opened the lid and yelled, "Bingo," as he reached down for the sticker. He then remarked, "Lickit-stickit," as he pressed on the picture sticker with his thumb in the upper-right quadrant of a 24×24 inch sheet of plain white paper that hung on the wall immediately behind the boxes. The controller terminated the trial by replacing the doll facing sideways on the container with the comment, "Look in the mirror," and made a final verbal response, "There."

The other model then took her turn and performed a different set of imitative acts but equated with the controller's responses in terms of number, types of response classes represented, structural properties, and interest value. At the starting point, for example, she remarked, "Get set, go," and walked stiffly toward the boxes repeating, "Left, right, left, right." When she reached the container she said, "Down and up," as she lay the doll down on the lid and opened the box. She then exclaimed, "A stick-eroo," repeated, "Weto-smacko," and slapped on the sticker with the open hand in the lower-left quadrant of the sheet of paper. In terminating the trial, the model lay the doll on the lid of the container with the remark, "Lie down," and returned with her hands behind her back, and emitted the closing remark, "That's it."

The two sets of responses were counterbalanced by having the models display each pattern with half the subjects in each of the three groups.

The models performed alternately for four trials. At the conclusion of the fourth trial the controller explained that he had to check some materials in his car and while he and the other model were away the child may take his turns. Before they departed, however, the experimenter administered a picture preference test in which the models were asked to select their preferred picture from six different stickers pasted on a 5×8 inch card, after which the child was presented a similar card containing an identical set of stickers and requested to indicate his preference.

In addition to the introductory block of four trials by the models, the child's 15 total test trials were interspersed with three two-trial blocks by the models. The models were always absent from the room during the child's test series. This procedure was adopted in order to remove any imagined situational restraints against, or coercion for, the child to reproduce the models' responses. Moreover, demonstrations of delayed imitation in the absence of the model provide more decisive evidence for learning by means of imitation.

The models always selected different boxes, the right-left position varying from trial to trial in a fixed irregular order, and the controller always took the first turn. Although the models received stickers on each trial, the child was nonrewarded on one third of the trials in order to maintain his interest in the cover task.

At the beginning of each of the blocks of subjects' trials, the experimenter administered the picture preference test and the selection of stickers that matched the models' choices was recorded. In addition, on the eighth trial the models removed their hats and hung them in different locations in the room. If the child removed his hat during the session and placed it along side one or the other of the model's hats, this imitative act was also scored.

At the completion of the imitation phase of the experiment, the children were interviewed by the experimenter in order to determine whom they considered to be the controller of resources, and to assess their model preferences. The latter data were used as an index of attraction to the models. In addition, for the children in the Adult Consumer condition, the session was concluded by providing them the same lavish treatment accorded their adult rival.

Children in the control group had no prior social interaction with the models but participated with them in the imitative learning phase of the study. The experimenter assumed complete charge of the procedures and treated the models as though they were naive subjects. This control group was included primarily to determine the models' relative effectiveness as modeling stimuli. In addition, the models alternated between subjects in the order in which they executed the trials so as to test for the possibility of a primacy or a recency of exposure effect on imitative behavior.

IMITATION SCORES   The imitation scores were obtained by summing the frequency of occurrence of the postural, verbal, and motor responses described in the preceding section, and the hat, color, and picture preferences that matched the selections of each of the two models.

The children's performances were scored by three raters who observed the experimental sessions through a one-way mirror from an adjoining observation room. The raters were provided with a separate check list of responses exhibited by each of the two models, and the scoring procedure simply involved checking the imitative responses performed by the children on each trial. In order to provide an estimate of interscorer reliability, the performances of 30% of the children were recorded simultaneously but independently by two observers. The raters were in perfect agreement on 95% of the specific imitative responses that they scored.

RESULTS

The control group data revealed that the two models were equally effective in eliciting imitative responses, the mean values being 17.83 and 20.46 for the male and female model, respectively; nor did the children display differential imitation of same-sex ($M = 22.30$) and opposite-sex ($M = 18.50$) models. Although children in the control group tended to imitate the second model ($M = 22.21$) to a somewhat greater extent than the one who performed first ($M = 16.08$) on each trial, suggesting a recency of exposure effect, the difference was not of statistically significant magnitude ($t = 1.60$).

Table 1 presents the mean imitation scores for children in each of the two experimental triads. A $2 \times 2 \times 2 \times 2$ mixed factorial analysis of variance was computed on these data in which the four factors in the design were sex of child, sex of the model who controlled the resources, adult versus child consumer, and the controller versus the other model as the source of imitative behavior. As shown in Table 2, the findings of this study clearly support the social power theory of imitation. In both experimental treatments, regardless of whether the rival adult or the children themselves were the recipients of the rewarding resources, the model who

TABLE 1. Mean Number of Imitative Responses Performed by Subgroups of Children in the Experimental Triads

Subjects	Objects of Imitation			
	Male Controller	Female Consumer	Female Controller	Male Consumer
Girl	29.00	9.67	26.00	10.00
Boys	30.17	18.67	22.33	16.17
Total	29.59	14.17	24.17	13.09
	Controller	Ignored	Controller	Ignored
Girls	22.00	16.17	31.84	22.17
Boys	29.17	16.67	26.83	34.50
Total	25.59	16.42	29.34	28.34

TABLE 2. Summary of the Analysis of Variance of the Imitation Scores

Source	df	MS	F
Between subjects	47	310.17	
Sex of subjects (A)	1	283.59	<1
Sex of controller model (B)	1	128.34	<1
Adult versus child consumer (C)	1	518.01	1.61
A × B	1	23.01	<1
A × C	1	1.76	<1
B × C	1	742.59	2.31
A × B × C	1	21.10	<1
Error (b)	40	321.49	
Within subjects	48	113.24	
Controller versus other model (D)	1	2,025.84	40.61***
A × D	1	297.51	5.96*
B × D	1	237.51	4.76*
C × D	1	396.09	7.94**
A × B × D	1	256.76	5.15*
A × C × D	1	19.52	<1
B × C × D	1	23.02	<1
A × B × C × D	1	184.00	3.69
Error (w)	40	49.88	

* $p<.05$.
** $p<.01$.
*** $p<.001$.

possessed rewarding power was imitated to a greater degree than was the rival or the ignored model ($F=40.61$, $p<.001$). Nor did the condition combining resource ownership with direct reinforcement of the child yield the highest imitation of the model who controlled and dispensed the positive rewards. The latter finding is particularly surprising since an earlier experiment based on two-person groups (Bandura and Huston, 1961) demonstrated that pairing of model with positive reinforcement substantially enhanced the occurrence of imitative behavior. An examination of the remaining significant interaction effects together with the postexperimental interview data suggest a possible explanation for the discrepant results.

The differential in the controller-other model imitation was most pronounced when the male model was the controller of resources ($F = 4.76$, $p < .05$), particularly for boys. In fact, boys who were the recipients of rewarding resources mediated by the female model tended to favor the ignored male as their object of imitation. In the postexperiment interview a number of boys in this condition spontaneously expressed sympathy for the ignored male and mild criticism of the controller for not being more charitable with her bountiful resources (for example, "She doesn't share much. John played bravely even though she didn't even share. . . . She's a bit greedy.").

As a partial check on whether this factor would tend to diminish the differential imitation of the two models, six children—three boys and three girls—participated in a modified Child Consumer treatment in which, halfway through the social interaction session, the ignored adult was informed that he too may have access to the playthings. He replied that he was quite content to read his book. This modified procedure, which removed the rivalry and the exclusion of the model, yielded four times as much imitation of the controller relative to the model who was ignored by choice.

The significant triple interaction effect indicates that the differential in the controller–other model imitation was greatest when the same-sex model mediated the positive reinforcers, and this effect was more pronounced for boys than for girls.

The data presented so far demonstrate that manipulation of rewarding power had produced differential imitation of the behavior exhibited by the two models. In order to assess whether the dispensing of positive reinforcers in the prior social interaction influenced the overall level of matching responses, the imitation scores in each of the three groups were summed across models and analyzed using a Sex $\times$ Treatment design.

The mean total imitative responses for children in the Child Consumer, Adult Consumer, and the Control group were 50.21, 40.58, and 37.88, respectively. Analysis of variance of these data reveals a significant treatment effect ($F = 3.37$, $.025 < p < .05$). Further comparisons of pairs of means by the t test show that children in the Child Rewarded condition displayed significantly more imitative behavior than did children both in the Adult Consumer treatment ($t = 2.19$, $p < .05$), and those in the Control group ($t = 2.48$, $p < .02$). The Adult Consumer and Control groups, however, did not differ from each other in this respect ($t = .54$).

The model preference patterns were identical for children in the two experimental conditions and consequently, the data were combined for the statistical analysis. Of the 48 children, 32 selected the model who possessed rewarding power as the more attractive, while 16 preferred the noncontrolling adult. The greater attractiveness of the rewarding model was significant beyond the .05 level ($\chi^2 = 5.34$). The experimental triad in which boys were the recipients of positive reinforcers while the male model was ignored, and the female consumer–girl ignored subgroup, contributed the highest preference for the noncontrolling adult.

In addition to the experimental groups discussed in the preceding section, data are available for 9 children in the Adult Consumer condition, and for 11 children in the Child Consumer treatment who revealed, in their postexperiment interviews, that they had actually attributed rewarding power to the ignored or the consumer adult despite the elaborate experimental manipulations designed to establish differential power status. A number of these children were firmly convinced that only a male can possess resources and, therefore, the female dispensing the rewards was only an intermediary for the male model (for example, "He's the man and it's all his because he's a daddy. Mommy never really has things belong to her. . . . He's the daddy so it's his but he shares nice with the mommy. . . . He's the man and the man always really has the money and he lets ladies play too. John's good and polite and he has very good manners."). This view of resource ownership within the family constellation was often directly reinforced by the mothers (for example, "My mommy told me and Joan that the daddy really buys all the things, but the mommy looks after things."). Children who attributed the resource ownership to the consumer or ignored female model had considerable difficulty in explaining their selection (for example, "I just knowed it does. . . . I could tell, that's how."), perhaps, because the power structure they depicted is at variance with the widely accepted cultural norm.

TABLE 3. Imitation as a Function of Attributed Rewarding Power to the Models

Treatment Condition	Objects of imitation			
	Female Controller	Male Noncontroller	Male Controller	Female Noncontroller
Adult consumer	24.0	12.3	29.8	14.6
Child consumer	18.2	6.7	35.5	16.2

As shown in Table 3, models who were attributed rewarding power elicited approximately twice as many matching responses than models who were perceived by the children as possessing no control over the rewarding resources. Because of the small and unequal number of cases in each cell, these data were not evaluated statistically. The differences, however, are marked and quite in accord with those produced by the experimentally manipulated variations in power status.

DISCUSSION

To the extent that the imitative behavior elicited in the present experiment may be considered an elementary prototype of identification within a nuclear family group, the data fail to support the interpretation of identificatory learning as the outcome of a rivalrous interaction between the child and the adult who occupies an envied status in respect to the consumption of highly desired resources. Children clearly identified with the source of rewarding power rather than with the competitor for these rewards. Moreover, power inversions on the part of the male and female models produced cross-sex imitation, particularly in girls. The differential readiness of boys and girls to imitate behavior exhibited by an opposite-sex model is consistent with findings reported by Brown (1956, 1958) that boys show a decided preference for the masculine role, whereas, ambivalence and masculine role preference are widespread among girls. These findings probably reflect both the differential cultural tolerance for cross-sex behavior displayed by males and females, and the privileged status and relatively greater positive reinforcement of masculine role behavior in our society.

Failure to develop sex appropriate behavior has received considerable attention in the clinical literature and has customarily been assumed to be established and maintained by psychosexual threat and anxiety reducing mechanisms. Our findings strongly suggest, however, that external social learning variables, such as the distribution of rewarding power within the family constellation, may be highly influential in the formation of inverted sex role behavior.

Theories of identificatory learning have generally assumed that within the family setting the child's initial identification is confined to his mother, and that during early childhood boys must turn from the mother as the primary model to the father as the main source of imitative behavior. However, throughout the course of development children are provided with ample opportunities to observe the behavior of both parents. The results of the present experiment reveal that when children are exposed to multiple models they may select one or more of them as the primary source of behavior, but rarely reproduce all the elements of a single model's repertoire or confine their imitation to that model. Although the children adopted many of the characteristics of the model who possessed rewarding power, they also reproduced some of the elements of behavior exhibited by the model who occupied the subordinate role. Consequently, the children were not simply junior-size replicas of one or the other model; rather, they exhibited a relatively novel pattern of behavior representing an amalgam of elements from both models. Moreover, the specific admixture of behavioral elements varied from child to child. These findings provide considerable evidence for the seemingly paradoxical conclusion that imitation can in fact produce innovation of social behavior, and that within the same family even same-sex siblings may exhibit quite different response patterns, owing to their having selected for imitation different elements of their parents' response repertoires.

The association of a model with noncontingent positive reinforcement tends to increase the incidence of imitative behavior in two-person groups (Bandura and Huston, 1961), whereas the addition of a same-sex third person who is denied access to desired rewards may provoke in children negative evaluations of the rewarding model and thereby decreases his potency as a modeling stimulus. These two sets of data demonstrate how learning principles based on an individual behavior model may be subject to strict limitations, since the introduction of additional social variables into the stimulus complex can produce significant changes in the functional relationships between relevant variables.

REFERENCES

BANDURA, A. Social learning through imitation. In M. R. Jones (Ed.), *Nebraska symposium on motivation: 1962.* Lincoln: Univer. Nebraska Press, 1962. Pp. 211–269.

BANDURA, A., and HUSTON, ALETHA C. Identification as a process of incidental learning. *J. abnorm. soc. Psychol.,* 1961, 63, 311–318.

BRONFENBRENNER, U. Freudian theories of identification and their derivatives. *Child Develpm.,* 1960, 31, 15–40.

BROWN, D. G. Sex-role preference in young children. *Psychol. Monogr.,* 1956, 70 (14, Whole No. 421).

BROWN, D. G. Sex-role development in a changing culture. *Psychol. Bull.,* 1958, 55, 232–242.

FRENCH, J. R. P., JR., MORRISON, H. W., and LEVINGER, G. Coercive power and forces affecting conformity. *J. abnorm. soc. Psychol.,* 1960, 61, 93–101.

FRENCH, J. R. P., JR., and RAVEN, B. The bases of social power. In D. Cartwright (Ed.), *Studies in social power.* Ann Arbor, Mich.: Institute for Social Research, 1959. Pp. 150–167.

FREUD, ANNA. *The ego and the mechanisms of defense.* New York: International Univer. Press, 1946.

FREUD, S. The passing of the Oedipus-complex. In, *Collected papers.* Vol. 2. London: Hogarth Press, 1924. Pp. 269–282.

FREUD, S. *Group psychology and the analysis of the ego.* London: Hogarth Press, 1948.

KAGAN, J. The concept of identification. *Psychol. Rev.,* 1958, 65, 296–305.

KLEIN, MELANIE. *The psycho-analysis of children.* London: Hogarth Press, 1949.

MACCOBY, ELEANOR E. Role-taking in childhood and its consequences for social learning. *Child Develpm.,* 1959, 30, 239–252.

MOWRER, O. H. Identification: A link between learning theory and psychotherapy. In, *Learning theory and personality dynamics.* New York: Ronald Press, 1950. Pp. 69–94.

MOWRER, O. H. Hearing and speaking: An analysis of language learning. *J. speech hear. Disord.,* 1958, 23, 143–152.

MUSSEN, P., and DISTLER, L. Masculinity, identification, and father-son relationships. *J. abnorm. soc. Psychol.,* 1959, 59, 350–356.

PARSONS, T. Family structure and the socialization of the child. In T. Parsons and R. F. Bales (Eds.), *Family, socialization, and interaction process.* Glencoe, Ill.: Free Press, 1955. Pp. 35–131.

SEARS, R. R. Identification as a form of behavioral development. In D. B. Harris (Ed.), *The concept of development.* Minneapolis: Univer. Minnesota Press, 1957. Pp. 149–161.

WHITING, J. W. M. Sorcery, sin, and the superego: A cross-cultural study of some mechanisms of social control. In M. R. Jones (Ed.), *Nebraska symposium on motivation: 1959.* Lincoln: Univer. Nebraska Press, 1959. Pp. 174–195.

WHITING, J. W. M. Resource mediation and learning by identification. In I. Iscoe and H. W. Stevenson (Eds.), *Personality development in children.* Austin: Univer. Texas Press, 1960. Pp. 112–126.

ZIPF, SHEILA G. Resistance and conformity under reward and punishment. *J. abnorm. soc. Psychol.*, 1960, 61, 102–109.

QUESTIONS

1. Carefully describe how the dependent variable is defined.
2. The experiment involves four dichotomous independent variables. What are they, and to what type of unit or case do they apply?
3. Carefully inspect Table 1 and describe the pattern of arithmetic means for the different experimental conditions. You may want to rearrange the table in order to bring out different contrasts among pairs of categories.
4. How is "postexperimental" interview material used to "validate" the efficacy of the independent variable manipulations? How do the results lead to further experimentation?
5. How might you conceive of using these experimental variables in a natural group setting, such as the child in interaction with his parents? What would be the advantages and the limitations of trying to use a natural group?

Physicians and Medicare:
A Before-After Study of the Effects
of Legislation on Attitudes
JOHN COLOMBOTOS

Research designs vary in how they handle the variable of time. In true experimental design, for example, the temporal sequence of independent and dependent variable is automatically known because of the experimenter's control over the independent variable (the "treatment"). In the vast bulk of survey designs in sociology, the subjects are questioned at only one point in time, and it becomes far more difficult to ascertain the temporal sequence of variables. In some instances, fairly viable assumptions can be made, such as sex precedes amount of education. Or we might use the respondent's own recall of past events to infer temporal sequence (for example, respondent's description of his early family life can be used to specify the pressure of parents in his childhood as preceding current voting behavior). However, little can be done from "cross-sectional" design to some variables to order them along a time dimension (for example, which comes first: attitudes toward marriage or degree of premarital sexual intimacy?). In an attempt to overcome this limitation of

Reprinted from *American Sociological Review 34* (1969), 318–334, with permission of The American Sociological Association.

survey research, the "panel" design has been introduced in recent years. Panel studies are very similar to survey research (a sample of respondents is queried about their behavior, mental states, and characteristics) with the important difference being that the respondents are reinterviewed at later points in time. And by comparing changes in that panel as well as having knowledge of intervening events it is now possible to have more confidence in the temporal sequence of variables.

An illustration of the "panel" technique is provided by the following study of physicians' attitude toward Medicare legislation. It might be helpful to review article 21, especially the discussion about threats to validity, before reading the present one.

■ Seldom has a law been more bitterly opposed by any group than was Medicare by the medical profession (see Harris, 1966; Feingold, 1966; Rose, 1967: 400–455). Just before Medicare was passed by Congress in 1965, there was even talk about a "boycott" of the program by physicians. This paper examines how individual physicians reacted, in their behavior and in their thinking, to Medicare after it became law.[1] The more general issue raised by this question is the role of law as an instrument of social change, an old sociological problem.

LAW AS AN INSTRUMENT OF SOCIAL CHANGE   One view, attributed to early sociologists such as Herbert Spencer and William Graham Sumner, is that law can never move ahead of the customs or mores of the people, that legislation which is not rooted in the folkways is doomed to failure. Social change must be slow, and change in public opinion must precede legislative action. In brief, "stateways cannot change folkways." This view was expressed by Senator Barry Goldwater in the 1964 Presidential campaign (The New York Times, Nov. 1, 1964:1): "I am unalterably opposed to . . . discrimination, but I also know that government can provide no lasting solution. . . . The ultimate solution lies in the hearts of men."

Others see law as a positive force in initiating social change (Allport, 1954:471): "It is a well known psychological fact that most people accept the results of an election or legislation gladly enough after the furor has subsided. . . . They allow themselves to be re-educated by the new norm that prevails."[2]

These are oversimplified statements of the role of law as an instrument of social change and miss the complexity of the problem. The question must be specified: Under what conditions do laws have what effects?

EFFECTS: BEHAVIOR VS. ATTITUDES   Sumner's negative position on law as an instrument of social change has been distorted, according to one reappraisal of his writings (Ball et al., 1962:532–540). Sumner (1906:68), in distinguishing between the effects of law on behavior and on attitudes, did not reject the power of law to influence men's behavior: "Men can always perform the prescribed act, although they cannot always think or feel prescribed thoughts or emotions."

This is in agreement with the views of the majority of contemporary politically liberal social scientists, who see law primarily as a way of changing behavior, not attitudes. For example: "[Legal action] cannot coerce thoughts or instill subjective tolerance. . . . Law is intended only to control the outward expression of intolerance" (Allport, 1954:477). And according to MacIver (1954:viii), "No law should require men to change their attitudes. . . . In a democracy we do not punish a man because he is opposed to income taxes, or to free school education, or to vaccination, or to minimum wages, but the laws of a democracy insist that he obey the laws that make provisions for these things. . . ."

The distinction between the effects of law on attitudes and on behavior is supported by empirical studies showing a discrepancy between the two (see Deutscher, 1966:235–254). In race relations, for example, study after study has shown that in concrete situations—in hotel accommodations (LaPiere, 1934:230–237), restaurant service (Kutner et al., 1952:649–652), department store shopping (Saenger and Gilbert, 1950:57–76), hospital accommodations, and school desegregation (Clark, 1953:47–50)—expressions of prejudice are not necessarily accompanied by discriminatory behavior. There are undoubtedly instances of the opposite, that is, verbal expressions of tolerance accompanied by discriminatory behavior, but they are not as well documented. The flight of white, liberal, middle-class families from the cities to the suburbs may be such an instance (Scott and Scott, 1968:46 ff.).

But to say that attitudes and behavior are not perfectly correlated is not to say they are unrelated, and there is evidence that change in behavior leads to change in attitudes. Studies of integrated army units, housing projects, and children's camps show that white people in these situations develop more favorable attitudes toward Negroes (Swanson et al., 1952:502; Deutsch and Collins, 1951; Yarrow, 1958). In an analysis of school desegregation, Hyman and Sheatsley (1964:6) describe the process thus: "There is obviously some parallel between public opinion and official action. . . . Close analysis of the current findings . . . leads us to the conclusion that in those parts of the South where some measure of school integration has taken place official action has preceded public sentiment, and *public sentiment has then attempted to accommodate itself to the new situation*" [emphasis added].

Other studies (Mussen, 1950:423–441; Campbell, 1958:335–340), however, have found that social contact has little effect in reducing prejudice.[3]

If indeed behavioral change does lead to attitudinal change, then law, by first changing behavior, may ultimately lead to changes in attitudes. As Allport says: "Outward action, psychology knows, has an eventual effect upon inner habits of thought and feeling. And for this reason we list legislative action as one of the major methods of reducing, not only public discrimination [behavior], but private prejudice [attitudes] as well" (1954:477). Berger, too, writes: "Law does not change attitudes directly, but by altering the situations in which attitudes and opinions are formed, law can indirectly reach the more private areas of life it cannot touch directly in a democratic society" (Berger, 1954:187). Clark (1953:72), among others, states the issue in more problematic terms: "Situationally determined changes in behavior [as in response to a law] *may or may not* be accompanied by compatible changes in attitudes or motivation of the individuals involved" [emphasis added].

Others, however, see law exerting a *direct* influence on attitudes, without necessarily changing behavior first. Law is conceived as a legitimizing and educational force, supporting one value or set of values against another. For example, according to Dicey (1914:465): "No facts play a more important part in the creation of opinion than laws themselves." And according to Bonfield (1965:111): "Past the change in attitude which may be caused by legally mandated and enforced nondiscriminatory conduct, *the mere existence of the law itself affects prejudice* [emphasis added]. People usually agree with the law and internalize its values. This is because considerable moral and symbolic weight is added to a principle when it is embedded in legislation."

The results of the few studies done on the effects of law on behavior and attitudes are mixed. Cantril (1947:228) notes: "When an opinion is held by a slight majority or when opinion is not solidly structured, an accomplished fact tends to shift opinion in the direction of acceptance. Poll figures show that immediately after the repeal of the arms embargo, immediately after the passage of the conscription laws, and immediately after favorable Congressional action on lend-lease and on the repeal of the neutrality laws [just before the United States' entry into World War II] there was invariably a rise of around ten per cent in the number of people favorable to these actions." And Muir (1967) found that the Supreme Court decision banning religious exercises in the nation's schools had an over-all positive effect on the attitudes and behavior of 28 officials in one public school system, though there was some evidence of a backlash.

Other studies, however, show that laws and court decisions have negligible effects on relevant attitudes. Hyman and Sheatsley (1964:3) and Schwartz (1967:11–12, 28–41) interpret the increasing acceptance of integration between 1942 and 1964 as a complex of long-term trends that are not easily modified by specific, even highly dramatic events, such as the Supreme Court decision of 1954. The physicians' strike against the province's medical care plan in Saskatchewan, Canada, in 1962 (Badgely and Wolfe, 1967) is an extreme case of noncompliance with a program implemented by a law.[4]

CONDITIONS FOR EFFECTIVENESS OF LAW   Three commonly cited factors determining the effectiveness of law are: (1) the degree of compatibility of the law with existing values, (2) the enforceability of the law, (3) the clarity of public policy and the diligence of enforcement.[5]

1. To say that a law must be compatible with some major existing values is not to say that it must be compatible with all values. In any society, especially in modern, industrial society, values themselves "are full of inconsistencies and strains, unliberated tendencies in many directions, responsive adjustments to new situations well conceived or ill conceived" (MacIver, 1948:279). A law, then, "maintains one set of values against another" (Pound, 1944:25). Thus desegregation and civil rights laws find support in the democratic creed and due process; Medicare finds support in the principle that adequate medical care is a right, rather than

a privilege. This position appears to be in agreement with Sumner's principle of a "strain toward consistency." There is an important difference, however. Whereas Sumner posed the question of compatibility between a new law and existing mores as one of all or nothing, the current view emphasizes conflicts and strains among a system of mores and poses the question of compatibility as a matter of degree (Myrdal, 1944:1045–1057).

2. In order for a law to be enforceable, the behavior to be changed must be observable. It is more difficult to enforce a law against homosexual behavior, for example, than a law against racial discrimination in public transportation.

3. The authorities responsible must be fully committed to enforcing the new law. One reason for the failure of Prohibition was the failure, or disinclination, of law enforcement agents to implement the law. Civil rights legislation runs into the same problem where local authorities, especially in the deep South, look the other way.

THE MEDICARE LAW   Medicare, signed into law in July, 1965, is a major piece of social legislation. It is often compared in importance with the original Social Security Act of 1935.

Medicare, Title 18 of the Social Security Amendments Act of 1965 (Public Law 89–97), established a new program of health insurance for people 65 years old or over. It has two parts: hospital insurance (Part A), applying automatically to almost all people 65 or over, which covers inpatient hospital services, outpatient hospital diagnostic services, and posthospital care in the patient's home or in an extended care facility (such as a nursing home); and medical insurance (Part B), a voluntary plan elected by over 90% of those eligible for Part A, which covers physicians' services wherever they are furnished, home health services, and a number of other medical services. Part A is financed by the same method that finances retirement, disability, and death benefits under Social Security, i.e., special Social Security contributions by employees and their employers. Part B is financed by a monthly premium of $3.00, from each participant who elects to pay, matched by $3.00 from the general revenues of the Federal Government.[6]

For twenty years the American Medical Association fought bitterly and effectively against such a Federal program of health insurance under Social Security. Now, however, that the program has become law, the question is: How have individual physicians reacted, in their behavior and in their attitudes, to Medicare?

RESEARCH DESIGN

Our data came from standardized interviews in 1964 and early 1965, before Medicare was passed, with 1,205 physicians in private practice in New York State (about 80% of a probability sample), and from reinterviews with subsamples of these physicians at two different points in time after Medicare was passed. The interviews were conducted mainly by telephone. An experimental comparison of telephone and personal interviews with small, random subsamples of physicians showed that the responses obtained by the two methods were essentially similar.[7]

The purpose of the first wave of interviews was to study physicians' political attitudes, their attitudes toward issues in the organization of medical practice, and their career values, and to examine the relationship between background characteristics, such as their social origins and specialties, and their attitudes.[8] Among the questions in the first wave of interviews was: "What is your opinion about the bill that would provide for compulsory health insurance through Social Security to cover hospital costs for those over 65—Are you personally in favor of such a plan, or are you opposed to it?"

The bill referred to was passed, as noted above, in July, 1965, as Part A of Title 18. Part B of Title 18, the voluntary insurance plan that pays for physicians' bills and other services, and Title 19, which provides for Federal matching funds to states for medical care for the "medically indigent," were not covered in the first wave of interviews because they were not introduced in the bill until the spring of 1965. Title 19, as a matter of fact, received little publicity until after the bill was passed. Title 19 is commonly called *Medicaid;* Title 18, Parts A and B, *Medicare.*

Thus, before the law was passed, measures were available of physicians' attitudes toward what was generally considered the major feature of the bill, hospital insurance for the elderly, and many related issues, providing a unique opportunity for a natural experiment of the effects of legislation on attitudes.

The 1,205 physicians were stratified on their initial attitude toward Title 18A (i.e., before it was passed) and on geographic area, religious background, and political ideology, all of which were highly correlated with their initial attitude toward Title 18A,[9] and randomly divided into two subsamples, one with 804 and the other with 401 physicians.

The first subsample of 804 physicians was contacted between the middle of May, 1966, and the end of June, 1966, nearly one year after Medicare was passed and just before it was to go into effect. The second subsample of 401 doctors was contacted between the end of January and April, 1967, a little over six months after the main provisions of the Medicare program had gone into effect. More than 80% of each of these subsamples—676 and 331, respectively—were successfully reinterviewed.

To summarize, 1,205 doctors were interviewed before Medicare was passed (call this Time 1). Of these, 676 were reinterviewed about ten months after the law was passed and just before its implementation (call this Time 2),[10] and another 331 were reinterviewed a little over six months after its implementation (call this Time 3).[11] Thus, differences in attitudes between Time 1 and Time 2 would reflect the effects of the Medicare law before actual experience with it; differences between Time 1 and Time 3 would reflect the combined effects of the Medicare law and short-term experience with the program. This design makes it possible to separate the effects on attitudes of the law itself from the effects of its implementation, that is, short-term experience with the program. The design is represented in Figure 1.

FIGURE 1: Research Design

PHYSICIANS AND MEDICARE

| Medicare Becomes Law (July 30, 1965) | Medicare Program is Implemented (July 1, 1966) |

Time 1	Time 2	Time 3
January to April, 1964; November, 1964, to March, 1965	May to June, 1966	January to April, 1967
Interviews with 1,205 physicians in private practice	Reinterviews with 676 of a stratified subsample of 804 from 1,205 interviewed at Time 1 [330 of a control sample of 472 also interviewed]	Reinterviews with 331 of remaining stratified subsample of 401 from 1,205 interviewed at Time 1

THE FINDINGS

Physicians' Behavior. As the Medicare bill was going through its final stages in Congress in June, 1965, resolutions were introduced at the semiannual meeting of the AMA's House of Delegates calling for a "boycott," or "nonparticipation," when it was passed (*The New York Times*, June 22, 1965:1). Immediately after the law was passed, the president of the AMA predicted that "quite a few" physicians throughout the country would refuse to participate in the program (*The New York Times*, August 18, 1965:55). By the following March, however, it was reported that "threats of a boycott, if not dead, are at least moot" (*The New York Times*, March 28, 1966:1). When the AMA House of Delegates met in June, 1966, a month before Medicare was to go into effect, there was little, if any, talk of a boycott.

There has been no boycott, that is, no concerted noncooperation on a large scale, to date.

Responses from the New York State private practitioners interviewed in this study are consistent with the evidence of nationwide compliance by physicians. In the fall of 1965, just a few months after the law was passed, the New York State Medical Society issued a statement that "now that 'Medicare' is an accomplished fact, [the Society] will cooperate in every way possible with the government. . . . As citizens and as physicians, the members of the State Society will obey, and assist in the implementation of the law of the land . . ." (*New York State Journal of Medicine*, 1965:2779).

The physicians interviewed were asked if they agreed or disagreed with their Society's policy of cooperation. (Note that the answers to this question indicate physicians' *attitudes* toward cooperation with Medicare. They are not reports of actual cooperation.) Ninety percent agreed at Time 2; 91% agreed at Time 3 (see Table 1).

At Time 2, 87% of those who had been asked to serve on a hospital utilization review committee for Medicare patients had agreed to serve; and of those not asked, 66% said they would serve if asked. Slightly higher proportions indicated willingness to serve at Time 3. Furthermore, a physician's refusal to serve on such a committee does not necessarily indicate protest against Medicare. He may refuse for other reasons (see note 12, below).

At Time 2, less than 5% said they would not accept patients who get benefits under Medicare. At Time 3, 6% of those who had any patients 65 or over had not treated any patients under Title 18B, but only one of the 331 physicians interviewed at that time had actually *refused* to treat any patients under Title 18B. That doctor explained he was in "semi-retirement" (he was 73 years old), and he wasn't "going to bother with this." The remainder of the 6% indicated that none of their elderly patients had come to them for treatment yet.

To sum up, despite what appeared to be threats of a boycott before Medicare was passed, practically all physicians complied after it became "the law of the land."[12]

PHYSICIANS' ATTITUDES   It is possible, of course, for physicians to comply with Medicare without changing their minds about it. What effects has Medicare had on physicians' attitudes toward the program? In 1964 and early 1965, before Medicare was passed (Time 1), 38% of the private practitioners in New York State were "in favor" of "the bill that would provide for compulsory health insurance through Social Security to cover hospital costs for those over 65," the bill that became Title 18A. This is a sizeable number, but nevertheless, a minority.

At Time 2, ten months after the law was passed, even before it went into effect, the proportion "in favor" jumped to 70%. At Time 3, a little over six months after the program went into effect, the proportion "in favor" again jumped, to 81%. At both Time 2 and Time 3, more than half of those in favor felt "strongly," rather than only "somewhat" in favor (see Table 2).

Table 3 shows that of those opposed to Title 18A at Time 1, more than half (59%) had switched by Time 2; 70% had switched by Time 3.[13] Very few switched from favoring it to opposing it.

Although the absolute percentage increase favoring Title 18A of Medicare is greater between Time 1 and Time 2 (from 38 to 70%), than between Time 2 and Time 3 (from 70 to 81%), it might be misleading, because of the operation of a "ceiling effect," to argue that the Medicare law itself had a stronger impact than experience of the physicians with the program implemented by the law.[14] What can be asserted, however, is that the law itself had a large effect on physicians' attitudes toward Medicare even before it was implemented.

THE EFFECTS OF IMPLEMENTATION ON ATTITUDES   Consistent with the increase in the level of physicians' support for Medicare between Time 2 and Time 3 is the fact that they were less worried about the consequences of Medicare at Time 3 than at Time 2. Their earlier fears simply did not materialize.[15]

TABLE 1. Responses of Physicians Indicating Compliance with Medicare at Time 2 and Time 3[a]

	Time 2	Time 3
Last fall the New York State Medical Society said it would cooperate with the Government on Medicare—do you agree or disagree with this policy?[b]		
Agree	90%	91%
Disagree	8	8
Don't know, no answer	2	1
	100%	100%
Weighted totals	(10,214)	(4,954)
Unweighted totals	(676)	(331)
(If the physician had been asked to serve on a utilization review committee under Title 18): Have you agreed to serve?		
Yes	87%	94%
No	10	6
Not decided	4	0
	101%	100%
Weighted totals	(1,810)	(1,441)
Unweighted totals	(156)	(123)
(If the physician had not been asked to serve on a utilization review committee under Title 18): If you were asked, would you agree to be a member of such a committee?		
Yes	66%	71%
No	27	26
Don't know	7	3
	100%	100%
Weighted totals	(8,323)	(3,513)
Unweighted totals	(516)	(208)

For example, the proportion who thought that the quality of care physicians give their elderly patients would be "not as good" under Medicare dropped from 28% at Time 2 to 8% at Time 3 (see Table 4). The proportion who thought there would be "a great deal" or "a fair amount" of unnecessary hospitalization under Medicare dropped from 69% at Time 2 to 38% at Time 3 (27% thought there had actually been "a great deal" or "a fair amount" of unnecessary hospitalization up to Time 3). The proportion who thought there would be "a great deal" or "a fair amount" of unnecessary utilization of physicians' services under Medicare also dropped from 77% to 36% (25% thought there had actually been "a great deal" or "a fair amount" up to Time 3). It is only in the questions about government interference under Medicare and its effects on physicians' income that there were not significant changes, but only 12% at Time 2 and 11% at Time 3 thought that they would earn less money under Medicare than before, compared with more than a third who thought they would earn more money.[16]

	Time 2	Time 3

According to your present thinking, do you plan to accept patients who get benefiits under Medicare, or not?[c]

	Time 2	Time 3
Accept (have treated)	93%	93%
Will not accept (have not treated)	4	6
Don't know, no answer	4	1
	101%	100%
Weighted totals	(8,941)	(4,345)
Unweighted totals	(609)	(299)

[a] "Time 1" in these tables refers to interviews conducted before the passage of Medicare, from January to April, 1964, and from November, 1964, to March, 1965; "Time 2," to interviews done after the passage of Medicare but before its implementation, from May to June, 1966; "Time 3," to interviews done after the implementation of Medicare, from January to April, 1967.

All percentages in these tables are based on the weighted figures, which estimate the total number of private practitioners in New York State. The weighted figures do not add up to the actual number of private practitioners in the state because of noninterviews. The sampling design was stratified on geographic area, size of city, and part-time participation in a health department. The unweighted totals represent the number of physicians in a given category actually interviewed.

[b] This is the Time 2 question. The Time 3 question was: "The New York State Medical Society has said it would cooperate with the government on both Titles 18 and 19. Regarding Title 18, do you agree or disagree with this policy?"

[c] This is the Time 2 question. The Time 3 question was: "Have you treated any patients who get benefits under Part B of Title 18, or not?" The figures for both questions exclude those physicians who indicated in a previous question that they had no patients 65 years of age or over.

Of the 18 physicians with patients 65 or over who had not treated any of these patients under Title 18B at Time 3, only one had actually refused. The others reported that no elderly patients had come to them for treatment since Medicare.

ALTERNATIVE INTERPRETATIONS

Let us consider some alternative explanations of the large shifts in attitude toward Title 18A:

1. It could be argued that the changes described above could have taken place without the Medicare law and its implementation; that the shift in physicians' attitudes toward Medicare is part of a general, long-term liberal trend in their thinking. Obviously, there is not available a control group of physicians from whom the facts of the passage of the Medicare law and its implementation could be withheld. The argument that the changes in attitude toward Medicare are due to the law, however, is supported by the following observations:

a. The change in attitude toward Title 18A is a large change—from 38% in favor to 70% to 81% in a period of no longer than three years. It is not plausible to argue that this is due to a general ideological trend unrelated to the passage and implementation of Medicare.

TABLE 2. Attitudes of Physicians Toward Medicare (Title 18A) at Time 1, Time 2, and Time 3[a]

	Time 1	Time 2	Time 3
Favor	38%	70%	81%
Strongly		38	45
Somewhat		31	33
Don't know, no answer		1	3
Oppose	54	26	19
Strongly		14	10
Somewhat		11	9
Don't know, no answer		1	*
Don't know, no answer	8	5	*
	100%	101%	100%
Weighted totals	(18,044)	(10,214)	(4,954)
Unweighted totals	(1,205)	(676)	(331)

[a] At Time 1, the question was: "What is your opinion about the bill that would provide for compulsory health insurance through Social Security to cover hospital costs for those over 65—are you personally in favor of such a plan, or are you opposed to it?" Respondents were not asked whether they were "strongly" or "somewhat" in favor or opposed at Time 1.

At Time 2, the questions were: "What is your opinion of Part A of Medicare—the part that provides for compulsory health insurance through Social Security to cover hospital costs for those over 65—are you personally in favor of this plan, or opposed to it?" "Would you say strongly (in favor) (opposed) or somewhat (in favor) (opposed)?" At Time 3 the words "Part A of Title 18" were substituted for the words "Part A of Medicare."

* Less than 0.5%.

b. The attitudes that do change are highly specific to Medicare. Physicians' responses to questions indicating their position on economic-welfare issues, political party preference, group practice, and colleague controls, all of which strongly related to their attitudes toward Title 18A at Time 1 (Colombotos, 1968), are relatively stable at Time 1, Time 2, and Time 3 compared with their responses to the question on Medicare. If the change in attitudes toward Medicare was part of a more general trend in physicians' thinking and unrelated to the passage of Medicare, then one would expect changes in attitudes toward these other issues as well.

2. It could be argued that the increasingly favorable medical opinion about Medicare and the passage of the Medicare law were both the result or part of a third factor occurring immediately before Medicare was passed. Strong public support for Medicare, for example, could have influenced both medical and legislative opinion. Data in the present study from two independent samples of Manhattan doctors who were interviewed at two different times before Medicare was passed are inconsistent with such an argument. The first sample of 70 physicians was interviewed from January to April in 1964, about 18 months before Medicare was passed. The second sample of 61 physicians was interviewed from November, 1964, to March, 1965, scarcely six months before the law was passed. There was essentially no difference in the proportion in favor of Title 18A in the two samples—53% in the first sample, 57% in the second.

TABLE 3. Attitudes of Physicians Toward Medicare (Title 18A) at Time 2 and
Time 3 by Their Attitudes at Time 1

	Time 1 Attitude Toward Medicare	
	Favor	Oppose
Time 2 attitude toward Medicare		
Favor	90%	59%
Strongly	59	25
Somewhat	30	33
Don't know, no answer	1	1
Oppose	11	40
Strongly	5	22
Somewhat	6	16
Don't know, no answer	0	2
	101%	99%
Weighted totals	(3,757)	(5,098)
Unweighted totals	(193)	(411)
Time 3 attitude toward Medicare		
Favor	98%	70%
Strongly	84	19
Somewhat	10	48
Don't know, no answer	4	3
Oppose	2	30
Strongly	*	17
Somewhat	2	13
Don't know, no answer	0	*
	100%	100%
Weighted totals	(1,877)	(2,787)
Unweighted totals	(95)	(213)

* Less than 0.5%.

3. It is possible that New York State physicians' acceptance of Medicare after the enactment of the law was influenced by their opposition to the State's Medicaid program. The New York State implementation of Medicaid was one of the most liberal in the country. The first version of the New York State program was signed into law on April 30, 1966. The program was amended and curtailed two months later after strong opposition in upstate New York and threatened boycotts by county medical societies.

At Time 2, just after the first version of Medicaid was passed by the state legislature, 42% of the doctors interviewed said they were in favor of the law. At Time 3, despite, or perhaps because of, the fact the program had been curtailed six months earlier, it was still only 42%.

On all other questions about Medicaid asked at Time 3, it was less well received than Medicare:

1. Forty-six percent thought that the Government would interfere "a great

TABLE 4. Perceived Effects of Medicare (Title 18A) at Time 2 and at Time 3

	Time 2	Time 3
Weighted totals	(10,214)	(4,954)
Unweighted totals	(676)	(331)

In your opinion, how will Medicare (Title 18) affect the *quality* of care doctors give their elderly patients—in general, will doctors give *better* medical care, or *not as good* care, or won't Medicare (Title 18) make any difference?

	Time 2	Time 3
Better	14	30
Not as good	28	8
No difference	54	60
Don't know	5	2
	100%	100%

In your opinion, will there be a great deal of *unnecessary hospitalization* under Medicare (Title 18), or a fair amount, or very little, or none at all?

	Time 2	Time 3
Great deal	32	12
Fair amount	37	26
Very little	18	38
None at all	9	20
Don't know	4	4
	100%	100%

Will there be a great deal of *unnecessary* utilization of *doctors' services* under Medicare (Title 18), or a fair amount, or very little, or none at all?

	Time 2	Time 3
Great deal	39	8
Fair amount	38	28
Very little	15	39
None at all	4	20
Don't know	4	5
	100%	100%

In your opinion, will doctors *earn more* money under Medicare (Title 18) than before, or less money, or won't Medicare (Title 18) make any difference?

	Time 2	Time 3
More	35	42
Less	12	11
No difference	41	38
Don't know	12	9
	100%	100%

In your opinion, will the Federal Government, under Medicare (Title 18), interfere with the individual doctor's professional freedom—Would you say a great deal, or a fair amount, or very little, or not at all?

	Time 2	Time 3
Great deal	17	21
Fair amount	37	26
Very little	25	31
Not at all	15	16
Don't know	6	6
	100%	100%

deal" with the individual physicians' professional freedom under Medicaid, compared with 21% for Medicare.

2. Fifty-nine percent thought that the State Medical Society should cooperate with the Government on Medicaid, compared with 91% on Medicare.

3. Fifty-five percent said they planned to accept (or had already accepted) patients under Title 19, compared with all but one physician under Title 18B.

It could be argued that the opposition to Medicaid in New York State had a "contrast" effect on physicians' responses to Medicare; that Medicare looked better to physicians than it would have looked had Medicaid not been passed, and that this "contrast" inflated the size of the oppose-favor switchers on Medicare. For example, at the height of the furor over Medicaid in the state, one county medical society in an advertisement in *The New York Times* agreed to "cooperate" with the "Federal Medicare Law, which provides a sensible and reasonable plan of medical care for all people over 65 . . . ," but found it "impossible to cooperate with the implementation of this State law [Medicaid] . . . as it is presently proposed. . ." (June 10, 1966:36). It called Medicaid "socialized medicine."

There is no evidence of such a contrast effect in our data. Rather, among those physicians who opposed Title 18A at Time 1, those who were in favor of Medicaid at Time 2 and Time 3 were much more likely to switch and favor Title 18A than those who opposed Medicaid.[17]

4. It could be argued that the physicians' attitudes toward Medicare expressed at Time 1, before its passage, were superficial and equivocal, and merely reflected official AMA policy, and that once the program became law, physicians felt freer to express their "real" attitudes toward Medicare. But this argument misses the point that law may "legitimate" opinion. The fact that the Medicare program was not law is as significant a part of the social situation at Time 1 as the fact that it had become law at Time 2 and Time 3. One could just as plausibly argue for the superficiality of attitudes expressed after the law, because of a "bandwagon effect," as for the superficiality of attitudes expressed before the law.

As a matter of fact, neither the attitudes toward Medicare at Time 1 nor at Time 2 and Time 3 appear superficial. The subquestion on intensity of feeling was not asked at Time 1. In the Time 1 measure, however, less than 8% were "don't knows." Also, attitude toward Medicare at Time 1 was strongly related to other political questions and issues in the organization of medical practice, as noted above (Colombotos, 1968), which argues against its being superficial. In the Time 2 and 3 measures, the number of "don't knows" was even smaller than at Time 1: at Time 2, it was 5%, and at Time 3, it was less than 0.5%. Also, of those in favor, more than half responded they felt "strongly" in favor, rather than only "somewhat" in favor.

5. Finally, a number of methodological problems in panel surveys may be involved:

a. Reinterview Effect. It could be argued that the Time 1 interview generated an interest in Medicare, thus influencing physicians' responses in the Time 2 interview. We found no difference between the responses to selected questions, including the one on Medicare, obtained from the reinterviewed sample at Time 2 and from a control sample of 330 physicians not interviewed before.

b. Change in the Interview Instrument, specifically in the sequence of the questions. The items preceding the question on Medicare in the Time 2 interview were different from those in the Time 1 interview. We found no difference between the responses obtained in two different versions of the interview at Time 2: one in which the repeat (retest) questions were mixed with new questions and one in which the repeat (retest) questions were asked first, followed by the new questions.

c. Mortality Effect. It could be argued that physicians in the panel not interviewed at Time 2 and Time 3 were less likely to be pro-Medicare than those who were interviewed. We found that physicians who could not be reinterviewed at Time 2 and Time 3 did not differ from those who were reinterviewed in either background characteristics or attitudes, including their attitude toward Medicare, expressed at Time 1.

SUMMARY AND CONCLUSIONS

Despite their opposition to Medicare before the law was passed in 1965, physicians are complying with the program. There may be individual instances of noncooperation, but they are rare, at least in New York State, and there has been no boycott in the sense of concerted noncompliance.

Consistent with their compliance with Medicare, a large number of physicians who were opposed to Medicare before it became law switched and accepted it after it became law. In New York State, the proportion in favor rose from 38% before the law was passed to 70% less than a year after it was passed, even before it was implemented, and once again to 81% six months after the program went into effect.[18] The first increase, from 38% to 70%, argues that for law to influence attitudes it does not necessarily have to change relevant behavior first. We have in physicians' response to Medicare a case in which attitudes adapted to the law even before it went into effect.

The ready accommodation, both in deed and in mind, of these physicians to Medicare contrasts sharply with their continuing opposition to Medicaid and, to take a more extreme example, with physician strikes, such as the one in Saskatchewan, Canada, in 1962, against the province's medical care program.

What accounts for such differences in response to a law? The following differences between Medicare and the New York State Medicaid law illustrate some of the conditions listed above and suggest others that promote the effectiveness of a law:

1. *The Content of the Program.* The direct impact on physicians' practice of Medicaid in New York State is much greater than that of Medicare.

a. The number of people covered under Medicare in the state (those 65 or over) is less than two million. Estimates in May, 1966, of the number eligible under Medicaid ranged from 3.5 to 7 million. Furthermore, the number covered by Medicaid could be increased by liberalizing the definition of eligibility.

b. The clients of Medicare are the aged and the program is based on the insurance principle. The clients of Medicaid are the "medically indigent" and the program is based on the welfare principle. Physicians may be more sympathetic to a program serving the medical needs of the aged through insurance than to a program serving the "(medically) indigent," classified with "welfare cases."

c. Medicaid provides more services than Medicare, including drugs, dental bills, and other services not covered by Medicare.

d. New York State's Medicaid affects the physicians' practice more directly than Medicare. Medicaid attempts to control the quality and cost of medical care: the quality, by establishing criteria for determining who can render care, thus limiting the free choice of physicians; and the cost, by paying physicians fixed fees rather than "usual and customary" charges. Medicare has attempted neither. The direct effects of Medicare on physicians' practice, as a matter of fact, are minimal. Somers and Somers (1967:1) put it this way:

The 1965 enactment of Medicare was heralded as "revolutionary." But, in fact, it was neither a sudden nor radical departure from the march of events in the organization and financing of medical care and government's growing participation. No existing institutions were overturned or seriously threatened by the new legislation. On the contrary, Medicare responded to the needs of the providers of care as well as those of the consumers. It was primarily a financial underpinning of the existing health care industry—with all that implies in terms of strengths and weaknesses.

As a matter of fact, Medicare supports the stability of physicians' income under Title 18B, without controlling their fees. As noted above, more than a third of New York State physicians interviewed thought that under Medicare physicians would earn more money than before, and only about 10% thought they would earn less; the remainder thought it would not make any difference.

Both in terms of consistency with their ideology and in terms of their self-interest, then, Medicare is more acceptable to New York State physicians than Medicaid.

2. *Degree of Popular Support.* Medicare was passed with overwhelming popular support. Two-thirds of the public were in favor of Medicare, according to a nationwide Gallup poll in January, 1965, six months before it was passed. The percentage was probably higher in New York State. In contrast, there was little awareness about Medicaid before it was passed, and there was strong opposition, particularly in upstate New York, from industry, farm organizations, and in the press, after the first version of the New York Medicaid law was passed in April, 1966.

3. *Medicare Is the Same Throughout the Country, Whereas Medicaid Varies Greatly from State to State.* It is possible that the opposition of New York physicians to their state's Medicaid program, the most liberal in the country, is reinforced by their feeling "worse off" than their colleagues in other states where the Medicaid programs are not as ambitious. A plausible hypothesis, setting aside regional and local differences in values that may or may not be congruent with a given law, is that a

national law is more "legitimate" and more likely to be effectively complied with than a state or local law.[19]

Outside the area of medical care, public response in many parts of the country to statutes and judicial decisions requiring the desegregation of schools and other institutions contrasts sharply with physicians' response to Medicare. The issues of desegregation and civil rights will not be taken up here in any detail, but some obvious differences between them and Medicare come to mind:

1. Despite the "American creed" and trends showing a reduction of prejudice and discrimination, at least up to 1964, "white racism" may be more firmly entrenched among large segments of the American public than the fear of Government participation in health care among physicians.

2. The distributions of opposition to desegregation and to Medicare are different. Social supports to segregationists are more widely available than social supports to physicians opposed to Medicare. The general public strongly supported Medicare, and it was the medical profession that was out of step.

3. Desegregation, like Medicaid, runs into a hodgepodge of inconsistent and contradictory local, state, and Federal laws concerning different facilities and institutions—schools, transportation, recreation, housing, employment, marriage. Some of these laws actually *prescribe* segregation. Consider a hypothetical situation in which some states had laws that made it illegal to provide hospitalization and medical care under the terms ultimately provided by the Federal Medicare law![20]

Having established in this [article] the fact that the passage and implementation of Medicare had a sharp effect in changing the attitudes of physicians toward the program, the next steps will be (1) to examine the *conditions* under which physicians make both short-term and long-term changes in their attitudes toward Medicare, (2) to examine the long-term effects of Medicare on physicians' attitudes toward the program and toward other related political and health care issues, and (3) to compare the long-term and short-term responses of physicians to Medicare and Medicaid. A fourth wave of interviews with our physician panel is being planned in 1970—five years after the passage of Medicare—to answer these questions.

1. The two major sets of conditions of individual change in attitudes toward Medicare we shall examine are attitude-structural and social-structural variables. The general assumption is that there is pressure toward both intrapersonal and interpersonal consistency. For example, among those opposed to Medicare before the law was passed, it is predicted that Democrats are more likely to change their attitudes toward Medicare than Republicans; that physicians in areas where support for Medicare was initially strong are more likely to change than those in areas where support was weak; and that physicians who perceive themselves as having different opinions from their colleagues are more likely to change than those who see themselves as being in agreement. Other variables such as physicians' knowledge about Medicare, their experience with it, and their perceptions of its effects on their practice will also be studied as conditions of change in their attitudes toward Medicare.

2. a. The short-term effects of the Medicare law and program on physi-

cians' attitudes toward it were indeed dramatic. What will be the long-term effects—five years later? Will opposition to Medicare continue to wither away, or will it stiffen?

b. We have found that the Medicare law had little short-term effect on physicians' attitudes toward other related political and health care issues. The stability of these attitudes, as a matter of fact, was offered to support the argument that the change in attitude toward Medicare was indeed an effect of the Medicare law and program rather than a part of a more general liberal trend in physicians' thinking. Katz observes that "it is puzzling that attitude change seems to have slight generalization effects, when the evidence indicates considerable generalization in the organization of a person's beliefs and values" (Katz, 1960:199). But our results, and Katz' observation, refer to the short-run. It is plausible to expect that a change in one part of an attitude structure will produce changes in other parts of the structure, but the generalization of change *may not take place immediately*. It may take some time for the structure to become reintegrated. Will physicians' acceptance of Medicare make them more liberal in the longer run in their thinking about political issues and about changes in the organization of medical practice, or will it make them more conservative and resistant to such changes, or will it simply have no effects?[21]

3. In contrast to the ready acceptance of Medicare, physicians continued to oppose Medicaid in New York State nearly a year after it was implemented. How will they feel four years later? What will be the conditions under which physicians make long-term changes in their attitudes toward Medicaid, and how will these conditions differ from those that distinguish changers and nonchangers on Medicare? A comparison of the dynamics of the short-term and long-term responses of physicians to Medicare and Medicaid represents a modest test of the conditions under which laws influence behavior and attitudes.

NOTES

1. It is of course necessary to distinguish between the attitudes of individual physicians toward Medicare and official AMA policy. The AMA leadership is commonly regarded as more conservative than the rank-and-file; however, the opposition of the AMA to Medicare before its passage apparently was supported by the majority of its membership. In a national poll of private practitioners in 1961, less than 20% were in favor of the program "to provide hospital and nursing home care for the aged through the Social Security System" (Medical Tribune, May 15, 1961).

2. Allport qualifies this remark elsewhere in his book. It is quoted here to state the issue in its sharpest form.

3. In Campbell's study of a desegregating school system, the results were mixed. White students who claimed Negroes as personal friends were more likely to show a reduction of prejudice than those without Negro friends, but the time order of these factors is ambiguous: Those who became less prejudiced may then have chosen Negro friends. Also, those who had many classes with Negroes were no more likely to become less prejudiced than those with few classes with Negroes.

4. In an experimental study, information that a behavior was illegal did not change the subjects' attitudes toward that behavior (Walker and Argyle, 1964: 570–581). In a follow-up experiment, however, it was found that knowledge of the law and knowledge of peer consensus did change attitudes, and, furthermore, these effects depended on the authoritarianism of the subjects (Berkowitz and Walker, 1967:410–422).

5. These conditions are discussed in the following: Berger, 1954:173–177; Clark, 1953:53–59; Allport, 1954:469–473; Roche and Gordon, 1955:10, 42, 44, 49; Rose, 1959:470–481; Evan, 1965:285–293; Bonfield, 1965:107–122; Mayhew, 1968:258–284. Problems of implementation, specifically, the work and effects of antidiscrimination enforcement agencies, are analyzed by Berger (1954) and Mayhew (1968).

Less commonly cited factors determining the effectiveness of law are: (1) The amount of opposition to the law and the distribution of this opposition. The stronger and the more concentrated the opposition in politically relevant units, along geographical or occupational lines, for example, the more effectively it can oppose the law (Roche and Gordon, 1955:341). (2) The quality of support. A law is more likely to be effective if supported than if it is opposed by community leaders (see Killian, 1958:65–70). (3) The tempo of change. It is argued that the less the transition time, the easier the adaptation to the change enacted by the law (see Clark, 1953:43–47; Evan, 1965:290; Badgley and Wolfe, 1967:45).

6. Amendments to the Social Security Act in 1967 made some minor changes in the Medicare program and included an increase in the monthly premium.

7. Reported in "The Effects of Personal vs. Telephone Interviews on Socially Acceptable Responses," presented by the author at the annual meeting of the American Association for Public Opinion Research, Groton, Connecticut, May 14, 1965.

8. Some of these data are reported in the following papers: Colombotos, 1968; Colombotos, 1969a; Colombotos, 1969b.

9. Physicians in New York City were more pro-Medicare than physicians in upstate New York; Jewish physicians were more pro-Medicare than Protestant physicians, with Catholics in between; and those who were Democrats and took a liberal position on economic-welfare issues were more pro-Medicare than those who were Republicans and took a conservative position (see Colombotos, 1968:320–331).

10. Actually, the 676 physicians interviewed at Time 2 include 100 who could not be reached by June 30 and were interviewed between July and October, after Medicare went into effect. Those interviewed after June 30 were a little better informed than those interviewed before June 30 about the services covered by the Medicare program, which is not surprising, but the patterns of change in the attitude toward Title 18A of the two groups were practically the same. The specific month within the Time 2 or Time 3 periods when respondents were interviewed also made no difference in the pattern of change in their attitude toward Title 18A.

11. The original plan of this phase of the study was to reinterview all 1,205 physicians just before Medicare went into effect and again three to four years after it had been in effect. It was decided, however, to set aside a third of this sample (401) to be reinterviewed six months after the law was implemented in order to test the *short-run* effects of implementation. The original sample of 1,205 was not reinterviewed both before and immediately after Medicare's

implementation because of the financial cost and because, with the two interviews coming so close together, of a concern about a high refusal rate in the third interview. Reinterviews with all 1,007 (676 plus 331) physicians, interviewed both before and after Medicare, are planned for 1970.

12. Our measures of compliance, apart from being reports of own behavior rather than observations of actual behavior, are admittedly simple measures of a complex variable. Consider the following: (1) A physician may provide some services under Medicare, but refuse to provide other services; (2) he may provide services to some patients, but refuse to provide them to other patients; (3) he may cooperate at one point in time after the program goes into effect, and not cooperate at another; (4) he may sabotage the program by "over-complying," that is, by providing more services than are medically indicated. Also, the question of compliance is irrelevant for physicians without patients 65 or over, such as pediatricians.

As a matter of fact, when the specific behaviors required of physicians under Medicare are examined, it is difficult to conceive what form a physicians' boycott of Medicare could have taken. What is a physician asked to do under Medicare?

1. He must certify that the diagnostic or therapeutic services for which payment is claimed are "medically necessary." Such certification can be entered on a form or order or prescription the physician ordinarily signs.

2. Under Title 18, Part B, the physician can choose between two methods of payment for his services: he can accept an assignment and bill a designated carrier (such as Blue Shield, or another private insurance company, depending on the geographic area), or he can bill the patient directly. If he takes an assignment, he agrees that the "reasonable charge" determined by the carrier will be his full charge and that his charge to the patient will be no more than 20% of that reasonable charge. If the physician refuses to take an assignment and bills the patient directly, the patient pays the physician, and then applies to the carrier for payment. Under this method, a physician is not restricted by the "reasonable charge" for a given service. The patient, however, will be reimbursed only 80% of the reasonable charge by the carrier. Although the Social Security Administration had hoped for wide use of the assignment method, the AMA's House of Delegates adopted a resolution at its 1966 meeting recommending the use of the direct billing method (The New York Times, June 30, 1966:1). Use of the direct billing method cannot be called "noncooperation," however, since the law provides for either method.

3. In order to promote the most efficient use of facilities, each participating hospital and extended care facility is required to have a utilization review plan. A committee set up for such a purpose must include at least two physicians. Many hospitals already had such review procedures before Medicare went into effect. One way in which a physician can protest against Medicare is to refuse to serve on such a committee if asked. But refusal to serve does not necessarily mean a protest against Medicare, anymore than unwillingness to run for a local Board of Education is an indication of protest against the public school system.

To sum up, the direct and immediate effects of Medicare on a physician's day-to-day practice are minimal. For the vast majority of services under Medicare, the physician is not required to do anything more or differently in treating patients than he did before Medicare was passed. One form a boycott of Medicare could have taken would be for physicians to have refused to treat patients

65 or over, most of whom are eligible for benefits under both Part A and Part B of Medicare. This, apparently, few physicians chose to do. Furthermore, it would be difficult to interpret such acts as "noncooperation," unless the physician himself said so. A physician's refusal to admit an elderly patient to the hospital, for example, could mean that, in his medical judgment, hospitalization was not necessary.

13. Physicians' attitudes toward Title 18B, highly correlated with their attitudes toward Title 18A, were also very favorable. Seventy-eight percent were "in favor" at Time 2 and 83% at Time 3.

14. The effect of an experimental variable on a group is limited by the initial frequency giving a certain response before exposure to that variable. Since the percentage in favor of Medicare is higher at Time 2 than at Time 1, there is "less room" for an increase in the percentage in favor between Time 2 and Time 3 than between Time 1 and Time 2. The statistical effect of this "ceiling" may be "corrected" by dividing the actual percentage difference by the maximum possible increase. Hovland et. al. (1949:285–289) call such a measure the "effectiveness index." Such an index for the Time 1–Time 2 change is $.52[(70-38)/(100-38)=.52]$. For the Time 2–Time 3 change it is $.37 \ [(81-70)/(100-70)=.37]$. The fact that the Time 1–Time 2 index is larger than the Time 2–Time 3 measure indicates that the larger increase in the percentage of those in favor of Medicare between Time 1 and Time 2 than between Time 2 and Time 3 cannot be explained away as being entirely due to a statistical ceiling effect.

There is another type of ceiling effect, this one due to *selection*. Those still opposed to Medicare at Time 2 are likely to include a higher proportion of "hard-core" opponents of Medicare than those opposed at Time 1. We found, however, that the Time 2 opponents of Medicare were no more conservative on other measures of political ideology at Time 1 than the Time 1 opponents.

The study design has a limitation, too. Since it provides for only one measure of the physicians' attitudes after the law was passed and before its implementation, it is not possible to assess the effect of time alone. It is possible that the change in attitude toward Medicare between Time 2 and Time 3 is a function of time alone and has nothing to do with the implementation of the program. As a matter of fact, the "transition probabilities" between Time 2 and Time 3 are the same as those between Time 1 and Time 2.

15. Clark (1953:47–50) reports a similar pattern in cases of desegregation.

16. There is no increase in the level of physicians' knowledge about the details of Medicare between Times 2 and 3—they are poorly informed at both times—and there is no association between their level of knowledge and the amount of experience with Medicare, on the one hand, and change in their attitude toward Medicare, on the other.

17. Another test of the effects of Medicaid on attitude change toward Title 18A would be to examine the problem in a state where physicians' attitudes toward Title 18A were similar to those in New York State, but where the Medicaid program did not arouse as much opposition as the one in New York State. Unfortunately, such data are not available.

18. The proportion of private practitioners in favor of Medicare was higher in New York State than in the country as a whole before Medicare was passed (see note 1). No post-Medicare data from a national sample of physicians are available, however. Note also that our New York State study sample excludes

physicians on full-time salary, who are more likely to be politically liberal and in favor of Medicare than private practitioners. (For data supporting the latter point, see Lipset and Schwartz, 1966:304).

19. In terms of these conditions, the prospects of the plan that physicians struck against in Saskatchewan in 1962 were, in retrospect, not good: (1) the plan's impact on physicians' practice was much greater than Medicare's, providing for universal coverage for all residents in the province and a comprehensive range of services; (2) public opposition to the plan appeared to be stronger and better organized than the opposition to Medicare; and (3) it was a provincial, not a national plan.

20. The effects of law on behavior and attitudes are interpretable in terms of cognitive dissonance theory. According to this theory, the greater the dissonance between an individual's continued opposition to a program, behaviorally and attitudinally, and other elements in his cognitive structure, the greater is the probability of his complying and accepting the program. If we conceive as elements in an individual's cognitive structures the passage of a law and the specific conditions for its effectiveness, then it follows that the more of these conditions that apply, the greater the dissonance and the greater the probability of compliance and attitudinal acceptance.

That part of the theory that focuses on the effects of compliance on attitude change and the conditions under which dissonance between these two elements is aroused, however, is not particularly relevant to our case, since we found a large shift in attitudes toward Medicare even before physicians had an opportunity to comply (unless planning to comply is seen as equivalent to complying). The effects of compliance on attitude change in terms of dissonance theory is explicitly applied to desegregation in Brehm and Cohen (1962:269–285).

21. Note that "short-term" and "long-term" in attitude change research mean quite different things depending on the perspective of the investigator and the design used. In experimental studies, "short-term" effects are measured within minutes, hours, or at most, a few days after the introduction of the experimental variable; "long-term" effects usually mean no more than a few weeks later. In panel surveys, the time intervals are longer.

REFERENCES

ALLPORT, GORDON W. 1954. *The Nature of Prejudice*. Cambridge, Mass.: Addison-Wesley Publishing Co.

BADGLEY, ROBIN F., and SAMUEL WOLFE. 1967. *Doctors' Strike, Medical Care and Conflict in Saskatchewan*. New York: Atherton Press.

BALL, HARRY V., GEORGE EATON SIMPSON and KIYOSHI IDEDA, 1962. "Law and social change: Sumner reconsidered." *American Journal of Sociology* 67 (March):532–540.

BERGER, MORROE. 1954. *Equality by Statute*. New York: Columbia University Press.

BERKOWITZ, LEONARD, and NIGEL WALKER. 1967. "Laws and moral judgments." *Sociometry* 30 (December):410–422.

BONFIELD, ARTHUR EARL. 1965. "The role of legislation in eliminating racial discrimination." *Race* 7 (October):108–109.

BREHM, JACK W., and ARTHUR R. COHEN. 1962. *Explorations in Cognitive Dissonance.* New York: John Wiley and Sons.

CAMPBELL, ERNEST Q. 1958. "Some social psychological correlates of direction in attitude change." *Social Forces* 36 (May):335–340.

CANTRIL, HADLEY. 1947. *Gauging Public Opinion.* Princeton: Princeton University Press.

CLARK, KENNETH (issue ed.). 1953. "Desegregation: an appraisal of the evidence." *The Journal of Social Issues* 9:47–50.

COLOMBOTOS, JOHN. 1968. "Physicians' attitudes toward Medicare." *Medical Care* 6 (July–August):320–331.

————. 1969a. "Physicians' attitudes toward a county health department." effects of early socialization." *Journal of Health and Social Behavior* 10 *American Journal of Public Health* 59 (January):53–59.

————. 1969b. "Social origins and ideology of physicians: a study of the (March):16–29.

DEUTSCH, MORTON, and MARY E. COLLINS. 1951. *Interracial Housing: A Psychological Evaluation of a Social Experiment.* Minneapolis: University of Minnesota Press.

DEUTSCHER, IRWIN. 1966. "Words and deeds." *Social Problems* 13 (Winter): 235–254.

DICEY, ALBERT VENN. 1914. *Law and Opinion in England during the Nineteenth Century.* Second Edition, London: Macmillan and Co., Ltd. [Printing used, 1963]

EVANS, WILLIAM M. 1965. "Law as an instrument of social change." Pp. 291–292 in A. W. Gouldner and S. M. Miller (eds.), *Applied Sociology.* New York: The Free Press.

FEINGOLD, EUGENE. 1966. *Medicare: Policy and Politics.* San Francisco, Cal.: Chandler Publishing Co.

HARRIS, RICHARD. 1966. *A Sacred Trust.* New York: The New American Library.

HOVLAND, CARL L., ARTHUR A. LUMSDAINE and FRED D. SHEFFIELD. 1949. *Experiments on Mass Communication,* Vol. III, Studies in Social Psychology in World War II. Princeton: Princeton University Press.

HYMAN, HERBERT H., and PAUL B. SHEATSLEY. 1964. "Attitudes toward desegregation." *Scientific American* 211 (July):6.

KATZ, DANIEL. 1960. "The functional approach to the study of attitudes." *Public Opinion Quarterly* 24 (Summer):163–204.

KILLIAN, LEWIS M. 1958. *The Negro in American Society.* Florida State University Studies, No. 28:65–70.

KUTNER, BERNARD, CAROL WILKINS and PENNEY B. YARROW. 1952. "Verbal attitudes and overt behavior involving racial prejudice." *Journal of Abnormal and Social Psychology* 47:649–652.

LaPIERE, RICHARD T. 1934. "Attitudes vs. actions." *Social Forces* 13 (March): 230–237.

LIPSET, SEYMOUR MARTIN, and MILDRED A. SCHWARTZ. 1966. "The politics of professionals." Pp. 299–310 in Howard M. Vollmer and Donald L. Mills (eds.), *Professionalization*. Englewood Cliffs, N.J.: Prentice-Hall.

MacIVER, ROBERT M. 1948. *The More Perfect Union*. New York: Macmillan.

————. 1954. Forward P. viii in Morroe Berger, *Equality by Statute*. New York: Columbia University Press.

MAYHEW, LEON H. 1968. *Law and Equal Opportunity*. Cambridge, Mass.: Harvard University Press.

MUIR, WILLIAM K., JR. 1967. *Prayer in the Public Schools: Law and Attitude Change*. Chicago: The University of Chicago Press.

MUSSEN, PAUL H. 1950. "Some personality and social factors related to changes in children's attitudes toward Negroes." *Journal of Abnormal and Social Psychology* 45 (July):423–441.

MYRDAL, GUNNAR. 1944. *An American Dilemma*. New York: Harper and Row.

New York State Journal of Medicine. 1965. Editorial. Vol. 65 (November 15): 2779.

POUND, ROSCOE. 1944. *The Task of Law*. Lancaster, Pa.: Franklin and Marshall College.

ROCHE, JOHN P., and MILTON M. GORDON. 1955. "Can morality be legislated?" *New York Times Magazine* (May 22):10, 42, 44, 49. In Kimball Young and Raymond W. Mack (eds.), *Principles of Sociology: A Reader in Theory and Research*. New York: American Book Co., 1966.

ROSE, ARNOLD M. 1959. "Sociological factors in the effectiveness of projected legislative remedies." *Journal of Legal Education* 11:470–481.

————. 1967. *The Power Structure: Political Processes in American Society*. New York: Oxford University Press. Chap. xii, pp. 400–455, "The passage of legislation: the politics of financing medical care for the aging."

SAENGER, GERHART, and EMILY GILBERT. 1950. "Customer reactions to the integration of Negro sales personnel." *International Journal of Opinion and Attitude Research* 4 (Spring):57–76.

SCHWARTZ, MILDRED A. 1967. *Trends in White Attitudes toward Negroes*. Chicago: National Opinion Research Center, University of Chicago.

SCOTT, JOHN FINLEY, and LOIS HEYMAN SCOTT. 1968. "They are not so much anti-Negro as pro-middle class." *The New York Times Magazine* (March 24):46 ff.

SOMERS, HERMAN M., and ANNE R. SOMERS. 1967. *Medicare and the Hospitals: Issues and Prospects*. Washington, D.C.: The Brookings Institution.

SUMMER, WILLIAM GRAHAM. 1906. *Folkways*. New York: The New American Library [printing used, 1960].

SWANSON, GUY E., et al. (eds.). 1952. "Opinions about Negro infantry platoons in white companies of seven divisions." *Readings in Social Psychology*. New York: Holt.

WALKER, NIGEL, and MICHAEL ARGYLE. 1964. "Does the law affect moral judgments?" *British Journal of Criminology* 5:570–581.

YARROW, MARION RADKE. 1958. "Interpersonal dynamics in a desegregation process." Special Issue, *Journal of Social Issues*, 14.

YOUNG, KIMBALL, and RAYMOND W. MACK. 1960. *Principles of Sociology: A Reader in Theory and Research*. New York: American Book Co.

QUESTIONS

1. What are some alternative explanations offered by Colombotos and how are they discarded?
2. Attempt to design a "cross-sectional" study to investigate the phenomenon. At what time (t_1, t_2, or t_3 in the present study) would you interview? What problems might you encounter in attempting to study the relationship between the passage of the Medicare law and attitudes toward the law? Is there any way you can make reasonable causal inferences from such a cross-sectional study?

Other-Directedness in Consumer-Goods Advertising: A Test of Riesman's Historical Theory

SANFORD M. DORNBUSCH and LAUREN C. HICKMAN

Much of contemporary research in the social sciences involves the study of research units that exist at the time they are being studied (for example, living persons, contemporary societies). Of course a large number of research designs are available for the study of contemporary phenomena (many of which are illustrated in the articles in this reader). The study of past phenomena poses special problems, however, primarily because many design alternatives cannot be considered (for example, experimentation). Thus those who desire to conduct "historical" research must seek alternative approaches. Dornbusch and Hickman illustrate one such alternative—the content analysis of published materials.

This study also provides us with a good example of an explicit test of a social theory and the related problems in such endeavors. Among others, these problems include the operationalizing of theoretical concepts and the locating of unambiguous evidence. Take special note of the authors' own attitude toward the adequacy of the test. It is usually a long and painful process before a theory receives sufficient testing to justify confidence in its validity.

■ Some of the most influential and scientifically significant theories in the social sciences are often difficult to formulate in terms amenable to empirical testing. Sewell notes the necessity for reformulation of the theory in order to derive testable hypotheses.[1] In this paper an attempt will be made to formulate and test the historical trend toward other-directedness in American life posited in the work of David Riesman.[2]

Although there are empirical studies applying Riesman's conceptual

Reprinted from *Social Forces* 38 (1959), 99–102, by permission of The University of North Carolina Press.

scheme to contemporary American society,[3] the authors know of no research on the historical aspects of his work. He assumes, with considerable illustrative material, a general trend in recent years away from a character structure based on internalized goals toward a social character emphasizing throughout life the guiding reactions of others. Since we cannot query the dead, it is obviously necessary to use an indirect set of data which can be assumed to bear some relationship to the hypothesized shift.

THE UNIVERSE UNDER ANALYSIS

A basic assumption of this research is the belief that a shift in the verbal themes of consumer-goods advertising is likely to reflect a corresponding change in the values of the audience for that advertising. Riesman himself makes more than twenty separate references to such advertising. The advertising in one magazine with a long period of uninterrupted publication was selected for analysis. All issues of the *Ladies' Home Journal* from 1890 to 1956 constituted the universe to be sampled. This magazine was chosen because it is essentially middle class in its orientation[4] and is directed solely at women. More than most journals, there appears to be stability in the type of readers, but it is obviously impossible to control the influence of changes in readership upon the themes to be analyzed. In our opinion, the findings reported below are of such magnitude that it is unlikely they are in any large measure a product of this uncontrolled variable.

THE SAMPLE

There were a total of 816 issues of the *Ladies' Home Journal* during this 67-year period. The sample of issues to be analyzed was drawn in the following manner. Each issue was assigned a number. By means of a table of random numbers, one issue from each year was selected for possible inclusion. The order in which the issues were to be analyzed was also assigned through a table of random numbers. Limitations of time and money permitted the analysis of issues from only 41 years.[5] This is a five percent sample of the total population.

It is important to note that the random assignment of the order in which these magazines were to be read effectively prevents changes in the perspective of the content analysts from producing shifts in the amount of other-directedness found in advertising. The trends noted below are not a function of changing standards of content-analysis procedure.

INDICES OF OTHER-DIRECTEDNESS

No indices of inner-directedness are employed in this study. Rather, the proportion of advertisements with some form of other-directed appeal is the basic measure. The hypothesis is that the proportion of other-directed advertisements will increase through time. The single advertisement is accordingly the basic context unit. No relationship was found between other-directed appeals and size of advertisement, so no bias is introduced by using this unit for the entire time period.

Six indices of other-directedness were used. They fall logically into two types: endorsements by persons or groups, and claims that use of a product is related to satisfactions in interpersonal relations.

Endorsements:
1. Testimonials ("Billie Burke wears Minerva Sweaters.")
2. Collective Endorsements ("Housewives like the Singer Sewing Machine.")
3. Quantitative Endorsements ("25 million men use Star blades.")

Interpersonal Satisfactions:
4. Positive Interpersonal ("He'll like you better if you use Revlon.")
5. Negative Interpersonal ("Her perspiration drove her friends away. She should have used Mum.")
6. Both Positive and Negative Interpersonal ("Jim lost his girl because poor breakfast foods gave him no pep. After eating Wheaties, he's won her back.")

These indices obviously bear only an indirect relationship to other-directedness as perceived by Riesman. They do have the advantage, however, of being sufficiently explicit to permit intersubjective reliability among coders. Indices 4, 5, and 6 are mutually exclusive, but more than one appeal per advertisement may be recorded among indices 1, 2, and 3. When combined into groups of indices, advertisements are simply viewed as containing an other-directed appeal or having no such appeal, thus eliminating any possible bias due to the coding of several appeals in a single advertisement.

RELIABILITY

Table 1 shows the number of advertisements with other-directed appeals which were found by two independent coders analyzing two issues randomly selected from the earlier period (up to 1921) and the more recent half of the sample.[6] The high level of reliability of coding for the different types of endorsements is obvious. Unfortunately, these two issues do not contain a sufficient number of advertisements with interpersonal appeals to test the reliability of such coding. Two additional issues, those of May 1926, and January 1936, were used for a separate study of the reliability of coding. These issues are the two which contain the largest number of references to interpersonal consequences of product use, according to the scores of the individual who coded all issues. A third person scored these issues, and a different measure of reliability was employed. Instead of comparing the frequencies for each issue, a reliability coefficient was computed for the percentage of agreement between coders on specific advertisements where either scorer found some

TABLE 1. Comparison of Frequencies Recorded by Two Codes Analyzing the Same Issues of the *Ladies' Home Journal*, October 1895 and July 1951

	1895		1951	
	Coder A	Coder B	Coder A	Coder B
Endorsements				
Any type of endorsement	9	10	24	27
Testimonial	2	3	9	9
Collective	7	7	14	14
Quantitative	2	2	7	10
Interpersonal				
Any type of interpersonal satisfaction	0	0	1	1

other-directed appeal. The level of agreement was very high. For the three endorsement indices, the reliability coefficients were .95, .89, and .89. For the interpersonal appeals combined, reliability was .80, based on 10 cases. There were not sufficient cases to provide reliability measures for the three specific types of interpersonal effects of product use.

These are extremely high reliabilities, reflecting the explicit character of the indices of other-directedness employed in this research. The reliability coefficients would be even higher if one considered the large number of agreements with respect to the lack of other-directed devices in most advertisements. The ads where other-directedness was at issue were only a minority of all advertisements; thus these high coefficients of reliability state the minimum level of agreement between the pairs of readers.

SUMMARY OF FINDINGS

The null hypothesis to be tested states, for each index and combination of indices, that the proportion of other-directed advertisements is the same in issues published up to 1921 and in issues appearing after that date. The year 1921 is the midpoint of our sample, therefore representing the best arbitrary cutting point. The chi square test, a nonparametric measure, is then used as the basic statistical tool. Eight separate analyses were undertaken: one for each of the six indices, one for the use of any endorsement device, and one for the use of any interpersonal appeal.

The results of this statistical analysis can be briefly stated. In each of the eight tests, the null hypothesis is rejected at the .001 level. To the extent that the indices formulated here reflect the position of Riesman, the results of these statistical tests lend empirical support to his approach. When one compares the advertising of consumer goods in the period 1890 to 1921 with the themes of more recent advertisements, there has obviously been a marked change in orientation closely related to the sphere of other-directedness.

A somewhat different statistical approach is even more indicative of the magnitude of the shift toward other-directed appeals. Each issue is scored as either above or below the median of the sample for each of two measures, the use of any endorsement technique or any mention of interpersonal satisfactions. Dividing the issues into an older group, up to 1921, and a more recent set, the identical results appear for each of the two measures. Of the 21 oldest issues, 19 are below the median in other-directedness. Of the 20 more recent issues, 18 are above the median in other-directedness. The null hypothesis of no shift in other-directedness through time can again be rejected at the .001 level. Even more definitive, the 19 earliest issues are the 19 lowest in the use of the endorsement technique. For the interpersonal approach, there is only one advertisement using such an appeal in the first 19 issues in the sample.

There is one aspect of the findings which was not an object of our study design. As can be observed in Table 2, all indices except Index 1, the use

TABLE 2. Proportion of Other-Directed Advertisements in the *Ladies' Home Journal* by Six Indices

		Endorsements			
Decade	Number of Advertisements	Index 1 (Testimonials)	Index 2 (Collective)	Index 3 (Quantitative)	Indices 1, 2, 3 (Any Endorsement)
1890–99	1697	.0283	.0301	.0159	.0660
1900–09	1296	.0262	.0502	.0262	.0965
1910–19	1138	.0158	.0475	.0404	.0975
1920–29	1569	.0656	.1173	.0969	.2390
1930–39	502	.0677	.1235	.0916	.2151
1940–49	1088	.0708	.0588	.0662	.1728
1950–56	1102	.0662	.0635	.0699	.1570

		Interpersonal Satisfaction			
Decade	Number of Advertisements	Index 4 (Positive)	Index 5 (Negative)	Index 6 (Positive and Negative)	Indices 4, 5, 6 (Any interpersonal appeal)
1890–99	1697	0	0	0	0
1900–09	1296	.0008	0	0	.0008
1910–19	1138	0	0	0	0
1920–29	1569	.0057	.0038	0	.0096
1930–39	502	.0179	.0100	.0100	.0378
1940–49	1088	.0074	.0028	.0046	.0147
1950–56	1102	.0027	.0018	.0018	.0064

of testimonials, show a sharp decline in other-directed themes from 1940 to 1956. No tests of statistical significance are appropriate here, since the choice of cutting point arose from inspection of the data. It is possible, however, to give one additional piece of evidence that indicates a decline in other-directedness since 1940, as measured by these indices. The peak of other-directed appeals is found for each of the six indices, respectively, in 1932, 1932, 1926, 1936, 1936, and 1936. This is certainly contradictory to the expectations of a continual increase in other-directedness in recent years.

DISCUSSION

We have found a dramatic shift in advertising themes in the *Ladies' Home Journal,* beginning about 1920. The direction of change is harmonious with the general orientation of Riesman and his associates, thus lending some empirical support to their position. It should be emphasized that the field of consumer-goods advertising is far removed from the central core of American values, and our findings should not be generalized beyond this consumption area. For ourselves, we must confess that our initial skepticism about the usefulness of Riesman's approach has been replaced by the view that it is testable, important, and has some predictive power.

The decline in other-directedness after 1940 which is indicated by our measures cannot be appropriately evaluated in the light of this first set of data. One view assumes the reality of the peak in the 1920's and 1930's, associating it with (a) the breakdown of fixed standards when the depression overthrew faith in the American economic system, and (b) the rise of feminism after World War I and woman's corresponding search for new values. A different interpretation relates the decline to increased subtlety of advertisers. Our measures are based on explicit statements by advertisers, partly because of our concern that reliability be high. Riesman comments, "Even though the social-class level of readers of the *Ladies' Home Journal* may not have risen, I would suspect that the educational level has risen considerably. . . . The ads and the articles, if not always the fiction, have gained in sophistication as the readership has gained in education and cosmopolitanism. . . . Is there more use now of polite implication rather than direct premise or direct threat?"[7] By this interpretation, the recent decline is a function of research technique rather than changes in the level of other-directedness in advertising. Only further research using different indices can answer this question.

NOTES

1. Wm. H. Sewell, "Some Observations on Theory Testing," *Rural Sociology,* XXI (March 1956), 1–12. An earlier paper by one of the present authors used a similar approach. See S. Frank Miyamoto and Sanford M. Dornbusch, "A Test of Interactionist Hypotheses of Self-Conception," *The American Journal of Sociology,* LXI (March 1956), 399–403.

2. David Riesman, Nathan Glazer, and Reuel Denney, *The Lonely Crowd* (New Haven, Conn.: Yale University Press, 1950).

3. Elaine Graham Bell, Inner-Directed and Other-Directed Attitudes (Unpublished Ph.D. dissertation, Yale University, 1955); E. G. Guba and J. W. Getzels, The Construction of an Other-Directedness Instrument, with Some Preliminary Data on Validity, paper read before the American Psychological Association, Sept.,

1954; Michael S. Olmsted, "Character and Social Role," *The American Journal of Sociology*, LXIII (July 1957), 49–57.

4. Riesman claims that it is the middle-class character which is in transition.

5. In the order of coding, the sample included one issue from each of the following years: 1926, 1920, 1902, 1908, 1922, 1917, 1953, 1950, 1914, 1899, 1932, 1939, 1954, 1903, 1952, 1909, 1890, 1897, 1907, 1936, 1931, 1940, 1894, 1910, 1929, 1927, 1912, 1943, 1924, 1915, 1895, 1891, 1944, 1893, 1921, 1941, 1900, 1896, 1951, 1923, 1946.

6. We are indebted to Caroline Roberts for her assistance in the reliability checks.

7. Personal communications, April 9 and April 11, 1957.

QUESTIONS

1. What considerations both conceptually relevant and irrelevant went into the selection of the *Ladies' Home Journal* as the magazine for study?
2. Would the choice of a second magazine over the same period of time provide further evidence on the hypothesis? What problems of "independence" might arise because the same advertisements appear in different magazines?
3. What are the problems of interpretation involved with the use of mass media to give evidence regarding changes in social character? What group of persons does this evidence actually apply to? What assumptions about the process of advertising are required?
4. What purpose is served by having two independent coders analyzing the same issues of the magazine? Which of Campbell's threats to validity does this type of operation speak to?
5. What theoretical proposition is being tested in this study? What are the key concepts? How are they operationalized?
6. Familiarize yourself with Riesman's complete theory of social character and indicate what aspects of that theory have not been tested in the current study. Suggest ways in which they might be tested.
7. Suggest some other data sources that might be used for testing the hypothesis being investigated in the Dornbusch and Hickman study.

The Lost-Letter Technique:
A Tool of Social Research

STANLEY MILGRAM, LEON MANN, and SUSAN HARTER

An important feature of research design is the extent to which we allow
the research subjects to know if they are objects of study. In some instances it
may be desirable to prevent the subjects from knowing they are in a research
setting because they may alter their behavior if they know they are being
studied. Techniques that are designed to accomplish this are referred to as
"unobtrusive." Many attempts have been made at developing "unobtrusive"
procedures (see Webb et al., *Unobtrusive Measures*), one of which is described
in the following article. [For further discussion of the "lost-letter" technique see:
Allan W. Wicker, "A Failure to Validate the Lost-Letter Technique," *Public
Opinion Quarterly* 33 (1969):260–262; Stanley Milgram, "Comment on 'A Failure
to Validate the Lost-Letter Technique,' " *Public Opinion Quarterly* 33 (1969):
263–264; and R. Lance Shotland, Wallace G. Berger, and Robert Forsythe,
"A Validation of the Lost-Letter Technique," *Public Opinion Quarterly* 34
(1970):278–281.]

■ This note describes briefly an experimental technique for assessing
community orientations toward political groups and other institutions.
The technique consists of dispersing in city streets (and other locations)
a large number of unmailed letters. The letters are enclosed in envelopes
that have addresses and stamps on them but that have not yet been
posted. When a person comes across one of these letters on the street, it
appears to have been lost. Thus he has a choice of mailing, disregarding,
or actively destroying the letter. By varying the name of the organization
to which the letter is addressed and distributing such "lost letters" in
sufficient quantity, it is possible to obtain a return rate specific to the
organization. The focus of the technique is not on the individual reaction
to the lost letters but, rather, on the rate of response for a particular
organization relative to other organizations that serve as controls.

In a first study, 400 stamped, addressed envelopes were distributed in
the city of New Haven, Connecticut. One hundred letters were assigned
to each of the following addresses:

Friends of the Communist Party
P.O. Box 7147
304 Columbus Avenue
New Haven 11, Connecticut

Medical Research Associates
P.O. Box 7147
304 Columbus Avenue
New Haven 11, Connecticut

Friends of the Nazi Party
P.O. Box 7147
304 Columbus Avenue
New Haven 11, Connecticut

Mr. Walter Carnap
P.O. Box 7147
304 Columbus Avenue
New Haven 11, Connecticut

Reprinted from *Public Opinion Quarterly* 29 (1965), 437–438, with permission of Columbia
University Press.

Research Design

The letters were systematically distributed in ten districts of the city and in four types of placement: street pavements, shops, telephone booths, and under automobile windshield wipers. (In this last case, the inscription "found near car" was written in pencil on each envelope.) Twenty-five envelopes with each address were distributed in each placement.

The following table shows the number of letters returned for each cell of 25. The last column gives the over-all percentage of letters returned for each address:

Address	Placement				
	Shops	Cars	Streets	Phone Booths	Per Cent Return
Medical Research Associates	23	19	18	12	72
Personal letter	21	21	16	13	71
Friends of the Communist Party	6	9	6	4	25
Friends of the Nazi Party	7	6	6	6	25
Total	57	55	46	35	48

The return rate for all 400 letters was 48 per cent, but this is of less interest than the relative return rates for the several organizations. Seventy-two per cent of the Medical Research letters and 71 per cent of the Personal letters were received in our post office box, but the Communist and Nazi Party return rates were each 25 per cent.

The substantive results do not tell us anything new or spectacular: it is no surprise that extremist political organizations should be less favored than a medical research group. But the experience does show the general feasibility of using the technique as a means of assessing community orientations toward social groups or organizations. Moreover, it now becomes possible to extend the technique to domains and issues where the answers are not so clearly known, or where it is desirable to conduct a study without directly questioning subjects.

Several new studies using the lost-letter technique have been completed, or are now underway. In a second study, a demographic variable was introduced; letters relevant to the racial integration question were distributed in North Carolina using neighborhoods of different racial composition. A third study is being conducted in Hong Kong to measure the orientation of overseas Chinese toward the Peking and Taiwan governments, and a fourth study is planned in which the response rates will be assessed against a criterion measure, namely the 1964 presidential election returns.

The lost-letter technique has many limitations, among them, a relative lack of control over the precise processes that mediate the return of the letters: one knows only the rate of response for any particular letter series. However, there are compensatory advantages: (1) the person who comes across the letter rarely if ever realizes he is a participant in a sociological survey, (2) an ordinary action is used as the basis of measurement, and (3) the responses can be gathered up conveniently in a post office box. With proper controls the technique can prove a useful and unobtrusive means of gathering information on selected social issues.

QUESTIONS

1. Primary data collecting techniques can be categorized easily as: (a) interviews or questionnaires, (b) observation, or (c) analysis of artifacts (for example, content analysis of published materials). In which category would you place the "lost-letter technique"?
2. What are the problems of interpretation associated with the lost-letter technique? Review the threats to validity listed by Campbell.
3. What are the reasons for varying the locations in which the letters were "lost"?
4. What kind of design does the research have?
5. What other phenomena might the lost-letter technique be used to study?
6. To what extent would you call the act of returning a "lost letter" a behavior in a natural setting or a research setting?
7. In this brief article is the principal theoretical interest in behavior or in attitudes? Discuss the difficulties in utilizing the lost-letter technique to collect data on mental phenomena.
8. Design a research project that might be utilized to compare the findings of a lost-letter procedure with one of the more conventional techniques (such as interviewing or questionnaires).

SUGGESTED READINGS

BACKSTROM, CHARLES, and HURSH, GERALD D. *Survey Research.* Evanston, Ill.: Northwestern University Press, 1967.

BRUYN, SEVERYN T. *The Human Perspective in Sociology: The Methodology of Participant Observation.* Englewood Cliffs, N.J.: Prentice-Hall, Inc., 1966.

CAMPBELL, DONALD T., and STANLEY, JULIAN C. *Experimental and Quasi-Experimental Designs for Research.* Chicago: Rand McNally, 1963.

GARFINKEL, HAROLD. *Studies in Ethnomethodology.* Englewood Cliffs, N.J.: Prentice-Hall, Inc., 1967.

HOLSTI, OLE R. *Content Analysis for the Social Sciences and Humanities.* Reading, Mass.: Addison-Wesley, 1969.

McCALL, GEORGE J., and SIMMONS, J. L. (eds.). *Issues in Participant Observation.* Reading, Mass.: Addison-Wesley, 1969.

RASER, JOHN R. *Simulation and Society: An Exploration of Scientific Gaming.* Boston: Allyn and Bacon, 1969.

ROSENTHAL, ROBERT. *Experimenter Effects in Behavior Research.* New York: Appleton-Century-Crofts, 1966.

SELLTIZ, C. et al. *Research Methods in Social Relations.* Rev. ed. New York: Holt, Rinehart & Winston, 1959. Appendix B: An Introduction to Sampling.

STEPHAN, FREDERICK F., and McCARTHY, PHILIP J. *Sampling Opinions.* New York: Wiley, 1958.

SUCHMAN, EDWARD A. "The Principle of Research Design and Administration," in John H. Doby (ed.), *An Introduction to Social Research.* 2nd ed. New York: Appleton-Century-Crofts, 1967. Chapter 13.

WEBB, EUGENE J. et al. *Unobtrusive Measures: Nonreactive Research in the Social Sciences.* Chicago: Rand McNally, 1966.